T0304789

Managing Portfolio Credit Risk in Banks

Credit risk is the risk resulting from uncertainty that a borrower or a group of borrowers may be unwilling or unable to meet its contractual obligations as per the agreed terms. It is the largest element of risk in the books of most banks and financial institutions. Potential losses due to high credit risk can threaten a bank's solvency. After the global financial crisis of 2008, the importance of adopting prudent risk management practices has increased manifold. This book is an attempt to demystify various standard mathematical and statistical techniques that can be applied in measuring and managing portfolio credit risk in the emerging market in India. It also provides deep insights into various nuances of credit risk management practices, which are derived from the best practices adopted globally with case studies and data support from the Indian banks. The book explains how a proper portfolio credit risk management framework enables banks to identify, assess and manage the risk proactively and enhance entity performance. The book has been designed to give readers – students of finance, bank personnel and practitioners – solid foundation knowledge of credit risk measurement and management.

Arindam Bandyopadhyay is Associate Professor in Finance and Associate Dean (Research and Consultancy) at National Institute of Bank Management (NIBM), Pune. He teaches risk management and research methodology subjects for NIBM's postgraduate course and has undertaken major consultancy research projects in risk management, banking, finance, and housing market. Dr Bandyopadhyay has publications to his credit in peer-reviewed journals in the areas of risk management and corporate finance. He is a trainer to bank executives and has conducted about 50 executive development programmes for banks at NIBM.

Managing Portfolio Credit Risk in Banks

Arindam Bandyopadhyay

CAMBRIDGE
UNIVERSITY PRESS

Shaftesbury Road, Cambridge CB2 8EA, United Kingdom

One Liberty Plaza, 20th Floor, New York, NY 10006, USA

477 Williamstown Road, Port Melbourne, VIC 3207, Australia

314–321, 3rd Floor, Plot 3, Splendor Forum, Jasola District Centre, New Delhi – 110025, India

103 Penang Road, #05–06/07, Visioncrest Commercial, Singapore 238467

Cambridge University Press is part of Cambridge University Press & Assessment, a department of the University of Cambridge.

We share the University's mission to contribute to society through the pursuit of education, learning and research at the highest international levels of excellence.

www.cambridge.org
Information on this title: www.cambridge.org/9781107146471

First published 2016

A catalogue record for this publication is available from the British Library

ISBN   978-1-107-14647-1   Hardback

Cambridge University Press & Assessment has no responsibility for the persistence or accuracy of URLs for external or third-party internet websites referred to in this publication and does not guarantee that any content on such websites is, or will remain, accurate or appropriate.

*To my wife Mousumi, whose encouragement
and support made it possible*

Contents

Tables, Figures, Charts

Tables

Annexures

Preface

Effective credit risk management has gained an increased focus of banks in India in recent years, mainly driven by the changing regulatory regime in line with Basel II advanced internal rating-based (IRB) approaches as well as Basel III. Regulatory capital standards based on internal credit risk models would allow banks and supervisors to take advantage of the benefits of advanced risk-modelling techniques in setting capital standards for credit risk. Banks in India should now have a keen awareness of the need to identify, measure, monitor and control credit risk as well as to determine that they hold adequate capital against these risks and that they are adequately compensated for risks incurred to survive during the downtime. In this light, this book provides a basic guide to understand various modelling requirements, and then focuses on the role these models and techniques have in measuring and managing credit risk under the advanced IRB approach which may be adopted by Indian banks.

Credit risk models are the tools that assist banks in quantifying, aggregating and managing risk across geographical and product lines. The outputs of these models also play increasingly important role in enhancing banks' risk management and performance measurement processes through customer profitability analysis, risk-based pricing, active portfolio management and crucial capital structure decisions. Credit risk models enable banks to assess internally the level of economic capital to be allocated to individual credit assets and the credit portfolio as a whole. And most importantly, validated credit risk models and their proper use tests are the basic building blocks to achieve regulatory compliance. An efficient management of credit risk is a critical component of a comprehensive approach to risk management and essential to the long-term success of any banking organization.

This book is an attempt to demystify various standard mathematical and statistical models that have been widely used by globally best practiced banks and demonstrates their relevance in measuring and managing credit risk in emerging Indian market. The book would help the academicians/ practitioners/risk managers/top executives in banks as well as students in the banking and finance area to understand the nuances of credit risk management that involves understanding modern tools and techniques in identifying, evaluating credit risk and its implications on profits and business strategies. The readers looking to learn how to build models may easily base their work in line with the given practices or methods shown and benchmark the outputs with the various published results given in book. This book is specially designed to enable the banks to prepare for eventual migration towards more sophisticated risk management framework under the Basel IRB approach set by the Reserve Bank of India.

This text is divided into eight chapters. Chapter 1 gives "Introduction to Credit Risk": Definition, major risk drivers, management concepts, the purpose of managing credit risk, its importance for bank performance and overall solvency. This chapter discusses key issues and challenges for banks in Indian measuring and managing credit risk in the backdrop of global financial crisis and recent macroeconomic scenario. This chapter also reviews banks' existing internal risk management culture, policies and procedures to manage risk, governance framework and so on, in line with Basel regulatory expectations.

Chapter 2 discusses the various types of "Credit Rating Models" used by rating agencies and banks to predict borrowers' risk of default. It describes Judgmental (or expert opinion based) as well as statistical scoring models and their usefulness in borrower risk assessment in Indian context as well as in other emerging market economies. This chapter provides detail about the risk factors which should be considered for the development of internal rating models for various categories of exposures. It brings together a wide variety of credit risk modelling framework for corporate loans, project finance, small and medium enterprises (SMEs), housing loans, agriculture loans, sovereign exposures and micro-financial institutions (MFIs), and more. Focus has been given to both corporate as well as retail credit-scoring techniques. Stress has been given on structural and hybrid scoring models to predict credit risk of large corporate loans. The intention is to provide the reader a concise and applied knowledge about statistical modelling for credit risk management and decision-making. The strengths and weaknesses of each model have also been discussed with examples. This chapter also explains minimum requirements for validating such models to test their effectiveness for internal use and also to meet the regulatory expectations for compliance.

Chapter 3 demonstrates the various approaches for measuring "Probability of Default" (PD), which is the most critical element in measuring credit risk capital. This chapter describes rating transition matrix analysis using rating agencies data as well as bank data and compares them. The analysis of rating agencies reported probability default estimates would help the banks to benchmark their internally generated PD figures. If rating data is not available, for example in case of retail loans, an alternative pooled PD method has been elaborated. Calculation of default rates across various sub-categories of portfolio (e.g. grades, industries, regions, etc.) enables more granular analysis of portfolio credit risk.

Chapter 4 discusses the techniques that are used to estimate "Exposure at Default" (EAD) and "Loss Given Default" (LGD). First part of this chapter describes the methodology for estimating EAD and the later part explains the LGD methodology. Estimation of EAD has been covered in detail for various loan facilities extended by commercial banks in India. It includes various off balance sheet products like cash credit, overdraft, revolving line of credit and working capital loans. The estimation of usage given default (UGD) or credit conversion factor (CCF) for non-fund-based facilities such as guarantees and letter of credits (LCs) are also explained in detail. This chapter also demonstrates how CCF/UGD can be used as an early warning signal for default prediction. LGD is of natural interest to lenders wishing to estimate future credit loss. LGD is a key input in the measurement of the expected and unexpected credit losses and, hence, credit risk capital (regulatory as well as economic). Data limitations pose an important challenge to the estimation of LGD in Indian banks. This chapter provides examples for the estimation of economic LGD through workout method. Using actual loss data of various Indian public sector banks, Chapter 4 deduces the methodology for computing economic LGD from the banks' loss experiences and assesses the various factors that determine LGD. Chapter 4 shows how such historical loss analysis can enable IRB banks to develop LGD predictor model for predicting future losses.

Banks need to invest time and technology into validating their model results. Back testing and validation are important criteria to check the robustness of the models. This is an important issue for many emerging markets like India, where the quality and scale of data are not comparable with most developed countries. Hence, these statistical models need to be properly validated with new outcomes, beyond the time horizons of the data series on which the models are constructed. The regulators through internal-rating-based approach (IRB) under Basel II and Basel III are emphasizing greater transparency in the development and use of credit risk models. The validation process should encompass both qualitative and quantitative elements as the responsibility is on the banks to convince the regulators that their internal validation processes are robust.

Chapter 5 covers in detail the model validation requirements and the best-practiced validation techniques which are also recognized under Basel

II/III. Besides discussions on various statistical parametric as well as non-parametric measures like Gini coefficient, ROC curve, CAP curve, Correlation method, Mean Square Error, Type I and Type II error tests, it also narrates regulatory validation criteria in terms of use tests, checking data quality and model assumptions. Several numerical examples have been constructed to provide hands on explanation of models' validation, calibration, back testing, benchmarking and stress-testing methodologies. The differences between point in time (PIT) and through-the-cycle (TTC) estimation techniques, the linkage between PD, LGD, and correlations with macroeconomic factors have also been addressed in this chapter. Understanding of these relationships will enable banks to create a sound framework to conduct scenario analysis and check the stability of rating models on a regular basis. This will make them more resilient to macroeconomic stress.

Chapter 6 explains the importance of measurement and management of correlation risk in the "Assessment Portfolio Credit Risk" in banks. It demonstrates the various methods to practically estimate default and asset correlations in the credit portfolio of banks. These correlation estimates will enable the portfolio managers to understand the linkage between banks' portfolio default risks with the systematic factors. This chapter also describes the various tools and techniques (like Gini coefficient, Expected Loss based Hirschman Herfindahl Index (HHI), Theil Entropy measure, setting risk-based limits, transition matrix, etc.) that are used for the assessment of portfolio concentration risk.

Chapter 7 is devoted to describe the various methods to estimate "Economic Capital and Risk-adjusted Return on Capital". Economic capital gives a clear answer to the most pressing question of all: Does a bank's available capital equal or exceed the capital necessary to ensure long-term survival? Using internal loss data of some leading PSBs in India, this chapter demonstrates how credit value at risk (Credit-VaR) method can be used to estimate the portfolio unexpected loss and economic capital (EC). This chapter also explains the most common ways to "stress test credit risk" elements in a dynamic framework (by incorporating macroeconomic framework) and understand their effects on risk capital. Finally, this chapter illustrates how Risk-adjusted Return on Capital (RAROC) can act as a powerful risk measurement tool for banks and FIs in measuring solvency and evaluating the performance of different business activities, thereby facilitating the optimal allocation of shareholders' capital.

Chapter 8 familiarizes the reader with the conceptual foundations, data requirements and underlying mathematical models pertaining to the calculation of minimum regulatory "Capital Requirements for Credit Risk under the Basel IRB Approach". The internal approach will allow the banks to use their own "internal" models and techniques to measure the major risks that they face, the probability of loss and the capital required to meet that loss subject to the supervisory expectation and review. This chapter explains the conceptual and the underlying mathematical logic behind the Basel IRB Risk Weight Functions for various exposure categories (sovereign, corporate, retail, SMEs, project finance, etc.) and demonstrates the methods for estimating risk-weighted assets as well as regulatory capital. This chapter is also intended to aid the bank to design a road map for the implementation of Advanced IRB approaches. Key pillar II supervisory review processes that will be faced by the IRB banks have also been discussed in this chapter (ICAAP under IRB section). Banking regulation pertaining to measurement and management of credit risk has progressed evidently since the 2008 subprime crisis. The changing regulatory regime in the form of Basel III expects the banks to develop and use better risk management techniques in monitoring and managing their risks. Basel III urges that systemically important banks should have loss-absorbing capacity beyond the existing Basel II standards to ensure financial stability. These new regulatory and supervisory directions have been addressed at the end of the chapter.

Acknowledgements

Many people have directly or indirectly helped during the process of thorough researching and working on this book. I wish to express my sincere gratitude to everybody involved in the completion of this project. I would particularly like to thank Shri Dhiraj Pandey, my editor, for his help and support. I am grateful to all the reviewers who read various chapters of the original manuscript and made many constructive comments and suggestions that led to further improvements in the final version. I wish to acknowledge Cambridge University Press for all their support to this project.

I am deeply grateful for the support of the National Institute of Bank Management (NIBM), Pune. I am very thankful to Dr Achintan Bhattacharya, director of NIBM, for his cooperation, encouragement and continuous support. Special thanks to my students Veeresh Kumar, Nishish Sinha, Mathew Joseph, Sonali Ganguly, Nandita Malini Barua, Hitesh Punjabi and Smita Gupta for their assistance. I am grateful to my banker participants for many fruitful discussions and suggestions during my class interactions. I would like to thank my colleagues Prof. Sanjay Basu and Prof. Tasneem Chherawala for many useful discussions, comments and suggestions.

I would like to acknowledge people from academics and practitioners for their constant support and guidance. I extend my gratitude to Dr M. Jayadev, John Heinze, Dr Jeffrey Bohn, Dr Soumya Kanti Ghosh, Saugata Bhattacharya, Pramod Panda, Ajay Kumar Choudhary, P.R. Ravi Mohan, Dr Asish Saha, Asit Pal, Krishna Kumar, Dr Rohit Dubey, Amarendra Mohan, Benjamin Frank, Mohan Sharma, Sandipan Ray, Sugata Nag, Anirban Basu, Allen Pereira,

Dr Debashish Chakrobarty, Dr Sachidananda Mukherjee and Mallika Pant. I am genuinely indebted to all of them.

This project would not have been possible had I not been constantly inspired by my wife Mousumi. I am grateful for her continuous support and encouragement. I also owe to her family members, Mukunda Debnath (Babu), Manjushree Nath (Maa) and Suman (Bhai) for their patience and encouragement. I nurture the memory of my father Late Satyendra Nath Banerjee and mother Late Uma Rani Banerjee and their blessings all the time. I am also indebted to my eldest sister Rajyashree Gupta and her husband Samudra Gupta for their support.

Abbreviations

AB	: Advance Bills
AC	: Asset Correlation
AIGV	: Accord Implementation Group Validation
AIRB	: Advanced Internal Rating Based approach
ALCO	: Asset Liability Committee
ANOVA	: Analysis of Variance
APRA	: Australian Prudential Regulation Authority
AR	: Accuracy Ratio
ARC	: Average Risk Contribution
ASRF	: Asymptotic Single Risk Factor
ATM	: Automated Teller Machines
AUROC	: Area Under Receiver Operating Characteristic
BCBS	: Basel Committee for Banking Supervision
BD	: Bills Discounted
BG	: Bank Guarantee
BIS	: Bank for International Settlements
BNM	: Bank Negara Malaysia
BOJ	: Bank of Japan
BOK	: Bank of Korea
BOT	: Bank of Thailand
BSM	: Black and Scholes and Merton Model
CAP	: Cumulative Accuracy Profile
CAPM	: Capital Asset Pricing Model
CASHPROF	: Cash Profit
CB	: Counter Cyclical Buffer
CBR	: Central Bank of Russia
CBRC	: China Banking Regulatory Commission
CC	: Cash Credit

CCB	: Capital Conservation Buffer
CCC	: Credit Control Committee
CCCB	: Counter Cyclical Capital Buffer
CCF	: Credit Conversion Factor
CCR	: Collateral Coverage Ratio
CD Ratio	: Credit Deposit Ratio
CDF	: Cumulative Default Frequency
CEO	: Chief Executive Officer
CET1	: Common Equity Tier 1 capital
CF	: Cash Flow
CHAID	: Chi-square Automatic Interaction Detector
CMIE	: Centre for Monitoring Indian Economy
CPD	: Cumulative Probability of Default
CR	: Current Ratio
CRA	: Credit Rating Agency
CRAR	: Capital to Risk-weighted Assets Ratio
CRE	: Commercial Real Estate
CRISIL	: Credit Rating Information Services of India Limited
CRM	: Credit Risk Mitigation
CRMC	: Credit Risk Management Committee
CRMD	: Credit Risk Management Department
CRO	: Chief Risk Officer
CS	: Credit Spread
CVA	: Credit Value Adjustment
DBOD	: Department of Banking Operations and Development (DBOD)
DBS	: Department of Banking Supervision
DC	: Default Correlation
DD	: Distance to Default
DP	: Default Point
DSCR	: Debt Service Coverage Ratio
EAD	: Exposure at Default
EBA	: European Banking Association
EBIDTA	: Earnings Before Interest Depreciation Taxes and Amortization

EBIT	: Earnings Before Interest and Taxes
EC	: Economic Capital
ECAI	: External Credit Agency Institutions
ECB	: European Central Bank
ECOLGD	: Economic Loss Given Default
EDF	: Expected Default Frequency
EL	: Expected Loss
ELGD	: Expected LGD
EMI	: Equated Monthly Instalment
EPD	: Expected Probability of Default
EPS	: Expected Probability of Solvency
EVA	: Economic Value Addition
FED	: Federal Reserve
FICO	: Fair Isaac Corporation
FIMMDA	: Fixed Income Money Market and Derivatives Association of India
FIRB	: Foundation Internal Rating Based approach
FRBNY	: Federal Reserve Bank of New York
FSR	: Financial Stability Report
FTP	: Fund Transfer Pricing
GDP	: Gross Domestic Product
GNPA	: Gross Non Performing Assets
GNPGR	: Gross National Product Growth Rate
GNPL	: Gross Non Performing Loans
HHI	: like Hirschman Herfindahl Index
HKMA	: Hong Kong Monetary Authority
HR	: Hurdle Rate
ICAAP	: Internal Capital Adequacy Assessment Process
IG	: Investment Grade
IRB	: Internal Rating Based approach
IRR	: Internal Rate of Return
JDP	: Joint Default Probability
JPMC	: JP Morgan & Chase
KFA	: King Fisher Airlines
KMV	: Kealhofer, McQuown and Vasicek model

KS	: Kolmogorov Smirnov test
LC	: Letter of Credit
LDP	: Low Default Portfolio
LEF	: Loan Equivalent Factor
LEQ	: Loan Equivalent
LGD	: Loss Given Default
LIED	: Loss in the Event of Default
LLCR	: Loan Life Coverage Ratio
LRPD	: Long Run Probability of Default
LTV	: Loan to Value Ratio
MAS	: Monetary Authority of Singapore
MDA	: Multiple Discriminant Analysis
MFI	: Micro Finance Institute
MIS	: Management Information System
MKMV	: Moody's KMV
MLE	: Maximum Likelihood Estimation
MPD	: Marginal Probability of Default
MRC	: Marginal Risk Contribution
MSE	: Mean Squared Error
MVA	: Market Value of Assets
MVD	: Market Value of Debt
MVE	: Market Value of Equity
NBFC	: Non Bank Finance Companies
NCAF	: New Capital Adequacy Framework
NHISTLGD	: Normalized Historical LGD
NIG	: Non Investment Grade
NPA	: Non Performing Assets
NPF	: Notice on Public Rulemaking
NW	: Net worth
NWK	: Networking Capital
OB	: Off Balance sheet
OCC	: Open Cash Credit
OD	: Overdraft
ODP	: Observed Default Probability

OE	:	Optimum Error
OLS	:	Ordinary Least Squares
OTC	:	Over the Counter
PAT	:	Profit After Tax
PBIT	:	Profit Before Interest and Tax
PC	:	Packing Credit
PD	:	Probability of Default
PDI	:	Perpetual Debt Instruments
PF	:	Project Finance
PIT	:	Point in Time
PLR	:	Prime Lending Rate
PNCPS	:	Perpetual Non-Cumulative Preference Shares
PSB	:	Public Sector Bank
QRRE	:	Qualifying Revolving Retail Exposures
RAPM	:	Risk Adjusted Performance Measures
RAROC	:	Risk Adjusted Return on Capital
RARORAC	:	Risk Adjusted Return on Risk Adjusted Capital
RBI	:	Reserve Bank of India
RCAP	:	Regulatory Consistency Assessment Programme
RCPS	:	Redeemable Cumulative Preference Shares
RETPROF	:	Retained Profit
RMA	:	Risk Management Association
RMD	:	Risk Management Department
RNCPS	:	Redeemable Non-Cumulative Preference Shares
ROA	:	Return on Assets
ROC	:	Receiver Operating Characteristic
ROCE	:	Return on Capital Employed
ROE	:	Return on Equity
RORWA	:	Return on Risk Weighted Assets
RRE	:	Residential Real Estate
RWA	:	Risk Weighted Assets
S&P	:	Standard and Poor's
SB	:	Supply Bills
SCB	:	Scheduled Commercial Bank

SD	: Standard Deviation
SME	: Small and Medium Enterprises
SOLVR	: Solvency Ratio
SREP	: Supervisory Review Process
TA	: Total Assets
TL	: Total Liability
TPM	: Transfer Pricing Mechanism
TTC	: Through the Cycle
UGD	: Usage Given Default
UL	: Unexpected Loss
VaR	: Value at Risk
WCDL	: Working Capital Demand Loan
WK	: Working Capital

## Chapter 1

Introduction to Credit Risk

C redit risk is the potential that a bank borrower or a group of borrowers will fail to meet its contractual obligations and the future loss associated with that. For most banks, loans are the largest and most obvious source of credit risk. However, other sources of credit risk exist throughout the activities of a bank, including the banking book and trading book, and both on and off the balance sheet. Banks are also increasingly facing credit risk in various financial instruments other than loans, including acceptances, interbank transactions, trade financing, foreign exchange transactions, financial futures, swaps, bonds, equities and options, in the extension of commitments and guarantees, and the settlement of transactions. Since the exposure to credit risk continues to be the leading source of problems in banks worldwide, banks and their supervisors should be able to draw useful lessons from the experiences. Banks should now have a keen awareness of the need to identify, measure, monitor and control credit risk as well as to determine that they hold adequate capital against these risks and that they are adequately compensated for risks incurred.

By definition, credit risk is the risk resulting from uncertainty in counterparty's ability or willingness to meet its contractual obligations. Credit risk relates to the possibility that loans will not be paid or that investments will deteriorate in quality or go into default with consequent loss to the bank. If credit can be defined as "nothing but the expectation of a sum of money within some limited time," then credit risk is the possibility that this expectation will not be fulfilled. Credit risk exists as long as banks lend money. Credit risk is not confined to the risk that borrowers are unable to pay; it also includes the risk of payments being delayed, which can also cause problems for the bank. The default of a small number of large exposures or cluster defaults in an important loan segment (e.g. housing loans, etc.) could generate very large losses and in the extreme case, could lead to a bank becoming insolvent. As a result of these risks, bankers must conduct proper evaluation of default risks associated with the borrowers.

The effective management of credit risk is a critical component of a comprehensive approach to risk management because lending is the core activity of the banking industry and, hence, such practice is necessary for long-run success in a more complex and competitive global market. The introduction of Basel II has incentivized many of the globally best practiced banks to invest in better credit risk management techniques and to reconsider the analyses that must be carried out to mitigate such risk of loss and benchmark their performance according to market expectations. More importantly, the recent US sub-prime crisis in the mortgage market has further stressed the importance of adopting a better risk management system (especially in the bank's loan book) with appropriate mix of quantitative and qualitative metrics, improved transparency in the decision-making process, and review valuation issues that enhance model validation and monitoring process. It has been observed in developed as well as emerging markets that rapid expansion of credit increases the possibility of relaxation of income criteria/lending standards. This is why, besides good models, due diligence in lending should continue to be the cornerstone of sound banking practices.

The interest in credit risk modelling and their conscious usage has grown significantly over the past few years and is attracting strong interest from all market participants, financial institutions (commercial banks, investment banks and hedge funds) and regulators. The need to react to market developments including venturing into new business or launching new products and services, business continuity issues and meeting the changing regulatory requirements, make risk management a dynamic exercise.

Major Drivers of Credit Risk

Credit risk arises because in extending credit, banks have to make judgements about a borrower's creditworthiness – its ability to pay principal and interest when due. This creditworthiness may decline over time due to change in its financials, poor management by the borrower or changes in the business cycle such as rising inflation, recession, weaker exchange rates or increased competition.

The major drivers of credit risks are:
- **Default risk:** Obligor fails to service debt obligations due to borrower-specific or market-specific factors
- **Recovery risk:** Recovery post default is uncertain as the value of the collateral changes unexpectedly
- **Spread risk:** Credit quality of obligor changes leading to fall in the market value of the loan
- **Concentration risk:** Over-exposure to an individual borrower, group, entity or segment
- **Correlation risk:** Common risk factors between different borrowers, industries or sectors which may lead to simultaneous defaults

Factors affecting credit risk (expected and unexpected losses arising out of adverse credit events) are as follows:
- **Exposure at default (EAD):** In the event of default, how large will be the expected outstanding obligations if the default takes place. The basis for EAD is the outstanding and the external limit booked in the official process systems. EAD has to be estimated on transaction level from historical default information available in the bank. For term loan with full utilization (e.g. bullet or amortizing loans), where there is no chance to further increase the loan exposure in excess of the set transaction limit, EAD = outstanding. However, for lending product facilities such as overdraft, revolving line of credit (viz. credit card) that are characterized by an external limit and average of the utilization of the month (outstanding), EAD = outstanding + UGD × free limit. Where UGD = usage given default or the credit conversion factor (CCF). A portion of the unutilized or free limit has been considered in EAD calculation is because it is expected that a counterparty close to default tends to increase its utilization, while the bank will work against this by reducing the available limits.
- **Probability of default (PD):** The probability that the obligator or counterparty will default on its contractual obligations to repay its debt. It is generally estimated by reviewing the historical default record of loans in a pool with similar characteristics (e.g. rating grades, asset class, industry, region, etc.) or from the temporal movement of gross non-performing assets from standard category of advances.
- **Loss given default (LGD):** The percentage of exposure the bank might lose in case the borrower defaults. Usually it is taken as: LGD comprises the fraction of exposure at default which will not be recovered by the bank following default. It comprises the actual

cost of the loss along with the economic costs (legal costs, interest foregone, time value for collection process, etc.) associated with the recovery process. Historical evidence shows LGD is lower for loans with higher value, more liquid and senior collaterals.

• **Default correlations:** Default correlation measures the possibility of one borrower to default on its obligations and its effect on another borrower to default on its obligations as well. This default dependence is due to common undiversifiable factors. Default events are not independent. Defaults may occur in clusters due to correlation across sectors, regions due to common systematic factors. Correlation of default adds to the credit risk when a portfolio of loans and advances is in consideration vis-à-vis single loans or advances. When many borrowers default together, correlation effects become more pronounced. Thus, the correlation contributions need to be considered carefully in the risk measurement and management of credit portfolios.

Credit risk is generally measured as a risk on individual counter-party transaction or default risk and portfolio risk. The credit risk of a bank's portfolio depends on both the external and internal factors. The elements identified for credit risk are shown in Chart 1.1.

Chart 1.1: Key Drivers of Credit Risk

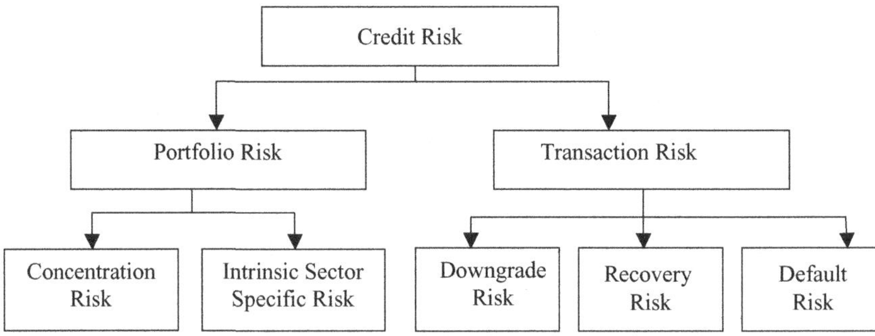

Source: Author's own illustration to explain different drivers of credit risk.

As a result of these risks, bankers must know which, when and how much credit risk to accept to strengthen bottom line, and also conduct proper evaluation of the default risks associated with borrowers. In general, protection against credit risks involves maintaining high credit standards, appropriate portfolio diversification, good knowledge of borrower's affairs (or behaviour) and accurate monitoring and collection procedures.

Based on the Basel Committee recommendations, encouraging banking supervisors to provide sound practices for managing "credit risk", Reserve Bank of India (RBI) has issued Guidance Note on Credit Risk and advised banks to put in place, an effective Credit Risk Management System.

Borrower Level Risk vs. Portfolio Risk

When making credit decisions during lending, there is always a risk that the borrower might default on its contractual obligations to repay principal and interest. The risk factors that are unique to the borrower causing them to default are called borrower-specific default risk. Borrower-specific risk can be measured by using credit rating (e.g. borrower-specific PD and facility-specific LGD) and tracking the borrower-rating movements. Portfolio risk arises from the composition of or concentration of bank's exposures to many assets to various sectors. Systematic factors are the external risk factors that affect the fortunes of a proportion of the borrowers in the portfolio. Concentration risk results from having a number of borrowers in the portfolio, whose fortunes are affected by a common factor. This common factor is also called correlation factor (default or asset correlation). Systematic factors correlate the portfolio risk to changes in macroeconomic environment (e.g. GDP growth rate, unemployment rate, fiscal deficit, etc.).

Credit-risk modelling is being extended into evaluating portfolio risk, especially in the areas of commercial and industrial loans, management of asset allocations in the loan portfolio and portfolio monitoring. The portfolio risk is influenced by idiosyncratic borrower-specific risk and external systematic risk. The internal borrower-specific risk can be managed by adopting proactive loan policy, good quality credit analysis, prudent loan monitoring and sound credit culture. The external risk factors can be managed by diversifying the portfolio, correlation analysis, setting norms for borrower and sector limits (VaR based or regulatory limits), and through effective loan review mechanism and portfolio management.

Importance of Management of Credit Risk in Banks

Lending is the major activity of banks and, thus, is the constant credit risk faced by them. Adequately managing credit risk in a bank is critical for its long-term survival and growth. Credit risk management is important for banks because of the following reasons:

A. Market realities

- **Structural increase in non-performing assets**: These result in massive write-downs and losses. The increase in stressed assets badly hit the banks as provision and capital requirements go up sharply, which squeeze their profit level. Subprime loans in the housing sector were one of the most important causes of the US financial crisis of 2008. Recently, a sector-wise analysis by RBI (2014) demonstrates the challenge of stressed assets in the Indian banking system intensified during 2013–14 due to the rising incidence of loan defaults in infrastructure, retail, small-scale industries (SSIs) and agriculture. This has resulted in slowdown in the system-level credit growth.
- **Higher concentrations in loan portfolios**: Over-exposure to a borrower or related group of borrowers can pose risks to the earnings and capital position of a bank in the form of unexpected losses. Higher loan concentration makes banks vulnerable during economic downturn due to incidents of clustered defaults.
- **Capital market growth**: It produces a "Winner's Curse" effect due to increased competition as many companies have alternate channels to raise funds (through bond and equity instruments).
- **Increasing competition**: Higher competition among banks to book big loans leading to lower spreads and net interest margin. This is a primary concern for top management in banks.
- **Declining and volatile values of collateral**: A decline or volatility in collateral value warrants greater amount of credit risk due uncertainty in loan recovery. Both the East Asian crisis (1997–98) and US subprime crisis (2008) have revealed that collateral value falls faster than the borrowers' increasing chance of default.
- **Growth of off-balance sheet credit products**: The rapid growth of off-balance sheet products like various structured products (e.g. collateralized debt obligations), credit derivatives (like credit default swaps), etc. to trade the credit risk positions has heightened the need for more prudent bank regulation.

B. Changing regulatory environment

- Basel II (pillar I, II and III requirements) and Basel III (dynamic provisioning, stress testing, counter cyclical buffer, etc.)

The regulatory compliance enables a bank to establish a risk management framework, set appropriate control process and improve corporate governance framework. The regulatory compliance is involuntary in nature and enhances a lot of values for the organization.

C. Institution's risk vision

- **Capital is a scarce resource, need optimal utilization:** The success or return in a project of a Financial Institution (FI) is observed by its stakeholders (market competitors, shareholders, debt-holders, etc.). If the FI is engaging into new business or expanding its existing business, it requires capital as a buffer against unexpected risk of losses.
- **Improve Risk-adjusted Returns on Capital (RAROC) and risk-based pricing:** A Risk Adjusted Performance Measurement Framework would guide it to link its business growth targets, risk management process and shareholders' expectations.

Combining the principles of risk management with those of shareholder value creation allows the lender to exploit the strengths of each for better strategic planning. In this regard, a risk adjusted performance measurement framework may act as a comprehensive tool for a financial institution. Risk management makes bankruptcy less likely, by making us aware of the volatility of overall cash flows. It reduces the cost of financial distress and gives a bank better access to capital markets. A comprehensive credit risk management framework is crucial for better reputation with the regulators, customers, shareholders and employees.

Role of Capital in Banks: The Difference between Regulatory Capital and Economic Capital

While housing prices were increasing in the US market, consumers were saving less and both borrowing and spending more.[1] Easy credit, and a belief that house prices would continue to appreciate, had encouraged many sub-prime borrowers to obtain adjustable-rate mortgages (ARM). The credit and house price explosion led to a building boom and eventually to a surplus of unsold homes, which caused the US housing prices to reach its peak and then begin declining in mid-2006. Refinancing became more difficult, once house prices began to decline in many parts of the US that resulted in higher loan to value ratios (LTV). Borrowers who found themselves unable to escape higher monthly payments began to default. The US sub-prime crisis has, thus, revealed the vul-

---

[1]   See Bureau of Economic Analysis – Personal Savings Chart (2009).

nerability of the financial institutions due to interaction between falling housing prices and homeowners' home equity lines of credit.[2] The fall in house prices led to sharp rise in mortgage defaults and foreclosures, which had increased the supply of homes on the market and caused house prices to fall further. The rising unemployment rate at a latest state has attenuated the trouble for the industry, and the economy was caught under a vicious cycle (Figure 1.1). To break this trap, the US government needed to step in with capital injections as revival measure for banks and the entire system.

Figure 1.1: Vicious Cycle of Capital Problem

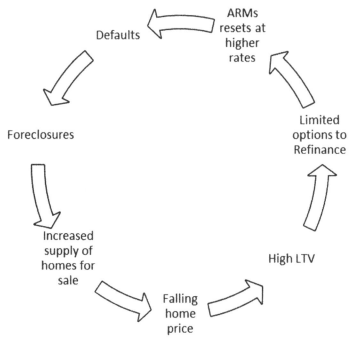

Source: Author's own summary of various causative factors that were responsible for the housing loan defaults in US and how increased foreclosures induced vicious cycle. This was indicated by various studies in the US done by Moody's, many reviews by Federal Reserve, USA; Dept. of Statistics and Operations Research (STOR), UNC; and also mentioned in Wikipedia..

---

[2] On a national level, housing prices peaked in early 2005, began declining since 2006. Increased foreclosure rates in 2006–07 by the U.S. homeowners led to a crisis in August 2007 for the sub-prime mortgage market that has triggered global financial crisis and recession.

A bank can also be trapped in such a vicious situation and hence veer towards bankruptcy due to rise in bad quality of assets. A significant deterioration in asset quality will increase the risk weighted assets and provisioning requirements and will thereby eat away its capital and profit. In order to assess the overall capital adequacy ratio (represented by CAR) of the bank, the risk weighted assets (RWA) are added up and then compared with the total available (eligible) capital. A fall in capital adequacy ratio (or CAR) will reduce bank's overall rating and erode the retained earnings due to rise in funding cost and will further worsen its solvency position. Recently, the financial stability report (FSR) of Reserve Bank of India (RBI, 2015) has raised concern over significant erosion in capital and profits of Indian Banks (especially the public sector) due to rise in bad debts and restructured assets. The NPA and restructured loans together increased to 11.1 per cent of the total advances at the end of December 2014. Most of the stressed assets were in five subsectors – mining, iron and steel, textiles, infrastructure and aviation that together constituted 25 per cent of the bank loans in India. An analysis of Table 1.1 containing quarterly data by bank groups shows that gross non-performing assets (GNPAs) have been increasing continuously since March 2012 for public sector banks (PSB) and old private sector banks. The FSR report has also noted that the gross non-performing assets (NPA) ratio for the Indian banking system could touch 4.8 per cent by September 2015 from current 4.6 per cent in March 2015. In view of these developments, it is vital for banks to understand the role and importance of capital for long-term survival.

Capital acts as a buffer to absorb future unidentified losses that protect the liability holders of a bank (depositors, creditors and shareholders). It plays the role a safety belt in the car (same concept like capital adequacy ratio (CAR)) as a protection against any accident. The concept of "Economic Capital" differs from "Regulatory Capital" measure. The Basel Accord uses a two-tier concept of regulatory capital, where core tier 1 consists of retained earnings, equity capital and free reserves, and tier 2 includes mainly borrowings.[3] Internationally, the total capital adequacy ratio is not

---

[3]   Additional tier 1 capital consists of certain debt capital instruments which have loss absorbance capacity. For example, Perpetual Debt Instruments (PDI) and share capital instruments like Perpetual Non-cumulative Preference Shares (PNCPS), etc. are considered as tier 1 capital. Similarly, provisions for NPA or loan loss reserves held against unidentified losses for standard assets, certain type of hybrid debt instruments and share capital instruments like Perpetual Cumulative

Table 1.1: Trends in Quarterly Gross Non-performing Assets of Indian Banks by Banking Groups (%)

Quarter	Mar-12	Jun-12	Sep-12	Dec-12	Mar-13	Jun-13	Sep-13	Dec-13	Mar-14	Jun-14	Sep-14	Dec-14
GNPL%												
All PSBs	2.68	2.93	3.30	3.42	3.30	3.91	4.31	4.63	4.49	4.74	5.09	5.49
PSB-Large	2.66	3.08	3.58	3.59	3.33	3.81	3.86	3.91	3.81	3.95	4.17	4.54
PSB-Medium	2.79	3.00	3.51	3.67	3.54	4.16	4.52	4.70	4.53	4.84	5.30	5.77
PSB-Small	2.60	2.81	3.03	3.16	3.13	3.79	4.39	4.94	4.79	5.08	5.40	5.78
New Pvt.	1.82	1.80	1.75	1.69	1.61	1.71	1.74	1.66	1.48	1.51	1.53	1.56
Old Pvt.	1.95	2.13	2.54	2.59	2.39	2.84	2.89	3.03	2.53	3.12	3.09	3.32
Credit Growth												
All SCBs	17.3	18.20	15.1	14.70	15.10	13.20	15.10	14.20	13.80	12.90	9.50	10.10
All PSBs	16.10	17.10	14.35	13.75	15.70	12.85	16.40	14.30	12.80	12.15	6.70	7.45
All Pvt.	21.80	22.40	21.30	21.80	18.50	17.00	13.20	14.30	16.10	15.20	16.70	17.10
CD Ratio												
All SCBs	77.50	76.70	75.40	77.70	78.10	76.50	77.80	76.90	78.00	77.20	75.90	76.40
IIP Growth	0.61	-0.24	0.43	2.07	2.22	-1.01	1.88	-0.75	-0.43	4.52	1.31	1.52
Non-food Credit Growth	16.97	18.13	15.94	14.27	13.52	13.48	18.17	14.83	14.30	12.97	8.64	9.76

Source: Author's own computations; compiled from CMIE Prowess and Ace-Equity database.

Note: PSB: Public sector banks, IIP: Index of industrial production allowed to fall below 8 per cent. In India, banks are under obligation to maintain minimum Capital to Risk-weighted Assets Ratio (CRAR) of 9 per cent and are encouraged to maintain a tier 1 of CRAR of at least 7 per cent. While "Regulatory Capital (RC)" is the mandatory capital, economic capital is the best estimate of the required capital that FIs use internally to manage their own risk. A proper economic capital model can enable the bank management to anticipate and safeguard themselves from potential problems. Economic capital (EC) is the actual amount of risk capital necessary to support the risk in the business taken on. It is purely a notional measure of risk capital but not of capital held. It does not involve the flow of funds or charge against profit and loss. However, the bank must know the inherent risks in their business and must assess the unexpected losses that could happen. Economic capital is generally used to evaluate the risk-adjusted performance. Moreover, EC measure typically takes into account a portfolio diversification benefit, which is not generally considered in the regulatory capital estimation. The major differences between economic and regulatory capital are nicely summed up by Michel Araten (2006). It was further emphasized that regulatory capital cannot be a substitute of economic capital since capital goals of supervisors and institutions are different. Risk taking is a natural part of banking transactions and banks are in the business of incurring, transforming and managing risk. They are also highly leveraged. The regulatory agency is responsible for creating a sound financial environment and level playing field by setting the regulatory framework where the supervisory agency monitors the financial viability of banks and checks compliance with regulations.

Credit Risk Management Framework

A financial institution or bank must know which, when and how much credit risk to accept to strengthen bottom line and also conduct proper evaluation of the default risks associated with borrowers. In general, protection against credit risks involves maintaining high credit standards, appropriate portfolio diversification, good knowledge of borrower's affairs (or behaviour) and accurate monitoring and collection procedures.

Preference Shares (PCPS) or Redeemable Non-Cumulative Preference Shares (RNCPS) or Redeemable Cumulative Preference Shares (RCPS) issued by banks are also part of tier 2 capital subject to some criteria set under the latest Basel III regulation.

In general, credit risk management for loans involves:

- **Borrower selection:** Selection of borrowers by using proper rating models, and the delegation of rules that specify responsibility for taking informed credit decisions.
- **Limit setting:** Set credit limits at various levels to avoid or control excessive risk taking. Most banks develop internal policy statements or guidelines, setting out the criteria that must be met before they extend various kinds of loan.
- **Portfolio diversifications:** Banks spread their business over different types of borrowers, sectors and geographical regions in order to avoid excessive concentration of credit risk problems and conduct proactive loan portfolio monitoring. In order to monitor and restrict the magnitude of credit risk, prudential limits have been laid down in the loan policy. The portfolio quality is evaluated by tracking the migration of borrowers from one rating category to another under various industries, business segments, etc.
- **Risk-based pricing:** Implementation of a more systematic pricing and adoption of RAROC framework enhances the organization value. A benchmark rate reflective of lending costs of the bank which can be used with an appropriate mark up (credit spread) to lend to various categories of borrowers. For example, a bank can formulate an interim risk pricing policy to price its borrowal accounts based on the rating category. A robust credit-risk-pricing model needs to generate a credit-term structure consistent with empirical properties. Banks should be looking to formulate pricing models that reflect all of the costs and risks they undertake. The pricing model should be realistic, intuitive and usable by the business people.

Credit risk management framework should enable the top management of banks to know which, when and how much credit risk to accept to strengthen bottom line. It constitutes of following steps:

- **Identify the risks:** Data capturing and identifying the drivers through various rating models
- **Measure the risks:** Assess in terms of size, timing and probability for which the bank should have proper systems and tools in place
- **Manage/control the risks**: Based on these measures, various reports can be generated that will help the management in avoiding, mitigating, off-setting and diversifying the credit risks in various portfolio segments

- **Monitor the risks:** Categorize significant changes in risk profile or controls

The critical element in successfully managing a credit risk portfolio is that one must manage the dynamics of credit risk. An understanding of risk-taking and transparency in risk-taking are key elements in the bank's business strategy. The bank's internal risk management processes support this objective. The bank's general ambition should be to match the best practices in risk management. Risk management is a process conducted independently of the business units of the bank.

The sound practices of credit risk management specifically address the following areas:

- Establishing an appropriate credit risk environment
- Operating under a sound credit-granting process
- Maintaining an appropriate credit administration, measurement and monitoring process
- Ensuring adequate controls over credit risk

Although specific credit risk management practices may differ among banks depending upon the nature and complexity of their credit activities, a comprehensive credit risk management programme will address the above four areas. These practices should also be applied in conjunction with sound practices related to the assessment of asset quality, the adequacy of provisions and reserves, and the disclosure of credit risk (BCBS, 2000).

The credit risk management process in a bank should aim at:

- Taking informed credit decisions
- Setting provisioning and reserve requirements against current/future levels of profitability in order to measure risk-adjusted performance
- Establishing minimum pricing levels at which new credit exposures to an obligor may be undertaken (termed as base rate)
- Pricing credit risky instruments and facilities (through estimation of credit spread)
- Measuring the Regulatory Capital (RC) charge following Standardized or IRB approaches
- Measuring the actual risk capital or Economic Capital (EC)
- Calculating the risk-adjusted performance measures such as RAROC

In order to facilitate compliance with Basel norms, Indian banks have made major investments in risk management systems, combining software tools with internal processes. For Credit Risk Management, most of the banks in India now have proper risk management policy that links with loan policy and robust credit rating models, especially for corporate and SME loans, and takes annual review of accounts. As a perquisite for establishment of an effective risk management system, a robust MIS data infrastructure has been set up in all Scheduled Commercial Banks in India. The risk management is a complex function and it requires specialised skills and expertise.

Banks have been moving towards the use of sophisticated models for measuring and managing risks.

A cornerstone of safe and sound banking is the design and implementation of written policies and procedures related to identifying, measuring, monitoring and controlling credit risk. A robust risk management framework can be effectively utilized to enhance the productivity of business activities in a bank. Today's risk managers have to be concerned with the downside of risk (unpleasant surprise component) as well as assess various opportunities for growth. Risk-adjusted return on capital (RAROC), which is the ratio of risk-adjusted net income to the level of risk that the asset or portfolio has, can be used as a tool to assess the profitability of a loan or a pool of loans on a risk-adjusted basis.

Management of credit risk in the bank is mainly governed by Board approved Credit Risk Management Policy, Loan Policy and Recovery Policy. The credit risk management committee (CRMC) formulates policies on standards for presentation of credit proposals, financial covenants, rating standards and benchmarks, delegation of credit-approving powers, prudential limits on large credit exposures, asset concentrations, standards for loan collateral, portfolio management, loan review mechanism, risk concentrations, risk monitoring and evaluation, pricing of loans, provisioning, regulatory/legal compliance, etc. The policy covers corporate, small and medium enterprises, retail, rural/agriculture and investment-related exposures. Credit Risk Management Department (CRMD) enforces and monitors compliance of the risk parameters and prudential limits set by the CRMC or CCC. The CRMD also lays down risk assessment systems (e.g. risk rating), monitors quality of loan portfolio, identifies problems and corrects deficiencies, develops MIS and undertakes loan review/audit.

The credit risk management process is generally articulated in the bank's loan policy, which is approved by the board. Following the RBI's guidelines, each bank has constituted a high level Credit Risk Management Committee (CRMC) or Credit Control Committee (CCC) headed by the Chairman/CEO/ED to deal with issues relating to credit policy and procedures and to analyse, manage and control credit risk on a bank-wide basis. Banks have also set up a credit risk management department (CRMD) independent of the credit administration department. The risk management activities in banks in India are mainly driven by the top management (top-down approach). At portfolio level, Chief Risk Officer (CRO), Risk Management Department (RMD) and Asset Liability Committee (ALCO) manage the overall risks in a banking institution through various committees by setting risk management policies and reporting framework. At transaction level, traders, swap dealers and loan officers manage the risk. The risk culture varies from bank-to-bank depending upon the nature and complexity of their business operations, risk appetite and ownership pattern.

Chart 1.2 explains the risk governance structure in a leading scheduled commercial bank (SCB) in India.

Chart 1.2: Risk Governance Structure in Leading SCB in India

Source: Risk management policy documents of various banks.

In order to ensure adequate control over risk, banks must establish a system of independent, on-going assessment of the bank's credit risk management process and the results of such analysis and reviews must be communicated directly to the board of directors and senior management (BCBS, 2000). The reporting process for sound and effective risk management control process and the role of the risk management department in an FI is illustrated in Chart 1.3.

Chart 1.3: Reporting Structure: Role of Risk Management Department in a Bank

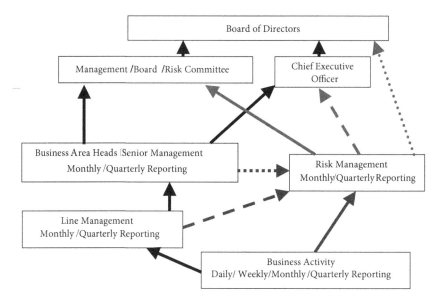

Source: ICAAP policy of various banks.

Management is ultimately responsible for understanding the nature and level of risks undertaken in various lending activities of the bank. Adequate oversight, monitoring and control of credit risk can be done through the involvement of the Board, the Risk Management Committee and the senior management in a bank. The risk management department must provide an independent view to the top management to ensure adequate risk oversight, monitoring, control and assurance. Periodic reporting should be sufficient to allow the board and management to assess risk exposures and decide whether the bank holds sufficient capital relative to identified risks. This enables the top management to develop strategy for maintaining capital levels consistent with risk profile and business plans.

As per the RBI's direction, primary responsibility for risk management must be vested with the Board of Directors (DBOD circular, 1999 and 2010). Banks must have an independent Risk Management Committee or an Executive Committee of Top Executives who will be primarily responsible for risk management function. The Committee will report to the Board. At a more sophisticated level, the bank should have core staff at head office trained in risk modelling and analytical tools. Banks in India have also recently set up a single committee for integrated credit and market risk management. Risk Management Committee is central to formulating and implementing risk management strategies in banks. Chart 1.4 shows the structure of credit risk management framework that integrates risk management activities in a bank to business decisions.

Chart 1.4: Structure of Credit Risk Management

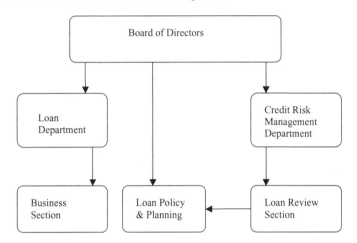

Source: Credit risk management policy of various banks.

The task of the credit risk management department is to identify, monitor and measure risk; develop policies and procedures; verify pricing models; review rating models; and set risk limits in terms of capital adequacy ratio or Value at Risk and portfolio monitoring. This Department is independent of Credit Administration Department and operates in the head office under the overall charge of General Manager to implement, execute and monitor work relating to credit risk management on day-to-day basis in coordination with other departments.

The key tasks for the credit risk management department (CRMD) are:

- Segmentation of the credit portfolio (in terms of risk but not size)
- Rating model requirements for risk assessments in various loan segments (e.g. corporate, SME, housing, personal loans, etc.)
- Collect and store necessary data for measuring risks
- Credit risk reporting requirements for regulatory/control and decision-making purposes at various levels
- Policy requirements for credit risk (credit process and practices, monitoring) for portfolio management

- Align Risk Strategy and Business Strategy to enhance stakeholders' value

The following instruments are used by CRMD to manage credit risk:
- Strengthening the credit approval process: Follow the proper standards
- Setting exposure limits: Either follow the prudential limits or set internal economic capital-based exposure limits
- Risk rating: Use credit risk rating models in assessing borrower risk
- Risk-based pricing: Incorporate risk into profit calculation and work out the loan pricing
- Portfolio management: Segmentation of credit portfolio in terms of risk and monitor the portfolio risk
- Loan review mechanism: Follow industry standards to monitor the risk

Credit risk models, in this regard, are intended to aid banks in accurately identifying and measuring the credit risk for each assets. The model outputs can be judiciously used to take informed credit decisions, compare risk positions, customer profitability analysis, risk based pricing and actively manage/control the risks. In order to ensure that banks do not fail, banking regulators regularly monitor the lending activities of the banks they supervise. Supervisor requires banks to hold capital against the amount of credit risk exposure they hold. The Basel Committee for Banking Supervision has issued a revised Basel II document in order to encourage banking supervisors globally to promote sound practices for managing credit risk. Basel II has made a real contribution by motivating an enormous amount of effort on the part of banks (and regulators) to build (evaluate) credit risk models that involve scoring techniques, default and loss estimates and portfolio approaches to credit risk.

Credit Risk Management: Emerging Challenges for the Banking Sector in India

In recent years, Indian banks have been making great advancements in terms of technology, quality as well as stability such that they have started to expand and diversify at a rapid rate. As a result of this, the needs for professional skills in the modelling and management of credit risk have rapidly increased and credit risk modelling has become an important topic in the field of finance and banking in India. While in the past, most interests were in the assessments of the individual creditworthiness of an obligor, more recently there is a focus on modelling the risk inherent in the entire banking portfolio. This shift in focus is caused, in greater part, by the change in the regulatory environment of the banking industry introduced by the Basel Committee on Banking Supervision (BCBS) in the form of Basel II and Basel III.

The introduction of Basel advanced approaches has incentivized many of the best-practiced banks in the Indian economy to adopt better risk management framework to evaluate their performance relative to the market expectations. From the recent US sub-prime crisis, we have learned that the effective management of risk and optimal allocation of scarce capital is a critical component of a comprehensive approach to risk management and also essential for long-term survival.

The BCBS had issued a revised framework on "International Convergence of Capital Measurement and Capital Standards" in June 2004 and later released the final draft of the same in January 2006. This revised capital accord intended to foster a strong emphasis on risk management practices and encourage ongoing improvements in banks' risk-assessment capabilities. In response to the change in global capital standards, the Reserve Bank of India (RBI) introduced new Basel II capital rule in April 2007 and indicated the bank's journey from standardized to more sophisticated advanced approaches. The foreign banks operating in India and the Indian banks having operational presence outside India were the first which migrated to Basel II with effect from 31 March 2008. Then, all other scheduled commercial banks migrated to these approaches with effect from 31 March 2009. All the scheduled commercial banks in India have been Basel II compliant as per the standardized approach with effect from 1 April 2009.

In July 2009, the timetable for the phased adoption of advanced approaches had also been put by RBI in public domain. Banks desirous of moving to advanced approaches under Basel II have been advised that they can apply for migrating to advanced approaches of Basel II for capital calculation on a voluntary basis based on their preparedness and subject to RBI approval. On 22 December 2011, RBI had released its final guidelines on adopting Basel II IRB approach. Since then, the Indian banks have started their preparations to move towards more sophisticated risk management framework such as Internal Ratings-based (IRB) approach of Basel II. Although the standardized approach retains the relative simplicity of Basel I while increasing the risk sensitivity of regulatory capital requirements, the IRB approach represents the major development from Basel I in calculating minimum capital requirements.

Enormous strides have been made in the art and science of risk measurement and management during the last two decades in line with the developments in the banking regulatory regime worldwide through Basel II and now Basel III capital accord. Due to these changes in the banking and finance industry, the use of internal risk measures in credit portfolio management has increased dramatically. One of the most popularly used risk measures is credit portfolio Value-at-Risk (VaR). It is a technique that uses the statistical analysis of historical data to estimate the likelihood that a given portfolio's losses will exceed a certain amount. There are various methods to calculate VaR, and these methods have a large impact on the way a bank manages its credit portfolio. Furthermore, VaR is incorporated in the Basel II IRB Capital Accord. The advanced approaches provide greater emphasis on banks' own assessment of risk. It encourages improvement of risk management, which also includes focused collation and analysis of data – data quality improves when used for decision-making. Regulatory capital standards based on internal credit risk models would allow banks and supervisors to take advantage of the benefits of advanced risk-modelling techniques in setting capital standards for credit risk. Integrated implementation in banks with wide geographical coverage is a phenomenal challenge. The transition to advanced approaches Basel II IRB would require that banks make fullest use of their newly created IT infrastructure to capture more granular data on a timely and ongoing basis.

The IRB advanced approaches under Basel regime would entail fundamental changes in their balance sheet management philosophy: From deposit taking to lending, from investments to diverse ancillary business, from pricing to capital allocation and stakeholder wealth maximization. The banks will have to incorporate model outputs in business decision-making. This will create a risk-sensitive framework to align capital more closely with underlying risks. Therefore, banks need to correctly assess the capital cushion that would protect them against various business risks in future.

The third Basel accord (or Basel III) was evolved in 2010 in response to the inadequacy in financial regulation revealed by the US financial crisis during 2007–08. After the US crisis, there is an increased focus on credit stress tests and search for more sophisticated approaches to model credit risk. The greatest challenge under Basel III regime is that banks will have to improve their balance sheet to attract shareholder capital, which is considered as core capital. In order to accomplish this, banks need to establish sound processes by which they can assign economic capital to transactions, products, customers and business lines, which is known as risk-based capital allocation. Better alignment of capital will increase productivity in banks' business through optimum and efficient decision-making. Nevertheless, in devising internal model capital standards specific to credit risk, banks and supervisors face significant challenges. These challenges involve the further technical development of credit risk models, the collection of better data for model calibration, the correct model specification and the refinement of validation techniques for assessing model accuracy.

Summary

Banking is a dynamic business where new opportunities as well as threats are constantly emerging. Banks are in the business of incurring, transforming and managing risk and are also highly leveraged. Only through steady progress in measuring and managing risk, the financial institutions can remain vibrant, healthy and competitive in the market. This perhaps has made risk management a dynamic exercise that needs continuous process updating. Credit risk is the largest element of risk in the books of most banks and financial institutions. Banks allocate greater proportion of their regulatory capital to credit risk. As a smart risk taker, banks need to manage the credit risk inherent in the entire portfolios as well as the default risk in individual credit or transaction level. The goal of credit risk management is to maximize risk-adjusted rate of return by maintaining credit risk exposure within acceptable parameters. Risk analysis, monitoring and reporting sends information to the top management of the organization to take strategic decisions through capital allocation, risk diversification or adopt risk mitigation strategies.

A proper credit risk management framework enables banks to identify, assess, manage it proactively and enhance performance at individual level or at entity level. Banks may follow risk-adjusted performance measures (RAPM) to compare loan portfolio performance. Board of directors of a bank have to take responsibility for approving and periodically reviewing credit risk strategy. Credit risk management department takes responsibility to implement the credit risk strategy. A centralized organization structure, comprehensive risk measurement approach, board-approved policies consistent with capital strength and business strategy, strong MIS system for reporting, effective and comprehensive risk-reporting framework and constant review and evaluation are the important parameters of risk management function.

In order to ensure banks do not fail, banking regulators regularly monitor the lending activities of the banks they supervise. The supervisor requires banks to hold capital against the amount of credit risk exposure they hold. The Basel Committee encourages banking supervisors globally to promote sound practices for managing credit risk. Basel II has made a real contribution by motivating an enormous amount of effort on the part of banks (and regulators) to build (evaluate) credit risk models that involve scoring techniques, default and loss estimates, and portfolio approaches to credit risk. Basel III necessitates the implementation of a strengthened operational management of collateral. Basel III further requires performing ongoing validation and back-testing of counterparty exposure models.

This book has been designed to give readers (especially students and practitioners) solid foundation knowledge on credit risk management. In view of this, the various chapters of this book will generally cover all aspects, steps, and issues that should be considered by the credit officer/analyst when undertaking credit risk management at a portfolio level. All these concepts with numerous practical examples will be discussed and elaborated in the backdrop of the Basel advanced approaches.

Key learning outcomes

After studying the chapter and the relevant reading, you should be able to:
- Define credit risk and its major elements
- Understand the major drivers of credit risk
- Understand the constituents of credit risk management
- Understand the importance of credit risk management in FIs
- Understand the role of capital in a bank

Review questions

1. What is credit risk? What are the major drivers of credit risk in Banks or FIs?
2. Explain the nature of credit risk.
3. Why is credit risk management an important component of FI risk management?
4. How do collaterals help protect an FI against default risk?
5. What are the key tasks of the credit risk management department?
6. What is the difference between systematic credit risk and borrower-specific credit risk?
7. What is the role of capital in a bank?
8. Is there any conceptual difference between the Regulatory Capital and Economic Capital?

References

Araten, M. 2006. "Economic vs. Regulatory Credit Capital", *RMA Journal,* March: 42–46.

BCBS. 2000. "Principles for Management of Credit Risk", Basel Committee on Banking Supervision, Basel, September.

Chorafas, D. 2000. *Managing Credit Risk – Volume 1: Analysing, Rating and Pricing the Probability of Default,* London: Euromoney.

Marrison, C. 2002. *The Fundamentals of Risk Measurement,* New York: McGraw Hill.

RBI. 1999. "Risk Management Systems in Banks", DBOD Circular.

RBI. 2010. "Master Circular – Prudential Guidelines on Capital Adequacy and Market Discipline – New Capital Adequacy Framework (NCAF), February 8.

RBI. 2011. "Implementation of the Internal Rating Based (IRB) Approaches for Calculation of Capital Charge for Credit Risk", DBOD, 22 December.

RBI. 2013. "Master Circular – Prudential Guidelines on Capital Adequacy and Market Discipline – New Capital Adequacy Framework (NCAF)", 1 July.

RBI. 2014. "Re-emerging Stress in the Asset Quality of Indian Banks: Macro Financial Linkages" by S.M. Lokare, working paper series (DEPR): March 2014. Available at: http://rbidocs.rbi.org.in/rdocs/Publications/PDFs/WSN03070214F.pdf

RBI. 2014. "Master Circular – Basel III Capital Regulations", 1 July.

RBI. 2015. "Financial Stability Report (FSR)", June.

Saunders, A. and Linda Allen. 2002. *Credit Risk Measurement: New Approaches to Value at Risk and Other Paradigms,* New York: John Wiley & Sons.

Saunders, A., and M. M. Cornett. 2000. *Financial Institutions Management: A Risk Management Approach,* third edition. New York: McGraw Hill.

Shimko, D. 2004. *Credit Risk-Models and Management,* second edition, London: RISK Books.

## Chapter 2

Credit Rating Models

redit ratings represent an opinion on the inherent credit quality of a borrower and act as a summary of diverse risk factors to indicate the default probability of the borrower. Risk assessment is the key objective and, hence, the assessment revolves around the measures of risk for creditors. The task for credit scoring is assigning a numeric formula to arrive at a summary number, which aggregates all the risks of default related to a particular borrower. The final score should be a relative indicator of a particular outcome (most often, creditworthiness or default probability of a borrower). However, as of now, credit-scoring models are not only limited to predicting credit worthiness but also used in predicting potential default.

Rating matters to ascertain the financial health of individual obligor, facilities and portfolios and thereby assist in lending decisions. Ratings allow to measure credit risk and to manage consistently a bank's credit portfolio, that is, to alter the bank's exposure with respect to the type of risk. Ratings are useful for pricing of a bond or a loan with respect to the type of risk. As Indian commercial banks start appreciating the need for a structured credit risk management framework, it is imperative for them to incorporate some systematic process that will comprehensively and objectively capture and evaluate the creditworthiness of the corporate/SME/retail clients of a bank in the perspective of changing market dynamics and to store the historic credit rating data for future generation of default and transition probability information.

Whether the credit granted is for working capital requirements or for project finance, it is important to take a long-term view of the industry as well as the business position of a company while rating it and not just the underlying financials of the company. While assessing the financials of the company, the bank's view on the trend in past financial performance, expected future financial performance, ability to raise funds and quality of financial statements submitted need to be taken into consideration. Also, it has been observed that management quality has a significant impact on a company's performance, irrespective of the industry and business characteristics. All these features need to be captured and analyzed in detail.

Credit scoring system can be found in all types of credit analysis from consumer credit to commercial loans. Risk assessment is the key objective and, hence, the assessment revolves around the measures of risk for creditors. The task is to assign a numeric formula to arrive at a summary number, which aggregates all the risks of default related to a particular borrower. The final score is a relative indicator of a particular outcome (most often, creditworthiness or default probability of a borrower). However, in a Basel II IRB (Internal Ratings-based) world, credit-scoring models are not only limited to predicting credit worthiness but also used in predicting potential default.

Benefits of Scoring the Borrower:

i.   As finance is risk management, scoring facilitates risk management;
ii. It quantifies risk as the percentage chance that something "bad" will happen;
iii. It makes risk evaluation explicit, systematic and consistent (not just loan officer's "gut feeling") and
iv. It quantifies risk's links with borrower characteristics.

A properly designed good credit scoring system allows creditors to evaluate thousands of applications consistently, impartially and quickly. Therefore, better risk management implies more loans with same effort, greater outreach, more market share and greater profits. The biggest benefit is that it strengthens the culture of explicit conscious risk management.

Rating is an objective assessment of the present and future economic situation (e.g. solvency) of customers. This assessment is often designated in a letter symbol, e.g. AAA, AA, A, BBB, BB, etc. Some banks give codes like CR1, CR2, CR3, ... or AB1, AB2, ..., AB7 or SB1, SB2,..., SB10; A++, A+, A, ..., etc. However, different rating levels have to be distinguished by a cardinal measure of risk instead of an ambiguous ordinal approach. Ratings should allow a bank to derive the implied probability of default (PD) and provide an early warning signal about deteriorating financial health of an individual obligor.

Many internationally active best practices banks are using in-house rating systems for an objective assessment of the client's default risk which is a perquisite for:

i.   Credit decisions and limit sanctioning
ii.   Margin calculation for granting loan
iii. Risk-based pricing decisions
iv.   Loan portfolio monitoring
v.   Estimation of expected loss (EL) and unexpected loss (UL) for analysis of the adequacy of loan loss reserves or capital
vi.   Measuring potential concentrations in loan portfolio
vii. Management of credit portfolio and credit allocation decision
viii. Meeting regulatory requirements

The rating system is expected to be applied to assess the creditworthiness of new customers, surveillance of portfolio quality and calculation of capital requirement. In connection with the calculation of regulatory capital according to IRB approach, it is essential to obtain an estimate of the probability of default (PD) for each rating class. This estimation process has been illustrated in Chapter 3. Furthermore, internal rating system often serves as a credible tool for credit policy within a bank. For example, senior management can stipulate some minimum rating as hurdle grade (or called passing grade), such as passing grade (or hurdle grade) BBB or above, might be required for sanctioning a loan. From the regulatory point of view, a bank must develop a systematic approach to measuring, monitoring and controlling credit risk within an institution. The rating systems should be based primarily on an institution's own experience (internal data). The rating system is a process that is embedded in the institution's credit culture. Irrespective of the regulatory compliance, ratings should become a central part of modern credit risk management within banks.

Types of Scoring Models

There are basically two broad categories of rating models that can be used by banks:

i. Custom Models
ii. Generic Models

Custom models are specific to a bank's internal loan portfolio history. But it is a time-consuming and costly exercise to collect and maintain relevant account level historical data. However, the accuracy of such models is potentially two or three times that of Generic Models. It is also fully understood by the user bank because it has been developed internally such that it fits the bank's own business culture. On the other hand, generic models are ready-made models developed by various agencies that are not bank specific. It has minimal data requirement and outcomes are generic and may have industry splits. It may be less powerful, but it is universally accepted. However, it needs proper customization.

The rating assignment techniques are broadly of two types:

i. Expert Judgement Systems: Credit officers have significant discretion to interpret key factors and assign ratings. However, different officers could reach different rating conclusions based on the same set of data and factors. This flexibility is both a strength and weakness of the process.

ii. Model-driven System: Rating assignment is based on model output. It is based on a very specific list of inputs (i.e. model drivers or factors) that are typically vetted statistically or mathematically. It can include quantitative as well as qualitative factors, but qualitative factors must be expressed quantitatively (using categorical scores or dummy variables). Ratings are replicable once the model is finalized.

The relative strengths and weaknesses of both the rating models have been given in Table 2.1.

Table 2.1: Expert Judgement System vs. Model-driven System Rating Model

Type of Rating Model	Strengths	Weaknesses
Expert-based judgement		
	Very (too) flexible	Lacks transparency
	Can incorporate different variables, depending on the situation	Subject to bias
		Expensive, time consuming
		Quality depends on analyst capabilities
Model-driven		
	Efficient	Less flexible

Table 2.1 contd.

Table 2.1 contd.

	Transparent	May not be designed to anticipate all situations
	Output is typically easy to understand	Difficult to incorporate qualitative factors
	Produces consistent results	Ratings quality dependent on quality of model

Source: Author's own summary from various rating techniques and based on industry feedbacks.

Different Rating Approaches

There exist a variety approaches to find and factor relevant information for assessing the creditworthiness of a borrower.

From a regulatory point of view, internal credit rating system means:

i. A systematic approach to measuring, monitoring and controlling credit risk within an institution. This should be properly customized with the bank's internal data

ii. A process that is embedded in the institution's "credit culture"

iii. A tool tailored to the institution's day-to-day credit risk management activities

Economists, credit analysts, and credit officers employ many different models to assess the default risk on loans and bonds. These vary from relatively simpler (qualitative or judgemental) to the highly quantitative advanced models. A credit officer/risk manager may use more than one model to arrive at a credit decision or pricing of loans. The factors that determine borrower default risk include "borrower-specific factors" that are idiosyncratic to the individual borrower and "market-specific (or systematic) factors" that are external to the borrower and have impact on all borrowers applying for credit. The scoring models then weight these factors to estimate an overall score to come to an overall credit decision. Borrower-specific factors are idiosyncratic in nature, which capture specific borrower problems like management factors (experience, ownership pattern, corporate governance, etc.), borrower-specific financial risk factors (volatility in earnings, leverage position, collateral, etc.) and borrower characters (age, ownership, constitution, demographic profile, job status, etc.). Default is also driven by market-specific factors like unemployment rate, macroeconomic growth rate, industry factors, changing market condition (recession, fall in demand, price, etc.), legal factors, environmental factors which are external to the borrower.

The four broad categories of scoring models used to estimate the client's probability of default (PD) are:

Expert Rating Systems

Expert rating systems are systems where the human experts' learning has been incorporated into a set of rules, some of which have been developed using inferences. This is a non-standardized approach as it is based on experts' opinion or analysts' opinion. Many experts can sit together and draft a rating model by sharing their credit experiences. Because of its reliance on many subjective judgements of the FI manager, this rating process is often called expert rating system.

Such rating model is generally based on "five common Cs" of credit analysis that are described by:

- **Character of a borrower:** How well you know the person or family or corporate group is a measure of the reputation, willingness to repay and repayment history of the borrower. This is a very important factor for evaluating firms as well as retail borrowers. For example, credit history or track record of the borrower, relationship between borrower and lender, age of the firm, etc. are factors that are generally qualitative in nature. Interestingly, the character factors can change over time and, therefore, banks need to track borrower information properly.
- **Capital structure:** This refers to how much is being asked for or the equity contribution of owner and its leverage position. For example, high leverage (i.e. higher debt to equity ratio) suggests greater chance of default than low leverage. Similarly, one can look into debt service coverage ratio, current ratio, interest coverage ratio, etc.
- **Capacity to pay or the repaying ability**: The ability of the borrower to repay can be captured through earnings and earnings volatility, asset growth, profitability ratios (e.g. return on asset, operating profit margin, etc.).
- **Collateral is** what is the applicant willing to put up from their own resources. In the event of default, a banker has claims on the collateral pledged by the borrower to limit its losses. The higher the value of the collateral (or margin) and its seniority standing, lower will be the exposure risk of the loan.
- **Cyclicality:** It means the conditions in the market, that is to say, the state of the business cycle (GDP growth rate, unemployment rate, demand growth, foreign exchange position, etc.). This is an important element in determining industry credit risk.

There is no fixed predetermined set of criteria the analyst recognizes. The criteria might be different for diverse individual counterparty depending upon their constitution and industry affiliation. This approach is easy to implement and depends on the knowhow of the analyst and the expert experiences. It is worthwhile to mention that a statistical credit scoring model can also be devised based on the above 5C's principle.

The expert judgement-based models have the following specific inputs towards lending decision as depicted in Chart 2.1.

Chart 2.1: Expert Judgement Rating Model

Source: Rating Manual of various banks in India and CRAs rating documents.

These rating systems are generally used by the banks. The crucial risk categories are listed below:

- **External/Industry Risk:** Industry outlook, competition, regulatory and environmental risks, contemporary issues, like WTO norms, their implications on industry prospects, etc.
- **Financial Risk:** Various ratios capture financial performance, like sales, profitability, cash flows, debt structure, earnings stability, liquidity and solvency of firms, etc. Since it is mainly based on financial performance of companies, auditors quality should also come into the assessment risk factors.
- **Business Risk:** R&D capabilities, capacity utilization, compliance to environmental norms, marketing and distribution network, user product profile, etc.
- **Management Risk:** Management track record, experiences, strategic initiatives, corporate governance, customer relationship, achievement of targets, length of the relationship with the bank, etc.
- **Facility Risk:** The presence of collateral as guarantee and its nature. Project risk is also part of it.

In assessing corporate rating, the impact of new project risk is also assessed in greater detail. Besides the purpose of the project, management experience and track record, the capital cost, fund raising ability, raw material sources, demand outlook, competitive environment, marketing arrangements, etc. are extensively analyzed. A common way of developing an expert judgement-based rating system is to ask the internal credit risk experts to rank the borrower characteristics according to their importance for credit risk prediction and suggest weights according to their importance. The performance of the weights can be validated by mapping with actual experiences through proper back testing. Statistical models may still play a role, though this may vary widely across institutions.

Internal Credit Rating System

Internal (in-house) credit rating system is a systematic approach to measuring, monitoring, and controlling credit risk within an institution. According to the regulator, it is primarily based on an institution's own experience and a process that is embedded in the institution's credit culture. Banks' internal rating models are of two types: expert-based judgemental rating model and statistical scoring model. Most of the public sector banks in India use expert systems either developed internally or provided by the vendors (e.g. RAM model of CRISIL) to evaluate the risk of corporate accounts. Chart 2.2 summarizes the types of credit assessment models generally used by internationally best practices banks.

Some leading private sector banks use a mix of heuristic (or expert-based) methods and other two quantitative models in practice for assessing the risk of commercial loans. A set of regression models and discriminant analysis may be very useful to serve the purpose. Waagepetersen (2010) had used a logistic model to capture the relation between the characteristics of the counterparty and the expert rating. A decision-tree-based classification model using various nodes is also used to develop judgemental rating models. The use of artificial neural networks is minimal in Indian banking industry as the interrelationship between the risk factors is not easily understood by the top management. Few private sector banks and foreign banks operating in India use option pricing models to closely monitor big corporates. This has been explained in the later part of the chapter.

Chart 2.2 Credit Scoring Model

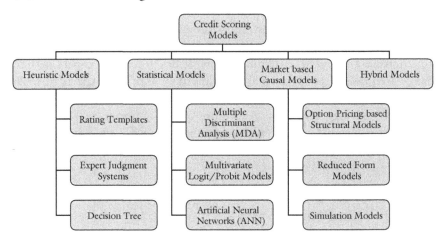

Source: OeNB (2004). Guidelines on Credit Risk Management-Rating Models and Validation. Oesterreichische National Bank (OeNB), Vienna, Australia.

In-house rating systems exist in most of the banks in India since the introduction of Basel II regulation by RBI in 2007–08. Banks have devoted considerable resources in developing internal risk models for approval of loans, portfolio monitoring, management reporting, etc. Rating templates allow banks to calibrate their internal rating process and also enable them to use in a consistent manner and monitor the portfolio. Most of the commercial loan rating models used by banks in India are judgemental type.

Table 2.2 is an illustrative example of a summarized rating template used by banks.

These rating sheets are used for borrower types to develop scores. Scoring factors are generally assigned linearly for each criteria (e.g. very good/excellent = 6; good = 5; satisfactory = 4; higher risk = 3; poor = 2 and very poor = 1 or a fixed multiple of these values (say multiple of 100). However, the chosen functions have to be justified logically by the experts and need to be properly calibrated. Maximum weightage is given to the financial risk factor. Note that the financial and management factors may impact differently on various industries. The business factors may also vary with sectors. The credit analyst bank personnel would enter his/her opinion on all relevant variables in the form of a score. All scores are then weighted to obtain overall score that is mapped to an internal rating category. The number of grades on internal scales may vary from bank to bank. The choice of weight is crucial. It can be either obtained statistically or through experiences of the key experts sharing their wisdom or a combination of both or through external mapping process. Some rating processes use statistical (MDA, regression analysis, etc.) or mathematical techniques (like decision tree, artificial neural network, etc.) to arrive at the weights. Like logistic regression, a number of corporate credit scoring models have been constructed using a decision tree structure following a classification rule. The weights need to be calibrated on a fairly large sample and back-tested regularly and should be consulted with the credit experts for their judgements.

Table 2.2: Example of an Internal Rating Template

Risk Factors	Factors	Weight	Scales (1–6)	Scores (50–300)	Risk weighted Score
Corporate Risk Score		A	B	C	=A×C
Industry (External) Risk	• Extent of competition • Industry outlook • Industry financials: e.g. return on capital employed (ROCE) • Earning stability • Cyclicality • Technology risk	15%		95	
Financial Risk	• Profitability-various ratios like return on assets (ROA), operating profitability (PBIT/TA), turnover ratio (Sales/TA) • Liquidity-working capital ratio (NWC/TA), current ratio (CA/CL), quick ratio [(CA-inventories)/CL], equity and reserves, etc. • Leverage-debt to equity (D/E), debt to tangible assets, debt to net-worth (TL/NW), etc. • Solvency-retained earning/TA, interest coverage ratio (PBIT/I), debt service coverage ratio (DSCR), etc. • Financial flexibility: Ability to raise capital from market • Financial Projection: 3-year projection • Quality of financial statement	45%		105	

Table 2.2 contd.

Table 2.2 contd.

Management Risk	• Management experiences • Group support (or group interlocking) • Management succession plan • Corporate governance: Ethics, disclosures • Management track record • Strategic initiatives • Achievements: Sales, profit, capital, etc. • Credibility: Goodwill • Relationship with the bank or track record	15%	110
Business Risk	• Market share analysis • Price flexibility to adjust cost • Raw material related risks • Distribution set up • Geographical diversity of markets • Consistency with quality • Advertising and promotional activities • R&D activities • Adoptions to patents	10%	80
Facility & Project Risk	• Collateral security position- security type, collateral coverage ratio (CCR), liquidity, seniority, etc. • Personal or corporate guarantee • Past payment record • Compliance with terms of sanction • Operations of the account • Asset coverage ratio, DSCR for the project (in case of term loan)	15%	100
Total		100%	101
Overall Rating			BB

Source: Rating Manual of certain banks in India.

Note: A factor score 6 indicates extremely favourable or lowest degree risk; a score of 1, on the other hand, entails maximum degree of risk or highly unfavourable position that could affect the company in a detrimental way. TA = Total assets; PBIT = Profit before interest and tax; I = Interest expenses; CA = Current assets; CL = Current liability. CCR = Approximate value of collateral/Loan balance.

Chart 2.3 shows the step-wise development process of an expert-based rating model in a bank.

Chart 2.3: Development Process of Internal Credit Rating Model in a Bank

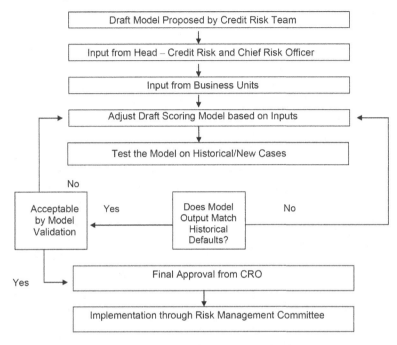

Source: Based of the feedback received from risk departments of some leading private sector banks in India.

The above exercise enables a bank to check how the rating model fits well with the existing credit origination and administration processes. The entire rating model implementation process needs to be clearly documented for obtaining supervisory approval. A more systematic methodology for incorporating expert judgement into credit risk assessment of a commercial exposure (corporate, SME, etc.) can promote accuracy, objectivity and consistency in the rating process and thereby make an institution more competitive and better able to meet regulatory expectations under the IRB approach.

One Tier vs. Two-tier Rating System

Rating is an opinion on the inherent credit quality of a borrower (say a company) and/or the credit instrument (e.g. bond or loan facility rating). The rating process may be one dimensional (borrower-specific obligor rating) or two dimensional (obligor as well as facility rating). One-dimensional rating mainly focuses on borrower risk. This type of rating was followed by most banks in India till 2008. A two-tier rating system has obligor rating as well as facility rating. Indian banks are now shifting to two-tier rating where rating criteria are applied separately to the borrower and the various facilities existing with the borrower. The main objective is to separate the default risk of the borrower from the recovery risk associated with each facility.

The obligor rating indicates that the chance of the borrower as a legal entity is defaulting. Facility rating indicates the loss of principal and/or interest on that facility. Risk characteristics are specific to the advance cum collateral. The obligor rating is an indicator of probability of default (PD) that evaluates the creditworthiness of an obligor (borrower). The facility rating is an indicator of loss given default (LGD) and evaluates the riskiness of a facility. It mainly checks the facility structure, the covenant's tightness and nature, type (seniority) and liquidity of the collateral. Covenants imply clauses in the lending contract. For example, a bank can set some benchmarks for the high risk companies (the limitations involve certain debt service and working capital requirement, repayment terms, use of collaterals, periodic reporting of stocks, etc.) and monitor performance against those benchmarks. The borrower rating and facility rating should be done independently to remove any bias.

A credit officer can arrive at either a numerical one-dimensional score or two-dimensional scores if the rating manual clearly specifies the respective weights and scores. For example, the obligor level one-dimensional total numerical score is 80 and it corresponds to a rating scale of III (or "A" grade) which has an implicit PD of 0.80 per cent. Similarly, two-dimensional rating also provides LGD rating of scale II which implies an expected LGD of 35 per cent. This LGD estimate may either be based on the expert opinion of the facility structure (collateral type, covenant tightness, seniority structure, guarantee coverage, legal enforceability of the security, etc.) and anticipation of recovery rate or by using statistically developed LGD predictor model.

Facilities proposed/sanctioned to a borrower are assessed separately under this dimension of rating. A bank can use one-dimensional rating for computation of IRB risk; weights provided rating reflects expected loss (EL). Two-dimensional rating is an improvement over one-dimensional rating because it separately addresses both PD and LGD which are the two important drivers of credit risk of a loan.

Table 2.3 illustrates how a two-dimensional rating can be used in credit management in a bank. Each loan may be evaluated on PD rating and LGD rating and then a credit decision may be made on both facility rating as well as borrower rating. The regulator may ask the banks to map the accounts based on borrower and facility rating in this two-axis table to check whether credit decisions have been made using two-tier rating system. However, this high-low risk scenario that has been described is perhaps the simplest scenario. Actually a bank may have to combine at least seven standard borrower grades and more than seven facility grades in taking the actual credit decisions. This may be specified clearly in the rating manual after following a proper calibration process.

Table 2.3: Use of Two-Dimensional Rating in Credit Management

Borrower Risk/ Facility Risk	Facility → Rating	Low Risk	High Risk
	Borrowing ↓ Rating	FR1	FR2
Low Risk	BR1	(BR_{LOW}, FR_{LOW})	(BR_{LOW}, FR_{HIGH})
High Risk	BR2	(BR_{HIGH}, FR_{LOW})	(BR_{HIGH}, FR_{LOW})

Source: Author's own illustration based on RBI's IRB guidelines (December 2011).

A rating model is a tool tailored to the institution's day-to-day credit risk management activities. From the risk management angle, internal ratings can be used for approving loans, portfolio monitoring and management reporting, analysis of adequacy of reserves and capital, and customer profitability and loan pricing analysis. These uses will definitely impact the rating system design. Banks need to ensure consistency and objectivity in assessing various risk components (with respect to the five Cs) such that common standards can be applied across lending officers. This makes comparability of risk rankings and decisions easier. In this regard, proper documentation of the rating process and use of ratings through credit policy play effective roles.

The regulator expects that a bank's rating system should be able to rate all past, current and future clients. It should be able to cope with all possible clients. A bank should make all possible efforts to ensure that its rating system is flexible enough to cope with all foreseeable types of risk. Banks need to use a common standard to mitigate the above problems. For banks that use either the standardized or the IRB approach, the method of assigning ratings is important because different techniques will require different validation processes and control mechanisms to ensure the integrity of the rating system. It is important for banks to select a transparent and objective methodology as a benchmark and compare their existing rating model and find ways to strengthen its approach. One good option is to mix the bank's existing expert judgement rating process with scorecards derived from statistical analysis of internal data. Scorecard simply acts as a framework for making sure that the right factors are considered in an objective manner and the right weights have been used. This can be done based on a fundamental analysis of the key credit risk drivers for each segment.

Rating Model for Project Finance (PF)

Project finance is limited resource funding typically used to finance large capital-intensive infrastructure projects through a special purpose vehicle (SPV). India spends almost 6 per cent of GDP on infrastructure. Most of the financing needs are in electricity, roads and bridges, telecom infrastructure, railways, chemical processing plants, mines, irrigation and water supply, and sanitation. The primary source of repayment is the income generated by the asset, rather than independent capacity of a broader commercial enterprise. Basel II IRB approach assumes a clear distinction between project and corporate loans. Unlike corporate lending, project performance is the core of project finance. The single asset nature, strong sponsors, priority of liens on and pledges of the project collaterals, loan syndication make project finance loans outperform corporate finance loans.

In project financing, the debt terms are not based primarily on the sponsor's credit support. The principle lender security is the future cash flows of the project itself and, hence, it is a cash-flow lending. Lender is usually paid back almost exclusively out of the money generated from the project (e.g., electricity sold by a power plant) and project assets are treated as security for the exposure. This type of financing is usually for large, capital-intensive projects that involve high cost installations. This might include power plants, mines, transportation infrastructure, telecommunication infrastructure and chemical processing plants. Amongst project finance, Green Field projects are new projects, while brown field is an upgrade or change in an existing project. In assessing risks involved in project finance, it is essential to understand the structure and implementation of the project (i.e. project structure, SPV, sponsors, lenders, suppliers, etc.).

The key risk areas for evaluation of a project are:

i. *Nature of the project* (hydel, thermal, nuclear, non-conventional, etc.)
ii. *Its technical characteristics* (use of technology, equipment quality, operating efficiency, environmental risk, land acquisition risk, etc.)

iii. *Project financials* (equity ownership, cash available for debt service, debt service coverage ratio for the project, internal rate of return, repayment period, total liability/total net worth, debt-equity ratio, etc.)

iv. *Credit-worthiness* of promoters (capability to implement projects, ability to infuse capital)

v. *Location* of the project (availability of inputs, skilled labour, nearness to market, etc.)

vi. *Infrastructure requirements* for operations

vii. *Fuel or input requirements*

viii. *Project implementation* schedule

ix. *Selling and distribution* arrangements

x. *Experience of the management team*

xi. *Political or regulatory risk* (risk of not getting approval due to political or environmental risk)

xii. *Operations and maintenance risk* (track record of the contractor, whether long term maintenance agreement & supply contract exists, off taker risk etc.)

xiii. *Security package* (quality, value and liquidity of assets, lender's control over cash flow, strength of the covenant package)

xiv. *Cash-flow* coverage (robust project model with cash flow, stress tested under a number of downside scenarios like reduced demand, rise in input price, macro-economic shocks), etc.

Following the BCBS (2006), RBI in its Basel II IRB guidelines has specified four supervisory rating grades (standard grades) for project finance exposure: strong, good, satisfactory and weak. Under the IRB approach, project finance (PF) falls under corporate class but in a specialized lending sub-class. The repayment of the exposure depends primarily on the project cash flow and on the collateral value of the project's assets rather than on a well-established end-user entity. Banks will have to conduct risk grading of the projects based on this supervisory slotting criteria that takes into account:

i. **Financial strength:** Market conditions, financial ratios, e.g. debt service coverage ratio (DSCR), loan life coverage ratio (LLCR), debt to equity ratio, etc., stress analysis (testing the project financials under stressed economic condition), etc.

ii. **Political and legal risk environment:** Risk arising out of government intervention and regulatory controls.

iii. **Transaction characteristics**: Technology risk, construction risk (e.g. status of permits), conduct of project operation, completion guarantee and track record of contractor.

iv. **Strength of the sponsor**: Track record, sponsor support, etc.

v. **Security package**: Type, value, liquidity of pledge of assets, covenant's strength.

Table 2.4 shows as to how various risk factors are weighted in assessing the risk of a thermal power project.

Table 2.4: Example of Project Finance Expert-based Rating Model
Case Name: LANCO-ANPARA POWER Pvt. Ltd. (Thermal Power)
Total Bank Exposure: ₹1500 Crore, both fund based and non-fund based

Risk Head	Weight (%)	Risk Score	Overall Weighted Risk Score
Industry risk	15	8.50	1.31
Business risk	30	5.68	1.83
Other key Risks – Build phase	20	6.00	1.20
Financial Risk–Build phase	30	5.10	1.53
Overall risk score	100%		5.87
Overall Rating			Moderate Risk
Key Financials:			
	IRR: 12.97	DSCR: 2.62	DER: 4.00

Source: Project Finance Rating Manual of a Scheduled Commercial Bank in India.

Scoring guide: Strong – Scores above 6; Weak – Scores below 4; Debt service coverage ratio (DSCR) threshold – Not less than 1.5; Internal rate of return (IRR) threshold – 4 per cent and above; Debt equity ratio range – from 2.5:1 to 4:1.

Finally, the internal risk ratings will have to be mapped into one of the four supervisory rating grades, and bank can apply risk weights to determine the required minimum capital as a cushion against unexpected loss. Only those banks that have good historical data (mainly PD) and properly validated internal scoring model can include project finance in the same category as the corporate portfolio to estimate risk weights. The risk weight's computation following supervisory slotting criteria for Project Finance (PF) loans has been shown in Chapter 8, where we have discussed IRB risk weight functions.

Rating Model for SMEs

SME (Small and Medium Enterprises) segment plays a vital role in the economic development of a nation. Credit risk assessment in this segment requires a specific approach, as the factors affecting the creditworthiness are somewhat different compared to those of large corporate entities. Besides financials, various non-financial factors like management risk, legal issues, industry and macroeconomic factors, track records, overriding factors, etc. play a crucial role in determining credit risk.

A rating system for small and medium enterprises (commercial exposures) has the following risk dimensions (see Chart 2.4):

Chart 2.4: SME Rating Chart

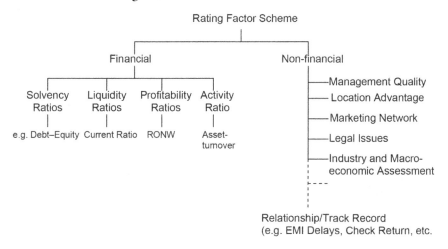

Source: Rating framework of a leading SCB in India.

Since the role of non-financial factors is significantly higher in determining the risk of SME loans (due to absence of audited balance sheet data), the risk officer should be well informed about any negative impact of the various events on the functioning of the SME. The rating obtained needs to be capped at a suitable level, if any of these overriding factors are present. Any news about insolvency, liquidation proceedings in court, petition filed for winding up, tax raid, cheque bounce incidents, fire instances affecting operations, employee fraud, cash adequacy, etc. are examples of such early warning signals.

Risk Rating for Microfinance Institutions (MFIs)

Credit risk rating measures the risk of default of a microfinance institution's (MFI) obligations. Chart 2.5 shows a comprehensive rating model developed by Morgan Stanley's Microfinance Institutions to evaluate risk of Microfinance sector and relative to other sector.[1] The analysis for this rating includes an examination of quantitative and qualitative factors that assess the institution's capacity to repay its financial obligations.

Chart 2.5: MFI Risk-rating Template

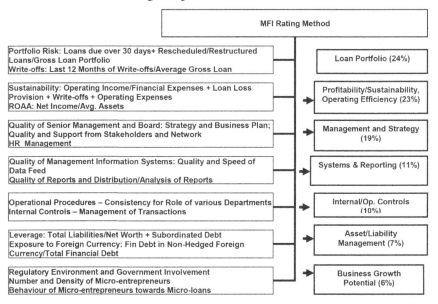

Source: Arvelo et al. (2008).

While loan portfolio risk field is capturing the credit risk part, market risk and liquidity risk segment is covered through asset–liability management field. Similarly, profitability, sustainability and operating efficiency measures the financial risk factor in MFIs. Internal or operational controls evaluate the operational risk. MFI's mission is to support financially excluded individuals with tailored financial services and offer a secure pathway out of debt and cash economy dependency on a sustainable basis. This rating methodology may be used by the banks as a benchmark to rate such loans. Using a similar

---

[1] See Morgan Stanley's "Approach to Assessing Credit Risks in the Microfinance Industry", *Journal of Applied Corporate Finance* 20 (1): 124–34, Winter 2008.

framework as described above, a bank can also develop a rating model for Non-bank Finance Companies (NBFCs) as well.

Country Risk Rating Model

Country risk forms an integral part of credit risk and refers to the possibility that sovereign borrowers of a particular country maybe unable or unwilling to fulfil their foreign currency obligations for reasons beyond the usual risks which arise in relation to lending. Assessment of country risk depends on the analysis of economic, social and political factors that relate to the particular country in consideration. Country risk element should be explicitly recognised while assessing the counterparty risk under the IRB approach.

With increasing international business of banks, the effective management of country risk has become a priority. An effective system aims to signal potential problems before they occur and facilitate the banks to minimize their exposure to these countries. Indian banks have been relying on external country rating agencies like ECGC, Euro money, Dun and Bradstreet, Institutional Investor, etc. for assessing the country risks. However, many cross-country empirical studies indicate that rating agencies are often merely reactionary and fail to predict crisis as was seen in the case of Asian crisis, Brazilian and Russian devaluation. The RBI has, hence, advised that banks must move towards an internal country risk assessment system.

Some of the different models used in country risk assessment are listed as follows:
- Scoring technique based on weighted average of various quantitative and qualitative parameters (judgemental method)
- Probability of default model using logit analysis (statistical method)
- Sovereign risk quantification model based on the expected default frequency over short- and long-term horizons (structural model)

The last two methods have been discussed in the later section of this chapter. The rating inputs can be utilised to set country-wise limits, estimating provisioning requirements and regulatory risk weight computation under IRB. The category limits and provisioning and regional limits will help the banks in avoiding the geographic contagion effect.

The parameters to be included in the model are to capture the different components of country risk, viz. transfer risk, sovereign risk, political risk, cross-border risk, currency risk and structural risks. Broadly, they can be captured by the following indicators:

- *Liquidity Risk Indicators*
  - Foreign exchange generating capability: Exchange rate, trade balance, external reserves, foreign investment positions, etc.
  - Obligations on external debt: Debt situation and debt maturity analysis
- *Domestic Economic Factors*
  - Economic indicators: Real GDP growth rate, investment/GDP, growth in money supply, fiscal balance/GDP, domestic savings, income distribution, etc.
  - Policy changes: Macro-policy changes, export–import policy, regulatory policy changes, price and wage policy
- *Social and Political Risk Factors*
  - Internal factors: Political climate, poverty, distribution of income and unemployment, foreign investment climate, etc.
  - External factors: External political threats, relationship with main trading partners, regional factors, etc.

The liquidity and domestic economic factors address the government's ability to repay its obligations. Social and political risk factors address the government's willingness to repay debt. Actually, these risk factors are interrelated.

In addition to quantitative aspects, it is extremely important to incorporate qualitative (judgemental) information as well. Qualitative analysis refers to the assessment of economic, financial and socio-political fundamentals of an economy that can affect the investment return prospect in a foreign country. The following six elements are important:

i. Social and welfare dimension of the development strategy; for example, geographic situation, natural resource endowment and self-sufficiency in raw material, physical infrastructure, population growth, labour force and unemployment, health care, GDP per capita, development indicators, etc.

ii. Macroeconomic fundamentals; for example, domestic economy assessment, macroeconomic policy evaluation, balance of payment analysis, etc.

iii. External indebtedness evolution, structure and burden; for example, solvency and liquidity position

iv. Domestic financial system situation; for example, efficiency of banking system, development of financial system, legal, accounting and supervisory infrastructure, etc.

v. Assessment of the governance and transparency issues; for example, transparency and corruption indicators

vi. Evaluation of political stability

External Credit Rating Systems

The most popular and long established credit rating systems are those of the external credit rating agencies (CRAs). The big three rating agencies are Moody's Investors Service, Standard & Poor's (S&P) and Fitch. The first two highly specialized agencies are based in the US, while Fitch has head-quarters in New York and London. In India, there are three major credit rating agencies: CRISIL of S&P, ICRA of Moody's, Fitch and CARE. Agency ratings aim at providing lenders and investors with independent and objective opinion of a borrower's creditworthiness. They publicly disclose the rating but not the detailed methodology. Companies with agency-rated debt tend to be large and publicly traded. The credit opinions are statements about loss given default (LGD) and default probability (PD), specifically expected loss, and thus act as combined default prediction and exposure models. Rating agencies analytical services are supposed to be based on independent, objective, credible and transparent assessment.

Rating agencies generally give their opinion about the creditworthiness of an obligor with respect to a particular debt instrument or loan facility (issue-specific credit ratings). A credit rating is based upon the relative capability and willingness of the issuer of the instrument to service the debt obligations (both principal and interest) as per the terms of the contract. The rating of a debt instrument broadly examines three factors: the probability of default, the terms and character of the security and the degree of protection that can be granted to investors if the security issuer faces liquidation. There is long-term as well short-term rating assessment depending upon the type of instruments.

The rating criteria adopted by the agencies are very strictly defined and constitute their intangible assets which have been accumulated over years of experience. The rating assessment is based on extensive human analysis of both the quantitative and qualitative performance of a firm. For companies, the analysis is divided among (a) **Business risk** (competitiveness, operations, cost control, etc.), (b) **Industry risk** (business fundamentals, regulatory actions, vulnerability to imports, demand–supply situation, overall prospects, etc.), (c) **Management risk** (quality of management and policies on leveraging, interest risks, currency risks, etc.), and (d) **Financial risk** (profitability, working capital intensity, debt structure–financial ratios, etc.). These risk factors may impact differently on various industries and accordingly they allow these variations. For example, higher weightage is given to business risk factors (e.g. R&D programmes, product promotions, patent expirations, etc.) to sectors like Pharmaceuticals and Property sectors in comparison to Airlines sector. On the other hand, financial risk (e.g. profitability, leverage, etc.) weight is high in Airlines in comparison to property, retail and pharmaceuticals sectors. As far as financial risk field is concerned, major ratios used by CRAs are: Funds from operations (FFO)/ Debt% (>60% for minimal risk and <12% for higher risk), Debt/EBITDA ($\times$) (<1.5 for minimal risk and >5 for highest risk), EBIT int. cov. ($\times$) (>10 for low risk and <1 for high risk), return on capital per cent (>20% for higher graded cos. and <10 for risky grades).[2] This has been elaborately described by Crouhy, Galai and Mark (JBF, 2001) and de Servigny and Renault (2004).

Basel II regulation requires homogeneity across CRAs' ratings. Wide discrepancies across agencies would induce banks to underestimate the risk. Table 2.4 suggests that rating agencies are relying on a similar set of explanatory variables. However, each rating agency's rating evaluation method is unique and it is their proprietary right and, hence, they don't share more details of their methodology.

The relevant risk factors used by CRAs are:

i. **Quantitative factors:** Turnover, earning ratio, gearing ratio, coverage ratio, cash flow, liquidity ratio, variations in working capital, capital spending, financial flows, foreign exchange effects, accounting effects, etc.

ii. **Qualitative factors**: Business sectors, market positions, geographical diversification, commercial strategy, barriers to entry, competitive advantage, management quality, financial policy, growth opportunities debt maturity, key characteristics of security, legal structure, ownership structure, corporate governance and regulatory framework.

CRAs' rating is meant to be forward looking and, thus, gives a forecast about a company's future risk. Rating agencies regularly publish company ratings and report observed default rates per rating category per year on a historical basis. They also estimate transition matrices and report probabilities of migrations from one rating category to another in a table. These give idea about system level risk position of corporates across industries and provide insight regarding trend in future probabilities of default of a loan.

Bank for International Settlement (BIS) in 2001 has set six criteria that external credit assessment institutions (ECAIs) must satisfy:

---

[2] EBITDA = Earnings before interest, taxes, depreciation and amortization. EBIT int. cov. (x) = interest coverage ratio = EBIT/interest expenses, where EBIT is the earnings before interest and taxes.

i. **Objectivity:** Rigorous methodology and historical validity of its credit assessments.
ii. **Independence:** Not subject to economic or political pressures.
iii. **International access/transparency:** Assessments available to both domestic and foreign institutions; the general methodology should not be publicly available.
iv. **Disclosure:** Both qualitative (e.g. definition of default, time horizon, etc.) and quantitative (default rates in each assessment category and transition rates from one rating category to another over time).
v. **Resources:** Sufficient resources to carry out high quality credit assessments, including ongoing contacts with the managements of the assessed entities; assessments to be based on methodologies combining qualitative and quantitative approaches.
vi. **Credibility:** Use of assessments by independent parties; existence of internal procedures to prevent the misuse of confidential information.

Source: BIS (2001).

External credit rating is a formal, independent opinion of a borrower's ability to service debt obligations. The credit rating agencies (CRAs) clearly emphasize this publicly. The CRAs use strictly defined criteria to assess the risk of a corporate. They broadly use similar methodologies in arriving at their issuer credit rating. The critical risk areas addressed by the popular rating agencies are presented in Table 2.5.

Table 2.5: Risk Criteria of Credit Rating Agencies (CRAs)

S&P	Moody's	Fitch
Financial Risk:	*Financial Risk:*	*Financial Risk:*
1) Balance Sheet and Profit and Loss	1) Profitability	1) Profitability
2) Financial Policy	2) Cash Flow	2) Cash-flow Measures (e.g. FFO, Interest Coverage Ratio, etc.)
3) Return	3) Liquidity	
4) Capital Structure (leverage)	4) Debt Structure	3) Financial Flexibility
5) Cash Flow	5) Equity and Reserves	4) Capital Structure
6) Financial Flexibility (access to debt and equity)	6) Financial Flexibility	
Business Risk:	*Competition & Business risk:*	*Business Risk:*
1) Industry Characteristics		1) Industry Fundamentals
2) Competitive Situation	1) Industry Risk	
3) Company Position	2) Relative Market Share, Competitive Position	2) Competition, Entry Barriers

Table 2.5 contd.

Table 2.5 contd.

4) Profitability, Peer Group Comparison	3) Concentration in the Industry 4) Barriers to Entry 5) Turnover, Costs 6) Sales and Purchases 7) Distribution Channels 8) Consolidation of Related Firms	3) Cyclicality 4) Diversification 5) Market Position 6) Distribution and Technological Capabilities 7) Regulatory, Legal Framework
Management Risk: 1) Management and Corporate Strategy 2) Corporate Governance	*Quality of Management* 1) Planning and Controlling 2) Management Track Record 3) Organizational Structure 4) Succession Plan	*Quality of Management:* 1) Corporate Strategy and Planning 2) Corporate Governance (per cent of Independent Directors, etc.) 3) Management Track Record

Source: Various reports on Corporate Rating Methodology of S&P, Moody's and Fitch.

Generally, the risk analysis is focused on three broad classes: Financial risk, business risk and management risk. These factors may impact differently across various industries. All ratings are monitored on a monthly basis. Rating agencies publish bond as well as loan ratings on a regular basis.

Resti (2003) had shown how a multinomial logistic regression model can be useful to test which ratios (profitability, liquidity, capitalization and debt service capacity) and aggregates (state and industry dummies) are statistically relevant in explaining agency ratings. However, differences in rating outcome may exist in certain instances and for certain sectors. This has been empirically observed by many researchers like Van Laere et al. (2012, RMI working paper), Ghosh (2013, Stern School of Business), etc.

Brief History about Rating Agencies in India

There are four popular rating agencies operating in India: CRISIL (now owned by S&P), ICRA (now owned by Moody's) CARE and Fitch. CRISIL (Credit Rating Information Services of India Limited) is the largest credit rating agency in India with a market share more than 60 per cent. It was established in 1987 to rate debt instruments and actively started its operations from 1991. Their bond ratings became public since 1992. Standard and Poor's now holds the majority of stake in CRISIL. ICRA was established in 1991 by leading Indian financial institutions and commercial banks.

International credit rating agency Moody's is its largest shareholder. Credit Analysis and Research Limited (CARE) was incorporated in 1993. It is promoted by financial and lending institutions like IDBI, Canara Bank, UTI, etc. It has completed over 7,564 rating assignments since its inception. Fitch is a global rating agency that provides independent credit opinion and it is part of Fitch Group operating in New York and London.

Issue Rating vs. Issuer Rating

Issuer rating focuses on the rated issuer's ability and willingness to meet its financial commitments in general as and when they arise and are not specific to any particular obligation. Issuer rating analyzes company credit worthiness and gives pure opinion about risk of default (PD). An issue rating, on the other hand, is assigned to a specific debt obligation of an issuer and is thus an opinion (expressed as a symbol) on the relative credit risk associated with that particular financial obligation.

Standard & Poor's perceives its ratings primarily as an opinion on the likelihood of default of an issuer, while Moody's ratings tend to reflect the agency's opinion on the expected loss (EL = PD × LGD) on a facility. However, recently (since 2007), S&P has incorporated recovery rating and took a combination of PD and LGD on its issue rating for speculative grades. Recovery rating makes the estimation of principal payment given default and gives pure opinion of risk of loss due to default (LGD).

Risk Differentiation

The long-term bond ratings of external rating agencies are divided into several categories, e.g. from AAA, AA, A, BBB, BB, B to CCC for Standard & Poor's and Aaa, Aa, A, Baa, Ba, B, Caa, Ca to C for Moody's. A rating of AA obtained by a firm and a rating of BBB obtained by another would indicate that the latter is 'more risky' than the former. But the 'AA' rating is not a guarantee that it will not default, only that, in their opinion, it is less likely to default than the 'BBB' bond. The rated universe is broken down into two broad categories: investment grade (IG) and non-investment grade (NIG), or speculative grade (combine risky grades). IG firms are relatively safer borrowers with moderate default risk are in the rating categories AAA to BBB of S&P's and Aaa to Baa for Moody's. The credit quality of firms is best (or low default risks) for AAA/Aaa ratings and deteriorates as ratings go down to the lower notches BB/Ba, B, CCC/Ca (categories with higher default risks). Rating agencies also give plus and minus notches in order to provide a more granular (or finer) indication of risk. The rating revisions (upgrades and downgrades) tend to impact the pricing of the debt as also the market sentiment. The transition probabilities captured in the transition matrix computed by the rating agencies quantify the likelihood that a company will change from one rating grade to another within a year.

Standard & Poor's in its public issue rating of NIG grades combines issuer rating (PD) and recovery rating (LGD). Issuer rating is the analysis of company creditworthiness. It is a pure opinion of risk of default (PD). Recovery rating is an estimate of principal payment given the default. It is a pure opinion of risk of loss (LGD). While evaluating LGD, the agency evaluates the post-default recovery prospect of the facility or issue (refer to the Chart 2.6). It considers security value, covenants, documentation and jurisdictional issues while making recovery expectations.

Chart 2.6: LGD Rating Scale

Scale	S&P's Recovery Rating	Indicative Recovery Expectations	Loan or Issue notching from CCR
1+	Highest expectation of full recovery	100%	+3 notches
1	Strong expectation of full recovery	90–100%	+2 notches
2	Substantial recovery	70–90%	+1 notch
3	Meaningful recovery	50–70%	0 (Un-notched)
4	Average recovery	30–50%	0 (Un-notched)
5	Modest recovery	10–30%	–1 Notch
6	Negligible recovery	0–10%	–2 Notch

Source: Standard & Poor's Ratings Direct, 31 January 2013.

Note: Recovery rating indicating recovery rate of principal plus accrued and unpaid interest at the point of default. LGD is 1-recovery rate. The normal recovery time frame is 2–3 years. Where recoveries may not be realized within this time frame, the RRs assigned may be lowered and the issue would not be notched up above the CCR level on the existing scale. + sign indicates notching up and – sign indicates notching down of the existing CCR. CCR = Corporate Credit Rating.
Source: S&P

The market responds to change in the rating of corporates. When there is a rating downgrade, the indication is that risk has gone up. So, market demands a higher risk premium for the corporate bond and price of the bond falls for the company. Credit Metrics (1997) model utilizes external credit rating to calculate yield spreads in the bond market to derive a value at risk

(VaR) figure for a bond portfolio. This is done by computing volatility in bond value caused by credit quality changes. The credit metrics approach has been explained in the next chapter.

Through the Cycle (TTC) vs. Point in Time (PIT) Rating Approach

The rating agencies (Moody's, Standard & Poor's) measure the future risk over one or more business cycles and use through the cycle ratings (TTC). CRAs' analytical focus is on fundamental factors that will drive an issuer's long-term ability to meet debt payments. Rating agencies encompass a long-time horizon (3–5 years) and look at the permanent components of the balance sheet. Rating agencies' long-term ratings factor the effect of business cycles (macroeconomic and industrial) and, hence, their ratings are more stable and through the cycle (TTC). The ratings therefore do not fluctuate much with short-term changes in business or supply demand cycles or reflect short-term market movements. This is the reason why most investors believe rating agencies are too slow in adjusting their ratings to changes in corporate creditworthiness. On the other hand, banks' internal credit rating is point in time (PIT) in nature and is based on financials for the latest year (Jayadev, 2006). Thus, bank ratings are volatile over time as it does not take long-term view. Stability is also an important property of a good rating system from the point of view of the regulator. One solution of this dilemma is to use both PIT and TTC ratings for better credit monitoring as well as to estimate regulatory capital under IRB approach. But one has to know the art of extracting TTC PD from PIT PD through a mapping process and then rightly balance between the two. This extraction process has been shown in Chapter 5.

Chassang and de Servigny (2002) have shown a way to extract TTC predictive default information from PIT financial input (say from Z-score or logistic score). They show that with a sufficiently large history of short-term PDs, it is possible to obtain TTC equivalent ratings, through a mapping exercise (based on mean, variance and skewness of PDs space). Resti (2003) in a multivariate logistic regression framework has empirically tested the key financial factors that drive agency rating movements for European firms. He finds that the probability of obtaining a higher grade is influenced by profitability (positive effect), indebtedness (negative effect), gross cash cycle (the average number of days the firm needs to produce its goods; the longer the cycle, the worse the rating), profit volatility (plays an extremely negative role) and state ownership (whether it enjoys the state's financial support). He finds that big, profitable, state-owned firms are more likely to get top ratings. On the other hand, slow, highly indebted and volatile companies will be poorly rated by the agency. Such empirical findings are very useful for the banks to fine tune their internal rating models. Similarly, Altman and Rijken (2006) have provided quantitative insights to combine rating stability, rating timeliness and rating performance in predicting future default.

Statistical Credit Scoring Models

While heuristic or judgemental credit assessment models rely on the subjective experience of credit experts, statistical models attempt to verify hypotheses using statistical procedures on an empirical database. In this case, econometric techniques are used to empirically determine which variables (quantitative and qualitative) characterize "good" (solvent) firms (or borrowers) from "bad" (defaulted or distressed counterparts). It also gives an estimate of what weight should be assigned to these variables to achieve the highest rate of discriminatory and predictive power. The final score can be used to discriminate between good (low probability of default) and bad (high probability of default) credits, to act as an early warning signal and to derive the implied PD.

Statistical procedures can be used to derive an objective selection and weighting of creditworthiness factors from the available borrower information. In this process, selection and weighting are carried out with a view to optimizing accuracy in the classification of solvent and insolvent borrowers in the empirical data set. The predictive power of such models depends on the quality of data used to build the model.

The goodness of fit of any statistical model, thus, depends heavily on the quality of the empirical data set used in its development. First, it is necessary to ensure that the data set is large enough to enable statistically significant statements. Second, it is also important to ensure that the data used accurately reflect the field in which the credit institution plans to use the model. If this is not the case, the statistical rating models developed will show sound classification accuracy for the empirical data set used but will not be able to make reliable statements on other types of new business.

Various types of statistical credit scoring models are available in the market. A good review of the worldwide application of multivariate credit scoring models can be found in Altman and Narayanan (1997).

i. Z-score Model: Edward Altman's (1968) original Z-score model is an empirical classificatory model for corporate borrowers that can be used to get a default prediction. Based on a matched sample (by year, size and industry) of 33 bankrupted (or failed) and 33 solvent firms, and using a multiple discriminant analysis (MDA) on a list of 22 potentially helpful financial ratios tested over a 20-year period (1946–65), Altman developed the best fitting scoring model (or equation) for commercial loans. MDA is a statistical technique used to classify an observation into one of several *a priori* groupings dependent upon the observation's individual characteristics. After groups (bankrupted or defaulted group vs. solvent group or standard group) are established, data variables are collected for the firms in the groups to derive a linear combination of these factors that best discriminates between the groups. This is a very standard statistical technique popularly used to derive such kind of statistical scoring models.

MDA models are developed in the following steps:

- Establish a sample of two mutually exclusive groups: firms which have "failed" and those which are still continuing to trade successfully.
- Collect financial ratios for each of these companies belonging to both of these groups.
- Logically, select financial ratios which best discriminate between groups (perform F-test/Wilk's Lambda, Canonical correlation test, etc.). Intuitively, a small Lambda signifies smaller within groups' dispersions and a between group (solvent vs. defaulted firms) mean difference of factors. Similarly, the higher the value, the more important is the independent variable to the discriminant function. The homogeneity of covariance matrices are checked by Box's M test. The larger the eigenvalue, the more of the variance in the dependent variable is explained by the discriminant function. The canonical correlation is the measure of association between the discriminant function and the dependent variable.
- Establish a Z score based on these ratios and functions.
- Compare alternative Z score models and their overall classification power.
- Select the relatively better one that has highest within as well as out of sample classification power.

The MDA models can be run in SPSS package. The discriminant weights are the mean difference (between solvent and defaulted group of firms) of each tested variables (or ratios) adjusted by their variance–covariance. Generally, Fisher's discriminant functions are used to separate two classes of customers as good borrowers and bad borrowers. Higher the discriminant score, greater the chance of solvency and lower the firm's default potential.

In order to arrive at a final combination of variables (or Z-score equation), the following procedures may be used:

i. Examination of the statistical significance of various set of variables and alternative functions in a step-wise manner;

ii. Determination of the relative contribution of each independent variable and their expected signs in predicting solvency;

iii. Evaluation of inter-correlations among the relevant variables so that almost similar factors or ratios are not included;

iv. Comparison of the predictive accuracy of various scoring models (or equations);

v. Overall judgement of the analysts.

The most famous application of MDA to credit scoring model is Altman's (1968) Z score. The final discriminant function obtained by Altman is given below:

$$Z = 1.2X_1 + 1.4X_2 + 3.3X_3 + 0.6X_4 + 0.999X_5 \qquad \text{Eq. 2.1}$$

Z = The final Z score function

X_1 = Net Working Capital (NWC)/Total asset (liquidity)

X_2 = Retained Earnings/Total Asset (cumulative profitability)

X_3 = Profit before Interest and Tax (PBIT)/total assets (productivity)

X_4 = Market Value of Equity/Book value of Liabilities (movement in the asset value)

X_5 = Sales/Total Assets (sales generating ability)

The first ratio (X_1: NWC to total assets) is a measure of short-term liquidity position of a firm. Net working capital is the difference between current assets and current liabilities. A firm with lower (or negative) working capital is likely to experience liquidity problems. By contrast, a firm with significantly positive working capital rarely has trouble meeting its obligations and, thus, has better asset liquidity. Thus, firms with higher NWC to total assets ratio are more solvent and can opt for more debt. Altman also tried current ratio and quick ratio; however, these were found to be less predictive in his MDA models.

The second ratio X_2 (retained earnings to total assets: RE/TA) is a measure of cumulative profitability over time. This ratio highlights the use of internally generated funds for growth (low risk capital). Generally, the older firms with higher credit standing have higher retained earnings ratio and, thus, have lesser debt in their capital structure. This is a long-term ratio, and it implicitly captures the age of the firm and the extent of the company's leverage. Companies with high RE/TA suggest a history of profitability and the ability to stand up to a bad year of losses.

The third ratio X_3 (earnings or profit before interest and taxes to total assets: PBIT/TA) is a good measure of firm's profitability. This ratio assesses a firm's ability to generate profits from its assets before interest and tax are deducted. Higher the ratio, stronger the earning power of the firm and lower is the credit risk. This ratio has the highest contribution to the overall discrimination power of the model.

The fourth ratio X_4 is the market value of equity to book value of liabilities (MVE/BVL). Market value of equity is the annual market capitalization of the firm, while liabilities include both current and long term. It is a measure of movement of market value of asset of firm which was subsequently used by Moody's KMV model as default predictor. This ratio shows how much the firm's assets can decline in value (measured by market value of equity plus debt) before the liabilities exceed the assets and the firm becomes insolvent. This ratio adds a market value dimension to the model and can be interpreted as the market's confidence in the company's financial position.

The fifth and final ratio X_5 is turnover ratio (Sales/TA) representing the sales-generating ability of the firm's assets. This is also a measure of management's capacity in dealing with competitive conditions. It also captures the industry effects as it will vary across industries. This ratio has a greater significance when it is used in a group because of its unique relationship to other variables in the model. This ratio ranks second in its contribution to the overall discriminating ability of the model.

Thus, from the original set of 22 variables, classified into five standard categories including liquidity, profitability, leverage, solvency and activity, he finally obtained five best predictive ratios and their based combination which has been captured in the above equation. Once the values of the discriminate coefficients (or weights) are estimated, it is possible to calculate discriminant scores for the existing or new borrowers, provided these five financial ratios are available.

If a credit officer gets information about the above five ratios from a borrower from its financials, he/she will be able to get an estimate of Z score after weighted by the estimated coefficients in the Z equation. Next, the resulted Z score needs to be compared with the following critical values:

If obtained Z score > 2.99, firm is in a good shape (Green signal);

If $2.99 > Z$ score>1.81 , warning signal about deteriorating health of the firm (Yellow signal);

If $1.81 > Z$ score, firm is in big trouble and could be heading towards bankruptcy (Red signal).

Therefore, the greater a firm's distress potential, the lower its discriminant score.

Altman had examined 86 distressed companies from 1969–75, 110 bankrupts from 1976–95 and 120 from 1997–99. The validation results reveal that the accuracy of his Z score model on sample of bad firms was in the range of 80–90 per cent. He had also used a more conservative cut-off score of 2.675 and found even better predictive accuracy of the Z score model (82–94 per cent). However, advocated using 1.81 is a more realistic cut-off Z score than the score 2.675.

In order to fit the un-listed firms into Z score model's prediction coverage, Altman had re-estimated his model and substituted the book values of equity for the market value in X_4. Accordingly, all coefficients were changed and that the classification criterion and related cut-off scores were also changed.

The revised Z score model for predicting bankruptcy risk of private firms is:

$$Z' = 0.717X_1 + 0.847X_2 + 3.107X_3 + 0.420X_4 + 0.998X_5 \qquad \text{Eq. 2.2}$$

The Z score equation now looks different to the earlier model.

A further revision of the Z score model was done by the author to adapt the model for non-manufacturers and include emerging markets in its coverage. This was done by dropping X_5 variable and including sample of firms of non-US corporates. Actually, Altman Hartzell and Peck (1995) had developed the enhanced Z'' score model to predict the default risk of emerging markets corporates specifically the Mexican firms that had issued Eurobonds denominated in US dollars. The book value of equity was used for X_4 in this case.

$$Z'' = 6.56X_1 + 3.26X_2 + 6.72X_3 + 1.05X_4 \qquad \text{Eq. 2.3}$$

Where Z'' scores below 1.10 indicate a distressed condition. Altman et al. further mapped and benchmarked these Z'' scores with S&P rating. The average Z score was 5.02 (with standard deviation 1.50) for AAA bond rating; 4.0 (with std. dev. 1.81) for AA; 3.60 (with std. dev. 2.26) for A; 2.78 (with std. dev. 1.50) for BBB; 2.45 (with std. dev. 1.62) for BB and 1.67 (std. dev. 1.22) for B. They had also added an intercept term +3.25 so as to standardize the scores with a score of zero mapped to a D rated bond. In that case, an AAA rating was mapped to EM score of 8.15; AA rating to 7.3; A to 6.65; BBB to 5.85; BB to 4.95; B to 4.15 and CCC to 2.50.

One can notice that all of the coefficients for variables X_1 to X_4 were changed as were the group means and cut-off scores. It can be noted that one of the main reasons for building a credit scoring model is to estimate the probability of default (PD). Though rating agencies (e.g. Moody's, S&P and Fitch) are not perfect in their credit risk assessments, in general it is believed that they do provide vital and consistent estimates of default via their published credit ratings. And since there has been a long data history and broad coverage of large number of defaults which had ratings, one can utilize this history by linking credit scores with these ratings and map them. Such mapping will enable us to derive the expected PDs for a fixed horizon of say one year.

In the emerging market score (EM score) model, Altman et al. (1995) also added a constant term +3.25 so as to standardize the scores with a score of zero (0) which was equated to a D (default) rated bond. This mapping was done based on over 750 US corporate bonds with rated debt outstanding in 1995. In this mapping, an AAA grade has corresponding average EM score 8.15; AA, 7.30; A; 6.65; BBB, 5.85; BB, 4.95; B, 4.15; CCC, 2.50. This way, Z-score model can be used as a default probability predictor model.

Limitations of the Z-score Model

A number of issues need to be addressed here about Z-score models. The model is linear in nature, where the path of bankruptcy may be highly non-linear (the relationship between X_i factors is likely to be nonlinear as well). Second, except the market value of equity term in the leverage ratio, the model is essentially based on accounting ratios which can be obtained annually. It is questionable whether such models can give signal about a firm whose condition is rapidly deteriorating, especially during the economic crisis period. Moody's KMV model, logistic regression models and artificial neural network are examples of nonlinear methods, which have been successfully applied to credit risk analysis. We have discussed these alternate models in the later section of this chapter.

Altman's original Z score and other modified scoring models were developed based on US market and some cases Mexican market data. As it can be seen, the weights and the variables of the Z-score equations change under different market and industry conditions. Moreover, the balance sheet sizes of firms across countries are also different. Therefore, banks and investors in India may not get accurate early warning signal about firm's deteriorating financial health unless it is properly customized and tested in Indian conditions.

Default Prediction Model for Indian Corporates

Bandyopadhyay (2006, JRF) has developed a new Z-score model for Indian corporates which is a better fit for the manufacturing firms in the Emerging Market like India than the Altman's models. This MDA model is based on a sample of 104 Indian corporates (52 solvent and 52 defaulted) financial data for the period of 1998 to 2003. The defaulted group is a class of manufacturers whose long-term bonds have been defaulted between 1998 and 2003. The solvent firms are chosen on a stratified random basis drawn from CRISIL rating database. The average asset size of the firms in the solvent group is ₹948.51 crore and that of the defaulted group is ₹818.62 crore. Here is his model:

$$Z_{NEW} = -3.337 + 0.736 \ (NWC\_TA) + 6.95 \ (CASHPROF\_TA) + 0.864 \ (SOLVR) + 7.554 \ (OPPROF\_TA) + 1.544 \ (SALES\_TA) \quad \text{Eq. 2.4}$$

Ratios used

i. NWK/TA: Networking capital by total assets ratio measures short-term liquidity position of a firm. Networking capital = current assets – current liabilities.

ii. CASHPROF/TA: Cash profit to total asset ratio is a measure of firm's cash flow. This ratio is profit after tax (PAT) plus depreciation and amortization divided by total assets.

iii. SOLVR: Solvency ratio measures the long-term solvency of the firm. This ratio is = total assets – revaluation reserves – misc. expenses not written off/total borrowings + current liability and provisions).

iv. OPPROF/TA = Operating profit to total assets measures the firm's earning capability. This ratio is profit before interest and tax (PBIT) to total assets.

v. SALES/TA = Total sales to total assets measures the sales generating ability of the firm's assets.

We predict a firm as solvent (or non-defaulting) if the final Z score obtained is positive [as for him, Prob. (solvent) > Prob. (defaulted)]. Similarly, the firm with a negative Z score is classified as one liable to default within a year horizon. Using Bayes' theorem, we can express a posteriori with a priori probabilities (here 50–50) to find out the conditional scores. This helps us to classify a firm to be in solvent group or in defaulted group. We express it as a likelihood ratio: $\text{EPS} = \dfrac{\exp(Z)}{1 + \exp(Z)}$. If EPS > 50 **per cent**, we classify a firm as solvent and if EPS < 50 **per cent**, it is predicted to be in the defaulted group.

Following the above approach, the model's predictive power has been tested on both within sample and hold out (or new borrower) sample. The hold out sample validation test result of 50 firms shows that the new Z-score model has 92 per cent correct prediction for defaulted firms (otherwise type 1 error) and 96 per cent correct prediction for solvent firms (otherwise type 2 error). A type 1 error is misclassifying a bad loan as good. A type 2 error is misclassifying a good loan as bad. It is important to note that when the least desirable bad borrowers (i.e. with high credit risk) become more probable to acquire loans than good credit risks, banks are subject to the adverse selection problem. That is why, validation check is important before using a scorecard in taking credit decision. This is also equally important for correct pricing of a loan.

Table 2.6 compares the predictive power of new Indian Z-score model with reconstructed Altman's original 1968 and emerging market Z-score on 104 Indian firms. Clearly, the new Z-score model has the highest classification power in predicting Indian firms. Thus, it is quite evident that the new Z-score model (developed by Bandyopadhyay, 2006) based on Indian data has the highest predictive power in comparison to other models. It better suits the Indian market.

Table 2.6: Comparison of Predictive Power of New Z-score vis-à-vis other Z-score Models

Model Type	per cent Correct Classification within Sample	
	Good	Bad
Alman Z-score 1968 Reworked with Indian Data:	84.00	82.00
$Z = -1.689 + 2.436$ (NWK/TA) $+ 8.158$ (RE/TA) $+ 3.73$ (PBIT/TA) $+ 0.037$ (MVE/BVL) $+ 1.602$ (SALES/TA)		
Altman Emerging Market Z-score 1995 (for Listed firms) Reworked with Indian Data:	88.20	75.90
$Z = -1.096 + 2.893$(NWK/TA) $+ 1.19$(RE/TA) $+ 11.711$(PBIT/TA) $+ 0.042$(MVE/BVL)		
New Z-score 2005 Developed on Indian Data (for both Listed & Private Firms)	85.20	91.00
$Z_{NEW} = -3.337 + 0.736$(NWK/TA) $+ 6.95$ (CASHPROF/TA) $+ 0.864$ (SOLVR) $+ 7.554$ (OPPROF/TA) $+ 1.544$ (SALES/TA)		

Source: Bandyopadhyay (2006).

The Z scores obtained for companies should be mapped with a bank's internal rating or external rating (CRAs rating) and respective PDs can be obtained. This finally can be used to estimate IRB risk weights.

Chart 2.7 shows how Z score can provide early warning signal about default status of a firm if it can be tracked over time. It can be seen why rating agency is slow to react to deteriorating health of the firm, the new Z score model was able to provide early warning signal about the company BPL Ltd is going to default well in advance. The credit rating agency CRISIL downgraded the company rating from A to D in the year 2003.

Chart 2.7: Checking the Early Warning Signal Power of New Z-score Model for Company – BPL Ltd.

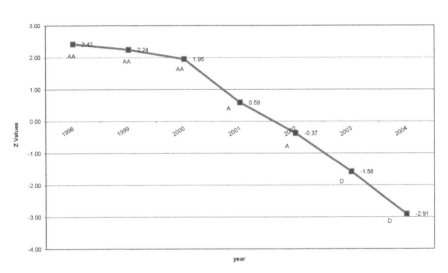

Source: Author's own computation using CMIE Prowess firm level balance sheet information and CRISIL's bond rating data.

Similarly, the new Z-score model has been also been tested on many recently defaulted Indian companies (i.e. during 2009–12). The results are quite satisfactory. One such example has been illustrated in Chart 2.7a. The company KLG Systel Ltd., a software development company (industry: engineering with NIC code 6201), was downgraded from BBB to BB in 2010 and finally to D in 2011 by CRISIL.

This kind of model can serve as a useful tool for quick evaluation of the corporate risk profile. Annexure 2.1A presents new Z score computation of a sample of Indian companies and its comparison with CRA published ratings. Using our new Z-score model, banks as well as investors can get early warning signals about the default status of Indian corporate firms and might reassess their magnitude of the default premium in pricing a loan.

Annexure 2A: New Z-score Computation of a Sample of Indian Companies

Co. Name	Year	Industry	Total Assets (Rs. Billion)	NWC /TA	CASH PROF /TA	SOLVR	OPPROF /TA	SALES/ TA	New Z-Score	CRISIL Rating
Asian Paints Ltd.	2010	Paints & Varnish	57.94	-0.373	0.180	3.775	0.258	1.253	4.786	AAA
	2011		57.94	-0.036	0.193	3.775	0.268	1.253	5.201	AAA
	2012		91.39	0.012	0.219	3.045	0.315	1.894	6.127	AAA
	2013		104.90	0.012	0.217	3.344	0.296	1.846	6.156	AAA
	2014		121.98	-0.017	0.210	3.269	0.288	1.806	5.900	AAA
Riga Sugar Co. Ltd.	2011	Sugar	2.63	0.037	0.027	1.179	0.074	0.473	-0.820	BB
	2012		3.14	-0.053	0.004	1.154	0.056	0.486	-1.178	D
	2013		3.03	-0.016	0.011	1.148	0.063	0.668	-0.775	D
	2014		3.33	-0.007	0.008	1.125	0.051	0.500	-1.152	D
Transstroy (India) Ltd.$	2010	Construction	7.82	0.224	0.121	1.651	0.187	1.308	2.527	BBB
	2011		16.26	0.092	0.074	1.490	0.133	0.945	0.995	BBB
	2012		24.96	0.016	0.061	1.537	0.135	0.834	0.729	BB+
	2013		38.70	-0.034	0.059	1.517	0.122	0.811	0.530	#(BLR)
	2014		52.80	-0.081	0.059	1.511	0.127	0.859	0.601	#(BLR)

Annexure 2A contd.

Annexure 2A contd.

Ultratech Cement Ltd.	2010	Cement	83.7							AAA
	2011		201.6	-0.050	0.101	2.652	0.146	0.742	1.868	AAA
	2012		230.9	-0.057	0.143	2.766	0.199	0.892	2.887	AAA
	2013		275.8	-0.061	0.136	2.685	0.183	0.829	2.545	AAA
	2014		299.3	-0.047	0.109	2.889	0.144	0.766	2.148	AAA
				-0.004	0.190	2.882	0.250	0.924	3.787	
Vardhman Chemtech Ltd.	2010	Drugs & Pharma	1.51							BBB
	2011		2.71	0.044	0.054	1.365	0.119	0.920	0.568	BBB
	2012		4.67	0.060	0.038	1.804	0.100	0.836	0.574	BB
	2013		4.40	0.048	0.023	1.955	0.095	0.944	0.728	D
	2014		4.56	0.204	-0.104	1.575	-0.041	0.692	-1.787	D
				0.040	0.090	1.426	0.164	1.406	1.964	

Source: CMIE Prowess and CRISIL data

Note: #(BLR) denotes rating suspended. $ The Company declared NPA in July 2015.

Chart 2.7a: New Z-score Model for Predicting Default Status of KLG Systel Ltd.

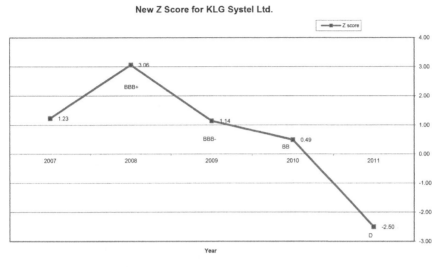

New Z Score for KLG Systel Ltd.

Source: Author's own computation using CMIE Prowess firm level balance sheet information and CRISIL's loan rating data.

The MDA-based Z-score model has another major problem that it is a linear probability model like ordinary least square (OLS) regression models. The regression approach to linear discrimination says the Z score is linearly related to borrower risk characteristics (X1, X2, X3,...., Xn factors). This has one obvious flaw of unboundedness as Z value can be of any range. Moreover, there may be non-linear relationship between risk factors and probability of default. In order to improve this, the left-hand side probability of default function is expressed as log of the probability odds (PD/PS). Note that PD + PS = 1. This leads to the logistic regression approach where one matches the log of the probability odds by a linear combination of the characteristics variables. This way, 'logit model' overcomes the weakness of 'unboundedness' problem of MDA and Linear Probability Models by restricting the estimated range of default probabilities to lie between 0 and 1.

Logit PD Prediction Model

Logit PD is a standard model for developing a statistical credit scoring model. The name Logit Model is because the borrower default prediction model is developed by applying Logistic Regression Technique. The contribution of financial as well as non-financial variables to model can be easily tested using statistical software like SPSS, STATA and SAS. Logit regression investigates the relationship between binary (default or not default) or ordinal response probability (rating changes, etc.) and explanatory variables (risk factors). The MDA and logit analysis have different assumptions concerning the relationships between the independent variables. While linear discriminant analysis is based on linear combination of independent variables, logit analysis uses the logistic cumulative probability function in predicting default.

The dependent variable is the natural log of the odd ratio: Default to Non-default.

The logit model can be written as:

$$Prob(Default) = \frac{e^{\alpha_0 + \beta_1 x_1 + \beta_2 x_2 + ... + \beta_k x_k}}{1 + e^{\alpha_0 + \beta_1 x_1 + \beta_2 x_2 + ... + \beta_k x_k}} \qquad \text{Eq. 2.5}$$

This implies a linear, monotone relationship between the Log Odd and the input accounting ratios along with various non-financial factors:

$$\text{LogOdd} = \alpha_0 + \beta_1 x_1 + \beta_2 x_2 + ... + \beta_k x_k \qquad \text{Eq. 2.5a}$$

A logistic model has the flexibility of incorporating both the qualitative and quantitative factors and is more efficient than the linear regression probability model. The final outcome of this model is a relative indicator of a borrower's chance of default.

Bandyopadhyay (2006) has also developed a logistic EPD ex-ante PD model for Indian Corporates from the same database of Z-score model. The model parameters and their weights have been illustrated in Table 2.7. Like the new Z-score model, this logit EPD model also has the capacity to give an early warning signal about the chance of default in advance.

Logit Score = Function {NWC_TA, CASHP_TA, SOLVR, MVE_BVL,
SALES_TA, ISOD, LN(Age), Industry Category}   Eq. 2.6

$$\Rightarrow LogitEPD = \left\{ \frac{1}{1 + e^{-(LogitScore)}} \right\} \qquad \text{Eq. 2.7}$$

where e is the exponential and its value is approximately 2.718281828. The model is estimated using the maximum likelihood technique (MLE).

This logit PD scoring model would enable the Indian banks to estimate a statistical ex-ante PD (or EPD) for its commercial loan exposures. It has been empirically observed that the inclusion of non-financial factors along with financial ratios improves the predictive power of a scoring model (both the explanatory power and predictive power of the model improves).

Hence, the output of this model is a statistical ex-ante or anticipated default probability (in per cent) which can be used by the bank for ascertaining credit rating (on the basis of default ranking) that can be finally used for regulatory capital computation. Both the models have a very good predictive power and have been properly tested on a huge set of corporate as well as SME accounts.

Table 2.7: Parameters of Indian Logit EPD Models

Items#	Logit EPD (DDEF = 1)	Coefficients	Variable Definition
1	NWC_TA	−10.35***	Networking Capital by Total Assets: it is equal to current assets minus current liabilities
2	CASHPROF_TA	−12.91***	Cash Profit by Total Assets: Profit after tax plus depreciation and amortization divided by total assets
3	SOLVR	−1.23***	Solvency Ratio: Total assets net of revaluation reserves, advance tax and miscellaneous expenses not written off divided by total borrowings plus current liabilities plus provisions less advance payment of tax
4	MVE_BVL	−1.74***	Market value of equity divided by book value of liabilities
5	SALES_TA	−1.67***	Sales by total assets
6	ISOD	−1.27***	ISO dummy capturing management quality (= 1 if certified; = 0 if not)
7	LN(AGE)	−1.66**	Natural Logarithm of the age of the firm since incorporation
8	INDUSTRY CATEGORY		Industry factors captured by respective industry dummies
8.1	IND1_FOOD	−1.114	If the borrower is in this industry, Food dummy = 1 and other dummies = 0
8.2	IND2_PAPER	−	Dropped, but in built in the model and added to the intercept (one can put zero value for this industry)
8.3	IND3_TEXTILE	0.45	Textile Industry Dummy = 1, otherwise, 0
8.4	IND4_CHEMICAL	1.27	Chemical Dummy = 1, otherwise, 0
8.5	IND5_ENGINEERING	2.48**	Engineering Dummy = 1, otherwise, 0

Table 2.7 contd.

Table 2.7 contd.

8.6	IND6_METAL&NONM	0.86	Metal and Non-metal industry Dummy = 1, otherwise, 0
8.7	IND7_AUTO & PARTS	0.46	Auto Dummy = 1, otherwise, 0
8.8	IND8_POWER	–	Dropped, but effect has been taken care off
8.9	IND9_DIVERSIFIED	1.49	Dummy for diversified industry
8.10	IND10_SERVICE	–3.52***	Dummy for service sector
8.11	IND11_OTHER	–	Dropped, but effect has been taken care of
9	Intercept	11.46***	Constant term, capturing other effects

Source: Bandyopadhyay (2006).

Note: *** denotes significance at 5% or better; ** denotes significance at 5–10% level. The overall R2 of the model is 0.70 with total number of observations = 518. The overall within sample predictive power of the model measured by ROC is: 97.2%. The out of sample predictive power on 50 firms is 94% correct for bad firms and 84% correct for good firms.

Instead of a logistic distribution function, one can also specify actual default events in a binary probit model framework. For example, Moody's RiskCalc (2002) for US private banks is estimated using a probit model that uses the normal or Gaussian cumulative distribution function.

Most Powerful Drivers of Default Risk in Corporate and SME loans

The most powerful drivers of default risk in corporate and SME borrowers that have been observed empirically by many researchers/analysts are listed below:

- **Volatility:** Equity, asset, sales volatility, etc.; higher volatility means higher insolvency risk.
- **Size:** Market cap, sales, assets; bigger companies are generally more diversified and, hence, relatively less risky.
- **Profitability:** Profit before interest and tax (PBIT)/sales, PBIT/total assets; retained profit/total assets, EBITDA/total assets, net income/assets, PBIT/debt, etc.; higher profit lowers default risk.
- **Operating/Activity Ratios:** Sales/total assets, expenses/sales, EBITDA/interest expenses. Operating ratios assist in the evaluation of management performance. Higher the ratio, better the management performance and lower the chance of default.

- **Coverage:** Debt service coverage ratio (DSCR), interest coverage ratio (PBIT/annual interest expenses), etc. Low debt coverage increases the probability of default.
- **Leverage/Gearing:** Liabilities/total assets; debt/assets; short-term debt/BV of equity, short-term debt/total debt, etc. Higher leverage implies higher default probabilities.
- **Liquidity:** Net working capital/total assets; current ratio (current assets/current liabilities); quick ratio (cash and equivalents plus net trade receivables/current liabilities), cash/total assets, cash/net sales, intangible/total assets, net sales/net trade receivables, etc. These ratios indicate the liquidity position of firms. Lower liquidity implies higher risk.
- **Growth:** Sales growth and export growth. Both rapid growth and rapid decline (negative growth) will tend to increase a firm's default probability, and stable revenue lowers a firm's default chance.
- **Inventories:** Inventory/sales; higher stock of inventories relative to sales imply higher default probabilities.

Jayadev (2006) had provided empirical evidence on the significance of selected financial ratios in predicting companies default and suggested careful selection of accounting ratios in designing internal rating models for Indian banks. This study further suggested that bank should internally develop statistical Z-score models for large corporate, mid corporate and SME borrowers and combine with internal ratings for IRB the purpose of graduating for the IRB approach.

Statistical Scoring Model for SMEs

Altman and Sabeto (2005) have developed an SME "Z" score model by utilizing a sample containing financial data for 2,010 US SMEs with sales less than $65 million (approximately €50 million). This data was gathered from US COMPUSTAT database over the period 1994–2002. The data consisted of 120 defaulted SMEs with no missing data. Then, they randomly selected 1,890 non-defaulted firms over the sample period in order to obtain an average sample default rate, which is closer to the expected average default rate for US SMEs (6 per cent). For each selected year, they calculated the number of non-defaulted SMEs in order to maintain the overall expected default rate of 6 per cent.

Out of 10 possible predictive ratios, they statistically derived five key ratios that together describe a company's financial risk profile: liquidity, profitability, leverage, coverage and activity. Applying a logistic regression analysis on logarithmic transformed financial variables (similar to Altman and Rijken, 2004), they developed the following SME scoring model:

$$\text{Log(PS/PD)} = \text{Logit } Z = 53.48 + 4.09 \times -\text{LN}(1-\text{EBITDA/Total Assets})$$
$$-1.13 \times \text{LN (Short-term Debt/Book Value of Equity)}$$
$$+ 4.32 \times -\text{LN}(1-\text{Retained Earnings/Total Assets})$$
$$+1.84 \times \textbf{LN}(\text{Cash/Total Assets})+1.97 \times (\text{EBITDA/}$$
Interest Expenses) $\hspace{4cm}$ Eq. 2.8

The dependent variable is a dummy dependent variable, where D = 0 for non-defaulted and 1 for defaulted. Note that PS + PD = 1. The above combination of five ratios best predicts the SME default.

Using the above scoring function (Eq. 2.1), the final score can be estimated for any new or existing firm by taking summation of the constant 53.48 and the product between the coefficients and the value of each of the predictor ratios. The estimated score approximates the probability that a firm does not default. A higher score indicates lower chance of bankruptcy and a lower score indicates rejection of the loan due to higher probability of default. Note that this model defines bankruptcy as the incident of default.

The overall accuracy (AR) of the model within as well as in a hold out sample (406 non-defaulted and 26 defaulted firms) is 87 per cent based on the logged variables. The type 1 error rate (where the model fails to predict defaulted firms) in the hold out sample randomly chosen by them is 11.76 per cent.

Credit Scoring Models for Retail Portfolio

Credit risk management in retail portfolios places a premium on a bank's ability to accurately differentiate the credit quality of borrowers to assess credit risk and to allocate their economic capital to different segments of their portfolios. The necessity to develop retail scoring model has been driven by the need to achieve automation in credit sanction process and to achieve more granular risk measurement.

Internationally active retail banking organizations use application scores to decide whether to approve facilities, limit setting and pricing process. Many of the best practices institutions also have behavioural risk scorecard that calculates a measure of credit risk according to the way the customer behaves. Both types of models (application scorecard as well as behavioural scorecard) can be developed using customer-level detailed data from banks and/or from credit bureau.

Retail lending differs substantially from wholesale lending, and while sophisticated scoring methods are employed for classifying and/or measuring delinquency and default probabilities for individual retail credits, internal economic capital models are less fully developed for retail. However, despite the emphasis on the commercial side, retail credit is a substantial part of the risk borne by the banking industry. Recognizing this, the industry has begun to develop more sophisticated credit-scoring models for measuring retail risk.

The credit evaluation procedure for retail lending in most banks is limited to assessing certain acceptance/eligibility criteria like income, age, document availability, etc. The framework for evaluation is largely subjective and judgemental, including rules and policies formulated based on past experience. A large number of other risk criteria are left out. There is a need to develop empirically derived, demonstrably and statistically sound credit scoring systems. This is a major challenge for most of the public sector banks in India as it requires relevant granular data on timely and ongoing basis.

How a Customized Retail Credit Scoring Model can be developed by Banks

Phase I

- *Evaluation of data availability for each loan scheme/segment:* Home loan, car loan, credit card loan, personal loan, education loan, small and medium enterprises (SMEs). Create sub-populations of retail portfolios; specify the objective and performance definition (growth, profitability, default or loss experiences). Designing a detailed data template is a must to collect necessary loan information to build a statistical credit scoring model.
- *Design Analysis Sample:* A sufficient, random and representative portion of recent accounts with known payment behaviour, plus declined and/or bad applications for each sub-population.
- *Selection of Parameters:* Selecting the risk parameters that may be predictive of default.
- *Model Construction:* Development of credit scoring model, setting cut-offs, risk bucketing.
- *Validation:* Model validation, testing and documentation of results.

Phase II

- **Risk Forecasting:** Probability of Default (PD) estimation through rating transition, retail pooled PD estimation.
- **Risk Bucketing:** Benchmarking and calibrating rating grades (AAA, AA, A, CCC) with the actual default experience of the bank (produce the predicted probabilities (PD) and align scoring benchmarks).

Risk Parameters

Based on the information from application form, it should be identified and categorized as following:

- **Borrower Character:** Age, education, occupation and nature of business, documents provided, and valid contact numbers provided, relationship with the bank, past credit history and payment behaviour.
- **Stability Characteristics:** Number of years at current business/job and residence, marital status and number of years account held at main bank.
- **Ability to Pay:** Ownership status of residence, number of dependents and number of children.
- **Capital Structure:** Annual income, expenditure, asset ownership and other outstanding loans or liabilities.
- **Collateral:** Primary security and collateral information, collateral value, whether guarantee is available, if yes, rating of the guarantor, etc.
- **Macro-economic Condition:** Regional location of the borrower, economic condition of the region (geographical data and socio economic conditions), growth rate of the economy during loan evaluation, etc.

It is important to note that such retail scoring model takes into account most of the information known about a customer or applicant at the point of application. This includes

- information from the application form
- information from a credit bureau (if it exists)

For the existing customers applying for additional product, information about the way in which the applicant has run his or her other accounts (behaviour of the account).

Estimation Method

It can be either statistical or judgemental model. The proper documentation of the weights and logic for the scores is needed for regulatory approval. If it is a statistical model, the stepwise methodology, statistical techniques used (MDA or logistic or artificial neural network, etc.) and choice of benchmarks should be clearly explained.

Key Decision Points Pertaining to Statistical Scoring Models

- *Sample selection*
  - How far back do you go to collect enough defaults?
    Keeping past history about account performance is important. An exposure is considered to be in default by the bank at the end of a quarter if account is tagged as NPA when customer is unlikely to pay. For retail exposures, the definition of default can be applied at the level of particular facility rather than at the level of obligor. If the customer is unlikely to pay or the account tagged as NPA or restructured are defined as defaults.
  - Ratio of defaults to non-defaults?
    Find all the loans that were in non-default status few years ago and track their performance over the following years. If you have a huge portfolio, you may want to take a random sample. One can also take industry expected default rate (say 5 per cent for housing loans) to select the non-defaulted random sample.
    The sample size could vary, but around 5,000 observations may be a good number to build the model. This is also termed as a development sample.
    Another 2,000 accounts (includes both defaulted and non-defaulted accounts) might be needed as a hold out sample to test the models predictive power.

- *Factor (or variable) selection*
  Now select relevant variables that you think might be predictive of default:
  - *Financial Factors:* Set of quantitative factors, for example, income, total income/debt, borrowing/assets, margin given, EMI/income, collateral value/loan amount, LTV, etc.
  - *Non-financial factors:* Set of qualitative inputs, for example, constitution of the borrower, age group, family size, employment status, reputation, education, marital status, ownership pattern, banking habit, loan type, etc.
  - *Collateral Factors:* One may also try to incorporate collateral factors like tangible/intangible security, collateral deposits, mortgage cover,

conduct of the account, etc., then regional information, etc. in predicting credit risk in bank loans.

As many as possible data fields required from the bank. Inclusion of additional information obtained from credit bureau (e.g. CIBIL in India) will further strengthen the explanatory power of the model.

- *Model selection*

  - Apply univariate statistical analysis (descriptive statistics, t-test, Chi-square test, ANOVA, etc.) to analyze single ratios or factors that may explain probability of default.
  - Run multivariate regression analysis (such as multiple discriminant analysis, logistic or probit regression) to select main driver variables and their significance. Neural networks and factor analysis can also be adopted to facilitate the process.
  - Specify the estimated function and define the scoring model. Define your dependent variable. Let's say a default is a loan that has NPA flags. Code an indicator variable for this with a 1 (default) or a 0 (non-default).

$$\text{e.g } EPD = \frac{1}{1 + e^{-\alpha_0 - \beta_1 x_1 - \beta_2 x_2 - \ldots - \beta_k x_k}}$$

EPD denotes the probability of a borrower to default on a loan; α is intercept, $x1, x2, \ldots, xk$ are set of exogenous variables (income/liability ratios and other quantitative ratios) and βs are their estimated coefficients.

An example of an estimated statistical scoring model:

Score (z) =

$w_1 \times$ **(Age of the borrower** + $w_2 \times$ **(Sector** or Business Type)

+ $w_3 \times$ (Years in business) – $w_4 \times$ (Past arrears)

+ $w_5 \times$ (no. of past loans) – $w_6 \times$ **(Indebtedness: liabilities/assets in per cent)**

– $w_7 \times$ (loan/income)

Low score means high risk, weights are determined statistically. Score (z) forecast risk at **per cent** probability. Define 'Bad' events (e.g., arrears 60 days in a row) to specify the dependent variable.

Note that a PD scorecard is a statistical method of providing a quantifiable risk to assess a customer or loan applicant. Credit scoring is a process whereby information provided is actually converted into a numerical formula to obtain numbers that are added together to arrive a score.

- *Model performance evaluation*

  - Produce the predicted probabilities (EPD) and align scoring benchmarks. For this, one can rank the customers in terms of score bands or EPDs.
  - Using the estimated model, one can conduct sensitivity analysis to assess the impact of each variable on the PD. This helps the analyst to understand the economic significance of each parameter in explaining default risk.
  - In-sample validation: This is also called goodness-of-fit test. For this, adjusted R^2, Hosmer Lomeshow Goodness of fit, Chi-square tests (predicted vs. actual default) are used to evaluate and compare the model performance. Power curves like cumulative accuracy profile (CAP), Gini coefficients are also estimated for development sample.
  - Out-of-sample analysis: This is also called hold out sample validation. This is done by checking the forecasting and discriminatory power of the model through Gini coefficient or accuracy ratio, AUROC, brier scores, etc. These validation techniques have been discussed in detail in Chapter 5.

Furthermore, population stability tests are also to be carried out to check the applicability of the model in current environment. Chart 2.8 summarizes the basic steps behind developing a retail scoring model under the Basel II IRB approach.

Chart 2.8: Steps in Developing a Basel II IRB Retail Scoring Model

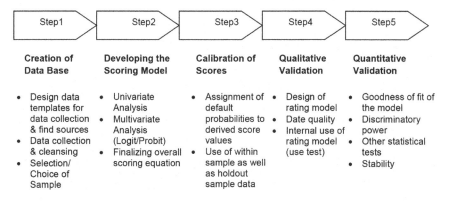

Source: OeNB (2004). Guidelines on Credit Risk Management-Rating Models and Validation. Oesterreichische Nationalbank (OeNB), Vienna, Australia.

Examples of Retail Scoring Models

A bank can use statistically derived scoring model to predict borrower level default risk which can be customized at the bank level for the use of credit sanctioning and also to study the customer behaviour. Such type of retail scoring model will also satisfy the requirements of an IRB approach under Basel II. Besides the IRB requirements, use of such scientific rating tools will improve risk management capability of the organization than mere complying with the regulations.

Application credit scoring and behavioural scoring models are the techniques that help organizations decide whether or not grant credit to consumers who apply to them. The first kind of decision that the lenders have to make is whether they should grant credit to new applications. The tools that aid this decision are called credit scoring methods. The second type of decision is how to monitor the existing customers.

Chart 2.9 summarizes various risk factors that may significantly impact residential housing loan default in India. This chart is based on housing market default risk study of 14,000 borrower data over 12 years period obtained from the housing finance companies and banks in India.[3]

Chart 2.9: Retail Credit Risk Model – Risk Factors in Housing Loan Illustration

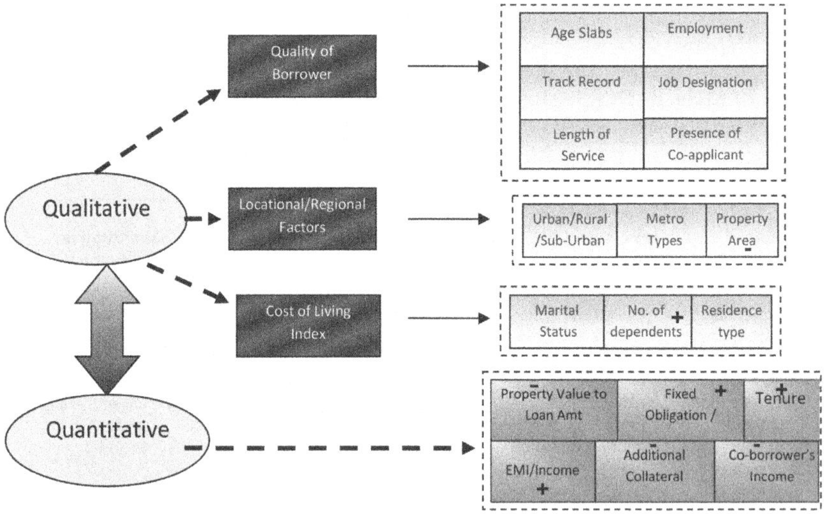

Source: Bandyopadhyay and Saha (2011).

---

[3]   For details, see Bandyopadhyay, A. and A. Saha (2011), JES paper.

The risk factors have been obtained through a set of logistic regression techniques. The positive sign of a factor is increasing the chance of a borrower to default (i.e. higher odds of default: D/S). The negative sign is reducing the borrower risk position. This study has also done some sensitivity analysis and finds that a 10 per cent decrease in the market value of the property vis-à-vis the loan amount raises the odds of default by 1.55 per cent. This implies deterioration in the credit rating of a borrower in the event of fall in margin. Similarly, a 10 per cent increase in EMI to income ratio raises the delinquency chance by 4.50 per cent. This captures the impact of interest rate movement on borrower rating. Such sensitivity analysis allows banks to constantly monitor the rating position of a borrower and take necessary follow up actions.

The above model's risk factors can be used to develop a housing application scorecard. This has been shown in Table 2.8. The weights and the coefficient signs have been obtained from a regression analysis that has been used in Bandyopadhyay and Saha (2011). As can be seen, all the attributes of this scorecard are intuitively sensible.

In Table 2.8, we have also shown how this retail scoring model can be used to predict borrower risk of default. For this, we have obtained information about two borrowers (borrower 1, which is actually a safe customer and borrower 2, who is risky) and applied the scorecard.

Table 2.8: Example of Statistically Derived Application Scorecard – Residential Housing Loan

Variables	Weight	Sign & Highly Significant?	Sample Values: Borrower 1	Sample Values: Borrower 2	Unit
Area (Log value of Sq. mt)	−0.599	negative & yes	5.70	4.25	Sq.mt.
EMI to Income Ratio	0.371	positive & yes	30%	60%	
Magin (*C/**E)	−0.169	negative & yes	140%	80%	
GDP Growth	−13.88	negative & yes	7.80%	7.80%	
No. of Dependent	0.06	positive & yes	1	4	
Additional collateral	−0.145	negative & yes	1	0	dummy=1 if yes,=0, if no

Table 2.8 contd.

Table 2.8 contd.

No. of co-borrower	−0.244	negative & yes	1	0	
Co-borrower's monthly Income	−0.0001	negative & yes	10,000	0	in Rs. Unit
Tenure (in months)	0.007	positive & yes	30	120	
Location: Sub-urban vs. Urban	0.622	positive & yes	1	0	dummy=1 if yes,=0, if no
Location: Rural vs. Urban	0.579	positive & yes	0	1	dummy=1 if yes,=0, if no
Mid Sized City vs. Big City	−0.136	negative & yes	1	0	
Small City Vs. Big City	−0.534	negative & yes	0	0	
Ageslab<40 vs. Ageslab50–60	−0.866	negative & yes	1	0	
Ageslab40-50 vs. Ageslab50–60	−0.429	negative & yes	0	0	
Ageslab>60 vs. Ageslab50–60	−0.228	negative & no	0	1	dummy=1 if yes,=0, if no
Employed vs. Unemployed	−0.362	negative & yes	1	0	
Self Employed vs. Unemployed	0.495	positive & yes	0	0	
Retired & Pensioners	−0.228	negative & yes	0	0	
Other Factors also include Age slab 50–60; BigCity & Urban factors	5.395	positive & yes			
Z			−1.091	3.286	
Expected Probability of Default (EPD) =			25.15%	96.39%	
		Rating	**V good**	**V risky**	

Source: Bandyopadhyay and Saha (2011).

Note: *C = collateral value; **E = exposure amount.

The odd of default (D/S) can be estimated by using function: $exp\,(Z)$.

The scoring model generates not only the Z scores, but also the expected probability (EPD) of default. The expected probability of default can be expressed by: EPD = $1/(1 + \exp(-z))$; where exp = 2.71828. If EPD > 50%, the borrower's chance of default is higher than its chance to remain solvent. Similarly, if EPD < 50%, its chance to remain solvent is higher than the chance of default. This way, borrowers can be classified and can be rated based on their Z scores. The odd to default ratio (D/S) is the probability of occurrence of default (or bad) to the solvency (good), which can be expressed by: D/S=exp(z).

Agriculture Rating Model to Evaluate Risk in Farm Loans

As the New Basel Capital Accord encourages financial institutions to develop and strengthen risk management systems, banks need to obtain a more objective rating of retail loan portfolios even for agriculture loans. Because agricultural credit conditions change rapidly, a more scientific risk rating process will enable the bank to estimate its credit risk more accurately. The traditional role of bank credit in agriculture in India has been to fund production of traditional and seasonal crops, development of lands and longer term investments in land, buildings, equipment and breeding stock. The repayment of agricultural loans depends primarily on the successful production and marketing of the product, and secondarily on the collateral taken for the loan. Credit risk is the most significant risk in agricultural lending. Therefore, while modelling credit risk for agricultural loans, one must account for the borrower-specific risk characters, like borrower profile, cost of living, banking habit, financial position, etc. The performance of the loan is also influenced by economic cycles and is highly correlated with crop type, seasonality and geographic location.

Chart 2.10 portrays the key risk factors in agricultural lending in India. These risk parameters have been obtained using zonal level agricultural loan data history of a leading public sector bank in India.

This model includes both qualitative and quantitative factors in assessing credit risk of agricultural loans. The sign of each factor shows its relationship with the borrower's default probability (i.e. the odds of default: ln(PD/PS)).

Because of broad spectrum of agricultural activities, the types of risks involved in agri-lending also vary. This is why facility risk component is very important. It is important that the lender should fully understand the critical factors and risk associated with each operation being financed.

Based on the analysis of the above factors, a statistically derived scoring model along with the weights has been documented in Table 2.9.

Chart 2.10: Risk Factors in Agri-loans

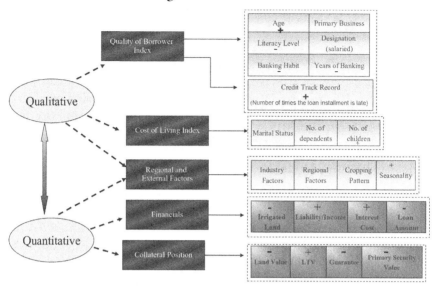

Source: Bandyopadhyay (2008).

Table 2.9: Statistically Derived Risk Weights in Agri-loans

Items#	Risk Parameters	Weightage Scheme	Weights	Significance
1	**Quality of Borrower Index**	=1.1+1.2+1.3	**3.74%**	
1.1	Age (+)		0.09%	Yes
1.2	Banking Habit (−)		3.48%	Yes
1.3	Age of the Relationship with Bank (−)		0.16%	Yes
2	**Cost of Living Index**	=2.1	0.05%	
2.1	Number of Dependents (+)		0.05%	No
3	**Regional & External Factors**	=3.1+3.2+3.3 +3.4+3.5	**34.57%**	
3.1	Crop Intensity (+)		1.37%	Yes
3.2	Regional Location		14.24%	Yes
3.3	Crop Type		9.97%	Yes
3.4	Yield of Food Crop (−)		6.92%	Yes
3.5	Yield of Cash Crop (−)		2.07%	No

Table 2.9 contd.

Table 2.9 contd.

4	Financials	=4.1+4.2+4.3	3.88%	
4.1	Loan size in log scale (–)		1.64%	Yes
4.2	Total Liability/Total Income (+)		0.29%	No
4.3	Interest Burden (+)		1.96%	Yes
5	**Facility or Security Information**	=5.1+5.2+5.3+ 5.4+5.5+5.6	**51.80%**	
5.1	Facility Characteristics		48.22%	Yes
5.2	Loan Tenure (–)		0.96%	Yes
5.3	Presence of Guarantor (–)		1.92%	No
5.4	Primary Security Type		0.24%	No
5.5	Primary Security Margin (+)		0.01%	No
5.6	Value of own Land/Land area in acres (–)		0.45%	No
6	**Other Factors**		5.97%	No

Source: Bandyopadhyay (2008).
Note: The above scoring model has been developed using a multivariate logistic regression method. The weights have been derived from the estimated regression coefficients (standardized). The term significance means the statistical significance of these parameters at 5 per cent or better level. The above model is constructed using the data sample of 800 borrowers (estimated sample observations = 448). The overall explanatory power of the model (measured by R^2) is 0.41. The overall discriminatory power of the model measured by the area under ROC curve is 0.8893.

We have developed this scoring model using a robust sample data of 800 loan accounts and borrower details collected from four circles of a leading public sector bank in India. The factors reported in Table 2.9 have a combined effect on the creditworthiness of a borrower applying for agriculture loan. This model is able to discriminate between the good customer and bad customer. The model's within sample discriminatory power is measured by the 'Area under ROC curve' whose value is 0.893, which means the model has good predictive power.

The prototype agri-scoring model reported in Table 2.9 may enable a credit officer to objectively assess risks in an agricultural loan proposal. It has been observed that regional and external factors and facility characteristics contribute a lot in determining the default risk of agriculture loans, and maximum weights have been given to these two risk fields. A credit officer also needs to look at the relevant documents submitted by the borrower, the presence of government subsidy, product market condition (especially the price movements) as additional factors to arrive at an overall assessment of the borrower. A rater can also slightly adjust the final grade up or down based on their judgement. For this, bank can explicitly assign a weight in the final rating (e.g. approximately 6 per cent weights given to incorporate other factors in Table 2.9). This way, one can also incorporate judgemental factors into a statistical model but to an explicitly limited degree.

After estimating the model, we have tested it on 800 sample borrowers to derive the predicted Z scores and corresponding expected probability of default (EPD). The predicted scores are then ranked in ascending order (low EPD to high EPD) to find EPD ranges through a percentile method. Finally, model output (EPD) is calibrated to sample default probabilities. The accompanying Table 2.10 illustrates the calibration process that was used to define the agri-scoring buckets. The rating scales have been assigned by comparing the predicted (ex-ante) EPD ranges with median realized (ex-post) default rates. Similar exercise needs to be done on a wider database of bank during customization process. The bank should have a sufficiently large data history of past PDs to stabilize the rating buckets. The calibration process has been discussed in detail in Chapter 5.

Table 2.10: Mapping Scores to PD

EPD Ranges	Rating Scale	Actual Median Default Rate
0.00–4%	AGR1 (Highest Safety)	0.00%
4–10%	AGR2 (Very Good)	0.00%
10–13%	AGR3 (Good)	0.69%
13–25%	AGR4	2.41%
25–27.3%	AGR5	2.76%
27.3–40%	AGR6 (Moderate)	4.83%
40–50%	AGR7	5.52%
50–61%	AGR8 (Early Warning)	7.24%
61–83%	AGR9 (Risky)	13.45%
83–95%	AGR10 (Very Risky)	15.86%
95–99%	AGR11 (Highest Risky)	17.24%

Source: Bandyopadhyay (2008).

After building the above type of internal scoring models, banks have to use them (a) to assess the creditworthiness of their borrowers during loan sanction process and (b) estimate regulatory capital and economic capital on a portfolio basis. After defining the rating scales, banks have to track the record of default rates per rating category, per region, per retail products to derive the portfolio benefit under the Basel II IRB capital rule.

Example of behavioural scorecard

Behavioural scoring systems allow lenders to make better decisions for the existing clients by forecasting their future performance. From a bank's point of view, it is critical to monitor the payment behaviour of its current customers in order to prevent them from defaulting later. Behavioural scoring is a method of updating the assessment of borrower risk in the light of the current and most up-to-date performance of the existing consumer. Borrower performance on one product may give good warning signals of their likelihood to default on other products. A behavioural scoring technique helps a bank to take decisions on various aspects, such as:

1. If an existing customer wants to increase his/her credit limits, whether the bank will agree to that?
2. What selling and pricing strategy should be taken for the safe customer?
3. What preventive actions should be taken if the borrower starts to show signs on problems?

The behavioural scorecards are used by few leading private sector banks in India (like ICICI Bank, HDFC Bank, etc.) that are highly focused in the retail business. It enables the bank to understand the dynamic behaviour of the customer and assess the survival of loans.

The extra information needed in behavioural model compared to application scorecard is the repayment history of the customer, which is available within the bank itself. The process for developing behavioural scorecards is similar to that for application scorecards, with the exception that the borrowers are the existing customers with sufficient credit history. Behavioural scorecard can be developed statistically using logistic or multinomial logit regression techniques.

There are six different types of scoring models that can be developed statistically:

*   **Model 1:** Predict the likelihood that a loan currently outstanding or currently approved for disbursement under standard loan evaluation process will have at least one spell of arrears of at least x days.

➔ This can be used to guide risk-based pricing or to mark potential loans for extra review or outstanding loans for a preventive visit from a loan officer before they fall into arrears.

- **Model 2:** Predict the likelihood that a loan x days in arrears now will eventually reach y days of arrears.

  ➔ This information can be used to prioritize visits by loan officers to delinquent borrowers.

- **Model 3:** Predict the likelihood that a borrower with an outstanding loan in good standing will choose not to get a new loan once the current one is repaid.

  ➔ This information can be used to offer incentives to good borrowers who are likely to drop out.

- **Model 4:** Predict the expected term of maturity of the next loan of a current borrower.

- **Model 5:** Predict the expected size of disbursement of the next loan.

- **Model 6:** The ultimate scoring model combines information from the 1–5 models with knowledge of expected revenue of a loan with a given term of maturity and disbursement and with knowledge of the expected costs of drop-outs, loan losses (or default) and monitoring borrowers in arrears (i.e. loan recovery).

Some typical characteristics that can be used in developing *behavioural score-cards* that better describes the conduct of the customer are:

- *Savings a/c Balance Information:* Monthly/quarterly trend in average balance and maximum and minimum levels of balance.

- *Loan Information:* Average balance to total value of credits ratio and their range; total number of credits (in a month/quarter); utilization pattern of the credit limit, number of collateral free loans, etc.

- *Debt proceeds:* Average balance to total value of debits ratio, minimum, maximum range.

- *Transaction data:* The way in which ATMs, credit cards, cheques, balance transfers, etc. take place as payment mechanism.

- *Mode of payments:* Cash payment, cheque payments, etc.

- *Signs of delinquent behaviour:* Number of missed payments, period of delays in the payment (no. of times and months of arrears due, maximum period of dues).

- *Borrower characteristics:* Age, job designation, marital status, relationship with the bank, residential status, etc.

A pure behavioural scoring model will only include variables related to customer's performance and variables obtained from the monthly credit bureau reports.[4] For example, in predicting delinquency of credit card loans, past delinquency of obligors and obligation to income ratio are considered most important. At the time of acquisition, Credit Bureau records past borrower behaviour in terms of repayment history and inquiries about income and obligation to income ratio for credit card borrowers. Banks also check balance carry to income ratio, total credit debt to income, etc. All these factors are considered while modelling. Behavioural scoring technique facilitates more practical loan monitoring process, predicts survival period of a loan, estimates the profitability of customers on a product, etc. Such calculations are required to predict how much the lender needs to provide to cover the expected loss of a loan. An IRB bank will have to mix application scores with behavioural scores for the existing customers in order to obtain a more stable estimate of grade-wise PDs for different retail sub-segments (e.g. housing, education, auto, credit card, personal loans, etc.).

Modern Methods

Structural Models like Moody's KMV, reduced form or intensity-based models, hybrid scoring models (statistical, includes a mix of structural, ratio-based and non-financial factors).

Market-based Corporate Default Risk Model

Mapping corporate drift towards default is a crucial part of any financial institution's credit risk measurement. Banks need to predict the possibility of default of a potential borrower before they extend a loan. This can lead to sounder lending decisions. Monitoring the likelihood of corporate default is essential not only for better pricing in a competitive environment, but also for estimating capital cushion needed in case of unexpected default that can erode capital to a potentially dangerous degree.

Academic belief is that default is driven by market value of firm's assets, level of firm's obligations (or liabilities) and variability in future market value of assets. As the market value of firm's assets draws near the book

---

[4]   Like Equifax, Experian and TransUnion, in the US, Credit Information Bureau India Ltd. (CIBIL) is the consumer credit reporting agency in India licensed by RBI. Credit Bureaus collect and maintain records of retail customers' payments pertaining to loans and credit cards.

value of liabilities, its relevant net-worth approaches zero and the default risk of firm increases. In the option pricing model (based on Merton's 1974 model), the loan taken out by the company is associated with the purchase of an option which would allow the equity investors to satisfy the claims of the debt lenders by handing over the company instead of repaying the debt in the case of default. The price the company pays for this option corresponds to the risk premium included in the interest on the loan. The price of the option can be calculated using option pricing models commonly used in the market. This calculation also yields the probability that the option will be exercised. This probability measure is termed as expected default frequency (EDF).

The main idea underlying option pricing models is that a credit default will occur when the market value of the firm's assets falls below the book value of its debt. KMV Corporation, now owned by Moody's (new name Moody's KMV) since 2002, has a procedure for estimating the PD of a firm that is based conceptually on Merton's (1974) option theoretic approach.

In this approach, a firm's relevant net worth = Mkt. Value of Assets – Default Pt. The firm will default, when relevant net worth => 0. The default point is the threshold value of firm's assets. It lies somewhere between total liabilities and current liabilities at which the firm defaults.

Basically there are three steps in estimating expected default frequency of a company:

i. Estimation of current market value of firm's assets and volatility of asset return by using market capitalization, stock return volatility and book value of liabilities.
ii. Calculation of distance to default (DD).
iii. Mapping expected default probability (EDF) from DD using normal distribution.

MKMV equations: Loans as options

Moody's KMV (or MKMV) provides a term structure of physical default risk probabilities using the Kealhofer, McQuown and Vasicek (KMV) models. Following the pioneering work of Black and Scholes (1973) and Merton (1974), KMV model recognizes that when a firm raises funds by issuing bonds or increasing its bank loans, it holds a very valuable default or repayment option. That is, if the firm's investment project fails so that it cannot repay the bank, it has the option of defaulting on its debt repayment and turning any remaining assets over to the debt holder. Equity is the most junior claim on the assets of the firm. Because of the limited liability for equity holders, the borrower's loss has limited downside risk by the amount of equity invested in the firm.

A firm defaults when the value of its business (i.e. MVA) falls below its liabilities (default point). On the other hand, if firm's investment project earns good returns, the borrower can keep most of the positive returns on asset invested after the promised principal and interest on the debt have been paid. As long as the value of the business is greater than the obligations due, the equity holders have the ability and the incentive to pay the debt obligations. Market value of assets is the net present value of the firm's future cash flows. It is not the book value of assets. If firm's assets have sufficient market value, the firm can raise cash and pay its debt by selling a portion of its assets or by issuing additional equity. The MKMV has used this relatively simple idea into a credit monitoring model based on the firm's market data which can be very frequently updated.

Market coordinates multiple and disparate sources of information about a firm. Market information can be updated on a more frequent basis than any other types of models. Many internationally best practices large financial institutions use market-based models (also termed as structural models) to determine the expected default risk frequency (EDF) of large corporations. EDF is the probability that a firm's future market value will be insufficient to meet its future debt obligations. Performance of these models is consistently found to be good.

Merton (1974) noted that when a bank makes a loan, its pay-off is isomorphic to writing a put option on the assets of the borrowing firm. If the value of the firm falls below a certain threshold, the shareholders will put the firm to the debt holders. The KMV model uses the following payoff equations based on five key variables:

Loan payoff = payoff to the writer (or seller) of a European put option on the assets of the borrowing firm.

Value of put option on stock $= f(S, X, r, \sigma, \tau)$; where S = stock price, X = exercise price, r = risk-free rate, σ = equity volatility, τ = time to maturity.   Eq. 2.9

Value of default option on risky loan $= f(A, B, r, \sigma_A, \tau)$; where A = market value of assets, B = face value of debt, r = risk-free rate (e.g. 364 T bills rate), σ_A = asset volatility, τ = time to debt maturity.   Eq. 2.9a

Note that function "*f*" is the Black and Scholes (1973) option function.

Payoff for the Borrower and the Creditor

The payoff is a function of the value of the firm V at the debt maturity. D is the principal of debt. Borrowing company has the option of defaulting on its debt repayment if its investment project fails. Since the company is owned by the equity holders, due to limited liability for equity holders, the borrower's loss is limited on the downside by the amount of equity invested in the firm. On the other hand, if the project return is good, the borrower can retain most of the upside returns on asset invested after the promised principal and interest on the debt have been paid. The KMV model of Moody's (KMV Credit Monitor) has used this theoretical relation to develop their credit monitoring model.

The left-hand panel of Chart 2.11 depicts the pay-off to the borrower. Where S is the size of the initial equity investment in the firm, D is the value of outstanding loan amount and V is the market value of the assets of the firm. If the investment project does badly such that its assets are valued at lower point V_1, the equity holders of the firm due to its limited liability will default on the firm's debt and turn its assets (V_1) over to the debt holder and lose only their initial stake in the firm (S). On the other hand, if the firm does well and the project return is good, asset value will be high (V_2) and the firm's stockholders will be able to pay off the firm's debt ($0D$ amount) and retain the difference ($V_2–D$). The value of the loan from the perspective of the borrower is: *max [D, V]*. Quite obviously, higher the values of V relative to D, the better off are the firm's stockholders. Thus, the borrower has a very large potential upside return if things turn out well but face only a limited downside risk which is analogous to buying a call option on the assets of the firm under uncertainty.

Similarly, the right panel of the Chart 2.11 explains the pay-off to the bank (the debt holder or the creditor) on the same loan, which is isomorphic to the payoff to the writer of a call option. The pay-off to the debt holder is bounded by the repayment of the principal D. The value of the loan from the perspective of the lender is: *min [D, V]*. That is, the payoff function to the debt holder is similar to writing a put option on the value of the borrower's assets with D, the face value of debt, as the exercise price. The firm will repay the loan if $V > D$ (i.e. say asset value is at V_2) and debt holder will receive its fixed return similar to the premium on a put option. However, if the value of the firm is below debt ($V < D$), the borrower defaults and then debt holder will exercise the option and will seize the entire value of the firm V. When asset value is at V_1, region left to D, the debt holder will receive back only those assets remaining as collateral and will lose $D–V_1$.

Chart 2.11: Pay-off Functions

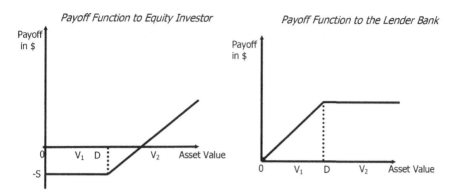

Source: Saunders and Allen (2002).

Strength of the option pricing model lies in the fact that it can be applied to any publicly traded firm. It is forward looking and has a strong theoretical underpinning where equity is viewed as a call option on the asset of the firm.

In general, for options on stocks, all five variables on the RHS of the equation 2.1 are directly observable. However, in the latter case, the market value of the firm's assets (A) and its volatility are not directly observable.

The real innovation of the KMV credit monitor model is that it turns the bank's lending problem around and considers the loan repayment incentive problem from the view point of the borrowing firm's equity holder.

In general terms, equity can be valued as a call option on a firm:

Equity valuation: $E = h\ (A, \sigma_A, B, r, \tau)$ Eq. 2.10

E is the market value of equity (or market capitalization) which can be obtained from the market. A is the market value of assets, which is not directly observable. σ_A is the asset volatility, r is the risk-free rate (e.g. 364 T bills rate) and τ is the time horizon (say 1 month or 1 year).

To solve the problem of A and std. dev. (A) or σ_A, the model uses (a) the structural relationship between the market value of the firm's equity and the market value of its assets and (b) the relationship between the volatility of a firm's assets and the volatility of the firm's equity. After the values of these variables are derived, an expected default frequency (EDF) measure for the borrower can be calculated.

The model brings another volatility equation to solve for A and σ_A:

$$\sigma_E = g(\sigma_A) \qquad \text{Eq. 2.11}$$

σ_E: Equity volatility which is the standard deviation of daily (or monthly) stock price return.

where h and g represents the cumulative normal distribution function. The debt value is given by $D = A-E$.

The simple BSM structural model formula expresses equity value today (E_0) as an option on the firm value. Equity holders get only an amount remaining after paying the debt holders on date T. The pay-off of the equity holders is like payoff from holding a long position in a call option on the firm's assets with strike price D and maturity:

$$E_T = Max(V_T - D, 0) \qquad \text{Eq. 2.12}$$

This way, Merton's (1974) model links the market value of equity and market value of the assets of the firm as follows:

$$E_0 = V_0 N(d_1) - De^{-rT} N(d_2) \qquad \text{Eq. 2.13}$$

Where

$$d_1 = \frac{\ln(V_0 / D) + (r + \sigma_V^2 / 2)T}{\sigma_V \sqrt{T}} \quad \& \quad d_2 = d_1 - \sigma_V \sqrt{T}$$

The Black and Scholes (1973) option pricing formulation has been mathematically illustrated in Hull (2007).

Today, the market value of debt is: $V_0 - E_0$; the value of risky debt can be given by

$$D_0 = V_0 - E_0 = V_0 N(-d_1) + De^{-rT} N(d_2) \qquad \text{Eq. 2.14}$$

The expression N is the cumulative density function of a standard normal distribution.

We can observe E_0 if the company is publicly traded. We can also estimate equity volatility from the daily/weekly/monthly stock return series of the company.

From Ito's lemma, we get:

$$\sigma_E E_0 = N(d_1)\sigma_V V_0$$

$$\sigma_E E_0 = \frac{\partial E}{\partial V}\sigma_V V_0 \qquad \text{Eq. 2.15}$$

Solving two simultaneous equations 2.13 and 2.15 of the form F(x,y)=0 and G(x,y)=0, using Newton Raphson Algorithm, we can solve for MVA (or A) and asset volatility (σ_v). The constrained optimization can be run using excel solver. The optimization problem can be written as: minimize $F(x,y)^2+G(x,y)^2$ with respect to V and σ_v. Here, we assume that the maturity period (T) is 1 year. However, one can also produce monthly EDFs by assigning $T = 1/12$. This optimization can be successfully conducted using excel solver. This optimization technique is similar to solving the problem of maximizing utility subject to the budget constraint which is popularly used in consumer theory in economics.

Now, we can solve for A and σ_A to obtain a Distance to Default

$$(DD) = \frac{A - D}{A \times \sigma_A}$$

The risk neutral probability of default on the debt is: $N(-d2)$ which has been worked out subsequently.

A firm's distance to default measures the difference between the estimated market value of the assets (A) and the total liabilities (D), scaled by the standard deviation of the assets' market value. Here, we numerically demonstrate how the market values of asset and the volatility of asset are estimated with an exercise.

Example: Let the values arising out of the equations 2.12 and 2.14 for any given firm with equity value $6 million, equity volatility 50 per cent and book value of debt $14 million (to be paid within 1 year) with a risk-free rate of 7.7 per cent be derived by an analyst. The obtained solutions are presented below:

The current year market value of asset A (or V_0) = $18.955 million
Asset volatility σ_A (or σ_v) = 15.936%.
The default boundary (D) = $14 million.

Assuming that the future value of the asset of the borrower is normally distributed around the firm's current asset value, one can directly measure the distance from default (DD) at the one-year horizon as:

Distance from default = (A–D)/std. dev. (A)
=(18.955 – 14)/(15.936% × 18.955)
= 1.64 (approximately)

This is a simple measure of DD. It implies that for the firm to enter the default region, the asset values would have to drop by $4.955 million which corresponds to 1.64 standard deviation. This means the firm is 1.64 standard deviation (σ) away from the default point (D). Assuming the asset value is normally distributed with 0 mean and 1 standard deviation, we know that there is 5 per cent probability that asset values will be below the default threshold. Therefore, the expected default frequency (EDF) for the company or obligor would be 5 per cent. Normality assumption plays a crucial role in the computation of the theoretical EDF.

In this exercise, the market value of debt (MVD) = MVA – MVE = $12.955 million. The present value of 1 year debt is $14e^{-0.077 \times 1} = \$12.962$ million. Therefore, the expected loss on debt = (12.962 – 12.955)/12.962 = 0.055%. The expected loss given default (LGD) would be = 0.055%/5% = 1.10%.

The KVM model differs from Merton model (1974) with respect to the default threshold and default probabilities. In KMV, default boundary is called default point (DP) and is not total debt (or total liability). KMV's DP is the sum of all the short-term debt (STD) and one-half of all the long-term debt (LTD) of the company. KMV model uses the default boundary or default point (DP, or D) as: DP = short-term debt + 0.5 × long-term debt. If the firm's asset return is good and stable, its distance to default (DD = difference between the asset's market value and the book value of liability to asset volatility) will be high and its expected solvency position would be good or EDF will be low.

The theoretical risk neutral probability of default (or EDF) = $\Pr(V_t \leq D)$

$$=N(-DD) = \frac{E[V_T] - DP}{\sigma_V}$$

$$= N\left\{-\frac{\ln(V_0 / D) + (r - \sigma_V^2 / 2)T}{\sigma_V \sqrt{T}}\right\} \qquad \text{Eq. 2.16}$$

where N{.} is the cumulative standard normal distribution. In excel, it can be written as "=normsdist(.)". Using the above expression, the EDF at the end of the year T for the previous example firm would be: 1.058 per cent. The other derived values are: $d_1 = 2.4644$ and $d_2 = 2.3050$. Hence, the distance to default (DD) at the end of maturity of loan period T is 2.305. Note that here DD is higher and EDF is lower since we have considered market value of assets to grow at a risk free rate.

One can also use asset drift (μ_v) instead of risk-free rate (r) to estimate the "real EDF". When we are pricing bonds, credit derivatives and other credit claims, we should use risk neutral default probabilities. However, for conducting loss scenario analysis on actual credit portfolios, we should use real EDFs. Note that, if asset drift is higher than the risk-free rate, real EDF would be lower than the risk neutral EDF. In practice, KMV (now of

Moody's) also transforms risk neutral probabilities into a BSM framework to real probabilities for various companies.

In case of real EDF measure, the risk-free interest rate r is replaced by the drift of the assets μ_v.

$$\therefore \; Real\ EDF = N\left\{-\frac{\ln(V_0 / D) + (\mu_v - \sigma_V^2 / 2)T}{\sigma_V \sqrt{T}}\right\} \qquad \text{Eq. 2.17}$$

The asset drift μ_v can be extracted from equity drift μ_e using a capital asset pricing model (CAPM): $\mu - r = \beta(\mu_M - r)$. Note that μ_M is the expected market return and Beta (β) measure the risk of the firm vis-à-vis the market return. For further details, see Bohn (2000), Farmen et al. (2004, 2007), Bandyopadhyay (2007).

However, KMV uses a large historic database of firm defaults and no default to estimate a company's real default probability. Unlike BSM model, KMV does not rely on the cumulative normal distribution N(.) to estimate the probability of default. The reason is default probabilities calculated as N(– DD) would be much lower than the actual PD due to normality assumption. KMV actually maps its EDF to match historical default frequencies recorded on its huge databases.

Chart 2.12 is a graph of the asset value process that follows a Brownian motion and the interpretation of EDF derived from it.

Chart 2.12: Market-based Corporate Default Prediction Model

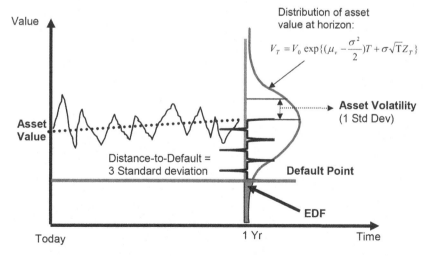

Source: Crouhy et al. (2000).

In the above diagram, we observe that if the future distribution of asset values at horizon of one year were known, the default probability (or EDF) would be the likelihood that the asset value after one year (V_T) falls below the default point (DP) at the analysis horizon. This tail region is marked by shades in the figure. Notice that the Expected Default Frequency (EDF) or PD of a company is thought of as distance from default driven by asset volatility and net worth. As distance to default comes down (DD $\downarrow$) and asset volatility goes up ($\sigma\uparrow$), the firm's chance of default (measured by EDF) goes up ($\Rightarrow PD \uparrow$).

Default occurs after ample early warning in Merton's (1974) structural model. That is, default occurs only after a gradual descent (diffusion) in asset values to the default point (equal to the debt level). The diagram shows the distribution of log normal distribution of the firm's value at a time t^5. Since asset return follows a Brownian motion, the probability of default of a firm (P_{def}) can be transformed into a normalized threshold "Z" such that the area in the left tail below Z measures the real probability of default (Crouhy et al., 2000).

$$\therefore P_{def} = \Pr\left[V_t \leq V_{def}\right]$$

$$= \Pr\left[\frac{\ln(V_0 / D) + (\mu_p - \sigma_V^2 / 2)T}{\sigma_V \sqrt{T}} \geq Z_t\right] \qquad \text{Eq. 2.18}$$

Distance to default DD is a normalized default threshold of asset (i.e. Z_t) such that the area in the left tail below DD is the probability of default.

$$\Rightarrow \Pr\left[Z_t \leq -\left(\frac{\ln(V_0 / D) + (\mu_p - \sigma_V^2 / 2)T}{\sigma_V \sqrt{T}}\right)\right] \equiv N(-d_2) \qquad \text{Eq. 2.19}$$

Where d_2 in KMV term is called distance to default or DD. KMV's empirical EDF utilizes its worldwide huge database of historical defaults to calculate PD. Note that here we are considering that the firm's assets will grow at μ_v rate over the next year and derive the relevant EDF at year end.

Example: Considering the case of same firm, we now have an estimate of asset drift μ_v = 8%, the firm's distance to default (DD) is 2.32 and corresponding real EDF is 1.007 per cent.

---

[5] Note that Market value of the firm is log normally distributed and at time horizon T is: $V_T = V_0 \exp\{(\mu_v - \frac{\sigma^2}{2})T + \sigma\sqrt{T}Z_T\}$; where V_0 is the initial market value of asset $(t=0)$, μ is the asset drift and σ is the asset volatility. Firm's expected market value of asset is $E(V_T)=V_0 \exp(\mu t)$.

Using the similar option pricing framework and asset drift, the credit spread (or the risk premium) can be computed as follows:

$$s = k(T) - r = -\frac{1}{T}\log\phi(d_2) + \frac{V_0}{D}\exp(\mu_v T)\phi(-d_1)$$ Eq. 2.20

The symbol "s" is the difference between yield on risky debt (k) and risk-free rate (r). Where V_0 is the initial asset value of the firm, D is the default barrier or DP for the firm. If the firm's asset value V is below D at the terminal date T (say, 1 month or 1 year), then the firm is in default. μ_v is the drift of the asset return and σ is the volatility of asset return. The symbol "ϕ" stands for cumulative normal distribution function. The expressions d_1 and d_2 are explained in equation 2.13.

Example: Continuing with the same example, the one-year credit spread using equation 2.20 is estimated as 2 per cent (approx.).

A further illustration about critical steps in computing Distance to Default and EDF of a corporate borrower has been shown in Table 2.11.

Table 2.11: Steps in Estimating EDF in MKMV Model

Variable	Value	Notes
Market value of equity	$22,572 billion	(Share Price)×(Share Outstanding)
Book liabilities	$49,056 billion	Balance sheet
Market value of assets	$71,994 billion	Option-pricing model
Asset volatility	10%	Option-pricing model
Default point	$36,993 billion	Liabilities payable within one year
Distance to Default (DD)	4.8	Ratio: $\dfrac{72-37}{72\times10\%}$ (In this example, growth in the asset value between now and the end of the year is ignored)
Normal EDF (one year)	3.4 bp	=N(-DD)
KMV–EDF (one year)	21 bp	Empirical mapping between distance to default and default frequency

Source: KMV (1993), Credit Monitor Overview, Mimeo, KMV Corporation (Revised: 2002).

KMV's EDF is calculated from DD through empirical mapping and not from standard normal distribution table. Firms can, therefore, be put in respective risk buckets based on their DD and empirical EDF can be obtained. For example, if 15 firms out of 1,000 with a DD of 2.32 have defaulted over a 1-year horizon, then the assigned EDF for the firm would be 15/1,000 = 1.50%. The EDF values may range from 0 per cent to 20 per cent or above depending upon the rating, industry affiliation and geographic location of the firm. A mapping of EDF to external rating done by Crouhy et al. (2000) has been shown in Chart 2.13.

Chart 2.13: EDF Mapping and S&P Rating

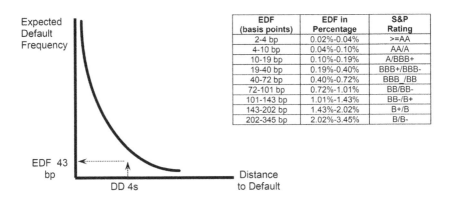

EDF (basis points)	EDF in Percentage	S&P Rating
2-4 bp	0.02%-0.04%	>=AA
4-10 bp	0.04%-0.10%	AA/A
10-19 bp	0.10%-0.19%	A/BBB+
19-40 bp	0.19%-0.40%	BBB+/BBB-
40-72 bp	0.40%-0.72%	BBB_/BB
72-101 bp	0.72%-1.01%	BB/BB-
101-143 bp	1.01%-1.43%	BB-/B+
143-202 bp	1.43%-2.02%	B+/B
202-345 bp	2.02%-3.45%	B/B-

Source: Crouhy, Galai and Mark (2000).

A mapping of DD with external agency rating reveals that a DD of 2.75 and above indicates a corresponding Standard & Poor's rating of BBB. Similar mapping of EDF (based on Merton Model) with CRIS-IL's PD for Indian corporates has been shown in Table 2.12. However, one should be cautious while mapping a point in time EDF measure of credit risk with a through the cycle credit ratings as rating horizons may be different.

Expected default frequency (EDF) is a forward-looking measure of the actual probability of default. EDF is firm specific may vary from industry to industry. The greatest advantage of KMV model over ratio-based or traditional rating models is that it uses timely information from the equity market and, therefore, provides a continuous credit monitoring process that is difficult to replicate using traditional credit analysis. Chart 2.14 documents how MKMV's Credit Monitor predicted the Bankruptcy of Enron.

Table 2.12: Calibration of Real EDFs with CRISIL Corporate Rating Grades

CRISIL rating	CRISIL's Annual PD%	Real EDF%
AAA	0.00	0.00
AA	0.00	0.04
A	1.00	1.62
BBB	3.40	5.75
BB	15.48	6.12
B & Below	29.41	19.57

Source: Bandyopadhyay (2007).

Chart 2.14: Default Example: EDF Mapping of Enron

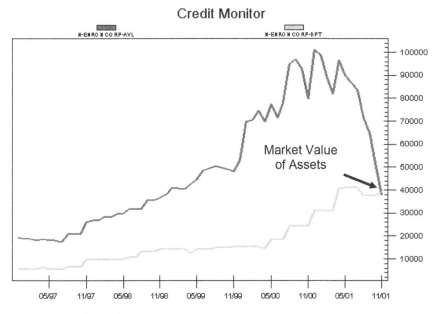

Source: KMV of Moody's.

On 2 December 2001, Enron Corporation filed for protection under Chapter 11 and became the largest corporate bankruptcy in the US history, which reported liabilities at the filing of over US$31 billion and revised liabilities of over US$60 billion. Enron was rated AAA in the end of 1999 and consistent BBB rating in 2000 end and then a B– to CCC+ rating just prior to the filing. Altman's Z score model (the four variable model for non-manufacturing) had Enron as BBB as of 1999 year end (as the rating agency predicted) but then showed a steady deterioration to B as of June 2001. Thus, both Z score and KMV monitor was issuing a warning long before the bad news hit the market.

Using the Merton (1974) model, similar to MKMV type, the default paths of two Indian companies have been mapped in Charts 2.15 and 2.16.

One can clearly notice from Chart 2.15 that the gap between the market value of assets (MVA) of BPL Ltd. and its default point (DP) sharply reduced in year 2003. This is the year when the company's bond received defaulted grade from CRISIL. Note that both the risk neutral EDF (dotted line) and real EDF (red line) shot up in 2003 which spells increase in default risk of the company. BPL Ltd. had reported a net loss of ₹41.59 crore during 2004–05 and its gross sales position was ₹64.45 crore.

Chart 2.15: Mapping Drift to Default of BPL Ltd.

Market Net Worth and EDFs of B P L Ltd.

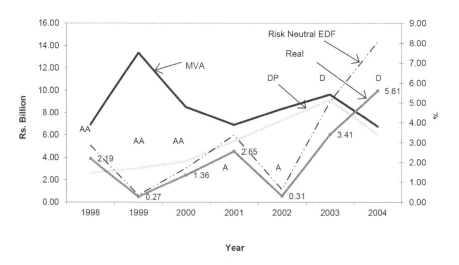

Source: Author's own computation based on Indian data.

Chart 2.16 shows the default path of Kingfisher Airlines which was established in 2003 and had started its commercial operations since May 2005.

Chart 2.16: Mapping EDF for KFA

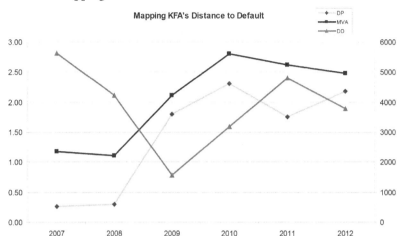

Source: Author's own computation based on Indian data.

One can notice that the gap between the company's market value of asset and default point decreased drastically in 2009. The firm's cushion between the asset and default point measured by distance to default (DD) quickly slipped to a very low level. This is the year when the company's instruments rating were below BBB. This was a clear sign that the company's future default risk has sharply gone up in 2009 itself. Due to a severe financial crisis faced by the airline, it had to finally shut down its operation in October 2012. Having said this, banks must also check whether the borrower engages in activities that make it less likely to repay the loan. Banks will have to be careful about such possibility in advance since such moral hazard activity of borrower may lead to huge losses for the bank.

Thus, these market-based tools certainly could provide an unambiguous early warning that the rating agencies were not able to provide. However, in a recent study, Jessen and Lando (2013) have suggested a volatility adjustment of distance to default measure that significantly improves its default prediction power. Hence, an objective model, based solely on publicly available accounting or market information or a mix of both including non-financial factors can better equip the bank to predict large corporate credit risk. However, it should be noted that although tools like Z score and MKMV EDF were available, losses were still incurred by even the most sophisticated investors and financial institutions. Thus, having these models is simply not enough, what is needed is a credit culture within these financial institutions whereby credit risk tools are listened to and evaluated in good times as well as in difficult situations.

Market-based Measure to Assess the Banks' Risks: Distance to Insolvency

Distance to default measure based on the structural approach of the BSM (1973 and 1974)'s option pricing model discussed above can be useful in predicting bank's failure or bank's insolvency. The distance to default illustrates the market's assessment of the probability that the bank will be able to honour its fixed liabilities (subordinated Tier II debt, borrowings and all deposits). It measures the changes (in number of standard deviation) in the market value of the assets that can be accommodated within the bank's buffer. Hence, it can be used as a measure of bank solvency.

Following this approach, we have estimated the distance to default of 11 major systematically important scheduled commercial banks in India for the year 2011–12 (see Chart 2.17). Tier I per cent is measured in the secondary (right) axis and DD is measured in the primary left axis. Bank's distance to default (DD) measures the difference between the estimated market value of the assets and the total liabilities (deposit and borrowings), scaled by the standard deviation of the assets' market value. If the bank's asset return is good and stable, its distance to default will be high and its expected solvency position would be good. This is a market-based measure of bank solvency (also term as economic capital) as opposed to regulatory capital.

Chart 2.17: Distance to Default as a Measure of Solvency of Indian Banks

Market Based Bank Solvency Position-2011-12

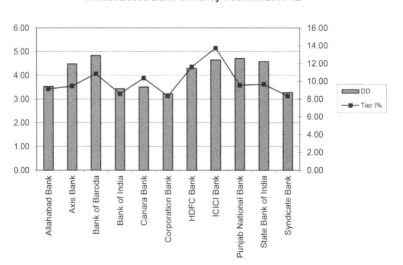

Source: Author's own computation based on stock market and audited balance sheet data.

A mapping of DD with external agency rating reveals that a DD of 2.75 and above indicates corresponding Standard & Poor's rating of BBB. This economic capital measure of banks is purely notional and it has been compared with actual Tier I per cent of these banks for the year 2011–12. However, a recent (2014–15) analysis reveals a significant deterioration in solvency position of certain leading public sector banks in India.

As the next task, we have mapped solvency status of two banks which had capital problems in the past and were taken over. The first bank is Global Trust Bank that had capital problems during the year 2004 and was finally amalgamated into Oriental Bank of Commerce through RBI intervention (Chart 2.18). The second bank United Western Bank Ltd. was in financial distress in 2006 and was finally acquired by IDBI Bank Ltd as a rescue measure instructed by RBI (see its default path in Chart 2.19).

Chart 2.18: Market-based Solvency Position of Global Trust Bank (GTB)

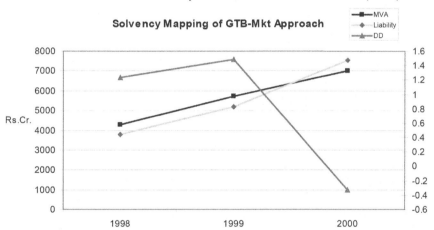

Source: Author's own computation based on stock market and audited balance sheet data.

Our market-based measures reveal that the first bank's DD fell very fast to a dangerously low level as the gap between its MVA and liability shrink (see Chart 2.18). DD became negative for GTB in the year 2000 and the bank was in severe capital shortage. One can also see that the yearly movements of its MVA, Liability and DD have been displayed in Chart 2.19. The bank's DD was just below 1.5 in year 2005 as an evidence of quick erosion of its capital.

Chart 2.19: Market-based Solvency Position of United Western Bank (UWB)

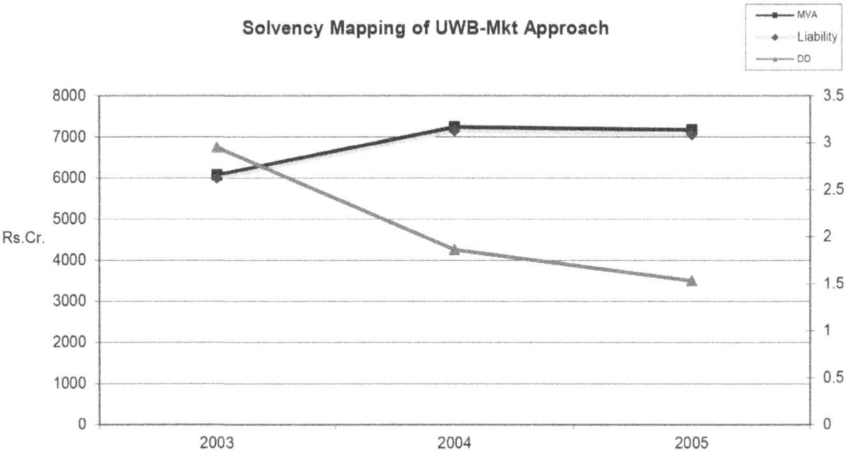

Source: Author's own computation based on stock market and audited balance sheet data.

Advantages of Market-based Model

Strength of the option pricing model lies in the fact that it can be applied to any publicly traded firm. It is forward looking and has a strong theoretical underpinning where equity is viewed as a call option on the asset of the firm. In comparison to traditional ratings, which is subjective and driven by fundamental analysis, EDF-based credit risk measure is more objective, precise and continuous, dynamic and provide full granularity.

Limitations of Structural Model

The structural model has few limitations. First, it is difficult to construct theoretical EDF without normality assumption. Second, it can be applied only to publicly traded firms whose stock price data is available. Private firms' EDFs can be calculated only by using some comparability analysis based on accounting data. Third, it does not distinguish between the different types of long-term bonds in terms of seniority, collateral, covenants or convertibility. Fourth, the structural model underestimates the probability of default over short horizons. Fifth, it understates PD since an asset's expected return is higher than the risk-free rate (real EDF vis-à-vis risk neutral EDF). However, using CAPM, one can remove risk-adjusted rate of return and can derive risk neutral EDF. Sixth, it works best in highly efficient liquid market conditions. Seventh, equity-based models are prone to overreact due to market noise and bubbles and, hence, unlikely to be favoured by the top management in banks. Eighth and last, structural models are based on variables that can be observed over time in the market. Asset values are inferred from equity prices. Structural models are difficult to use if capital structure is complicated and asset prices are not easily observable.

In a recent study, Milne (2014) empirically tested the usefulness of market-based measures of distance to default (DD) in predicting future bank failure. Using share prices as well as accounting ratios data of 41 failed as well solvent global banks, he finds that distance to default responds quickly to new information and can be a useful early warning indicator of imminent failure. However, his paper suggests for developing a more sophisticated version of the contingent claim models by allowing for the possibility of default over many periods and incorporate dynamic evolution of asset prices uncertainty. Thus, these models should be more consciously used by the bank managers as well as shareholders.

Overall, the equity-based structural model reflects the market's view about the probability of default of a company and provides valuable early warning signal about corporate drift to default. The structural model can be a useful complement to an analysis of a firm's fundamentals to get a better foresight.

Reduced Form or Intensity-based Credit Scoring Models

Reduced form models start with the observed debt price or credit spreads and infer PD without knowledge of the firm's balance sheet and internal structure. Intensity-based reduced forms of models are fundamentally empirical as they use observable risky debt prices (credit spreads) in order to ascertain the stochastic jump process governing default. Intensity-based models decompose observed credit spreads on defaul table debt to ascertain both the PD (conditional on there being no default prior to time) and the LGD. These models to estimate default probabilities were originally pioneered by Jarrow and Turnbull (1995), Jarrow, Lando and Turnbull (1997), and Duffie and Singleton (1998, 1999). This approach assumes that a firm default time is unpredictable and driven by a default intensity that is a function of latent state variables. Hull and White (2000) have given detailed explanations of several well-known reduced-form modelling approaches. Jarrow and Protter (2004) have argued that reduced-form models are more appropriate in an information theoretic context given that we are unlikely to have complete information about the default point and expected recovery.

Whereas structural models view default as the outcome of a gradual process of deterioration in asset values, intensity-based models view default as a sudden, unexpected event, thereby generating PD estimates that are more consistent with empirical observations. In contrast to structural models, intensity-based models do not specify the economic process leading to default. Default events are assumed to occur unexpectedly due to one or more exogenous events (observable and unobservable), independent of the borrower's asset value. Defaults occur randomly with a probability determined by the intensity or "hazard" function.

Intensity-based models use observed risky debt (e.g. bonds, credit derivatives) prices and are better able to reflect complex term structures of default than the structural models. The observed credit spread (defined as spread over risk-free rate) is viewed as a measure of expected cost of default using the following expression:

$$CS = PD \times LGD \qquad \text{Eq. 2.21}$$

Credit spread measures the excess return on a corporate bond permitted to an investor as a compensation for taking the credit risk. It is used as a forward-looking risk measure. Different assumptions are used to separate out the PD from the LGD in the observed credit spread. Jarrow, Lando and Turbull (1997) model utilises corporate bond credit spreads to estimate implied PD for corporate borrowers.

However, due to lack of liquid credit spreads, reduced form models may not be applicable in Indian market condition to predict corporate defaults. Although structural models have solid theoretical base, the intensity-based approach is more ad hoc.

Hybrid Credit Scoring Models

Hybrid credit scoring models combine two or more credit risk modelling approaches. For example, a researcher or a credit risk modelling expert can combine the features of a structural model based on Merton's options – theoretic view of firms with an accounting ratio in a multivariate statistical modelling framework. Researchers have proved that such mixture models have better power in predicting potential defaults. The Sobehart & Stein (2000) of Moody's has developed a hybrid RiskCalc® model to predict default risk of public firms. Researchers have found that market information of a firm is more useful when also coupled with fundamental information on the firm and its business environment. Moody's model incorporates the variants of both a contingent claims model and a statistical reduced form model using a non-linear probit regression approach. Using its huge credit research database (CRD), RiskCalc combines several relationships between ratios and default frequencies in a consistent and objective credit risk measure. It uses similar financial statement ratios to those used by credit analysis.

The logit model based on a combination of financial, non-financial and market-based factors developed by Bandyopadhyay (2007) is another example of a hybrid credit-scoring model. This model predicts corporate defaults probability in India. Using data of 150 publicly traded Indian corporates over 7 years (1998–2005) in a logistic modelling framework, it has been found that a mix of parameters obtained from structural model along with financial and non-financial factors can more accurately classify firms in terms of credit risk. Table 2.13 describes the Indian hybrid corporate scoring model.

Table 2.13: Example of Hybrid Corporate Logit Model for Indian Public Firms

Factors #	Variables	Coefficient (or weight)	Description
1	DD	−0.59***	Distance to Default: (MVA-DP)/Asset Volatility
2	NWK/TA	−4.68***	Net working capital over total assets
3	CASHPROF/TA	−6.12***	Cash profit to total assets
4	MVE/BVL	−3.66***	Market value of equity to book value of liabilities
5	SALES/TA	−1.7***	Turnover ratio: sales to total assets
6	LN(TA)	−0.26*	Natural log of total assets measures the firm size
7	DUMMY_TOP50	−1.17***	Dummy representing top 50 business group firms (D=1 for top 50 firms, D=0 for other firms)
8	GNPGR	−0.25***	Annual GNP growth rate at current price capturing the effect of macro cycle.
9	Intercept	4.7***	Constant term capture the other factors that may affect default

Source: Bandyopadhyay (2007).
Note: Included number of observations = 948 with 0.61 R2. Industry effects have been incorporated (not reported). Sample observation is 100. ***, ** and * denote significance at 1 per cent or better, 1–5% and 5–10% level, respectively. The overall accuracy of the model is 92 per cent measured by accuracy ratio.

The key inputs to this hybrid model were: credit rating, return on assets (net income/assets), firm size (log of assets), operating liquidity (working capital/assets)leverage (market value of equity to book value of liabilities), Management factor (represented by group dummy), distance–to–default (obtained from Merton's 1974 option pricing model) and macroeconomic factor (annual GNP growth rate). These variables were able to significantly differentiate between defaulting and non-defaulting firms.

In a recent study, Gupta et al. (2013) have made an attempt to combine financial factors and market-based variables of firms to predict the default risk of 1,392 listed companies in India. These companies issued long-term bond were also rated by rating agency CRISIL. In a set of logit regressions, the researchers have tried to establish a linkage between implicit default probability obtained from KMV model (firm's distance to default) and balance sheet ratios (liquidity, profitability and leverage) and thereby assess these ratios' predictive power. This study also finds that inclusion of market variables along with the accounting variables significantly improves the predictive ability of the model to forecast default risk of firms. The study further confirms that neither the market-based model nor the accounting model is sufficient in predicting the default risk, but a combination of both provides a blend of the merits of both.

Summary

This chapter has provided detailed discussions about various forms of credit rating models used by banks as well as rating agencies. Banks need to develop internal credit risk rating models for different types of exposures under the IRB approach. These models are supposed to play a crucial role in their measurement and management of credit risk at a portfolio level. Credit risk assessment tools assist banks in measuring and aggregating risks across geographical and product lines. A good credit rating system can provide a competitive edge to a bank. Credit-scoring models facilitate objective assessment of loan risk. This benefits both the borrowers as well as the bank. Risk models also help banks to assess precisely the level of economic capital to be allocated to individual credit assets and the credit portfolio as a whole.

The rating agencies' ratings also convey system level, through the cycle information about credit quality of corporate clients. The external ratings can be used by banks for benchmarking their internal rating grades. Bank rating approach differs from rating agencies in architecture and operation design as well as in the uses of ratings. Internal ratings guide a bank for loan origination, portfolio monitoring, loan pricing, limit setting and management reporting. Credit-scoring models are not only limited to predicting credit worthiness but also used in predicting potential default. Banks will have to rightly balance their short-term (PIT) and long-term (TTC) objectives in designing various credit scoring models for regulatory capital estimation.

Banks will have to build up internal risk management capabilities at Head Office (HO) level. More than having the right policies, risk culture needs to be established. A proper documentation of the weights and the logic followed to obtain scores and final uses of these ratings in day-to-day management of credit is very essential for getting the supervisory approval. A more scientifically developed credit-scoring model clearly reduces costs and increases transparency in loan origination and holding. Besides using standard two-tier internal rating models, banks will need KMV-type default prediction models for closely monitoring the default potential of large corporate loans. Recent post-financial crisis credit risk research results reveal KMV-type model has a year forward prediction to the global financial crisis. Studies also show that KMV model is still useful to credit risk management of emerging markets like India and China. Since the KMV model needs capital market data and the listed company's annual report, it can provide timely and more objective prediction about probable default status of large listed companies. The same model can also be used by IRB banks to assess the probability of default for sovereign as well as bank exposures.

Lastly, as most of the banks are now focusing on retail business, they require to develop more scientific IRB retail scoring models and frequently update their loan ratings for measuring and managing credit risk of sub-portfolios (such as housing loans, car loans, credit card and personal loans). It is necessary to optimally combine the outputs from the application and behavioural scorecards and the credit bureau information to provide single measure of PD. While application scorecards are being used to facilitate informed credit approvals, behavioural scorecards enable banks for collection prioritization and pre-delinquency management. The risk analysis of retail loans will enable the banks to better understand the credit needs of the borrowers and extend need-based credit to the desired segment. A bigger challenge will be to compile and maintain such big customer database (application as well as behavioural data), update and validate models and make models useful in taking day-to-day business decisions.

Key learning outcomes

- Structure of credit rating process, its usage
- One-tier vs. two-tier rating system
- Difference between external rating and internal rating process
- Financial risk vs. business risk criteria of credit rating Agencies (CRAs)
- Credit scoring models for corporate and SMEs–Altman Z score, Logistic and Hybrid models
- MKMV market-based default predictor model
- Relationship between option pricing and loan default
- Mapping distance default (DD) with expected default frequency (EDF)
- Market-based measure for predicting bank solvency
- Risk rating for project finance
- Credit-scoring models for retail customers
- Application scoring model vs. behavioural scoring model
- Through the cycle vs. point in time rating

Review questions

After studying the chapter and the relevant reading, you should be able to answer:

1. What is credit scoring system? Mention and discuss the different types of credit-scoring models.
2. What are the differences between external rating and internal rating processes?
3. How can one check whether a bank rating is PIT or TTC?
4. Mention few borrower-specific and market-specific risk factors in predicting default risk.
5. Mention the various uses of credit rating system.
6. Which credit risk models discussed in this section are really forward looking?
7. What is the link between a firm's asset volatility and its expected default frequency?
8. Which ratio in the Altman's original Z score appears most important in assessing credit risk of a loan applicant?
9. What is the difference between application scorecard and behavioural scorecard?

10. List out three strengths and three weaknesses of statistical models vis-à-vis judgemental models.
11. What are the salient features of an infrastructure rating model?
12. Why is SME credit risk assessment different from the corporate?
13. A company has assets of $400,000 and total debts of $160,000. Using an option pricing model, the implied volatility of the firm's assets is estimated as 20 per cent. Using Merton's model (KMV type), estimate the firm's expected default risk.

References

Agarwal, V. and R. Taffler. 2008. "Comparing the Performance of Market-based and Accounting-based Bankruptcy Prediction Models", *Journal of Banking and Finance* 32: 1541–51.

Altman E.I. 1968. "Financial Ratios, Discriminant Analysis and Prediction of Corporate Bankruptcy", *Journal of Finance* September: 189–209.

——— 2000. "Predicting Financial Distress of Companies: Revisiting the *Z* Score and ZETA Models", Working paper (New York: Stern School of Business).

Altman, E.I. and H.A. Rijken. 2006. A Point-in-Time Perspective on Through-the-Cycle Ratings, *Financial Analysts Journal* 52(1): 54–70.

Altman, E.I., J. Hartzell and M. Peck. 1995. *Emerging Markets Corporate Bonds: A Scoring System* (New York: Salomon Brothers.

Arora, N., J.R. Bohn and F. Zhou. 2005. Reduced Form vs. Structural Models of Credit Risk: A Case Study of Three Models, *Journal of Risk Finance* 7(3): 255–72.

Arvelo, M., J. Bell, C. Nova, J. Rose and S. Venugopal. 2008. "Morgan Stanley's Approach to Assessing Credit Risk in the Microfinance Industry", *Journal of Applied Corporate Finance* 20(1): 124–34.

Bandyopadhyay. 2006. "Predicting Probability of Default of Indian Corporate Bonds: Logistic and *Z*-score Model Approaches", *The Journal of Risk Finance* 7(3): 255–72.

——— 2007. "Mapping Corporate Drift towards Default – Part 1: A Market Based Approach", *The Journal of Risk Finance* 8(1): 35–45.

——— 2007. "Mapping Corporate Drift towards Default – Part 2: A Hybrid Credit Scoring Model", *The Journal of Risk Finance* 8(1): 46–55.

——— 2008. "Credit Risk Models for Managing Bank's Agricultural Loan Portfolio", *ICFAI Journal of Financial Risk Management* 5(4): 86–102.

Bandyopadhyay, A. and A. Saha. 2011. "Distinctive Demand and Risk Characteristics of Residential Housing Loan Markets in India", *Journal of Economic Studies* 38(6): 703–24.

Bank for International Settlements, Basel Committee on Banking Supervision. 2001. The Standardized Approach to Credit Risk, Supporting Document to the New Basel Capital Accord, Consultative Document, January.

Black, F. and J. Cox. 1976. "Valuing Corporate Securities: Some Effects of Bond Indenture Provisions", *Journal of Finance* 31: 351–67.

Black, F. and M. Scholes. 1973. "The Pricing of Options and Corporate Liabilities" *Journal of Political Economy* 81: 637–59.

Bohn, J.R. 2000. "A Survey of Contingent Claims Approaches to Risky Debt Valuation", *The Journal of Risk Finance* 1(3): 53–78.

Bouchet, M.H., E. Clark and B. Groslambert. 2003. *Country Risk Assessment – A Guide to Global Investment Strategy* (New York: John Wiley & Sons Ltd).

Chan-Lau, J.A. and N.R. Sy Amadou. 2006. "Distance-to-Default in Banking: A Bridge too Far?" Working Paper, IMF.

Chassang, S. and A. de Servigny. 2002. "Through-the-cycle Estimates: A Quantitative Implementation", Working Paper, Standard & Poor's.

Chorafas, D. 2000. *Managing Credit Risk – Volume 1: Analysing, Rating and Pricing the Probability of Default*, Euro Money.

Crouhy, M., D. Galai and R. Mark. 2000. "A Comparative Analysis of Current Credit Risk Models", *Journal of Banking and Finance* 24(1–2): 59–117.

———— 2001. "Prototype Risk Rating System", *Journal of Banking and Finance* 25: 47–95.

de Servigny, A. and O. Renaut. 2004. *Measuring and Managing Credit Risk* (New York: McGraw Hill).

Duffie, D. and K.J. Singleton. 1998. Simulating Correlation Defaults. Bank of England Conference on Credit Risk Modeling and Regulatory Implications, London, 21–22 September.

———— 1999. "Modeling Term Structures of Defaultable Bonds", *Review of Financial Studies* 12: 687–720.

Farmen, T.E.S., S. Westgaard and N. van der Wijst. 2004. "An Empirical Test of Option Based Default Probabilities using Payment Behaviour and Auditor Notes", Mimeo.

Farmen, T.E.S., S. Westgaard, S.E. Fleten and N. van der Wijst. 2007. "Default Risk and its Greeks under an Objective Probability Measure", SSRN working paper.

Ghosh, S. 2013. "A Study on Differences in Standard & Poor's and Moody's Corporate Credit Ratings", Mimeo, The Leonard N. Stern School of Business.

Gupta, V. 2013. A Unified Credit Risk Model for Predicting Default, *PRAJNAN – Journal of Social and Management Sciences* 42(3): 215–45.

Gupta, V., R.K. Mittal and V.K. Bhall. 2013. "Estimating the Default Risk of Public Limited Companies in India Using Structural KMV Model", *PRAJNAN – Journal of Social and Management Sciences* 41(4): 283–311.

Hull, J. 2007. *Options, Futures, and Other Derivatives,* Sixth ed. (Saddle River, NJ Prentice-Hall College Div).

Hull, J. and A. White. 2000. "Valuing Credit Default Swaps: No Counterparty Default Risk", Working Paper, University of Toronto.

Jarrow, R. and P. Protter. 2004. "Structural versus Reduced Form Models: A New Information Based Perspective", Working Paper, Cornell University.

Jarrow, R., D. Lando and S. Turnbull. 1997. "A Markov Model for the Term Structure of Credit Spreads", *Review of Financial Studies* 10: 481–523.

Jarrow, R.A. and S.M. Turnbull. 1995. "Pricing Derivatives on Financial Securities Subject to Credit Risk", *Journal of Finance* 50: 53–85.

Jayadev, M. 2006. "Predictive Power of Financial Risk Factors: An Empirical Analysis of Default Companies" *Vikalpa* 31 (3): 45–56.

——— 2006. "Internal Credit Rating Practices of Indian Banks", *Economic and Political Weekly* 18: 1070–78.

Jessen, C. and D. Lando. 2013. "Robustness of Distance to Default", SSRN Working Paper, August.

KMV. 1993. Credit Monitor Overview, Mimeo, KMV Corporation.

Laere, V., J. Vantieghem and B. Baesens. 2012. "The Difference between Moody's and S&P Bank Ratings: Is Discretion in the Rating Process Causing a Split?" RMI Working Paper, No. 12/05, September.

Merton, R. 1974. "On the Pricing of Corporate Debt: The Risk Structure of Interest Rates", *Journal of Finance* 29(2): 449–70.

Milne, A. 2014. "Distance to Default and the Financial Crisis", *Journal of Financial Stability* 12: 26–36.

Moody's KMV. 2003. "Modeling Default Risk", Technical Working Paper No. 18, December, MKMV.

Moody's RiskCalc. 2002. "Model for Privately Held U.S. Banks", July. Available at: https://riskcalc.moodysrms.com/us/research/crm/usbanksmethod.pdf

Ohlson, J.A. 1980. "Financial Ratios and the Probabilistic Prediction of Bankruptcy", *Journal of Accounting Research* 18(1): 109–31.

Ong, M.K. 2002. *Credit Ratings: Methodologies, Rationale and Default Risk* (London: Risk books).

Resti, A. 2002. "Replicating Agency Ratings through Multinomial Scoring Model", in *Credit Ratings Methodologies, Rationale and Default Risk*, ed. Michael Ong (London: Risk books), Chapter 10.

Roszbach, K. 2003. "Bank Lending Policy, Credit Scoring and the Survival of Loans", Sveriges Risksbank Working Paper Series 154.

Saunders, A. and L. Allen. 2002. *Credit Risk Measurement: New Approaches to Value at Risk and Other Paradigms* (New York: John Wiley and Sons, 2nd Edition).

Saunders, A. and M.M. Cornett. 2003. *Financial Institutions Management: A Risk Management Approach*, Fourth Edition (Boston, MA: McGraw-Hill).

Sobehart, J.R. and R.M. Stein. 2000. Rating Methodology – Moody's Public Firm Risk Model: A Hybrid Approach to Modeling Short Term Default Risk, Moody's Global Credit Research.

Waagepetersen, R. 2010. "A Statistical Modeling Approach to Building an Expert Credit Risk Rating System", *The Journal of Credit Risk* 6(2): 81–94.

Westgaard, S. and N.V. Wijst. 2001. "Default Probabilities in a Corporate Bank Portfolio: A Logistic Model Approach", *European Journal of Operational Research* 135: 338–49.

## Chapter 3

Approaches for Measuring Probability of Default (PD)

P robability of default (PD) quantifies the likelihood of a borrower that he will not be able to meet its contractual obligations and will default. Default does not necessarily lead to immediate losses, but may increase the likelihood of bankruptcy and, hence, subsequent losses. Default is uncertain. For the correct estimation of credit risk, banks first need to estimate the chance that the borrower will default over a certain time horizon. PD can be termed as the first dimension of measuring credit risk under the Basel II IRB approach. The internal ratings based (IRB) on the new Basel II accord allows banks to use their own internal credit ratings. Banks need to estimate rating-wise PD for the calculation of regulatory capital. The prime objective in modelling default risk is to measure credit risk in terms of default probabilities rather than ordinal rankings. By providing a PD for loan obligor, one is providing a forecast of the likelihood of default over the specified horizon (e.g. one year). This is true even if the historical default experience is used. PD can be estimated at an individual borrower level or at a portfolio level. The probability of default (PD) depends on borrower-specific factors such as the source of finance, financials, firm size, competitive factors, management factors as well as market-specific factors like business environment, unemployment rate, interest rate movements, etc. When credit quality of a borrower worsens, the probability of future default also increases.

The incident of default can be defined in several ways: missing a payment obligation, filing bankruptcy procedure, distressed exchange, breaking a covenant, etc. The definition of default employed in Basel II is based on two sets of conditions (at least one of the conditions must be met): first that "the bank considers that the obligor is unlikely to pay [in full]", and second, that "the obligor's past due is more than 90 days on any material credit obligation". The first is a subjective condition. The second is an objective condition, where the minimum number of days past due date that triggers default is 90 days, and the minimum past due threshold amount is the level of materiality fixed by the bank.

Correct estimation of default probabilities is becoming an increasingly important element of bank's measurement and management of credit exposures as wrong estimates of PD could lead to inappropriate capital allocation and as a consequence, destroy shareholder value due to default.

Methods for Estimating PD

There are broadly two data sources used to compute obligor PD: (a) internal data and model/ internal ratings and (b) external reference data/external ratings. Bank will likely use a bit of both. For middle market and small business, no public rating is available for banks. So, they have to rely on internal ratings history only. However, for large corporate, public ratings are available for benchmarking or calibration of internal ratings.

Default is an extreme event of credit migration. The credit migration or transition matrix describes the likelihood of migrating to any other state, including default, for a given rating. Transition matrix can be constructed through mortality analysis/cohort analysis of rating movements. Cohort is the most popular method for estimating transition matrix. It uses Markov (1907) chain process. Under the Basel II IRB approach, different borrowers are evaluated by internal credit rating models (judgemental/statistical) and then grouped or pooled into various grading buckets (AAA, AA, A, BBB,...., CCC, etc.). Obligors falling into the same bucket are assigned the same pooled average PD which will be the basis for computation of IRB risk weights. However, this grouping can be extended to industry categories, regions (e.g. industry-wise, rating-wise pooled PD) for portfolio segmentation. There needs to be a meaningful distribution of number of borrowers across sub-pools. It is important to note that in order to have a more stable estimate of PD; it is desirable to have a higher number of borrowers in each bucket. If the bucket range is too wide, IRB capital charges would be significantly overestimated.

Transition Matrix

Default is not an abrupt process, a firm's credit worthiness and asset quality declines gradually. Transition probability is the chance of credit quality of a firm improving or worsening. The transition matrix, thus, represents moving probabilities from one rating level to all other ratings, including default for a given rating and time horizon (say one year). It shows the complete possible states that a rating can take over a given time horizon and, therefore, provides detailed information on rating movements. Changes in distribution of ratings provide a much richer picture of changes in aggregate credit quality. When credit quality of corporate bonds worsens, the probability of future default also increases. Default is an ultimate event of credit migration. The last column of the transition matrix represents probabilities of default.

Rating agencies (Standard & Poor's, Moody's, Fitch internationally, in India, CRISIL) provide worldwide valid transition matrices, which could be directly applied for specific markets or industry branches to understand the system-level portfolio risk position of corporates. These published rating transition matrices are useful representations of the historical behaviour of ratings. They can also be used as a benchmark for internal models. Further, if a national bank institution intends to rate the credit standing of counterpart within own rating system, a procedure for synthetic transition matrix generation is needed.

Tasks for computing PDs

The following steps are used to calculate PD:

Step 1: Rate the obligor using one of the following:
- Expert judgement with the given criteria
- Score from a quantitative model
- PD from a quantitative model directly estimating PD

Step 2: Bucket the obligor into one of the seven or more grades

Step 3: Estimate PD for each bucket using one of the following:
- External historical loss data such as rating agencies
- Internal historical loss data for obligors in each bucket

Step 4: Determine the weighted average PDs for obligors in each bucket.

Method for estimation of PD through transition matrix

The transition matrix provides the profile of credit quality changes or migrations that have taken place for the selected credit portfolio between any two years that are selected. The transition matrix is a summary of how all the rated borrower accounts in the user's credit portfolio have migrated (within various standard account categories as well as to default or NPA category) between the selected two years. Normally, the traditional transition matrices provided by rating agencies are in discrete time, typically with a one-year horizon. It is customary to use a one-year horizon in credit risk management. Lando and Skodeberg (2002), Schuermann and Jafry (2002), Schuermann and Hanson (2004), Servigny and Renault (2005) present and review several approaches to estimating these migration matrices. Broadly, there are two approaches: cohort approach and duration (or hazard) approach. The cohort approach counts the observed proportions from the beginning of the year to the end as estimates of annual migration probabilities. Any movements within the year are not accounted for. The duration approach counts all rating changes over the course of the year and divides by the time spent in the starting rating to obtain the migration intensity which is finally transformed into a migration probability. We will mainly focus on the most popular parametric discrete cohort time homogeneous Markov chain approach, which is also approved by the Basel committee.

Chart 3.1 demonstrates some important features of a rating transition matrix. It shows the complete possible states a rating can take over a time horizon say one year. Such a square array is termed as the matrix of transition probabilities.

Chart 3.1: Transition Matrix Approach of Computing PDs

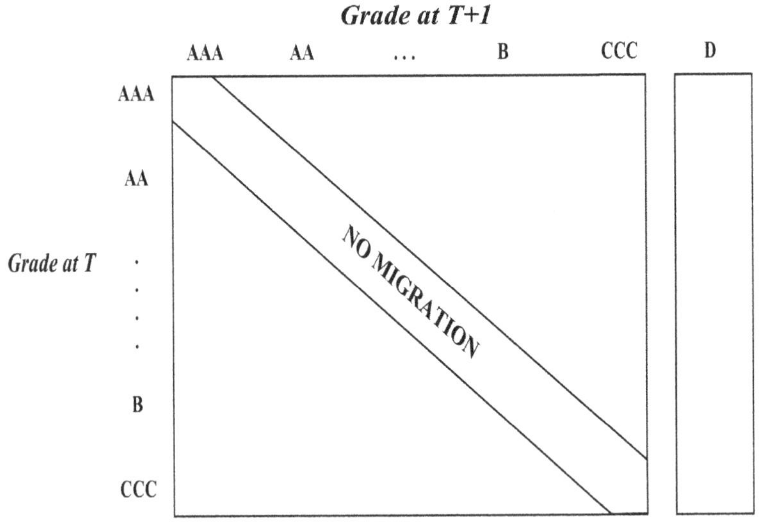

Source: Author's own illustration.

Information at only two dates for each year of data is necessary to calculate such a transition matrix. The rows of a transition matrix in any year show the beginning of year rating (i.e. grade at T) and the columns show the end of year rating (i.e. rating at period T + 1). The diagonal portion of the migration matrix captures the cells where no rating migrations take place. These are also the number of accounts counted for each rating grade where rating retention is taking place. Any movement to the right side of the diagonal for each grade captures the rating slippage. Any movement to the left-hand side from the diagonal position captures the rating up-gradation.

To construct a one-year average transition matrix over several periods (say 10 years), as a first step, one has to do mortality rate analysis of yearly cohorts of companies for at least two years to find the number of firms in each rating class (say AA) in each cohort moving towards default category (D) or any other class (e.g. AAA, or BBB and so on). Each yearly cohort comprises all the companies which have a rating outstanding at the start of the cohort year. From these cohorts produced by pivot tables in excel, we calculate year-wise transition probabilities (including default probabilities) for different rating grades.

Let's understand the method in detail. Say there are $T_{i,j}$ number of firms migrating to default category out of N_i number of firms in the ith rating grade over a one-year period, where the subscript i represents the rating grade (or industry) at the start of the period and the subscript j represents end year rating grade. The first year migration probability would be $P_{i,j}^1 = \dfrac{T_{i,j}^1}{N_i^1}$ for $i=1, 2, 3, ...,n$ and $j=1, 2, 3,..., n$ type of grades. In the same fashion, the marginal probability of default in a particular year (i.e. PD of the ith rating grade) is estimated by counting the frequencies: $P_{i,D}^1 = \dfrac{T_{i,D}^1}{N_i^1}$.

Since we have a sample with several periods (say k years of data, here, k = 10), then we can calculate k number of marginal migration probabilities including defaults. That means, we can derive $P_{i,j}^2 = \dfrac{T_{i,j}^2}{N_i^1}$ for the second year; $P_{i,j}^3 = \dfrac{T_{i,j}^3}{N_i^1}$ for the third,......, $P_{i,j}^k = \dfrac{T_{i,j}^k}{N_i^1}$ for the last year k.

Finally, one-year average unconditional migration probabilities across rating grades are computed as:

$$P_{i,j} = \sum_{t=1}^{k} w_i^t \frac{T_{i,j}^t}{N_i^t} \qquad \text{Eq. 3.1}$$

for i = 1, 2, 3, ..., n and j = 1, 2, 3,...., n and t = 1, 2, 3, ..., k and $\sum_{t=1}^{k} w_i^t = 1$.

Each period's marginal probabilities are weighted by its relative size in terms of rated observations. This approach is also followed by Standard and Poor's.

Following this procedure, the average one-year default probability for the ith rating grade (PDi) is also obtained by this weighted average method. The weights are the number of firms in the "i"th rating class in a particular year divided by the total number of firms in all the years.

Therefore, long-run PD for the "i"th grade can be expressed as:

$$PD_i = \sum_{t=1}^{k} w_i^t \frac{T_{i,D}^t}{N_i^t}$$

Eq. 3.2

where w_i^t is the weight representing the relative importance of a given year and $w_i^t = \dfrac{N_i^t}{\sum\limits_{s=1}^{n} N_i^s}$.

This method can be easily understood if we do some numerical exercises. Table 3.1 reports the number of defaults and the number of accounts in AA and BBB grades as well as accounts with missing/withdrawal grades in respective years. These numbers have been obtained through cohort analysis. The yearly discrete transition matrices can be constructed using "PIVOT Table" in Excel.

Table 3.1: Historical Rating-wise Default Statistics

	2007–08	2008–09	2009–10	2010–11	2011–12
AA:					
No. of Defaults	3	7	4	2	8
No. of Accounts#	300	250	200	220	300
# Missing/Withdrawal	30	20	15	10	15
BBB:					
No. of Defaults	15	20	10	15	40
No. of Accounts#	500	550	580	600	650
# Missing/Withdrawal	10	20	10	15	20

Source: Author's own numerical illustration.

The five-year PD for AA:

$$\frac{3+7+4+2+8}{300-30+250-20+200-15+220-10+300-15}$$

$$=> PD_{AA} = 1.98\%$$

Similarly, five-year PD for BBB:

$$\frac{15+20+10+15+40}{500-10+550-20+580-10+600-15+650-20}$$

=> PD_{BBB}=3.57%

Following the above approach, one derives the rating-wise yearly PD estimates. It is important to note that we have made adjustment for missing or withdrawn ratings. This adjustment is adopted by rating agencies and is performed by ignoring the firms that have their rating withdrawn during a given period.

These rating-wise internal PD estimates will act as a critical element for computation of borrower-wise risk weights under IRB. Using the similar method, one can also derive average transition probabilities of companies moving from one grade to any other grade besides default and thereby fill up all the cells of a transition matrix. This can be used to measure and understand the change in portfolio risk position of assets. Default is just one state into which the borrower can move when their credit quality changes. Companies' ratings can be upgraded, downgraded or remain unchanged. The IRB banks need to estimate rating-wise, region-wise, industry-wise PDs to more granularly measure the borrower-level credit risk. These additional fields need to be added to the PIVOT table layout to construct the desired transition matrices. For this, a data template will have to be created to systematically record the information about company name, industry type, regional location and the grades (rating symbol – AAA, AA, A, BBB, etc.) obtained over the years. Estimation of multiple PD numbers will help the banks to not only more granularly measure risks but also derive the benefit of portfolio diversification. For example, consider a bank has eight grades and loans are distributed across 20 regions and across 15 industries. Using the transition matrix analysis, it is possible to estimate 8 × 20 × 15 = 2,400 borrower-wise PDs.

Following this discrete cohort approach, we have studied the yearly rating migration pattern of 572 corporate bonds rated by CRISIL (of S&P) for the period 1995–96 to 2008–09 and constructed a one-year average transition matrix presented in Table 3.2. CRISIL also started publishing loan rating information of the listed Indian companies. Accordingly, we have collated the loan rating history of 426 Indian companies rated by CRISIL and studied their yearly rating migration pattern from 2009 till March 2015. Utilizing this recent loan rating data, we have constructed another six- year average transition matrix that represents corporate rating movements in recent years (Table 3.2a). These migration matrices represent the corporate portfolio risk position in India. Rating-wise average one-year default probabilities (see the last column) are obtained by weighted average method. The weights represent the relative importance of each year as given by the cohort size for each rating grade at the beginning of each year.

Both Table 3.2 and 3.2a show that as credit quality worsens, the default probability (PD) increases. The average default rate for investment grade companies is significantly lower (PDIG = 1.13%) than the speculative grade companies (PD$_{NIG}$ = 24.01%). This has been estimated after considering their combined rating movements over a longer data period from 1992–93 to 2012–13. We can see that higher ratings also have greater stability (or higher inertial frequency) than lower grades. However, the corporate rating stability (or rating retention) declines as the credit quality worsens. As a company moves down the rating scale, the likelihood of a multi-notch change (up or down) also increases. The lower rated companies are not only more volatile but also have relatively default probability. This is quite evident if we see their rating movements in recent years. If we add up all the column probabilities for a particular grade (say AA), we will obtain 100 per cent probability which is the total probability space available in the transition matrix.

Table 3.2: Average One-year Rating Transition of 572 Indian Corporate Bonds Rated Externally by CRISIL, 1992–2009

Withdrawal Adjusted, Figures in per cent

From/To	AAA	AA	A	BBB	BB	B	CCC/C	D
AAA	96.05	3.95	0.00	0.00	0.00	0.00	0.00	0.00
AA	2.81	89.74	6.20	0.68	0.39	0.10	0.00	0.10
A	0.00	3.99	83.71	7.12	2.70	0.32	0.54	1.62
BBB	0.00	0.51	5.09	75.83	10.69	1.53	2.80	3.56
BB	0.00	0.70	0.00	1.41	59.86	3.52	7.75	26.76
B	0.00	0.00	0.00	7.41	0.00	40.74	22.22	29.63
CCC/C	0.00	0.00	0.00	2.13	0.00	0.00	53.19	44.68

Source: CRISIL's monthly rating scans of several years, author's own analysis.

Table 3.2a: Indian Corporate Loan Rating Movements in Recent Years, 2008–15

Withdrawal Adjusted, Figures in per cent

From/To	AAA	AA	A	BBB	BB	B	CCC/C	D
AAA	99.04%	0.96%	0.00%	0.00%	0.00%	0.00%	0.00%	0.00%
AA	0.68%	95.56%	3.07%	0.00%	0.34%	0.00%	0.00%	0.34%
A	0.43%	4.74%	89.22%	4.31%	0.43%	0.00%	0.00%	0.86%
BBB	0.00%	0.00%	4.35%	83.07%	10.07%	0.00%	0.69%	1.83%
BB	0.00%	0.00%	0.84%	8.44%	70.04%	6.33%	3.38%	10.97%
B	0.00%	0.00%	0.00%	0.70%	12.68%	68.31%	4.23%	14.08%
CCC/C	0.00%	0.00%	0.00%	0.00%	5.00%	15.00%	55.00%	25.00%

Source: Compiled from CRISIL's published loan rating data of 426 Indian companies.

CRISIL publishes its own historical migration matrix based on similar cohort analysis from 1989–2008 on a cumulative basis. In Table 3.3, we have reproduced the original transition matrix that CRISIL publishes in their annual default studies. It is worthwhile to mention that the transition matrix produced by us also looks similar to the one-year average rating transition matrix published by CRISIL. However, CRISIL does not report industry-wise PDs.

Table 3.3: CRISIL's Published One-year Indian Corporate Transition Matrix

(Withdrawal Adjusted) (per cent), 1989–2008

From/To	Sample Size	AAA	AA	A	BBB	BB	B	CCC/C	D
AAA	752	96.30	3.70	0.00	0.00	0.00	0.00	0.00	0.00
AA	1572	2.20	90.80	6.00	0.50	0.30	0.10	0.00	0.00
A	1495	0.00	3.80	83.10	7.10	4.20	0.20	0.70	0.90
BBB	648	0.00	0.30	5.60	73.90	13.60	1.20	2.00	3.40
BB	342	0.00	0.60	0.00	2.30	74.90	1.80	5.30	15.20
B	34	0.00	0.00	0.00	5.90	0.00	55.90	8.80	29.40
CCC/C	82	0.00	0.00	0.00	1.20	0.00	0.00	70.70	28.10

Source: CRISIL.

We have also compared the Indian corporate risk behaviour with the global corporates. Table 3.4 displays global transition matrix reported by Standard and Poor's (S&P). Interestingly, ours or CRISIL's reported bond rating migration pattern and PDs across rating grades is markedly different from

Standard and Poor's transition matrix. The risk differentiation across grades is more pronounced in S&P migration table than the CRISIL's. It is quite evident that the probability of default (PD) of Indian corporates rated below investment grades (i.e. below BBB) is significantly higher than the global corporates. One can compare that our below BBB firms are as risky as S&P CCC firms. Thus, we can conclude that S&P grades are more granularly capturing the default risk of companies than the CRISIL grades.

Note that in many transition matrices, the last row is added such that the matrix is a square. Its interpretation is that default (D state) is a self-absorbing state; i.e. a firm in default has 100 per cent probability of remaining in default.

Table 3.4: S&P Global Corporate Transition Matrix in % (1981–2012)

From/ To	AAA	AA	A	BBB	BB	B	CCC/C	D	NR
AAA	**87.17**	8.69	0.54	0.05	0.08	0.03	0.05	0.00	3.38
AA	0.54	**86.29**	8.36	0.57	0.06	0.08	0.02	0.02	4.05
A	0.03	1.86	**87.26**	5.53	0.36	0.15	0.02	0.07	4.71
BBB	0.01	0.12	3.54	**85.09**	3.88	0.61	0.14	0.22	6.39
BB	0.02	0.04	0.15	5.18	**76.12**	7.20	0.72	0.86	9.71
B	0.00	0.03	0.11	0.23	5.42	**73.84**	4.40	4.28	11.68
CCC/C	0.00	0.00	0.16	0.24	0.73	13.69	**43.89**	26.85	14.43

Source: S&P CreditPro Default Study 2012.

Note: Figures have been rounded off; NR is not rated or withdrawn rating.

The rating transition matrices shown in Tables 3.2 to 3.4 are very useful representations of the historical behaviour of ratings. It is also clear that transitions occur mostly in the neighbouring class of ratings. The likelihood of a multi-notch change is very less in higher rating grades. But likelihood of two notch upgrades or downgrades is high in lower grades (especially in NIG level). Transition Matrices act as indicators of the likely path of a given credit at a given horizon. A correspondence can be drawn between the bank's own internal rating scale and the agencies' rating scales and a link between internal ratings and historical default probabilities can be established. Under IRB approach, the regulator expects that the entire matrix of transition probabilities between and within rating classes must play an essential role in the calculation of regulatory capital, credit approval, risk-based pricing, portfolio risk management and corporate governance functions of banks.

The rating agencies regularly publish system level information on companies rated and the number of defaults per rating category, year, per industry and also per geography. These studies provide vital information on system-level portfolio risk position in a country. This also enables a bank to compare its business position with industry trend and thereby can conduct better business and capital planning. Table 3.5 presents such average PD estimates for 15 industries computed by the author. Using the same rating data of 426 Indian companies in Table 3.2a, we obtain the industry default rates for IG and NIG grades. The Indian corporate default rates by industry category are reported in Table 3.5. Investment grade ratings correspond to ratings from AAA to BBB, while non-investment grade ratings (NIG) are from BB to C. As would be expected, the PD for most of the industries is higher for NIG class in comparison to their IG counterparts. The corporate PD for the IG class as a whole (all industries) is 0.94 per cent and the PD for NIG class is 13.90 per cent. The overall average corporate industry PD is 4.47 per cent. The highest default probabilities are observed in infrastructure, construction and engineering, electronics and electricals, paper and paper products, leather products and other sectors. Such industry differences in PD estimates would guide the top management of banks to more granularly compare corporate portfolio risk positions and conduct conscious credit planning.

Table 3.5: Annual Industry PDs (%) for Different Loan Grades

SL#	Industry Name	IG	NIG	Total
1	Auto & Parts	0.00	26.67	3.74
2	Chemical	1.92	12.50	3.91
3	Construction & Engineering	1.89	14.29	6.17
4	Electronics & Electricals	0.00	14.63	4.72
5	Food & Products & FMCG	0.00	12.07	4.32
6	Gems & Jewellery	0.00	2.78	1.35
7	Infrastructure	2.29	30.43	6.49
8	IT	1.35	15.38	3.45
9	Leather & products	0.00	12.50	6.25
10	Metal & products	1.18	13.51	4.92
11	Non-metal	2.17	8.33	3.45
12	Other	0.00	25.00	6.45
13	Paper & Products	0.00	18.00	7.02
14	Plastic & products	0.00	3.45	1.41

Table 3.5 contd.

Table 3.5 contd.

15	Rubber & products	0.00	8.33	3.03
16	Services	0.00	16.00	2.56
17	Textiles	3.39	8.33	4.82
	Overall	0.94%	13.90%	4.47

Source: CRISIL's loan rating data.

Note: The above estimates are borrower weighted yearly PD estimates obtained from historical rating transition history for the period 2008 to 2015. FMCG: Fast Moving Consumer Goods; IT: Information Technology; IG: Investment Grade and NIG: Non-investment Grade.

The link between observed default rates and rating grades published by rating agencies is an important source of information for banks to benchmark their internal ratings with the agency rating. The historical rating movement analysis and stability analysis of the grades over the long run empower a bank to obtain ex ante vision regarding future probabilities of default or movement. Hamilton (2002) has done a fascinating study on Moody's corporate rating migration pattern from 1984–2001. It reveals many interesting features of CRA's rating system. The study finds that higher ratings have generally been less likely to be revised over one year than lower ratings. Higher ratings also have greater stability (or higher retention rate) than lower grades. For ratings in the middle of the ratings scale, the likelihood of a rating upgrade and a rating downgrade is roughly symmetrical. Sudden rating changes occur infrequently: just 8.6 per cent involved rating changes of more than one rating category excluding defaults and withdrawn ratings). As one goes down the rating scale, the probability of a multi-notch movement in rating (up or down) rapidly increases. The study also observes that there is serial behaviour to rating changes which may not be completely conveyed by average one-year rating migration matrices. That means there is higher chance of credit migration in the same direction than for opposite direction in consecutive years. Companies that have been recently downgraded by the agency are almost one and a half times more likely to be downgraded again. These companies are five times more likely to default than companies that experienced no prior rating change. Moreover, these companies are also three times more probable to be downgraded again and almost eight times more likely to default than companies that have recently been upgraded. Volatility of rating is highest for borrowers who were downgraded last year. Default rate is highest for borrowers who were downgraded in the prior year (5.78 per cent).

The "Rating watchlist" is an important leading indicator of future Moody's rating changes. It is an important source of information for market participants interested in measuring credit risk.

It is important to note that rating agencies generally follow through the cycle (TTC) approach in their rating process. On the other hand, bank rating is point in time (PIT) in nature as they give lot of importance to the latest balance sheet data of a firm in evaluating risk. This is why rating agencies' ratings are expected to be more stable than the bank ratings. Based on Moody's database, Carrey and Hrycay (2001) estimate that a historical sample between 11 and 18 years should be necessary in order to test the validity and stability of internal ratings. Standard and Poor's (S&P) believes that a time period of 10 years should be considered as a minimum for investment grade (IG) securities, while five years should be enough to back-test non-investment grade (NIG) issues.

Table 3.6 reflect the rating-wise portfolio risk position of a leading public sector bank in India. The reported transition matrix summarizes the frequency and magnitude of rating changes in the banks' corporate credit portfolio.

Table 3.6: One-year Corporate Transition Matrix of a Bank in India, 2003–09 (%)

Rating	R 1	R 2	R 3	R 4	R 5	R 6	R 7	R 8	Default
Year: T	T+1								
CR 1	**55.00**	12.86	10.50	8.42	7.97	4.53	0.36	0.00	0.36
CR 2	4.52	**74.80**	13.79	4.26	2.40	0.00	0.00	0.00	0.23
CR 3	1.76	4.60	**72.27**	14.10	5.00	1.57	0.10	0.00	0.60
CR 4	1.21	3.71	11.13	**56.86**	17.90	7.42	0.82	0.04	0.91
CR 5	0.52	1.87	6.25	14.36	**62.82**	11.63	1.04	0.22	1.30
CR 6	0.35	1.29	4.43	9.01	15.14	**62.35**	3.09	0.90	3.44
CR 7	0.00	0.00	1.94	3.40	8.25	19.90	**52.43**	5.34	8.74
CR 8	0.00	0.00	0.00	0.00	2.03	12.50	12.50	**52.00**	20.97

Source: Bank's corporate rating data.

Note: This has been constructed after tracking seven years of rating transition from 2002–03 to 2008–09 using the bank's 3,000 borrower rating sample (loan exposure above Rs. 5 crore).

The above migration matrix will help the banks to validate their rating models. Notice that there is a significant difference in migration pattern of bank ratings and agency ratings. More importantly, estimation of rating-wise, industry-wise and region-wise borrower PDs are critical inputs for the estimation of economic capital as well as IRB regulatory capital. The estimation of the probability of default for each credit dimension class, industry sector and region enables bank to more granularly measure the credit risk of a borrower. The transition matrix can be used across branches/regions/industry to track slippage rates. It is an effective portfolio monitoring tool that can limit the banks' vulnerability towards concentration risk.

It is important to note that corporate rating transition matrix may be influenced by the changes with macroeconomic conditions. Although rating agencies claim to have through-the-cycle (TTC) rating approach, it has been historically observed that they actively downgrade companies during downtime where target metrics are not maintained. As corporate credit quality worsens, the default probability (PD) peaks up. Therefore, it is necessary to study the change in rating migration pattern with alteration in business cycle. This helps us to understand the effect of rating drift on portfolio quality and, hence, risk-weighted assets. A positive drift (when upgrades are higher than the downgrades) indicates a stable credit environment. Alternatively, a negative drift signals overall deterioration in portfolio credit quality. From risk management point of view, generating the rating transition matrices under various macroeconomic scenarios is a prudent way to adjust the PD changes. Stress testing can also be conducted based on these historically generated scenarios. This has been discussed in the stress testing section of Chapter 7.

PD Estimation for a Low Default Portfolio (LDP)

Under Basel II IRB framework, the PD estimation requirement is applicable to all classes of assets. In some categories of exposures, historical default experiences may be very less or rare (e.g. sovereign, banks, big infrastructure companies or some asset categories). The portfolios with such very limited default events are defined as low default portfolio (LDP). Estimation of PD for such LDP portfolio has been a great challenge to both the regulator and banks. The regulator is very much concerned about the underestimation of credit risk for such portfolios due to scarcity of data. Pooling of data with other banks or using external rating agencies data as benchmark or market-based indicators (like MKMV type) or some proxy approach (like 60 days past due rather than 90 days or lowest non-defaulting rating) may be considered to complement default data as suggested by BCBS (News Letter no. 6, September, 2005). A degree of conservatism is expected to be maintained in cases of "low default" portfolios.

A prudent scaling-based PD estimation principle by using a confidence interval for various rating buckets has been suggested by Pluto and Tasche (2005). Many IRB banks are using this technique for calibrating PDs for loan portfolios with very few defaults (e.g. banks and sovereign exposures). This method uses an upper confidence interval of 95 per cent to appropriately order the PDs in terms of credit quality as indicated by the rating grades. Similarly, cumulative accuracy profile (CAP) or power curve can also be used as an effective tool of calibrating PD for low default portfolios. This method has been demonstrated in Van Der Burgt, 2008 for an LDP of sovereigns. The details about CAP curve in performing model validation and calibration have been discussed in Chapter 5. By drawing a set of CAP curves from different rating buckets, calibrated default rates can be arrived through a variation in concavity parameter after setting appropriate granularity criteria in risk buckets. The concavity parameter measures the model's discriminatory power. The authors have also established a relationship between concavity and accuracy ratio (AR) in describing the calibration method. This method has been further numerically elaborated in Chapter 5. A more conservative hybrid Maximum Likelihood PD model on a virtual sovereign portfolio has also been recently proposed by R Roengpitya and P Nilla-Or (2011). Tasche (2013) in a recent paper has suggested a Bayesian approach to estimate PD for an LDP. In this method, a prior distribution of PD is considered which can also be taken from expert judgement. However, this may produce less conservative estimates. The most conservative approach can be appropriate for IRB capital computation and less conservative estimates can be applicable for provisioning and pricing of loans.

Cumulative Probability of Default (CPD)

The cumulative probability of default gives an idea about a borrower's chance of default over a longer time horizon (of say five years or longer time). This can be obtained from the analysis of survival rates for various grades through yearly mortality analysis over a longer time horizon (e.g. $3/5/10$ years). This helps a risk analyst to compare default rates over multi-year horizons.

In order to estimate CPD, we have to assume conditional independence among each yearly cohort of rating movements. The following expression may be used to estimate a five-year CPD of a grade i:

$CPD_n^i = 1 - \text{Sn}$

Sn: Survival rate at the end of year "n"

$\text{Sn} = (1 - pd_1) \times (1 - pd_2) \times (1 - pd_3) \times (1 - pd_4) \times (1 - pd_5)$

$\therefore CPD_i = 1 - \{(1 - pd_1) \times (1 - pd_2) \times (1 - pd_3) \times (1 - pd_4) \times (1 - pd_5)\}$

Eq. 3.3

The cumulative default probability until time 5 is the probability of defaulting at any point in time until time 5.

Given a constant one-year probability of default of 10, the cumulative probability of default two years is 0.19.

The survival rate up to "n" years is as thus:

$(1 - \text{cn}) = (1 - \text{cn} - 1) \times (1 - \text{dn})$ 　　　　　Eq. 3.4

Where

cn = cumulative probability of default (CPD_n) in n^{th} year; dn = pd (probability of default in n^{th} year.

cn – 1 = cumulative probability of default in n – 1th year

Using the above expression, one can convert cumulative PD into probability of default in a particular year.

Now, using the default numbers reported in Table 3.7, we can obtain yearly PDs (or call marginal PDs) as well as cumulative PDs (CPDs).

Table 3.7: Historical Rating-wise Default Statistics

	2007–08	2008–09	2009–10	2010–11	2011–12
AA:					
No. of Defaults	3	7	4	2	8
No. of Accounts#	300	250	200	220	300
# Missing/Withdrawal	30	20	15	10	15
Yearly PDs (pd)	1.05	2.92	2.16	0.95	2.76
BBB:					
No. of Defaults	15	20	10	15	40
No. of Accounts#	500	550	580	600	650
# Missing/Withdrawal	10	20	10	15	20
Yearly PDs (pd)	3.06	3.77	1.75	2.56	6.35

Source: Author's own numerical illustration.

Using the yearly PD figures, we can now estimate five-year cumulative PD for AA:

$CPD5^{AA} = 1 - \{(1 - 1.05) \times (1 - 2.92) \times (1 - 2.16) \times (1 - 0.95) \times (1 - 2.76)\} = 9.48$

This gives an estimate of cumulative probability of default for AA borrowers at the end of the fifth year.

Similarly, three-year cumulative PD for BBB would be:

$CPD3^{BBB} = 1 - \{(1 - 3.06) \times (1 - 3.77) \times (1.75)\} = 8.36$

This gives an estimate of cumulative probability of default for AA borrowers at the end of the third year.

Similarly, five-year CPD for BBB would be = 16.38

Cumulative PD captures the incremental default probability of a borrower over a longer time horizon. As a prudent risk management practice, during loan sanction, a risk manager has to estimate the probability of default for a loan over a longer time horizon.

Table 3.8 illustrates the pattern of historical PD and CPD of a bank on a portfolio of corporate loans with exposures above ₹1 crore. One can check the annual PD and CPD numbers across different time horizons of AA and A ratings.

Using equation 3.4, one can obtain the figures in the blanks of Table 3.8. This will enable us to better understand the relationship between PD and CPD. Notice that the five-year survival probabilities for AA and A loans are 97.575 per cent and 97.473 per cent, respectively. Similarly, one can check that the four-year cumulative default rate is higher for an A rated borrower than an AA rated borrower.

Table 3.8: Relationship between Yearly PD and Cumulative PD (CPD)

Rating		Time Horizon				
		Year 1	Year 2	Year 3	Year 4	Year 5
AA	Annual default (PD)	0.100	0.250	0.600	0.697	0.800
	Cumulative default rate (CPD)	0.100	0.350	0.948	1.640	2.425
A	Annual default (PD)	0.050	0.400	1.000	0.400	0.700
	Cumulative default rate (CPD)	0.050	0.450	1.445	1.840	2.527

Source: Author's own numerical illustration.

Table 3.9 documents the global corporate average cumulative PDs as given by the Standard and Poor's across grades for different time horizons. These CPDs have been estimated using historical PDs across rating grades from 1981 till 2012.

Table 3.9: Default Rates for Different Horizons

S&P Global Corporate Average Cumulative PDs (1981–2012) (%)

Rating	Time Horizon (years)									
	1	2	3	4	5	6	7	8	9	10
AAA	0.00	0.03	0.14	0.25	0.36	0.48	0.54	0.63	0.69	0.76
AA	0.02	0.04	0.09	0.24	0.39	0.53	0.68	0.80	0.91	1.03
A	0.07	0.18	0.28	0.43	0.59	0.80	1.01	1.20	1.44	1.71
BBB	0.20	0.52	0.81	1.26	1.73	2.18	2.60	3.01	3.47	3.93
BB	0.71	2.21	4.29	6.22	8.05	9.60	10.98	12.16	13.18	14.04
B	5.10	11.20	16.04	19.47	22.04	24.44	25.95	27.04	28.02	28.87
CCC	26.85	35.94	41.17	44.19	46.64	47.71	48.67	49.44	50.39	51.13
IG	0.11	0.31	0.54	0.82	1.12	1.41	1.68	1.94	2.19	2.45
NIG	4.11	8.05	11.46	14.22	16.44	18.30	19.85	21.16	22.36	23.46
All	1.55	3.06	4.40	5.53	6.48	7.29	7.98	8.58	9.12	9.63

Source: S&P.

One can notice in Table 3.9 that the upper graded corporate CPDs are generally lower than their lower graded counterparts. The default rates are closer to zero, especially over short horizon. However, as time horizon increases, the rate of change in CPD for investment grades (IGs: AAA–BBB) are much faster than the rate of change in non-investment grades (NIGs: BB–CCC). This is the reason why BCBS has imposed a higher capital charge for better rated assets as for longer maturity loans. Historical evidence indicates long-term credits are riskier than short-term credits. Generally, PDs are lower for better graded borrowers. But as time horizon increases, these grades have to pass through many rating transitions and, hence, their CPD will rise at a faster rate. Downgrades from one rating category to a lower one are more likely for long-term credits. This is quite evident in Table 3.9. Thus, maturity effects are stronger for obligors with low probability of default. Consistent with these considerations, the Basel Committee has proposed a maturity adjustment (m_i) to be multiplied with each term of the regulatory capital computed for corporate and bigger SME borrowers (that are treated as corporates).

Table 3.10 documents the rating-wise CPD estimates of Indian corporates obtained from CRISIL's transition matrices from 1988–2011. Here also the rates increase over longer horizon (two years and above) and the increase is faster in upper grades than the lower grades.

Table 3.10: CRISIL's Indian Corporate Cumulative PDs (Withdrawal Adjusted) (%)   Year: 1988–2011

Rating	Issuer months	Time Horizon (Years)		
		1	2	3
AAA	11,846	0.00	0.00	0.00
AA	24,368	0.04	0.40	1.09
A	25,694	0.82	3.52	7.66
BBB	29,366	1.89	5.34	12.27
BB	22,685	5.80	12.52	24.58
B	11,489	8.25	17.89	37.90
CCC	2,350	21.36	37.23	50.79

Source: CRISIL.

Cumulative probability of default has uses in pricing long-term loans and in studying the risk behaviour of various grades over different maturity horizon. One can notice from Tables 3.9 and 3.10 that there is a striking difference in CPD trends between investment grade and non-investment grade corporates. It is quite evident that there is a historical inverse correlation between rating level and defaults. However, as the time increases (and the maturity of the loan), the cumulative default probability of IG grades increases more rapidly than the NIG grades. This perhaps is again capturing the maturity effect of a bond on default risk. Better rated corporates are less risky and have low PD. However, as time horizon increases, their risk of default also increases as their ratings will have to pass through different phases of macroeconomic cycle.

Pooled PD for Homogenous Buckets of Retail Exposures (Tracking the Numbers)

Under the IRB approach, a bank will be expected to assign a pooled PD to each of its risk buckets. These pooled PDs should reflect the central tendency (the mean or the median) of the PDs of the individual obligors contained in each bucket. In practice, of course, IRB banks will need to estimate pooled PDs from the available data. Bank supervisors and risk managers will be tasked with evaluating PD quantification methodologies to ensure that those methodologies produce accurate estimates of pooled PDs. The revised framework also outlines approaches to quantifying pooled PDs. Banks may use any one approach for estimating pooled PDs.

Under a historical default experience approach, the pooled PD for a risk bucket is estimated using historical data on the frequency of observed defaults among obligors assigned to that bucket.

The following section describes other two pooled PD approaches which may be adopted by banks.

Retail Pooled PD Approach

The historical default experience approach is most appropriate for quantifying pooled PDs for point in time retail buckets. It will be most accurate when long-run average default rates are calculated over a number of years. A bank may either follow frequency-based measure or rupee-weighted exposure-based measure to compute-pooled PD.

Frequency-based Measure

The probability of default (PD) for a retail pool/bucket is defined as the observed default rate for the bucket over a fixed assessment horizon (usually one year). That is:

$$PD_t = D_t / N_t$$

Where D_t is the number of defaults observed for a bucket over year t and N_t is the total number of obligors assigned to that bucket at the beginning of year t. The pooled PD for a risk bucket can be interpreted as an ex-ante forecast (which is also called the expected default frequency or EDF) of the one-year-ahead ex-post observed default frequency for that bucket. However, because default events are generally correlated across obligors, it is unlikely that in any given year, a bucket's pooled PD (actually observed) will closely match its observed default frequency. Here, we are trying to find out long-run PD from the observed default frequencies. During the years when aggregate economic conditions unexpectedly improve the observed default frequency for a risk bucket will tend to fall below its dynamic pooled PD. During the years when economic conditions unexpectedly deteriorate, observed default frequencies will tend to lie above forecasts. In such a situation, the long-run average default probability (LRPD) is considered as a close proxy of the pooled PD for the retail bucket.

The long-run default frequency (LRPD) for a risk bucket is simply the average of that bucket's annual default rates taken over a number of years. In symbols:

$$LRPD = \sum_{t=1}^{T} PD_t \qquad\qquad \text{Eq. 3.5}$$

Where T = total number of years in the data history

Table 3.11 demonstrates the data requirements and methodology for estimation of pooled PDs for retail buckets.

Table 3.11: Estimation of Frequency-based Pooled PD for Homogeneous Retail Buckets (Personal Loans) – Illustration 1

Units in Number

Year	2006	2007	2008	2009	2010	2011	2012
Total no. of accounts Outstanding	8000	10000	12000	15000	18000	20000	22000
No. of accounts defaulted out of the no. of accounts Outstanding in the previous year		300.0	450.0	500.0	450.0	500.0	520.0
Yearly Default Probability (PDt)		3.33	4.50	4.05	3.00	2.83	2.60
LRPD=pooled PD							3.40

Source: Author's own computation (illustrative).

The bank may compare January 2006 with January 2007 or may follow financial year March 2006 to March 2007 for tracking default numbers and no. of accounts outstanding.

The bank should make adjustments every next year because portfolio will change. For example, exclude those accounts outstanding in 2006 and maturing in 2007, and exclude those accounts of 2006 which have defaulted in 2006. Include those accounts of year 2006 which have not matured or defaulted and may still be outstanding in year 2007. This may be repeated for other years as well. Include the new accounts which have been sanctioned in 2006. A bank can also track NPA exposure (in rupees) movements (ratio of

GNPA additions to three year average gross advances) if no data is missing. However, one should use a more conservative method.

Over time, year-to-year differences between unstressed pooled PDs and observed default frequencies should tend to cancel out, and the LRPD for a retail bucket can be expected to converge towards the long-run average pooled PD for that bucket. This implies that given a sufficiently long history of performance data, the historical default experience approach can provide an effective means of quantifying pooled PDs that reflect obligor PDs for the retail bucket.

Exposure-based Rupee (or $) weighted pooled PD:

We also outline below another proxy method for estimating historically de-rived pooled PDs for retail portfolios in case number of accounts data is not available. This is called exposure-based method for computing pooled PD. In this method, PD can be estimated for the entire pool from its yearly (or quarterly) movements of gross non-performing assets (GNPA).

One should first estimate yearly (or quarterly) marginal PDs by using a moving average method as shown in the following equations:

$$MPD_t = \frac{\Delta GNPA_t}{(\sum_{t=-2}^{t} Advances_t) / 3}$$ Eq. 3.6

$\Delta GNPA_t$ is the additions in gross NPA in the current year. This information can be obtained from historical yearly (or quarterly) gross NPA movements of banks.

Finally,

$$PD = \sum_{t=1}^{T} \frac{MPD_t}{T}$$ Eq. 3.7

Where, T is the total number of periods. A 10-year average will give us a long-run estimate of annual PD. In some cases, where enough NPA history cannot be obtained, a minimum five-year data should be used to get a long-run estimate of pooled PD.

In this method, the bank's credit analyst will track the yearly additions of gross NPA amounts (denoted by $\Delta GNPA_t$) and divide it by the three years' average gross advances and estimate marginal PDs. Repeating the same exercise for other years, one can finally find the long-run average PD by taking five- or ten-year weighted average of yearly marginal PDs (i.e.

MPDs). This gives us an estimate of rupee weighted average long-run PDs for the entire retail pool.

A minimum of five years of data is required to arrive at a long-run average pooled probability of default. However, the longer the time series taken, the better will be the statistical reliability of the pooled PD estimate. Table 3.12 defines the data requirements and methodology for the estimation of pooled PDs for retail buckets using the proxy approach.

Table 3.12: Estimation of Long-run Average Pooled Probability of Default for Homogeneous Retail Pool (Personal Loan) – Illustration 2 (Exposure-based Method)

Year	2006	2007	2008	2009	2010	2011	2012
Gross Advances	313	280	320	480	550	620	729
Incremental GNPA		13.0	12.0	18.0	17.0	18.0	24.0
MPD		4.39	3.95	5.00	3.78	3.27	3.79
LRPD = pooled PD							3.96

Source: Author's own numerical illustration.

Note: LRPD is the long-run PD which is the average of five yearly MPDs.

A bank may have to compare both the methods (frequency vs. exposure measure) and must choose the most conservative estimate of pooled PD for the risk weight calculation. A polynomial trend regression equation may also be used to obtain a smooth long run pooled PD estimate.

A bank may also follow other methods for computing retail PDs:

Under a statistical model approach, predictive statistical models are used to estimate a PD for each obligor currently assigned to a bucket. The bucket's pooled PD is then calculated as the average of the obligor-specific PDs.

Under an external mapping approach, a mapping is established that links each of a bank's internal risk buckets to external rating grades. Pooled default probabilities for the external grades are calculated from external data and then assigned to the bank's internal grades via mapping.

Each of these approaches has important strengths and weaknesses that depend on the dynamic characteristics of the pooled PDs being estimated.

Summary

Estimation of PD is the first crucial element in measuring credit risk under the Basel II IRB approach. Transition matrices act as indicators of the likely path of a given credit at a given horizon. Rating transition matrices produce cardinal inputs that can be used by banks to measure and monitor credit risk in a loan portfolio. They are useful indicators of historical behaviour of ratings. Default rates do not remain constant over time and these shifts should be captured in the transition matrices. This information can be obtained from the leading rating agencies as they have a longer rating history. A point-in-time philosophy (PIT) groups obligors according to one-period-ahead predicted default frequencies. A through-the-cycle (TTC) philosophy groups obligors according to stress-scenario default probabilities. Many researchers find that keeping more grades (especially in the high-risk segment) reduces the concentration of borrowers and enables banks to distinguish the borrowers more granularly. Clearly distinguishable grades both in taker (investment grade) and non-taker (non-investment) grades are important for more granularly measuring risk in a bank's credit portfolio. Grouping exposures into homogeneous retail pool is an important requirement of Basel's retail IRB approach. An yearly/quarterly tracking of incremental NPAs across sub-portfolios (e.g. products/industries/regions etc.) would provide crucial early warning signals to the credit risk management department. Portfolio segmentation in terms of PD estimates will also reduce the capital requirements due to the diversification effect.

Key learning outcomes

- Concept of probability of default (PD)
- Methods for estimating rating-wise probability of default (PD)
- Transition matrix and its usage
- Sectoral PD estimation
- Retail-pooled PD estimation
- Low-default portfolio
- Cumulative probability of default and its importance

Review questions

After studying the chapter and the relevant reading, you should be able to tell:

1. What is probability of default (PD)? Why is the estimation of PD important?
2. What is rating transition matrix? How can this be used to estimate PD?
3. What are the uses of transition matrix?
4. How industry-wise PDs can be estimated?
5. What is the relationship between PD and cumulative PD?
6. What is the use of cumulative PD?
7. What is retail-pooled PD? How can it be estimated?

References

BCBS. 2005. Validation of Low Default Portfolios in the Basel II Framework, Basel Committee News Letter no. 6, September.

Carey, M. and M. Hrycay. 2001. "Parameterizing Credit Risk Models with Rating Data", *Journal of Banking and Finance* 25: 197–270.

Craig, B.A. and P.P. Sendi. 2002. "Estimation of the Transition Matrix of a Discrete-time Markov Chain", *Health Economics* 11: 33–42.

Davis, P.O. and W. Darrin. 2004. "Credit Risk Measurement: Avoiding Unintended Results: Part 4: Loan Loss Reserves and Expected Losses", *The RMA Journal* 87 (2).

de Servigny and A. Renault. 2004. *Measuring and Managing Credit Risk* (S & P), Chapters: 2, 3 and 5.

Hamilton, D. H. 2002. "Historical Corporate Rating Migration, Default and Recovery Rates", in Credit Ratings: Methodologies, Rationale and Default Risk, ed. Michael K. Ong, . Chapter 2 (London: RISK publisher).

Lando, D. and Skodeberg, T. 2002. Analyzing Ratings Transitions and Rating Drift with Continuous Observations, *Journal of Banking and Finance* 26(2/3): 423–44.

Pluto, K. and D. Tasche. 2005. "Estimating Probabilities of Default for Low Default Portfolios". SSRN Working Paper, May.

Roengpitya, R. and P. Nilla-Or. 2011. "Proposal of New Hybrid Models for PD Estimates on Low Default Portfolios (LDPs), Empirical Comparisons and Regulatory Policy Implications", in *First International Conference on Credit Analysis and Risk Management*, ed. Joseph Callaghan and Austin Murphy, Chapter 12 (Newcastle: Cambridge Scholars Publishing), 18 October. https://find.bibliothek.tu-ilmenau.de/Record/73362331X/TOC

Saunders A. and M M Cornett (2003), *Financial Institutions Management: A Risk Management Approach*, McGraw-Hill, Fourth Edition, Chapters: 11, & 20.

Schuermann, T. and S. Hanson. 2004. Estimating Probabilities of Default, Staff Report no. 190. Federal Reserve Bank of New York.

Schuermann, T. and Y. Jafry. 2003. Measurement and Estimation of Credit Migration Matrices, Working Paper, Wharton.

Tasche, D. 2013. "Bayesian Estimation of Probability of Default for Low Default Portfolios", *Journal of Risk Management in Financial Institutions* 6 (3): 302–26.

Van der Burgt, M.J. 2007. "Calibrating Low-Default Portfolios using the Cumulative Accuracy Profile", *The Journal of Risk Model Validation* 1 (4): 17–33.

## Chapter 4

Exposure at Default (EAD) and Loss Given Default (LGD)

E AD and LGD estimates are key inputs in measurement of the expected and unexpected credit losses and, hence, credit risk capital (regulatory as well as economic). These are the second dimensions of Basel II IRB formula. To estimate LGD and EAD under advanced approach, each bank has to rely on its internal data on defaulted accounts. Basel II specifies that "LGD estimates must be grounded in historical recovery rates" – thus excluding any subjective choice of LGD estimates by banks. Building a drawing power and recovery predictor model from loss perspective side is hard because of non-availability of data within the banks in India. The banks also may not know in which format they should record and collect the relevant data for estimation of these two key risk parameters. This section provides a detailed explanation about EAD and LGD concepts, their estimation methodologies and data collection procedure. It also covers various studies related to EAD and LGD, provides interesting statistics about them, and discusses crucial factors that drive these two risks.

What is Exposure at Default (EAD)?

EAD is the amount of loss that a bank may face due to default. Since default occurs at an unknown future date, this loss is contingent upon the amount to which the bank was exposed to the borrower at the time of default. This is commonly expressed as exposure at default (EAD). In the case of normal term loan, exposure risk can be considered small because of its fixed repayment schedule. This is not true for all other lines of credit (e.g. guarantee, overdraft, letter of credit, etc.). The borrower may draw on these lines of credit within a limit set by the bank as and when borrowing needs arise.

Credit line usage has cyclical characteristics, i.e. the use increases in recessions and declines in expansions. The usage rate increases monotonically as the borrower becomes riskier and approaches towards default risk. Banks as a lender need to closely monitor the potential exposure to assess the credit risk more prudently. It is in this sense that the estimation of EAD is absolutely necessary for computation of regulatory as well as economic capital. As credit exposure varies from product to product, banks will have to track the drawing power of various facilities both on and off balance sheet based on historical data. A longer time series analysis is always preferred by the risk experts. It is worth to note that the tendency to allow ad hoc over drawings to address the so-called operational problem of the borrowers may result in deeper default outstanding in the later stage.

Based on Basel guidelines, EAD for loan commitments measures the amount of facility that is likely to be drawn if a default occurs. Under Basel regulation, a bank must provide an estimate of the exposure amount for each transaction (commonly referred to as EAD in banks' internal systems. All these loss estimates should seek to fully capture the risks of an underlying exposure.

Critical components of exposure at default (EAD)

The exposure at default is the outstanding amount at the time of default. Bigger the size of EAD, higher is the expected loss. For a term loan, the exposure amount is set by the amortization plan and the exposure is assumed to be fixed for each year. In such a case, the pattern of disbursements and repayments is fixed and known on the day of closing the deal. However, for a line of credit (also known as revolver or a commitment), only a maximum amount is set in advance. The type of commitment given by the bank to the borrower sets an upper limit on the possible future exposures. The party then draws on the line according to its needs and repays it when it wishes. This means that the bank cannot be certain about the exposure at default (EAD). How much credit exposure a bank may have to a particular borrower at the time of default is dependent on three things:

- **Outstanding (or drawn amount):** The portion of the bank asset that has already been extended to the borrower or is the drawn amount. In case of default, the entire outstanding amount is exposed.

- **Balance amount (or free limit):** The un-drawn portion of the loan (difference between the line of credit and outstanding amount which has already been disbursed). The borrower can draw from it whenever it faces financial distress. This portion is also called balance portion.
- **Covenants:** Terms and conditions/options that determine or draw down under commitment (or Usage Given Default or UGD). Covenants are designed to aid the active monitoring of risks and thus trigger pre-emptive actions when a borrower becomes risky.

Thus, exposure at default can be expressed as:

Exposure at Default (EAD) = Outstanding + UGD × (Credit Line − Outstanding)   Eq. 4.1

In the above formulation, the outstanding is the amount that the customer has currently borrowed (or drawn amount). This is also termed as the current balance by banks. Credit line is the maximum amount that the customer can borrow. The difference between credit line and outstanding is termed as the unused line of credit. The usage given default (UGD) is the likely draw down prior to default. UGD is also termed as CCF (credit conversion factor) under Basel II Standardized Approach and FIRB Approach. The CCF values are prescribed by the regulator under both regimes.

Different approaches for estimating exposure at default (EAD)

In the standardized approach as well as in FIRB of Basel II, CCFs are supplied by the regulator. However, in the Basel II IRB advanced approach (IRBA), the bank itself determines the appropriate EAD to be applied to each exposure, on the basis of robust data and analysis which is capable of being validated both internally and by supervisors.

If the draw down and repayment schedule of term loans are known and it has generally no chance to further increase its exposure in excess of the set transaction limit, long term loans can be repaid in a series of annual, semi-annual or monthly payments. EAD can be derived from the existing amortizing plan. BCBS (2006) document (paragraph 137) states: "For fixed exposures such as term loans and instalment loans, each loan's EAD is no less than the principal balance outstanding." In such a case, no model is required as the draw down schedule is known.

Hence, in the event of default, the exposure for such transactions is given by the current outstanding in every year.

EAD = Outstanding   Eq. 4.1a

However, for large infrastructure projects where the borrower needs the bank's explicit approval for drawn down in the subsequent stages in the long run, the bank would have to consider drawn and undrawn portions pertaining to the stage under implementation for estimating regulatory capital under the standardized approach.

However, the off balance sheet (OBs) lending products like cash credit, overdraft, revolving line of credit (e.g. credit card) and working capital loan facilities are characterized by an external limit. The draw down rate of the credit limit may have uncertainty. An obligor close to default generally tends to increase its utilization, while the bank will have to reduce the available limits to control its exposure risk. From risk management point of view, in order to have a more realistic prediction of exposure, the bank has to predict a portion of the free limit and include it in the EAD estimation.

In such cases of off balance sheet exposures

$EAD = Outstanding + CCF \times Free\ Limit$ Eq. 4.1b

CCF is also termed as usage given default (UGD) or the loan equivalency factor (LEF or LEQ).

Free limit is the balance limit which is the difference between the current line of credit minus the availed amount.

$Free\ Limit = Max\ \{0;\ Limit - Outstanding\}$ Eq. 4.1c

For off balance sheet exposures (OBs), the unutilized "free limit" portion will have to be converted into the equivalent credit exposure by applying a regulatory prescribed credit conversion factor. In India, banks are using credit conversion factors (CCFs) for non-market-related OBs as per the table 8 provided in latest NCAF (2014) and Basel III (2014) circulars.

For example, in case of a cash credit (OCC) facility of ₹100 lakh (which is not unconditionally cancelable), where the drawn portion is ₹60 lakh, and the un-drawn portion of ₹40 lakh will attract a relatively lower CCF of 20 per cent. This is due to the logic that cash credit facility is subject to review or renewal normally once a year. The credit equivalent amount will be = 20% × ₹40 lakh = ₹8 lakh. This amount will be assigned the appropriate risk weight as applicable to the borrower rating to arrive at the Basel II/III standardized risk weighted asset for the undrawn portion. The drawn portion (₹60 lakh) will attract a risk weight as applicable to the counterparty/rating.

For bonds, warrants, standby letters of credit related to particular transactions, CCF = 50 per cent. For direct credit substitutes like LCs, guarantees of loans, CCF = 100 per cent. Moreover, commitments that are unconditionally cancellable at any time by the bank without prior notice or that effectively provide for automatic cancellation due to deterioration in a borrower's credit worthiness, CCF = 0 per cent. These are clearly stipulated in Basel II (NCAF) and III guidelines of RBI (2014).

Under the AIRB approach, the banks themselves determine the appropriate EAD to be applied to each exposure. EAD is calculated taking account of the facility type and commitment details. The motivation for estimating CCF comes from the fact that if an account defaults in the future, the balance at default is expected to equal the balance today plus a fraction of the undrawn amount. For example, an overdraft typically becomes defaulted because the balance has exceeded the limit by a material amount for three consecutive months. Thus, the exposure of the overdraft facility at default is expected to be greater than the current balance because not only has none of the current balance been repaid but additional withdrawals may further increase the loan outstanding amount. In sum, the EAD should be the drawn amount plus the estimated amount of future draws. A bank can also internally calculate unpaid interest and fees which can be further added to the EAD value.

Under AIRB, exposure amounts will have to be calculated from internal historical experience regarding balances at default relative to current balances and/or relative to the amount of the line of credit. Such data cover periods of time that range widely from 1 to 7 years. Finally, EADs will have to be measured for various "segments" of accounts. Segments, in turn, are defined by various factors such as rating, facility default status (or reason), constitution, region, security, etc.

Facility-wise UGD or CCF for various customers can be estimated based on historical information of a bank. A bank can initially start the analysis with a yearly cohort approach. The following formula may be used to estimate the realized CCF (or UGD) from the past default history data.

$$CCF = \left\{ 0; \frac{Outstanding_d - Outstanding_{d-1}}{Limit_{d-1} - Outstanding_{d-1}} \right\} \qquad \text{Eq. 4.2}$$

Thus, the CCF shows the proportion of free limit being utilized by the borrower during default. d is the time of default and $d-1$ is the preceding year of default. Thus, CCF is like a ratio of increase in exposure until default year to maximum possible increase in exposure until default year. This approach is also termed as discrete cohort method which is accepted by the supervisor. When the facility data is more frequently available, then the bank can even move to a superior quarterly and monthly cohort approach.

The cohort analysis has been illustrated in Chart 4.1. Since credit line utilization increases significantly as borrower credit quality deteriorates, the amount outstanding might become significantly higher in the event of default, resulting in an EAD much higher than outstanding at the time of capital calculation.

Chart 4.1: EAD Forecast by Applying Realized CCFs for One-year Time Window

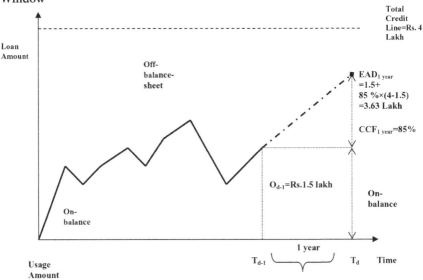

Source: Author's own illustration adapted from Valvonis (2008).

Chart 4.1 shows how CCF would be used to forecast the exposure at default (Valvonis, 2008). CCFs must be expressed as a percentage of the undrawn (off-balance) amount of the commitment. A time interval of one year has been used to derive ex-ante EAD. In the similar fashion, CCFs need to be estimated for each facility over different time periods. Banks are expected to estimate CCFs on the basis of the average CCFs by facility grade (pool) using all observed defaults with the data source. For AIRB risk weight estimation purpose, facility grade (pool) average CCFs are used for every non-defaulted exposure to obtain EADs. It is imperative to note that EAD may include the estimated future accrued but unpaid interest and fees. Banks need to validate CCFs and EADs before finalization of numbers. The articles by Asarnow El-liot and James Marker (1995), Ross Taplin, Huong Minh To and Jarrad Hee (2007), Vytautas Valvonis (2008), etc. discuss the estimation of UGD, CCF and EAD following the similar methodologies.

Historical studies have found that borrowers going into default tend to draw down more than healthy companies. Table 4.1 shows the rating-wise corporate historical UGD pattern of a US bank. This table is based on the EAD analysis done by Asarnow and Marker (1995) based on a sample of 50 large corporate loans at Citibank from 1988 to 1993. The EAD was estimated as the average use of the credit line plus the additional use at the time of default. They found that EAD depends on the initial credit grade. Lower credit quality borrowers had higher utilization and appeared to have lower UGD due to stricter monitoring by the bank. On the other hand, higher quality borrowers had lower utilization (or drawn per cent) but higher UGD because they were subject to fewer restrictions and covenants and less strict monitoring. That means, though the current utilization of the limits for better graded customers may be low, it peaks up when they are near the default boundary. The inverse relationship between loan equivalents (LEQ) and credit quality was also confirmed by Araten and Jacobs Jr. (2001) for revolving credits and advised lines. More interestingly, they observed that the decline in LEQ with increasing risk grade is most evident in the shorter time to default categories (1–2 years).

Table 4.1: UGD per Rating Class on Bank's Loan Commitments

Rating Class	Drawn Amount (a)	UGD (b)	EAD (c)=(a)+(b)[1-(a)]
AAA	0.10%	69.00%	69.03%
AA	1.60%	73.00%	73.43%
A	4.60%	71.00%	72.33%
BBB	20.00%	65.00%	72%
BB	46.80%	52.00%	74.46%
B	63.70%	48.00%	81.12%
CCC	75.00%	44.00%	86%

Source: Asarnow and Marker (1995).

Banks need to take these thresholds as an additional early warning signal of defaults for their parties.

The author has conducted an EAD survey of Indian banks in 2012–13. The following data fields were asked from the banks and are presented in Chart 4.2:

144 Managing Portfolio Credit Risk in Banks

Chart 4.2: Snapshot of an EAD Template

1. Name of the party (or borrower) – A bank may also provide borrower code.
2. Line of Business – Retail/SMEs/Corporate, etc. This information is needed to derive UGD numbers at sub-portfolio level.
3. Constitution of the borrower – Proprietorship/Pvt. Ltd. or Government, etc. This is also required to differentiate UGD numbers across borrower type.
4. Region/branch location – Location of the borrower as well as the sanctioning branch.
5. Name of the facility – Open cash credit (OCC)/overdraft (ODs)/S bills, etc. This field collects information about the nature of the facility. A bank may also group the facilities into fund-based and non-fund-based limits and give separate codes. A single borrower may have multiple facilities and this differentiation should be recorded properly.
6. Dealing with since, number of years of banking – This enables a bank to understand whether longer track record with the borrowers matters in EAD.
7. Date of last sanction – It should be collected in date format Day/Month/Year.
8. Limit at sanction – The total sanctioned limit either in rupees full unit or in rupees lakh.
9. Outstanding amount at sanction time – The sanction amount in rupees lakh.
10. Credit rating at sanction time – Internal/external credit rating of the borrower.
11. Date of default – The NPA date (year format is also fine).
12. Balance outstanding at default – The amount due at the time of default. This may include principal outstanding and interest suspense (say three months interest due).
13. Limit previous year of default – That is 1 year back; if default is on 31st March 2007, then what the limit was in 31st March 2006. A bank should also know whether limit has been changed during the one-year gap.
14. Balance outstanding preceding year of default.
15. Collateral type – Details about collateral information of the facility, whether secured/unsecured loan, type of collateral, etc.
16. Value of the collateral – The latest market value of the collateral in rupees lakh.

Source: Author's own designed data template.

The template for collecting account level as well as aggregate level EAD data has been given in the Annexure 4.1A and 4.1B. Banks can use these templates for their internal EAD studies. The EAD study has obtained the following estimates of UGD or CCFs for various pools of facilities that are reported in Tables 4.2 and 4.3.

It is quite evident from Tables 4.2 and 4.3 that EAD numbers will be different across different facilities. Cash credit limit is made available as a running limit and is freely available for drawls in the absence of any strict covenants. Hence, the UGD percentage is relatively higher than the packing credit (PC). PCs are reviewed regularly at the grant of every fresh PC. Hence, when the overdue is observed, an early checkpoint is placed restricting further drawls. The S Bills/F Bills/BEs are reviewed on a fortnightly/monthly basis and overdue bills are recovered from the party's operative accounts.

Table 4.2: Facility-wise CCF/UGD (%) Estimates of a Large Indian PSB

Facility Name	Facility Code	No. of Facilities	Mean UGD	Std. Dev.
Cash Credit	CC	128	37.23	42.07
Overdraft	OD	7	21.78	23.27
Packing Credit	PC	25	25.00	41.39
Supply Bills	SB	2	42.23	13.97
Total		162		

Source: Author's own study.
Note: Study period: 2002–08.

Table 4.3: Facility Pool-wise UGD/CCFs of another Large PSB

Facility Name	Facility Code	No. of Facilities	Mean UGD%
Bill of Exchange	BE	1	2.00
Devolve Guarantee	DG	2	79.50
F Bills	FB	3	49.00
Open Cash Credit	OCC	38	33.60
Packing Credit	PC	8	4.5
Supply Bills	SB	3	36.00
Total		55	34.1

Source: Author's own study.
Note: The facility number weighted average UGD is 31.43%. Study Period: 2001–07.

Similarly, the difference in UGD estimates across rating grades has also been examined. This has been documented in Table 4.4. Such sub-grouping of EAD figures will more granularly capture the risk and give diversification reward points to the banks. One can notice that the upper grades' mean utilization rate of loan limits during sanction is relatively lower than the risky grades. The risky grades' UGD rates are also comparatively higher than the upper grades.

Table 4.4: Rating-wise UGD Estimates of a Large PSB

Internal Rating	N	Mean Utilization during Sanction	Mean UGD	SD of UGD
R2	4	41.62	18.30	32.20
R3	19	65.30	30.42	42.95
R5	46	74.29	36.85	43.10
R6	24	98.10	28.66	37.51
R7	8	65.26	54.94	46.44
R8	11	74.29	35.75	40.79
Total	112		34.53	41.35

Source: Author's own estimate.
Note: R2, R3 are upper (safer) grades and R7, R8 are lower (risky) grades
Study period: 2002–08.

A bank using internal EAD estimates for capital purposes will have to differentiate EAD values on the basis of a wider set of transaction characteristics (e.g. product type) as well as borrower characteristics.

Description about Loan Facilities of Banks in India

Various types of credit facilities extended by a commercial bank are classified as follows:

A. **Fund-based**: It involves certain movement of funds, e.g. cash credit (CC), overdraft (OD), packing credit (PC), bills purchased (BP), bills discounted (BD), term loan (TL), working capital demand loan (WCDL) and advance bills (AB).

B. **Non-fund-based**: Actual funds are not involved as it comes in the form of commitments by the bank to the party and are fee-based. However, there is movement of funds only in case of default. These facilities are categorized as bank guarantees, letters of credit, etc.

Fund-based facilities

- **Cash credit (CC):** This is a working capital facility for the purpose of carrying on business. The borrower can draw up to a pre-fixed limit, can repay part or full of whatever he has borrowed, then can again draw up to the pre-fixed limit so on, so forth. CC can be against inventory and book debt. Open cash credit (OCC) is granted against hypothecation of stock such as raw materials, work in process, finished goods and stock in trade including stocks and spares. Cash Credits are, in theory, payable on demand. These are, therefore, counter part of demand deposits of the Bank. Drawings are regulated within the drawing limit permissible against stock of goods. Cash credit company utilizes the sanctioned limit as and when required in parts, and in cash credit sale, proceeds are deposited by company to CC limit.
- **Overdraft (OD):** The overdraft facility is permitted to meet the day-to-day operational expenses of civil contractors, manufacturers and traders where the goods cannot be hypothecated. This is granted by way of running limit and collaterally secured by immovable property, fixed deposits or other acceptable securities. Clean overdrafts are also issued by banks. Drawings can be made up to a sanctioned limit and interest is charged on the daily debit balance. The difference between cash credit and overdraft is very slight and relates to the operation of the account.
- **Packing credit (PC):** It has the same characteristics as described above, but the limit is extended only to exporters as a pre-sale (pre shipment) facility. PC is granted against hypothecation of stocks such as raw materials, work in process, finished goods used in the manufacture of goods meant for exports. This facility is made available by way of a single transaction loan on an order to order basis within the overall limit sanctioned. Borrower can deposit and withdraw again. RBI also allows running PC facility to established exporters.
- **Bills purchased (BP):** This facility is against bills of exchange raised by a seller. This is a receivable (current assets) financing. Usually it is covered by a charge on goods sold. The facility has a pre-fixed limit.
- **Bills discounted (BD):** Post-sale facility for usage bills. One bill discounted at a time. Aggregate not to exceed a pre-fixed limit. Usually it is not covered by a charge on goods sold. It is also a receivable (current asset) financing.
- **Term loan/loan (TL):** Term loan is instalment-based credit facility repayable over a period of 3–7 years, depending on due cash flows

of the unit. It is usually granted for the creation of fixed assets (e.g. machinery) as opposed to current assets, which are financed by CC/ OD/BP/BD. These are generally mid-term or long-term loans for acquisitions of fixed assets, usually granted by way of single transaction loans. This also includes home loans and car loans. The repayable interest is charged on monthly basis and, hence, depending on the repayment terms, the principal amount keeps reducing and cleared in full within the stipulated period.

- **Working capital demand loan (WCDL):** It is a short-term working capital facility enjoyed by company which is availed as lump sum and repaid in lump sum. It has a fixed limit and one disbursement followed by repayment/s. There is no opportunity of repaying and drawing again. This facility is given to medium and large companies against fixed assets or current assets. In WCDL facility, if a limit of ₹30 crores is sanctioned, the company will have to avail entire 30 crores of it at once for the period allowed and no further credit can be made to WCDL. Bank normally allows WCDL for a period of 30/45/60/ 90/180 days. The fixed amount is used for a pre-defined period. At the end of this period, the company will have to repay the entire amount. The company can again avail this ₹30 crore facility after this fixed period after repaying once. Hence, the facility is known as revolving. The company has the option of not revolving or rolling over.
- **Advance bills (AB):** Bank offers post-sale credit against bills. This facility is extended to corporate or non-corporate clients to ease the pressure on their cash flows. AB is the fund exposure arising out of LC devolvement or non-payment by customer on due date. Advance bill is, therefore, a sort of overdue arising out of liquidity mismatch of customer. If advance bills are adjusted within 15–30 days, banks treat it as acceptable and as normal. However, if it is not adjusted within 90 days, the account will have to be treated as NPA.

Non-fund-based facilities

- **Bank guarantee (BG):** A bank guarantee is a non-fund-based line of credit that guarantees a sum of money to a beneficiary. It is a commitment of the bank in writing to the beneficiary to make payment of the amount specified in the BG documents on or before the due date. It could be granted by way of single transaction limit or running limit. Unlike a line of credit, the sum is only paid if the opposing party does not fulfil the stipulated obligations under the contract and, thus, insure the beneficiary from loss due to nonperformance by the other party in a contract.

- **Letter of credit (LC):** Banks offer letters of credit facility to their clients for procurement of goods and other raw material imports as per their needs and ensure sellers that they will get paid. Letters of credit are common in international trade (call trade LCs) because the bank acts as an uninterested party between the buyer and the seller. For example, in trade, LC guarantees payment from a local importer to an overseas exporter. If the importer fails to pay, the bank will pay and then try to reclaim the amount from the importer. For the bank, this creates a short-term exposure to the local importer. LC normally has a usance period of 90 days. The bank faces the full default risk from its customer and has the same risk as if it had given the customer a direct loan. LC is a pure non-fund-based facility but when it devolves (i.e. when customer fails to make payment after usance period), bank makes the payment on behalf of the customer to the beneficiary of LC and an advance bill is opened for that amount. Frequent LC devolvement is an early warning signal for default. Entire non-fund-based exposure of a company can become fund-based exposure due to LC devolvement.

Application of CCF for non-fund-based facilities

Assume a bank has given a credit limit (for 6 months) of 100 crores for issuance of financial bank guarantees to a borrower. The borrower has got financial bank guarantee (BG) issued for ₹60 crores, whereas for the remaining ₹40 crores, the BG is yet to be issued. It is worth noting that the unavailed portion of the sanctioned limit has also the potential to be drawn on and that is why a bank needs to apply applicable CCF to arrive at the potential credit exposure. The risk weight depending upon the borrower rating applies after this.

In this case, the credit equivalent calculation will be as follows:

- On ₹60 crores for which the BG has already been issued, the CCF applicable will be 100 per cent, i.e. the credit equivalent will be 60 × 100 per cent = 60 crores.
- On the 40 crores, the CCF applicable will be 20 per cent (since it is a commitment for less than 1 year), i.e. the credit equivalent will be 40 × 20 per cent = ₹8 crores

The total credit equivalent will be = 60 + 8 = ₹68 crores.

Please note that in case there is a clause saying that the limit for which BG has not been issued can be unconditionally cancelled by the bank, then in that case no CCF needs to be applied on the remaining portion (₹40 crores in the above example).

Under the advanced approach, banks will have to track the drawal rates from the unavailed portion from the NPA history. Default implies that non-fund facility has got converted into funded facility. When the borrower defaults in completing with the terms of the LC or BG and the counterparty invokes his claim, the liability gets capitalized into a fund liability when the claim settled by the bank. The devolved liability is to be repaid by the party. When devolved guarantee phenomenon happens, the chance that the entire non-fund-based liability gets crystallized to a fund-based liability. As a result, UGD percentage may become higher. In such cases, the non-fund-based outstanding at the observation point and the amount converted into default (i.e. the devolvement amount) need to be recorded properly to correctly estimate the UGD (or CCF). In order to obtain a more stable CCF estimate, quarterly rolling estimate should be made for both undrawn and non fund based facilities. For traded products, EAD is determined by the expected future exposure (EFE) obtained from the mark-to-market value over the time period.

Factors that Determine EAD or CCFs

Empirical evidence from various studies worldwide suggests that the following factors drive CCFs or EAD:

- *Firm-specific risk:* Riskier borrowers' less UGD suggests bank monitoring;
- Credit lines with shorter maturities have higher UGD – longer maturities allow for better monitoring of the borrower;
- *Bank-specific risks:* Higher the NPA ratio, higher is the UGD number;
- *Borrower's liquidity situation:* Borrowers in tight liquidity condition will draw more;
- *Overall liquidity condition in the market:* The draw down rates in a revolving line of credit peak up as a firm approaches to default (Moody's research, 2008);
- *Macroeconomic fluctuations:* UGD peaks up during bad time (captures pro-cyclicality);
- *Loan size:* For a given time to default, larger credit lines are drawn less, due to better bank monitoring.

In our EAD survey of Indian banks, it has been observed that accounts with higher limits show lower UGD percentage. This could be probably because higher limits are under the sanctioning powers of higher authorities and are subject to regular scrutiny. Hence, the tendency to allow ad hoc over drawing to regularize the operational problem of the limit is also less at default. A bank can control the CCF through better monitoring and proper due diligence on the customer.

The above set factors may be used to develop an EAD prediction model using best fitting regression models. Studies by Min Qi (2009), Volvonis (2008) can be taken as a useful benchmark to develop banks' EAD models. Finally, the predicted EAD estimates need to be back tested to validate the accuracy of EADs on a portfolio basis.

Further tasks for the banks under IRB approach

A bank using internal EAD estimates for capital purposes might be able to differentiate EAD values on the basis of a wider set of transaction characteristics (e.g. product type, secured/unsecured, etc.) as well as borrower characteristics (e.g. rating wise, constitution wise, etc.). As with PD and LGD estimates, these values would be expected to represent a conservative view of long-run averages, although banks would be free to use more conservative estimates.

In terms of assigning estimates of EAD to broad EAD classifications, banks may use either internal or external data sources. Given the perceived current data limitations in respect of EAD (in particular external sources), a minimum data requirement of 7 years has been set.

A bank wishing to use its own estimates of EAD will need to demonstrate to its supervisor that it can meet additional minimum requirements pertinent to the integrity and reliability of these estimates. For a risk weight derived from the IRB framework to be transformed into a risk weighted asset, it needs to be attached to an exposure amount. Any error in EAD calculation will directly affect the risk weighted asset, thereby affecting both regulatory as well as economic capital requirement.

Loss Given Default (LGD)

Loss-given-default (LGD) is an important determinant of credit risk. It is an estimate of the extent of uncertainty about how much the bank will not be able to recover its loan past due if a borrower defaults. It actually measures the severity of the default loss. If ₹100 is the default outstanding amount and bank is able to recover ₹30, the recovery rate (RR) is 30 per cent and loss given default (LGD) will be 70 per cent. Thus, LGD estimates the magnitude of likely loss on the exposure, expressed as a percentage of the exposure at default. Facility level LGD estimates across borrower/industry/regions are key inputs in measurement of the expected and unexpected credit losses and, hence, credit risk capital (regulatory as well as economic). Banks must measure this loss arising from counterparty default in order to graduate towards the more sophisticated Basel II internal rating-based (IRB) approach.

Methods for estimating LGD

LGD can be estimated broadly using three different methodologies:

1. **Market-based LGD:** These are observed from market prices of defaulted bonds or marketable loans soon after the actual default event. For example, Altman, Cooke and Kishore (1999) estimated that when firms defaulted on their bonds in 1998, the investor lost on an average around 63 cents on the dollar (i.e. LGD = 63% and recovery rate RR = 37%.

$$LGD = \frac{Value\ before - Value\ after}{Value\ before}$$

Value refers to the valuation before and after the time of default. Most recovery studies conducted by rating agencies are based on this approach.

2. **Spread-based Implied LGD:** One can theoretically infer market-expected LGD for the listed bonds using information on the spreads. In this approach, LGDs are derived from risky (but not defaulted) bond prices (credit spreads) using a theoretical asset pricing model.

The FI manager would set the expected return on the bond (say BBB rated) to equal the risk-free rate in the following manner:

$$(1 - PS) \times RR(1 + r^*) + PS(1 + r) = 1 + r \qquad \text{Eq. 4.3}$$

The first term of the left-hand side of the above expression is the pay-off the FI expects to get if the borrower defaults.

$$\Rightarrow\ r^* - r = \phi = \frac{(1 + r)}{RR + PS - PS \times RR} - (1 + r) \qquad \text{Eq. 4.4}$$

The symbol "ϕ" is the observed credit spread which is the difference in yields between bond- and risk-free treasury rate. To derive the implied LGD, one has to solve for the risk premium between r^* (the required yield on risky corporate debt) and r (the risk-free rate of interest).

For example, if r = 10% and PS = 95% as before, but now the FI can expect to collect 90 per cent of the promised proceeds if default occurs (RR = 90% or LGD = 10%), then the required risk premium or credit spread = 60%.

Expression 4.4 of credit spread may be used to estimate the expected recovery Rate (RR) or loss given default rate (LGD) if spreads and risk-free rate are known. For example, say FIMMDA one year BBB corporate bond spread (over zero-coupon) is 267 bps (as on 2005) and one year treasury rate is 7 per cent. The one-year BBB probability of default is 5.17 per cent (i.e. PD = 5.17% obtained from CRISIL's average one year rating transition matrix). Then the expected RR would be 52.91 per cent and estimated LGD = 47.09 per cent. One can check the estimate by plugging in these values in equation 4.4.

This is applicable for the traded debts only.

3. **Workout LGD:** This can be estimated from the historically observed NPA loan loss data of banks at the end of workout and settlement process. The set of estimated cash flows resulting from the workout and/or collections processes are factored into the analysis and estimates are properly discounted and divided by the estimated exposure. These cash flows are the principal recovery; the carrying costs of non-performing loans (e.g. interest income foregone and workout expenses like collection charges, legal charges, etc.)

To estimate workout LGDs, each bank has to rely on its internal data on defaulted accounts and the positive (recovery against principal and interest) and negative (recovery costs-legal procedure, etc.) cash flows associated with these defaulted accounts.

Because of non-availability of data of post-defaulted bond price and bond spread and since most of the loan products are not tradable, the workout LGD estimation approach is more suitable for Indian banks. However, it needs extensive data requirement at each facility level and the data template should be broken down into various sub-clusters – clusters – e.g. type of collateral, short term vs. long term, fund based vs. non-fund based, presence of any guarantee, region, industry factors, etc. so that they significantly explain the difference in LGD.

Workout LGD estimation: Historical vs. economic LGD

The historical LGD (or accounting LGD) is the percentage of a loan that is actually lost and it equals 100 per cent – historical recovery rate (RR). The historical RR is the sum of the cash flow received from defaulted loans divided by total loan amount due at the time of default (EAD). Most bank records generally focus on charge-offs and recoveries (i.e. reversals of charge-offs) and are the source of data for calculating an "accounting" LGD or "net charge-off". The accounting loan recovery rate (RR) is the total amount recovered over the entire recovery cycle (sum recovered) divided by the outstanding exposure at default (EAD). The formula for estimating historical LGD can be expressed as:

$$HistLGD = 1 - \frac{\sum Total\ Recoveries_t}{EAD} \qquad \text{Eq. 4.5}$$

Where EAD = interest suspense plus principal outstanding at the year of default. Total recoveries comprise of principal recovery and interest recovery.

This is a straightforward traditional accounting measure of LGD. However, to better capture the actual loss experience of a defaulted loan, recoveries should be assessed in an economic sense rather than only from the accounting standpoint. The actual default loss of a loan should take into account the length of the collection period, direct and indirect costs associated with the collection of recovery costs and payments which banks actually incur.

Economic LGD is the economic loss in the case of default, which can be different from the accounting one. Economic means that all costs (direct as well indirect) related to workout process have to be included, and that the discounting effects have to be integrated. Accounting LGD differs from economic LGD in which it does not take into account the length of the workout period, and it does not include certain costs and payments that banks actually incur. For both internal economic capital estimation and Basel II IRB purposes, banks need to determine an "economic" LGD. The banks need to integrate a part of the legal department costs (legal/litigation expenses, advertisement cost, cost of repossession, etc.) and of the credit or risk department costs (operational costs, credit analyst, risk monitoring, audit, etc.).

Because loan recovery periods may extend over several years, it is necessary to discount post-default net cash flows to a common point in time (the most suitable being the event of default). The LGD on defaulted loan facilities is thus measured by the present value of cash losses with respect to the exposure amount (EAD) at the defaulted year. This can be estimated by calculating the present value of cash received post-default over the year's net discounted cost of recovery. If we divide this net discounted recovery by the exposure amount at default time (EAD), we get the recovery rate. Say, a bank holds a defaulted senior secured loan in its loan book in 2008 with an outstanding due of ₹8 crore. A total recovery amount of ₹2 crore 40 lakh in five years' time (till 2013) was done with total costs of ₹50,000. Suppose that both the recoveries and the costs are entirely obtained and paid at the end of the fifth year. Using an 8 per cent discount rate (which is the average risk free rate with a spread), the value of Eco–LGD at the time of default would be 79.63% = $1 - \dfrac{(240\text{-}0.50)/800}{(1+8\%)^5}$

=100%–29.94%×0.6806.

Otherwise, the simple accounting or historical LGD for this loan would be just 70% = $1 - \dfrac{240}{800} = 100\% - 30\% = 70\%$.

This value is lower than the economic value of the loss.

The basic equation for computing economic LGD is as follows:

$$ECOLGD = 1 - \frac{\sum \dfrac{\text{Re cov}\,eries_t - Costs_t}{EAD}}{(1+r)^t} \qquad\qquad \text{Eq. 4.6}$$

Where r is the discount rate, EAD is the exposure at default or outstanding due at the time of default (principle due plus interest suspense) and t is the workout period till an account is settled.

Total recoveries (*recoveries*) may be obtained in the form of cash recovered from the borrower and from the sale of collateral whose market value can be estimated. The cost part (*costs*) includes direct and indirect costs attributable to the recovery of the facility. Thus, the term "economic" (ECOLGD) means that all related costs of recovery (legal and courts and maintenance expenses, etc.) have been included and the discounting effects due to delay in recovery have been integrated. This is a comprehensive definition of LGD and is in line with Basel II IRB definition.

Table 4.5 illustrates a straightforward calculation of the historical recovery rate and economic LGD of a 10 year defaulted corporate term loan.

Table 4.5: Illustrative Example for Computing Historical and Economic LGD

Units in ₹ Million, others in per cent

Default year	2004	2004–05	2005–06	2006–07	2007–08	2008–09	2009–10
							(Settled & written off)
Principal Outstanding	750						
Interest due	50						
Principal Recovery		60	80	30	40	10	80
Interest Recovery		10	5	4	1		
Direct & Indirect Cost		50	20	5	3	5	20
Total Recovery		70	85	34	41	10	80
Total Due (EAD)	800						
Total historical Recovery							320
Historical Avg. Recovery Rate							40.00
Historical Avg. LGD							**60.00**
Net Recovery		20	65	29	41	5	60
Discount Rate (@ %)	5						
Net- Recovery Rate (NRR)							20.52
Economic-LGD							**79.48**
Discount Rate (@ %)	10						
Net- Recovery Rate (NRR)							15.52
Economic-LGD							**84.48**

Source: Author's own illustration.

The default occurs on corporate term loan facility in the year 2004. At the time of default, the bank has estimated that the total loan outstanding due is Rs. 800 lakh (see Table 4.5). The recoveries gained from the selling of collateral as well as through direct cash entries and transfers have recorded as principal/interest recoveries over various years. The account was finally settled in 2010 and was written off by the bank. The historical recovery rate (RR) of 40.00 (historical average LGD of 60.00 from 1-RR) are obtained by adding the year wise-recovery entries (both principal and interest recoveries) and then dividing by the amount outstanding (or EAD) at the time of default. The economic LGD is also estimated from net charge off amount using the write-off history of defaulted loans. This has been shown in Table 4.5 by applying different discount rates. As can be noticed, Economic LGD significantly differs from the Historical Avg. LGD estimates. The effects of delay of recoveries due to default has been incorporated in Economic LGD by discounting the net recoveries post default by a discount factor. The discount factor has to be risk adjusted to incorporate the opportunity cost. Higher the discount rate, higher is the Economic loss rate (i.e. Economic-LGD).

Asarnow and Edwards (1995) of Risk Management Association (RMA) had conducted a Citibank loss study and derived a definition of economic loss in the event of default (LIED). They had analyzed Citibank data over a 24-year period (1970–93) using this approach to derive economic LGD estimates from the write-off taken subsequent to default. The LIED (synonymous with LGD) components are given below:

$$LIED = \frac{W + ID - IC - R - MSC}{IDA}$$
Eq. 4.7

Where W is the present value (PV) of dollar amount of each write-off amount subsequent to default which is calculated to the date of default; ID is interest drag (the total dollar amount of foregone interest on the outstanding default balance) based on a monthly PV calculation for each default; IC is dollar amount of each cash interest payment also estimated on a PV basis; R is the PV of dollar amount for each unanticipated principal recovery, MSC is the PV of dollar amount of other income (or expense) events; and IDA is the initial dollar amount for the default (similar to EAD).

Finally, the LIED is defined as the simple average of LIED$_i$ across all defaults. By employing this discounted cash flow LIED method, Asarnow and Edwards (1995) obtained 34.79 per cent average LGD for C&I loans and 12.75 per cent LGD for structured loans.

Choice of discount rate in economic LGD estimation

One of the critical factors in computing economic LGD is the choice of appropriate discount rate to be used for recoveries. A discount rate should reflect the time value of money and the opportunity cost of funds to apply to recoveries and costs. Most banks do not report cash flow actually received on defaulted loans. However, cash flow can be reconstructed from a combination of periodic reported book values, charge-offs (total amount due) and recoveries of charge-offs (recovery). The charge-off net of recovery is the loss given default (LGD). Once the cash flows on defaulted loans are evaluated, they are then discounted at an appropriate discount rate. Discount rates chosen can vary anywhere between the risk-free rate and then yield that a buyer of distressed assets at the time of default would require to obtain the cash flows projected. It may not be appropriate to use the original contract rate of interest, as there is substantial risk that cash flows projected at the time of default may not be accurate.

Choosing the appropriate discount rate to post-defaulted cash flows is not straightforward and still is an unsettled issue among researchers, practitioners and regulators. Many studies have applied three different discount rates: the interest rate before the default date to each facility, an average discount rate for all facilities, and a forward looking rate. The bank's top management can also think and decide about what should be the appropriate discount rate. BCBS (2005) suggests that the discount rate should reflect the cost of holding defaulted assets over the workout period. That includes an appropriate premium. When there is no uncertainty in recovery streams (may be during upturn of the business cycle), net present value calculations only need to reflect the time value of money and a risk-free discount is appropriate. However, a risk-adjusted discount rate (sum of risk-free rate and a spread) will be appropriate for the risk of the recovery and cost cash flows during economic downturn. Empirical evidence suggests that the discount rates vary pro-cyclically and they increase with industry default rates. The choice of discount rate is important in the sense because of the high volatility of LGD rate with respect to the discount rate.

In addition to the exposure and cash flow received, demographic information pertaining to the borrower (e.g. rating, constitution, regional locations, etc.), industry affiliation, constitution, borrower rating, its leverage position, facility type, nature of collateral (mortgage, pledge, hypothecation, etc.), seniority of collateral, etc. need to be collected by the banks in order to derive segment-wise many LGD estimates according to these characteristics. Although historical data on collateral are often not captured, it is important to differentially determine LGD based on collateral. A further breakdown of LGD by type of collateral (e.g. cash and marketable securities, accounts receivables, inventory, fixed assets, mortgages, etc.) is also required to get a better insight about difference in loss experiences. This segmentation of LGD database into various sub-clusters will allow banks to more granularly differentiate the risk of loan losses and, thus, derive diversification benefits under the AIRB approach. These additional data fields are also necessary to analyze the determinants of loss severity and, thus, develop a more scientific statistical LGD predictor model.

The LGD estimates also vary across banks, which depends on the fact as to how proactive are the banks in recovering such loans. This tells us that the advantages lie in IRB approach where bank can utilize these statistics for getting capital benefits.

Past studies on LGD

The first study on bank-loan recovery rates was done by Carty and Lieberman (1996) using Moody's data on syndicated lending. They estimated LGD based on the discounted cash flows associated with recoveries that occurred after default. Subsequently, Carty (1998) updated the study where secured and unsecured loans were treated separately. He observed that secured loans, actual recovery rate (86.7 per cent), were significantly higher than the unsecured rate (79.4 per cent).

Asarnow and Edwards (1995), of RMA, studied the Citibank's internal loss data over a 24-year period and estimated the economic cost of default for structured and commercial and industrial loans. Their study covers 831 defaults over a 24-year period ending 1993. The study obtains an average LGD (or LIED) of 34.8 per cent. They find that LGD vary significantly by the size of the default. In particular, interest drag is much larger part of large defaults than small ones.

Gupton and Stein (2005) analyzed the recovery rate on over 1,800 corporate bond, loan and preferred stock defaults from 900 companies using Moody's LossCalc® model for predicting LGD immediately and in one year. However, in his sample, share of unsecured loan's portion was significantly less (approximately 10 per cent).

Some of the public studies on LGD available in the literature are summarized in reverse date order (i.e. recent to past) in Table 4.6.

An 18-year (1982–99) study (see Araten, Jacobs and Varshney, 2004) conducted at JPMC covered 3,761 defaulted loans and resulted in a 39.8 per cent average economic LGD, with a standard deviation of 35.4 per cent. The sensitivity to the discount rate was such that using a 10 per cent discount rate resulted in an average LGD of 36.2 per cent and using a 5 per cent discount rate resulted in an average LGD of 31.9 per cent. Therefore, higher the discount rate, higher is the LGD. The average "accounting" LGD or the average net charge-off rate, determined without any discounting, resulted in a 27 per cent LGD.

Table 4.6: List of Popular Public Studies on Loan LGD

Author	Data Time Period	Sample	LGD type	Statistics/Findings
Min Qi and Xialong Yang (2009)	1990–2003	data of 241,293 mortgages loan recovery data from settled insurance claims	Workout	– Average LGD is 30.53% – Avg. LGD is 49.2% in high LTV & 14% in low LTV – LGD varies with property types, loan purpose
Dermine and de Carvalho (2006)	June 1985–Dec 2000	371 defaulted loans	Workout	– Bi-modal LGD – Size and collateral effects on LGD, etc.
Gupton and Stein (2005), Moody's Investor Service, Global Credit Research	1981–2004	3,026 defaulted loans, bonds and preferred stocks	Market based approach	– Beta distribution fits recovery – Small number of LGD < 0
Araten, Michael, and Peeyush (2004)	1982–99	3,761 large corporate loans of JP Morgan	Workout	– Average 39.8% – St.dev. 35.4%
Gupton, Gates and Carty (2000)	1989–2000	Secondary market price of 181 defaulted bank loans of 121 defaulted issuers	Secondary Market Price Data	– Average LGD is 30.5% for Senior Secured & 47.9% for Sr. Unsecured Loans
Ciochetti (1997), Real Estate Finance, vol. 14 (Spring), pp. 53-69	1986–95	2,013 commercial mortgages	Workout	– Average 30.6% – Min/Max (annual) 20%/38%
Asarnow and Edwards (1995)	24 years Citibank data	831 commercial & industrial loans & structured loans (highly collaterlized)	Workout	– Average LGD is 34.79% for C&I loans – For structured loans: 12.75%

Source: Author's own review.

Many recovery studies have shown that recovery rates (and, hence, LGD rates) vary across industries. A wide range of differing recovery rates by industry will give diversification benefit to the banks under the AIRB approach. Another issue has been highlighted in many studies is that recovery rate is dependent upon the seniority and the presence of collateral. The studies of Altman and Kishore (1996), Gupton, Gates and Carty (2000) provide empirical evidence that seniority is a collateral matter in debt recovery. The greater the equity cushion (i.e. seniority charge of the collateral), the more likely there will be assets of value that will be recovered under absolute priority as they go first in liquidation.

LGD statistics for Indian banks

At the moment, there are only two studies available on LGD in India. Bandyopadhyay (2007) conducted an LGD survey of seven Indian public sector banks for the first time and reported bank-wise LGD numbers for retail and commercial loans. In another study, Bandyopadhyay and Singh (2007) studied the LGD experience of a major public sector bank in India. A Snapshot of the first round of LGD survey results is given in Table 4.7.

Table 4.7: First Round LGD Survey Estimates for Indian Banks: Commercial and Retail Bank Loans, 1998–2007

Panel A: Commercial Loans (Exposure>₹50 Lakh)

Bank Code	Default Number	Historical LGD (%)	Economic LGD (%)	Default Weights: Hist-LGD (col.2×col.3)	Default Weights: Eco-LGD (col.2×col.4)
1	101	62.59	78.08	6321.59	78.8608
2	22	81.06	87.19	1783.32	19.1818
3	972	84.91	90.46	82532.52	87.7462
4	78	73.76	80.36	5753.28	62.68.8
5	200	64.65	81.69	12930	163.38
6	127	80.55	84.91	10229.85	107.8357
7	66	66.50	76.50	4389	50.49
Total	1566			123939.56	136170.03
Simple Average		73.43	82.74		
Default Wtd. Avg.				79.14	86.95

Source: Author's own survey results conducted at NIBM (Bandyopadhyay, 2007).

Table 4.7 contd.

Table 4.7 contd.

Panel B: Retail Loans

Bank Code	Default Number	Historical LGD (%)	Economic LGD (%)	Default Weights: Hist-LGD (col.2×col.3)	Default Weights: Eco-LGD (col.2×col.4)
1	283	65.33	71.67	18488.39	20282.61
2	22	60.02	64.90	1320.44	1427.8
6	127	80.55	84.91	10229.85	10783.57
8	66	83.41	87.21	5505.06	5755.86
Total	498			35543.74	38249.84
Simple Average		72.33	77.17		
Default Wtd.Avg.		71.37	76.81		

Source: Author's own survey results.

Note: i. Bank names are not disclosed for confidentiality; ii. A discount rate of 10.5 is used which is the historical average of bank PLR (including a credit spread); iii. Borrower weighted historical LGD is estimated by dividing col. 5 total by col. 2 total; iv. Commercial loan exposures include defaulted corporates, commercial SMEs, NBFCs and commercial real estate exposures. Retail loan exposures include housing loans, auto loans and other consumer loan exposures, including student and personal loans, and defaulted credit card exposures.

The Indian experience in this survey suggested that LGD rates were higher (average historical LGD is 73.43 per cent for corporate and 64.74 per cent for retail segment) than those globally. Moody's 1970–2003 study of US bank loans shows an average LGD rate of 36.10 per cent, of which corporate LGD was 60.09 per cent. The high LGD rate comparison to the international number is a sign of weakness in the recovery mechanism of Indian banks.

The high economic LGD figure may be because of the time lag in recovery process. As the time of collection increases, the value of the recovered amount falls and recovery cost (cost of litigation) increases and, hence, the loss rate goes up. The survey has found that shorter the collection process' length (or how quickly recovery took place), better is the chance of recovery and, hence, lower LGD. Higher the value of the collateral in proportion to the exposure amount (loan to value ratio), better is the recovery rate. The data reveal that liquidity of the collateral, industry tangibility and regional factors also matter in recovery and, hence, LGD.

However, at that time, the LGD concept was not yet formalized in India as banks were in Basel I era. Very few financial institutions in India have ample data on recovery rates by asset-type and by type of collateral. Therefore, developing an LGD predictor model, as an input for their internal rate based (AIRB) models, is a daunting task for Indian banks. The awareness about collecting loss data has been significantly improved after the implementation of Basel II standardized approach in India since 2008. Moreover, the Securitization and Reconstruction of Financial Assets & Enforcement of Security Interest (SARFESI) Act, 2002 has enabled banks to recover their dues speedily. In view of these, the author has conducted a second round LGD survey during 2010–12 in India to further bridge this gap. The purposes of the second round survey were manifold:

1. Maintain a historical data pool on LGD of bank loans
2. Obtain system level LGD statistics for various types of loan facilities and derive segment-wise LGD numbers (e.g. industry-wise, collateral-wise, region-wise estimates)
3. Study the crucial factors that determine LGD
4. Develop a prototype LGD predictor model

The following LGD data fields were asked from the banks and are listed in Chart 4.3:

Chart 4.3: Snapshot of LGD Template

1. **Borrower details:** Name/code, borrower rating, branch/ region location, loan type (commercial loans or retail), industry information, constitution of the borrower, number of years of relationship with the borrower, etc.
2. **Facility details:** Type of facility (fund based or non-fund based), date of sanction, date of default, limit sanction, lending rate, loan tenure, reason of default, amount of loan outstanding due (principle due and interest suspense at the time of default), type of primary security, collateral type and collateral value, seniority of the claim (first charge or second charge), presence of guarantor, etc.
3. **Recovery history:** Yearly recovery of principle and interest due, in absence of yearly break up of recovery, aggregate recovery and number of years of recovery should be given; cost of recovery, amount written off, in case of compromise and the compromised amount with date must be given.
4. **Other details:** Banks are also advised to give details of all the settled accounts since this will give a complete picture of recovery. However, in case of absence of a large sample of settled accounts, partially settled accounts data may also be given.

Source: Author's own designed data template.

The loss data on defaulted loans was collected from eight scheduled commercial banks and one leading housing finance company in India. These banks have given their data to our satisfaction. But all data received from these banks was not usable for the final analysis. Even if Excel templates were given to the participating banks, the data obtained from some of these banks was in a very raw format and a lot of efforts had to be given for cleaning and compiling to make it usable. Data sorting, codification, matching, etc. were done to maintain data consistency.

Finally, a sorted sample pool of 823 commercial loans and 7,267 retail defaulted facilities were created and used to analyze the NPA recovery experiences of Indian banks. We have also retained some data points obtained in our firs round of LGD survey in the updated final data pool. The commercial loan data sample period is from 1989 to 2012. The retail pool data period is from 1994 to 2012. During data sorting, observations were further segmented along line of business, facility type, borrower industry, constitution, geographic region, default year, collateral type to study LGD differentiation.

LGD study results for commercial loan pool of banks in India

Table 4.8 documents historical as well as economic LGD estimates for the entire commercial loan pool. The economic LGD is estimated by discounting the net recovery. The corporate loss severity is relatively higher than the other commercial loans. In commercial loan LGD study of Indian banks, it has been observed that collateral liquidity and marketability have great influence on loan recovery.

Table 4.8: LGD (%) Statistics for Defaulted Commercial Loans in India: Second Round Survey Results

Sector	Sector Code	No. of Facilities	No. of Borrowers	Mean EAD (₹ lakh)	Mean Hist- LGD	Mean Eco- LGD @7.21	Mean Eco- LGD @10.5
Agri & Allied-Commercial	1	62	33	149.9161	65.987	76.682	79.761
Corporate[$]	2	355	253	388.9208	71.397	79.944	82.501
SME	3	241	198	273.9394	57.136	66.477	69.156
SSI-Commercial	4	165	87	276.3364	71.834	81.392	84.081
Total		823	571	314.6739			

Table 4.8 contd.

Table 4.8 contd.

Expos. Wtd. Avg.	67.644 76.649 79.279
Borr. wtd. Avg.	66.206 75.306 77.956

Source: NIBM LGD survey conducted by the author (Bandyopadhyay, 2013).
Note: Corporate and Institutional and Large and Medium Industry and NBFCs; Discount rate 7.21% is risk-free rate (average 364 T-bills rate from March 1998– March 2013), Discount rate 10.5% is average base rate of banks with a risk spread.
$^\$$ Corporate & Institutional and Large & Medium Industry and NBFCs are combined.

The presence of security can be an important distinction in the estimation of LGD. LGDs on secured exposures averaged 62.03 per cent, while LGDs on unsecured exposures averaged 78.01 per cent. A statistical mean comparison *t*-test has been used to check and it was found that the difference is statistically significant. The result shows there is a clear statistically significant difference between the secured and unsecured LGD figures at the 1 per cent level. Loans with good collateral and higher market value have shown better recovery and, hence, lower LGD. The difference is statistically significant for both historical as well as economic LGD (Table 4.9). These findings are in line with other international studies.

Table 4.9: LGD (%) Statistics for Commercial Loans: Secured vs. Unsecured Loans

		No. of Facilities	Mean	SD
Historical LGD:				
	Secured	565	61.940	33.15
	Unsecured	258	77.770	30.44
	Difference		−15.83*** (−6.52)	
Economic LGD (discount rate: @10.5%:				
	Secured	565	72.099	28.57
	Unsecured	258	84.686	23.84
	Difference		−12.587*** (−6.16)	

Source: NIBM LGD survey conducted by Bandyopadhyay (2013).
Note: The figures in the parentheses are the t-values, *** denotes significance at 1% or better.

Moody's 1985–2009 study of North American and Europe bank defaulted corporate loans show average LGD for senior secured loans is 44.50 per cent in Europe and 31.1 per cent in North America. LGDs for senior unsecured loans were shown at higher side: 57 per cent in Europe and 43.8 per cent in USA. Moody's recent default and recovery study of big project finance loans (Moody's Investor Service, 2013) reveals that project finance lending exhibits high recovery rates. The study is based on an aggregate global data pool from banks that includes 4,067 projects over a 28-year period. The mean recovery rate is almost 80 per cent (LGD = 20%). However, the economic recovery rate is estimated as 63.6 per cent (Eco–LGD = 36.4%). The study also shows that marginal annual default rates for project finance bank loans are consistent with high speculative grade credit quality during the initial three-year period following financial close. However, these default rates fall significantly after this period.

The LGD study of Indian banks conducted by the author finds that LGD amount for secured commercial loans varies inversely with the security margin. Higher the value of collateral margin of a loan exposure (C/E), lower is the LGD. The evidence has been documented in Table 4.10 results. This is the reason why the Basel committee and the Reserve Bank of India in their Basel II IRB circular (RBI circular paragraph 47–49) have stipulated that FIRB–LGD for collateralized exposures (under eligible collaterals) should be based on the collateral margin (C/E). The prescribed minimum LGD is inversely related to the exposure margin. This issue has been addressed later in Chapter 8.

Table 4.10: Margin-wise LGD (%) Statistics–Secured Commercial Loans

	C/E	Percentiles	No. of Facilities	Mean	SD
Historical LGD:					
	<35%	<25 percentiles	138	67.536	31.08
	35%–72%	25–50 percentiles	137	62.555	27.51
	>72%	>50 percentiles	290	58.985	36.16
Eco-LGD (@7.21%)					
	<35%	<25 percentiles	138	77.674	25.24
	35%–72%	25–50 percentiles	137	76.121	22.55
	>72%	>50 percentiles	290	67.546	31.76
Eco-LGD (@10.50%)					
	<35%	<25 percentiles	138	80.488	23.51
	35%–72%	25–50 percentiles	137	79.257	21.66
	>72%	>50 percentiles	290	70.377	30.20

Source: LGD survey conducted by Bandyopadhyay (2013).

Table 4.11 differentiates the LGD by collateral categories. The magnitude of LGD increases as the quality of the collateral security decreases. LGD values are lower for loans with mortgage/liens on real property and if collateral are in the form of financial instruments. On the other hand, LGDs are higher for fixed assets and machinery and agricultural land as collaterals.

Table 4.11: Collateral-wise Secured Commercial Loan LGD (%)

Collateral Type	Collateral Category	No. of Facilities	Historical LGD	Eco-LGD @7.21%
Agriculture Land	1	6	72.683	81.973
Financial Instruments	3	11	58.078	65.228
Fixed Assets & Machinery	4	66	77.245	85.151
Mortgage of Property$^\$$	2, 7 & 8	265	58.504	73.032
Other/Uncategorized	5 & 6	349	62.994	70.068
Total		697	62.642	72.649

Source: LGD survey conducted by Bandyopadhyay (2013).
Note: It includes commercial as well as residential real estate; Eco–LGD is estimated using discount rate @7.21%, which is the average risk-free rate.

Thus, the distinction between secured and unsecured in determining LGD is quite evident. Banks need to collect and record the collateral information in estimating workout LGD. Moreover, the collection time also has an importance in recovery. A lesser delay in the collection process yields lower economic LGD. The average length of time to NPA settlement is 4 ½ years. LGD rates are also lower for settled accounts than the unsettled accounts. International experience suggests that the collateral value falls faster than the health of the account. That is why banks need to frequently value and rate the collateral attached to a loan. Results by industry and region show that significant variation in LGD is also quite evident in our study.

LGD study results for retail loan pool

The overall results of the study for 7,267 defaulted and settled retail loans have been documented in Table 4.12.

Table 4.12: Historical LGD (%) for Retail Loans: Secured vs. Unsecured Loans

SL#Exposure Type	No. of Facilities	Mean	Mean Difference (Secured-Unsecured)	Median	Median Difference (Secured-Unsecured)	SD
1 Auto Loan:	106	68.878		90.11		38.39
Secured	42	50.779		50.676		40.42
Unsecured	64	80.755	−29.976*** ($t = -4.237$)	100.00	−49.324*** ($Chi^2(1)=12.78$) ($z = -4.415$)	32.12
2 Education Loan:	480	62.112		76.542		37.71
Secured	51	29.182		7.145		33.17
Unsecured	429	66.027	−36.845*** ($t=-6.911$)	80.054	−72.91*** ($Chi^2(1)=33.369$) ($z = -6.302$)	36.31
3 Housing Loan:	6181	38.833		39.009		32.61
Secured	6119	37.952		38.351		32.34
Unsecured	62	75.675	−37.723*** ($t=-9.123$)	100.00	−61.649*** ($Chi^2(1)=26.081$) ($z = 8.373$)	36.94
4 Personal Loan:	282	68.850		91.304		41.19
Secured	13	66.702		80.757		34.34
Unsecured	269	68.953	−2.251 (-0.192)	92.857	−12.100 ($Chi^2(1)=3.848$) ($z=-0.3516$)	41.55
5 Other category	218	71.158		93.599		37.29
Secured	106	57.711		69.165		38.99
Unsecured	112	83.886	−26.175*** (-5.521)	100.00	−30.835*** $Chi^2(1)=35.55$) ($z = -5.517$)	30.73
Total Pool:	7267	42.516		45.542		35.05
Secured	6331	38.356		38.822		32.68
Unsecured	936	70.651	−32.295*** ($t=-27.659$)	89.591	−50.769*** ($Chi^2(1)=297.01$) ($z = 26.745$)	37.53

Source: Author's own LGD survey results (Bandyopadhyay, 2013).
Note: A common retail pool has been created to conduct the statistical test; Auto loan also includes two-wheeler loans; other category includes retail SSI, agriculture, credit card loans and other retail loans. Figures in the parentheses of columns 6 and 7 are t values, Pearson Chi-square and Rank-sum test z values, respectively. *** denotes significance level at 1% or better. LGD and SD values are in per cent, t and z values are in fraction.

The mean, median, standard deviation of estimated LGD values across five re-tail categories and their statistical significance are shown in this table. Reported t values are the result of a parametric mean comparison test with equal vari-ance.[1] Chi-square values are the result of a non-parametric median equality test. Similarly, z values are the outcome of a Wilcoxon rank-sum (Mann–Whitney) non-parametric U test.[2] This test checks the difference between rank sums.

Table 4.12 results indicate that both mean and median LGD of secured retail loans (38.356 per cent, 38.822 per cent) are significantly lower than its unsecured counterparts (70.651 per cent, 89.591 per cent). Then, the results are further broken out by exposure types. The difference in ex-post LGD is more pronounced for housing loans (37.952 per cent vs. 75.675 per cent) because they are mostly secured by mortgage of the property and have good collateral value. The unsecured loans like Personal loans (70 per cent), credit card loans (91.9 per cent) and smaller sized education loans have very high loss severity. We have found two-wheeler loans recovery rate (LGD = 55.44%) is better than the four-wheeler loan recovery rate (LGD = 73.70%). SSI retail loans, which we have put in other category, have LGD of 34.09%.

Most of the residential housing loans (RRE) are secured by mortgage of the property and have significantly lower LGD. On the other hand, personal loans and credit card loans are unsecured ones and have very high LGD.

LGD predictor model

The ex-post LGD (pertaining to already defaulted facilities) is defined as "1-Recovery Rate". The ex-ante LGD (pertaining to standard accounts) can be predicted by applying statistical models which incorporate information at

---

[1] Two independent sample mean test is used when we compare the mean LGDs of secured and unsecured loans. The test statistic, with equal variance is:

$$t = \frac{(x_1 - x_2)}{\sigma\sqrt{(1/n_1)+(1/n_2)}}$$

[2] To test the difference between rank sums, we have used the following statistics:

$$U = T - E(T), \text{ where } T = \sum_{i=1}^{n} R_{1i}$$

$$E(T) = \frac{n_1(n_1+n_2+1)}{2} \text{ and } Var(T) = \frac{n_1 n_2 s^2}{(n_1+n_2)}; \text{ where } E(T): \text{ Expected}$$

Rank & s is the standard deviation of combined ranks of two groups n_1 & n_2. The Mann and Whitney rank-sum test statistic is: $z = \frac{T-E(T)}{\sqrt{Var(T)}}$; & $z \sim N(0,1)$.

different levels: collateral, instrument, firm, industry, country and the macro-economy. Such a methodology is a significant improvement over the use of historical recovery averages to predict LGD. This way, a bank can also develop its LGD rating model.

The purpose of developing models for predicting LGD is to produce the estimates of LGD for defaults occurring immediately and for defaults occurring in one year. In building an LGD predictor model (or facility rating model) for standard accounts, banks need to assess causative parameters that determine loan recovery. Statistical models incorporate information at different levels: collateral, instrument, firm, industry, country and the macro-economy to predict LGD. Such a methodology significantly improves on the use of historical recovery averages to predict LGD, helping institutions to better price and manage credit risk.

Evidence from many countries in recent years (refer to Table 4.6) suggests that the following factors contribute to recovery and LGD:

- *Facility characteristics:* Size of the loan has a positive impact on LGD; fund-based loans have relatively lower LGD than non-fund-based loans; LGD is high for multiple loan defaulters.
- *Bank-specific factors:* The bank's behaviour in terms of debt renegotiation with debtors, compromise and settlements may significantly impact recovery rates and hence LGD. It has been found defaulted loans with shorter settlement period and compromised loans have resulted in lower LGD.
- *Collateral security:* The presence of security and the nature of the collateral obtained can be an important distinction in the estimation of LGD. The quality of collateral attached to loans – higher the margin, lower the LGD; more liquid collaterals have low LGD; senior collaterals have lower LGD. International experiences suggest that the collateral value falls faster than the health of the account. Therefore, it is enough not only to know the chance of default of a borrower, but also to understand the collateral cycle and the expected future recovery rate.
- **Firm-specific capital structure**: Seniority standing of debt in the firm's overall capital structure, asset to liability ratio, etc. The assets to liabilities ratio acts like a coverage ratio of the funds available versus the claims to be paid. A higher ratio of assets to liabilities is better. Low leverage borrowers have low LGD; similarly, higher the current ratio, lower the LGD.
- **Industry factors**: It is the value of liquidated assets dependent on the industry of the borrower, industry growth, competitiveness, etc. More competitive industries are associated with stronger recoveries. Assets

that can be readily reused by another party have higher liquidation values and help increase recovery rates.

- **Regional factors (location):** Local or situational factors influence LGD. Regional social, legal framework and economic conditions matter in LGD.
- **Macroeconomic factors:** IIP growth rate, GDP growth rate, unemployment rate, interest rate and other macro-economic factors that capture economic cycle effect have strong influence on LGD (LGD is high during economic stress time!). Higher PD may influence LGD. The dependence between PD and LGD can be modelled simultaneously.
- **Country risk:** LGD figures may vary across countries due to changing macroeconomic environment, legal structure and banking behaviour. The Asia Pacific Banking Outlook 2004 estimate shows higher LGD in Singapore, Hong Kong and Malaysia by 25 per cent, 50 per cent and 55 per cent, respectively, where the number is quite high in Indonesia (85 per cent), Philippines (75 per cent) and in India (70 per cent).

According to the Basel II AIRB approach, banks can opt to provide their own LGD rate forecasts for the regulatory capital estimation. Thus, there is an urgent industry need for LGD modelling.

Multivariate modelling approach

Siddiqi and Zhang, 2004; Rosch and Scheule, 2005, Gupton and Stein (2002 and 2005) have applied multifactor statistical models to incorporate loan level, borrower level as well as macroeconomic factors in predicting LGD. It is a misconception that borrower-specific factors should not be incorporated in independent facility-specific LGD model under AIRB. The uncertainty of forecast losses and the economic capital measured decreases when systematic risk drivers are taken into account.

In building a statistical LGD predictor model (or facility LGD rating model) for standard accounts, one has to focus only on past information related to post-defaults or NPAs. Simultaneously, banks need to collect necessary parameters that may help in recovery. Since the dependent variable (LGD) is not a binary (0/1) variable as in the default model (default/no-default), simple linear regression (which uses the method of least squares to compute the weights for the prediction equation) may not be applicable as it may produce biased prediction. Linear regression can only estimate a linear relationship between the independent variable (factors that may influence recovery) and the loss rate (LGD). Unfortunately, even if the relationship is really non-linear (S-shaped or U-shaped), linear regression will provide only a linear approximation to the curve.

Tobit regression can be thought of as a hybrid between a linear regression model and logistic regression's twin brother, probit regression and it can predict future probability of recovery. Probit regression is similar to its logistic sibling, but it is based on a slightly different S-shape distribution. Tobit regression's edge over the other methods is that it was designed to handle cases where the dependent variable is clustered around limits such as 0. Zero or negative recovery has a great role in LGD predictor model because LGD value would be the maximum in such case and the facility would get the worst rating. If there are many observations where the per cent recovered was 0 or even negative (as it might come obviously), then estimating the model using linear regression could produce biased, less accurate results. Maximum likelihood estimation (MLE) process is used to estimate the regressor parameters and the residuals (See Greene, 1997).

Three multivariate Tobit regression models are applied to estimate the determinants of the LGD for our commercial loans LGD data pool. Through multivariate Tobit regression analysis, we are able to investigate which are the important factors contributing to the bank's net recovery rate and, hence, LGD. These continuous censored regression models may be taken as examples of LGD predictor models. Three different dependent variables have been used to model LGD. The first regression model uses economic LGD as dependent variable (Eco–LGD, using a discount rate of 7.21 per cent). Second model estimates the historical LGD (Hist–LGD).

A beta distribution has also been used to model LGD in the third regression exercise following Gupton and Stein (2002). This approach assumes that the dependent variable LGD has a beta distribution which is best suited to LGD distribution because it ranges from 0 to 1 and can have highly skewed shapes similar to actual loss distribution. The beta transformation is very useful for LGD modelling and it is easy to further transform LGD into a normal kind of distribution. Accordingly, we first calculate α (location) and β (scale) parameters from the underlying historical LGD distribution. We then transform the Historical LGD (Hist–LGD) data series into a beta distribution (BetaHistLGD) using the following expression:

$BetaHistLGD=betadist(HistLGD, \alpha, \beta, 0, 1)$ Eq. 4.8

Where α and β are generalized beta distribution parameters; other two values are minimum and maximum values.

Finally, we further convert BetaHistLGD into a normal distribution (NHISTLGD) to make it suitable for use in Tobit regression using the following function:

NHistLGD = norminv(BetaHistLGD, Mean, SD)   Eq. 4.9

Where $Mean = \dfrac{\alpha}{\alpha + \beta}$ & $SD = \sqrt{\dfrac{\alpha\beta}{(\alpha + \beta)^2(\alpha + \beta + 1)}}$

The notations α and β are parameters of beta distribution from LGD data.

Also, there are other models with ordinal responses where dependent variable is six or seven discrete LGD grades. Such models are appropriate where default cases are homogeneous within the LGD grade but may vary across the grades.[3]

The LGD model takes the following form:

$$LGD = \alpha + \beta_1 X_1 + \beta_2 X_2 + \ldots\ldots + \beta_k X_k$$

Eq. 4.10

As a next step, we test the statistical significance of the factors that determine loss given default rate of a loan facility and finally develop a predictive LGD model following the step-wise regression methods. In estimating an LGD model by running the appropriate regression method like Tobit, one can drop insignificant variables and include variables that have predictive power. The sign of the regression parameters have been examined to understand the logical relationship between dependent and independent variables. The interplays of these factors (policy factors as well as real factors) would help banks to predict recovery prospects of yet undefaulted loans (standard assets) on an ex-ante basis. The multivariate regression results are documented in Table 4.13.

The regression results show that commercial loan LGD rate is significantly influenced by collateral and their priority claim (lien) position. There exists a significant relationship between loan size (LNEAD[4]) and LGD. In the regression context, collateral margin (C/E) significantly explains LGD. It is observed that higher the value of the collateral in proportion to the outstanding at default (i.e. security margin, C/E), lower is the LGD. This is an important explanatory variable. We have also found that presence of collateral security (collateral dummy, COLLD), liquidity of the collateral (or seniority of the charge, SENIORITY), presence of guarantor (represented by dummy, DGUR) significantly determine LGD.

---

[3] One can also transform LGD variable using a logistic normal process: $LGD^* = \dfrac{\exp(LGD)}{1 + \exp(LGD)}$, following Dullmann & Trapp (2004)

[4] LNEAD is the log value of EAD.

Table 4.13: LGD Predictor Models – Multivariate Tobit Regression Results

Independent Variable	Model 1: Dependent Variable: ECOLGD	Model2: Dependent Variable: NHISTLGD	Model3: Dependent Variable: NHISTLGD
Loan Size (LNEAD)	0.03264*** (4.95)	0.02021*** (2.56)	0.04189*** (4.00)
Facility Character (DFUNDBASED)	–	−0.10738*** (−2.58)	−0.14118** (−2.18)
Presence of Collateral (COLLD)	−0.10744*** (−4.82)	–	–
Collateral Margin at default (C/E)	−0.01788** (−2.20)	−0.09460*** (−5.38)	−0.04914** (−2.40)
Presence of Guarantee (DGUR)	–	−0.07384*** (−2.54)	−0.10932*** (-2.65)
Collateral Seniority (SENIORITY)			-0.105235*** (3.14)
Default Reason (DEFREASON)			-0.05452*** (-2.81)
Settlement (SETDUM)	−026137*** (−4.00)	–	–
REGIOND1_CENTRAL	−0.07875 (−0.71)	0.00930 (0.09)	−0.07270 (−0.70)
REGIOND2_EAST	0.10063*** (2.97)	0.09614** (2.16)	0.10166* (1.66)
REGIOND3_NORTH	0.06076** (2.32)	0.05999** (2.04)	0.09067** (2.30)
REGIOND4_SOUTH	−0.00768 (−0.31)	0.01053 (0.28)	−0.04049 (−0.86)
Constant	0.71879*** (19.83)	0.73777*** (13.87)	1.12303*** (6.95)
No. of Obs.	800	501	241
LR Chi^2 (d.f.)	106.60*** (8)	52.63*** (8)	59.59*** (10)
Pseudo R^2	0.32	0.26	0.70

Source: LGD data of Schedule Commercial Banks (SCBs) in India obtained from Author's own survey conducted in 2013. The recovery time period covered in the analysis is 1989–2012.

Note: This table reports the estimation results from a set of regression of LGD on independent variables. The dependent variable is left censored at zero. *, *** and *** indicate the coefficient significant at 10%, 5% and 1% levels, respectively. Five region dummies have been used and "REGIOND5_WEST" (represent West India) have been dropped to avoid dummy trap.

We have assigned five dummy variables (REGIOND1–REGIONDD5) for demographic locations to see whether region locations are truly significant contributors to the model. On further analysis, it has been observed that the defaulted accounts that were compromised and settled (SETDUM) have lower LGD than the partially settled accounts (whose recovery is still in progress). Banks have higher recovery rates (hence, low LGD) in case of fund-based facility than in case of non-fund-based sanctions. This is captured by DFUNDBASED dummy variable. We see that LGD is also explained by default reason (represented by dummy DEFREASON). Loss severity is higher if default is due to systematic reason than due to borrower-specific idiosyncratic problems.

The estimated multivariate regression equations may be used to produce the estimated (or predicted) values of LGD. One can simply multiply the coefficients (or weights) by the value of the independent variables and add them together along with the intercept (or constant term) to obtain predicted value of LGD. One can see that regression results not only fit well with the data, but also the sign of coefficients are quite intuitive and have statistical as well as economic significance.

Before using the LGD predictor model, it has to be validated. For this, one has to look at R2 or the explanatory power of the model (say F values or Chi-square values). If R2 is good (say above 25 per cent), or Chi-square value is high (significant at 1 per cent or better), then the model's predictability would be good. There are also other tests like Chi-square test or Mean Square Error test that can also be applied for validation purpose. The predicted LGD figures need to be obtained for a wider set of loan facilities whose actual LGD experiences are also known for back testing. The third model fits the data reasonably well and it includes more explanatory variables.

LGD for standard loan accounts can be predicted using any of the models presented in Table 4.13. If we select regression Model 3, then we can predict the LGD for standard/restructure assets if we have information on values of all the regression factors. In order to obtain the predicted LGD estimate, we have to multiply these factor coefficients by the value of the variables add them with the constant term.

Finally, one has to discount this predicted LGD rate (1-RR) to factor into business cycle condition. This can be done by using the transformation:

$Discounted\ LGD = 1 - (RR \times e^{-r \times T})$ Eq. 4.11

Where r is the discount rate; it may be the lending rate (or base rate plus a risk spread) that the bank charges to the borrower. T is the number of years over which recovery is expected to happen (bank has to set a time horizon for that). The symbol e is the exponential; the value is 2.718281828 (approx.). The discounted LGD can be termed as economic LGD.

For example, using model 3, the loss given default rate for an exposure is estimated as 60 per cent. Thus, recovery rate (RR) = 40%. The borrower rating is BBB rating, for which interest rate was 11 per cent (base rate = 10%, spread 1% say) so r = 11%. Let us also assume that the bank expects to be able to recover from this borrower over a 3 year period, so T = 3 years.

Thus, Discounted LGD = $1-\{40\% \times (2.718281828)^{-3\times11\%}\}$
= 100%–28.76%
Therefore, Discounted LGD = 71.24%
This can be treated as stressed LGD.

Some leading private sector banks in India are using "Chain ladder projection" technique to project monthly recoveries in future. It is a step-wise prediction rule which assumes that the cumulative monthly recoveries develop consistently. In this way, to predict LGD, banks must imagine the circumstances that would cause default and the condition of the obligor after such default. A facility LGD rating model would not only benefit them for Basel IRB compliance but also walking out (loan recovery) bad loans. This loss research in banks and LGD prediction would also enable them to negotiate their bad loans with other banks that are the takers of such loans and, hence, will improve the banks' overall capital structure. LGD rating for standard accounts should seek to incorporate key factors affecting recovery prospects after default. This requires data archiving with great care and tracking of exposure and collateral received throughout the life of a loan.

Pooled LGD approach

If banks do not have enough data as mentioned above for each facility level, but very eager to know a rough LGD estimate, they may take help of the following method, as illustrated in Table 4.14:

Table 4.14: Estimation of Long-run Average LGD for a Retail Pool
Units in Rupees Lakh, others in percentage

Items/Year	2004	2005	2006	2007	2009	2009	2010
Gross NPA Outstanding	1,500	1,700	1,900	2,000	1,500	1,800	1,900
Cash/Other Recoveries	600	800	900	700	500	400	450

Table 4.14 contd.

Costs against Recovery	25	20	50	60	40	30	40
Net Recoveries (Rupees)	575	780	850	640	460	370	410
Ex-post Recovery Rate for each year	38.33%	45.88%	44.74%	32.00%	30.67%	20.56%	21.58%
Average Recovery Rate	33.39%						
Pooled LGD	66.61%						

Source: Author's own illustration.

Notes: 1. The field "Cash/Other Recoveries" represents both normal principal payments and any principal recoveries through legal or OTC settlements or other means or income received from the sale of one or more collateral as reported or any principal payments received from the guarantor of a facility aggregated for the entire pool for that year.

2. The field "Costs against Recovery" represents fees or other costs that the institution is unable to bill to the retail customers in the pool. This should not include internal overhead costs.

The approach mentioned in Table 4.14 to LGD estimation bank portfolio does not require any discounting of cash flows. The reason is that the aggregate recoveries are considered for the portfolio as a whole for the entire year, irrespective of the timing of the recovered amounts during that year and assuming that the recovered amounts will get adjusted in the Gross NPA amounts outstanding for the next year. This a purely accounting (or historical) measure of LGD. The estimated pooled LGD is also exposure weighted. This methodology of estimating Bank LGDs using historical loss experience is a very crude measure. Ultimately a bank has to analyze it segment wise.

This exercise can be further segmented into retail and commercial portfolio and at regional level depending on the bank's requirement. A sufficiently long-time series of data on recoveries and costs against recoveries (7 years or more) is necessary to derive an LGD estimate for the portfolio as a whole which covers at least one complete economic cycle.

IRB requirement for bank level LGD computation

Those banks planning for Advanced IRB approach should know that they will be allowed to use their own estimates of LGDs, provided they can demonstrate to the regulatory supervisors that their internal models are conceptually sound and historically consistent with their past experience. To demonstrate this, data on historical recovery rates must be collected and archived. This includes data on the different components of the recoveries experienced on defaulted exposures. For instance, amounts recovered; source of recovery (e.g. collaterals and guarantees; type of liquidation and bankruptcy procedures); time period elapsed before the actual recovery and administrative costs, etc. Note that all relevant information must be retained on a single-facility basis. Aggregated cash flows recovered from a given defaulted borrower must, therefore, be broken down, giving separate evidence to the partial recoveries associated with different loans issued to the same counterparty.

The Basel Committee and RBI also require that the LGD estimates produced by banks be long-run estimates, accounting for the possible correlation between recovery rates and default frequencies. This implies that the estimates must be based on the average economic loss of all observed defaults in the bank's database as shown in Table 4.15.

Bank should weight their LGD estimates with the number of defaults to take a more conservative view. Moreover, the default-weighted average might be replaced by an even more conservative estimate ("downturn LGD") if the bank feels that an economic downturn is approaching.

It is important to note that the independence between probabilities of default (PD) and loss given default (LGD) is questionable. A failure to take these dependencies into account will lead to inaccurate forecasts of the loss distribution and, hence, the estimated capital.

Table 4.15: LGDs: Simple vs. Weighted Average by Default Year (Corporate Loans)

Year	Number of Defaults	Eco-LGD (%)	GDP Growth Rate (%)
1997–98	44	87.68	4.30
1998–99	55	73.92	6.70
1999–2000	40	84.90	6.40
2000–01	33	81.18	4.40
2001–02	41	72.13	5.80
2002–03	24	85.36	3.80
2003–04	23	69.73	8.50
2004–05	26	67.33	7.50
2005–06	13	77.20	9.50
2006–07	9	70.51	9.70

Table 4.15 contd.

Table 4.15 contd.

2007–08	35	67.31	9.20
2008–09	39	58.72	6.70
Simple Average		74.66	
Default Weighted Average LGD		75.00	

Source: Default and Loss Data of SCBs in India.

Usefulness of LGD Computation for Banks

Indian banks must develop internal database and undertake loss research to identify the key recovery drivers for different asset classes and borrowers and thereby determine ex-ante LGD. The breakdown of LGD estimates into various sub-clusters will allow banks to more granularly differentiate the risk and, thus, derive portfolio diversification benefits. These additional data fields are also necessary to develop a more scientific statistical LGD predictor model. Banks intending to move towards more sophisticated Basel II Internal Rating Based (IRB) approach will have to determine the appropriate LGD to be applied to each exposure, on the basis of robust data and analysis.

The internal LGD study by banks would also help them to negotiate their bad loans with other banks and those who are the takers of such loans and, hence, will improve the bank's capital structure. Because of illiquidity of the collateral and rigidity in the legal system, banks hardly find any exit route on their defaulted loans.

Summary

In this chapter, we have discussed the concepts, methods and usefulness for calculating the exposure at default (EAD) and loss given default (LGD). These are two important drivers of credit risk other than PD. Uncertainty in EAD and LGD is an important driver of portfolio credit loss. The industry estimates of these two important parameters are presented in this chapter and their causative factors have been assessed. Understanding facility-wise, industry-wise, region-wise EAD and LGD factors and their relationship with PD will enable a credit portfolio manager to estimate the expected and unexpected loss of the portfolio to derive economic capital. These estimates will also give an idea about deriving portfolio diversification strategy.

We have shown how EAD can be estimated through a yearly cohort approach. Besides regulatory compliance, the internal EAD analysis can benefit the IRB banks to better understand the risk associated with unused commitments and can adopt prudent due diligence techniques in lending. The EAD model should look at the borrower's ability to increase its exposure while approaching default. This will be dependent on the type of facilities the borrower has taken from the bank and bank's ability to prevent excessive draw down on facilities (i.e. covenants). The EAD model results can be incorporated into the pricing decisions and capital allocations.

The loss given default analysis should be done in economic sense rather than as a straightforward accounting exercise. The time value of money held during the collection process and costs of recovery need to be factored properly in economic LGD estimation. We have shown that LGD is mostly computed via discounted net cash flow analysis where timing of all costs and recoveries, proper discount rate and proper measure of exposure are considered. The facility-wise recovery entries (both principal and interest recovery), direct and indirect cost of recovery, time period for collection, discount effects must be taken into account in computing ex-post LGD. Going to the advanced approach requires a sophisticated system and history of loss-given default data management.

The IRB banks must develop internal database and carry out loss research to determine the key factors contributing to LGD. The dynamic character of bank loan management requires developing a facility-wise recovery rating (or LGD rating) besides having a borrower-specific obligor rating system. Statistical models can incorporate information at different levels: collateral, instrument, firm, industry, country and the macro-economy to predict LGD. The LGD estimates derived from the model should be grounded based on actual historical recovery rates and not based solely on collateral value. Such a methodology is definitely a significant improvement over the use of historical recovery averages to predict LGD and will help institutions to better price and manage credit risk. However, achieving the required degree of accuracy for the LGD rating model requires sufficient availability of bank's historical data.

Key learning outcomes

After studying the chapter and the relevant reading, you should have clear understanding about:
- Concept about UGD, CCF, LEQ, EAD, LGD and LIED

- EAD and LGD data collection process
- Methods for estimating EAD and LGD
- Difference between loan limit and UGD
- Difference between accounting LGD and economic LGD
- Meaning of discount rate for computing economic LGD
- Different methods in estimating LGD
- Determinants of LGD
- Developing ex-ante LGD predictor model

Review questions

1. What is exposure at default? Why is it important for banks? How can it be estimated?
2. What are fund-based and non-fund-based facilities? And how can their exposure be mapped to predict risk?
3. Can you differentiate between the three types of credit exposures – derivative product, bullet term loan and overdraft?
4. How can EAD for non-fund-based exposures be estimated?
5. If CCF goes up, what will happen to EAD? If credit line changes, what will happen to CCF and EAD?
6. What are Asarnow and Marker (1995) observations on EAD?
7. What is LIED? Can you elaborate this?
8. What is economic LGD? How can it be estimated?
9. A bank is working out recovery calculation for its defaulted corporate loan facility. The loan defaulted in the year 2008 was a secured and senior one. The defaulted outstanding is Rs. 16 crore. A total recovery amount of Rs. 8 crore 50 lakh up to year 2014 was completed with total costs of Rs. 1 lakh 25 thousand. Suppose that both the recoveries and the costs are entirely obtained and paid at the end of the 2014. Using an 10% discount rate (which is the average risk free rate with a spread), can you estimate the value of Eco–LGD at the time of default? What happens to Economic LGD if recovery settlement time is delayed?
10. Write down at least five factors that may affect LGD of a loan?
11. What is the difference between ex-ante LGD and ex-post LGD?
12. What is downturn LGD?

References

Altman E. and V.M. Kishore. 1996. "Almost Everything You Wanted to Know about Recoveries on Defaulted Bonds", *Financial Analysts Journal* Nov/Dec: 57–64.

Altman, E., D. Cooke and V. Kishore. 1999. Defaults & Returns on High Yield Bonds: Analysis Through 1998 and Defaulted Outlook for 1999-2001. NYU working paper no. S-CDM-99-01.

Altman, E.I., B. Brady, A. Resti and A. Sironi. 2005. "The Link between Default and Recovery Rates: Theory, Empirical Evidence and Implications", *Journal of Business* November, 78 (6): 2203–27.

Araten, M., M. Jackobs Jr. and P. Varshney. 2004. "Measuring LGD on Commercial Loans: An 18-year Internal Study", *The RMA Journal* May: 96–103.

Asarnow, E. and J. Marker. 1995. "Historical Performance of the US Corporate Loan Market: 1988–1993", *The Journal of Commercial Lending* 10 (2): 13–32.

Asarnow, E. and D. Edwards. 1995. "Managing Loan Loss on Defaulted Bank Loans: A 24-year Study", *Risk Management Associates: Journal of Commercial Lending* 77 (7): 11–23.

Bandyopadhyay, A. 2007. "Poor Default History", Business Standard, December. Available at: http://www.business-standard.com/india/news/arindam-bandyopadhyay-poor-default-history/308756/

Bandyopadhyay, A. 2013. "Handling Irrecoverable Losses", *Financial Express*, November. http://archive.financialexpress.com/news/handling-irrecoverable-losses/1192595

Bandyopadhyay, A. and P. Singh. 2007. "Estimating Recovery Rates on Bank's Historical Loan Loss Data", MPRA working paper no. 9525.

BCBS. 2006. Internal Convergence of Capital Measurement and Capital Standards – A Revised Framework, BIS, June.

Ciochetti, Brian A. 1997. "Loss Characteristics of Commercial Mortgages", *Real Estate Finance* 14 (Spring): 53–69.

Dermine J. and C.N. de Carvalho. 2006. "Bank Loan Loss Given Default: A Case Study", *Journal of Banking and Finance* 30 (4): 1219–43.

Dullmann, K. and M. Trapp. 2004. "Systematic Risk in Recovery Rates: An Empirical Analysis of U.S. Corporate Credit Exposures", Discussion Paper, Series 2: Banking and Financial Supervision, no. 02/2004.

Gupton, G.M., D. Gates and L. Carty. 2000. "Bank Loan Loss Given Default", Moody's Investor Service, Global Credit Research, November.

Gupton, G.M. and R.M. Stein. 2002. "LossCalc™: Moody's Model for Predicting Loss Given Default (LGD). Moody's Investors Service.

Gupton, G.M. and R.M. Stein. 2005. *Loss Calc V2: Moody's Model for Predicting Loss Given Default (LGD)* (New York: Moody's KMV).

Huang, X. and C.W. Oosterlee. 2012. "Generalized Beta Regression Models for Random Loss Given Default, *The Journal of Credit Risk* 7 (4): 45–70.

Qi, M. 2009. "Exposure at Default of Unsecured Credit Cards", OCC Economics Working Paper 2009-2.

Qi, M. and X. Yang. 2009. "Loss Given Default of High Loan Value Residential Mortgages", *Journal of Banking and Finance* 33 (5): 788–99.

RBI. 2007. Guidelines for Implementation of the New Capital Adequacy Framework, Basel II Final Guidelines, April.

RBI. 2011. Implementation of the Internal Rating Based (IRB) Approaches for Calculation of Capital Charge for Credit Risk, DBOD Circular, December 22.

Rosch, D. and H. Scheule. 2005. "A Multifactor Approach for Systematic Default and Recovery Risk", *The Journal of Fixed Income* September: 63–75.

Schuermann, T. 2004. "What Do We Know About Loss Given Default", Working Paper, Federal Reserve Bank of New York.

Siddiqi, N.A. and M. Zhang. 2004. "A General Methodology for Modeling Loss Given Default", *The RMA Journal* May: 92–95.

Taplin, R., H.M. To and J. Hee. 2007. "Modelling Exposure at Default, Credit Conversion Factors and the Basel II Accord", *Journal of Credit Risk* 3 (2): 75–84.

Valvonis, V. 2008. "Estimating EAD for Retail Exposures for Basel II Purposes", *Journal of Credit Risk* 4 (1): 79–109.

Annexure 4.1A: EAD Excel Data Template – Account Level Data

Name of the Party	Name of the Branch	Line of Business	Constitution	Facility Type	Date of last sanction	Limit at last sanction (Lac)	O/s at sanction	Rating at sanction	Loan Rate%	Date of default	Bal O/s at default	Limit preceding up of default	Bal. O/s preceding default	UGD
1	coded	Mechanical	Propritorship	DG	8/17/2002	10			0.16	24/11/-3	5.88	10	0	58.80%
2	coded	Whole Sale	Propritorship	SB	10/21/2002	10	9.66	NA	0.1875	9/30/2003	9.77	10	9.66	32.35%
3	coded	whole sale coffee	Propritorship	OCC	22/03/02	70	37.926	na	0.1255	11/1/2003	67.46	70	66.06	35.53%
5	coded	MFR TEXTILES	PARTNERSHIP	PC	22/9/02	22	24.16	NA	0.09	31/12/02	45.47	40	3.18	114.86%
8	coded	MFR TEXTILES	partnership	OCC	3/10/2001	35	25.86	NA	0.15	4/1/2001	28.37	35	28.18	2.79%
9	coded	TRADERS	Propritorship	OCC	28-09-02	30	29.66	NA	0.15	11/1/2003	24.28	30	20.29	41.09%
10	coded	GRANITES EXPORTS	partnership	PC	16-02-04	25	19.06	NA	0.08	30-03-06	19.05	25	18.19	12.63%
11	coded	TEXTILES	Propritorship	OCC	15-02-06	15	15.96	NA	0.15	28-03-07	18.56	20	18.5	4.00%
12	coded	EXPORTER -GRANITES	PVT LTD CO	PC	2/2/2002	105	103	NA	0.145	31-03-03	64.51	105	60.89	8.21%
14	coded		PROP	OCC	2/2/2002	40	32.86	NA	0.1335	31-03-03	35.44	40	30.48	52.10%
15	coded	TRADERS	partnership	OCC	10/7/2005	10	9.2	na	0.16	30-09-06	28.77	30	28.5	18.00%
18	coded	TRADERS	PROP	OCC	20-01-2000	20	16.8	NA	0.165	31-03-06	10.48	20	10.2	2.86%
21	coded	TRADERS	prop	SOD	6/1/2005	8	6.32	NA	0.125	31-03-06	6.31	8	6.2	6.11%
23	coded			OCC	7/11/1997				0.1625	1/4/2003	76.27	80	76.79	-16.20%
24	coded	TRDER	PROP	OCC	2/1/2005	17.5	17.5	NA	0.1265	1/10/2005	17.79	17.5	15.02	111.69%
25	coded	HOTEL	PVT LTD CO	OCC	19-09-05	2	2.74	na	0.125	1/4/2006	0.01	2	0	0.50%
26	coded			TL	19.09.06	80	76.05	NA	0.1405	1/4/2006	62.12	80	60.05	10.38%
27	coded			DPN	26-12-05	10	6	NA	0.1475	1/4/2006	5.88	10	6.1	-5.64%
28	coded	MFR OF CEMENT	LTD CO	DPN	7/3/1990	31	0	NA	0.2125	4/1/1993	90.06	90	86.35	101.64%
29	coded			OCC	7/3/1990	60	55.67	NA	0.2325	4/1/1993	49.26	31	47.31	-11.96%
31	coded	MERCANTILE PRO	PVT LTD CO	OCC	10/8/2000	1.5	1.52	NA	0.1325	1/10/2003	26.31	30	19.29	65.55%
32	coded			SB	10/8/2000	10	0	NA	0.131	26-03-04	8.94	10	5.6	75.91%
33	coded			BE	10/8/2000	10	0	NA	0.131	26-03-04	0.19	10	0	1.90%
35	coded	TRADERS	PVT LTD	OCC	10/2/2005	5	0	NA	0.1325	1/10/2005	7.74	10	5.09	53.97%
36	coded	MFRS	PROP	OD	15-03-2001	5	4.99	NA	0.145	1/10/2003	4.48	5	4.09	42.86%
37	coded	MFR WOOD	partnership	OD	17-02-01	2	0	NA	0.1425	31-03-05	4.54	5	4.43	19.30%

Source: A sample data collected from a large public sector bank using the author's designed template.

Annexure 4.1B: EAD Excel Data Template – Aggregate Level Data

Facility Type	Year1 M1 (Month End)			Year1 M2 (Month End)			Year1 M3 (Month End)			...	For 4 years
	Sanction Limit	Limit Utilized	Rating Grade	Sanction Limit	Limit Utilized	Rating Grade	Sanction Limit	Limit Utilized	Rating Grade		
1. CC											...
2. BP											...
3. BD											...
4. BG											...
5. LC											...
6. LG											...
7. PC											...
Any other...											...

Source: Template designed by the author.

Note: For commercial exposures for at least last 4 year months, end data should be collected.

If rating has undergone a change, especially in case a standard account has become NPA, it needs to be mentioned as well.

## Chapter 5

Validation and Stress Testing of Credit Risk Models

The term "validation" is defined in the minimum requirements of the Internal-rating-based (IRB) approach as follows:

> "The institution shall have a regular cycle of model validation that includes monitoring of model performance and stability; review of model relationships; and testing of model outputs against outcomes." (BCBS, 2004).

The topics of "Model Validation" and "Model Risk Management" have received considerable attention globally in recent years. The US subprime crisis has revealed the necessity of the financial institutions to perform model validation on a regular basis. The Fair, Isaac and Company (now Fair Isaac Corporation or FICO) score was designed to measure risks on credit cards and other short-term consumer credit, but was also used for mortgage lending during good time (Luci Ellis, BIS, 2008). The short-term characteristics of the FICO credit-scoring model developed by the Fair Isaac and Corporation could not predict the actual default risk of subprime mortgage loans in reality. The improper uses of the models and failure to capture important risk drivers in lending products by banks have also been blamed to be responsible for causing the financial crisis in the US. Many researchers and analysts have shown that FICO scores did not indicate any relationship between the borrowers' credit scores and default incidents during the crisis. Wrong application of models, relaxation of lending standards and lack of due diligence in credit led to financial losses and damaged many banks' reputation. These issues have accelerated taking up of model governance initiatives across the banking industry. In this context, Federal Reserve released US SR11-07 guidance on model risk management which provides useful information for banks for adopting a model validation policy.[1] In India, the rising level of non-performing Assets (NPA) and quantum of restructured loans in banks in recent years (especially during 2013–14) are a key concern for the regulator (RBI). This further necessitates checking the predictive power and efficacy of rating models used by banks.

The ability of the bank in managing its credit portfolio depends on the quality of its rating system and its usage for taking conscious credit decisions. The supervisor seeks to encourage banks to develop and use better risk management techniques in monitoring and managing their risks and ensure that they have placed a rigorous process for determining the adequacy of their capital to support all risks to which they are exposed. It is of paramount interest to a bank to know the risk its assets carry. Ratings allow to systematically measure credit risk and to manage consistently a bank's credit portfolio. Model validation has been a key task for risk focused management for internal management of risk across various business lines. Reliable rating systems require efficient validation strategies. It plays a very important role in Basel II IRB framework as banks are allowed to use their own internal estimates of credit risk parameters as primary inputs to the capital computation. The Basel II IRB approach assumes that the key credit risk parameters PD, LGD and EAD are estimated correctly. If these factors are undercounted, capital will be undercounted. There is a powerful incentive for banks to undercount risk. This will be balanced by Pillar 2 and 3 of Basel II regulation. A proper credit scoring model will clearly reduce the cost and increase the transparency in loan origination and holding. The supervisory body, therefore, encourages banks to adopt a sound validation policy as a means to prevent the occurrence of model risk.

The primary purpose of validation is to examine whether the internally constructed scoring model can fully explain the credit status of borrowers. The validity of a rating model is judged from five dimensions:

1. **Consistency:** Rating model across different client groups and should conform to accepted theories and methods;
2. **Objective assessment:** Whether common standards have been applied in choosing weights to risk factors;
3. **Discriminatory power:** Whether the model passes the accuracy tests ' in differentiating good vs. bad borrowers and predicted rankings are in proper order

---

[1]   See SR Letter 11-7 on Supervisory Guidance on Model Risk Management, 4 April 2011 released by Federal Reserve Board, USA.

4. **Out of sample performance:** Testing the predictive power of the model using unknown sample and out of time.
5. **Independent review:** Independent model validation, compliance and model governance. The validation team must be independent of other functions. This review can also be done by an independent third party.

Validations are of Two Types

1. **Quantitative:** Includes all validation procedures in which statistical indicators for the rating procedure are calculated and interpreted on the basis of an empirical data set. Suitable indicators include the model's standard errors (SE), R^2 model fitness, the difference between the forecast and realized default rates of a rating class (i.e. error rates), Gini coefficient and Area under Receiver Operating Characteristics (AUROC) as measures of discriminatory power, etc.
2. **Qualitative:** Understanding of the model design and applicability of the quantitative methods in business practice.

These two aspects of validation complement each other. Chart 5.1 summarizes the important aspects of model validation.

Chart 5.1: Basel II IRB Rating Model Validation

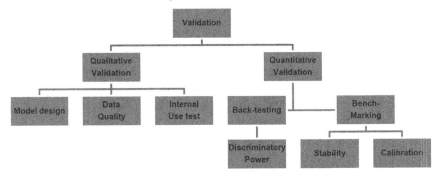

Source: BIS (2005).

Validation is not just numerous statistical tests to check the predictive power of the models. A check of the data utilized to form the model, clarity about the model design and assumptions, whether the data sample was sufficient enough to arrive at results, practical use of models in taking business decisions are also important part of the validation process. A rating procedure should only be applied in practice if it receives a positive assessment in the qualitative area. A positive assessment only in quantitative validation is not sufficient. Therefore, the validation report by the IRB bank must entail a clear relationship between model output and internal decision-making. The self-assessment could be conducted by an independent risk assessment team with support of auditors (if necessary) also including the participation of external auditors and consultants.

With regard to regulatory requirements, the entire validation process must be described in the rating model's documentation. In Rating System Design, we need to ensure:

1. The rating-grade PD and LGD values are correctly calculated and they are consistent with the actual default experience.
2. The process assigning the obligor ratings is appropriate to the obligors, reasonably constructed, consistently applied and have discriminatory ability.
3. Rating-grade PDs are representatives of actual experience and are granularly capturing the borrower risk.
4. LGD grades and judgements are based on the actual loss experience.
5. EAD calculations are correctly calculated and it is consistent with the actual exposure experience.

Banks need to ensure that the validation methodologies and standards are in line with industry best practice. Model validation exercise verifies whether rating models are practically working as anticipated and that the model usage is in line with the corporate business expectations and policies.

Galindo and Tamayo (2000) had precisely defined five key requisite qualities for choosing an optimal scoring model. These requirements are:

1. **Accuracy:** Low error rates arising from the assumptions in the model.
2. **Parsimony:** Not using too many explanatory variables that may over fit the model.
3. **Non-triviality**: Producing interesting and meaningful relationship.
4. **Feasibility**: Running in a reasonable amount of time (in a step-wise manner with many trials) and using realistic resources.
5. **Transparency and interpretability:** Providing high level insight into the data relationships and trends and clear understanding about the model output.

The Basel Committee on Banking Supervision (BCBS, 2005) had originally delineated several principles underlying the concept of validation that should be followed by the banks:

- **Principle 1:** Validation is fundamentally about assessing the predictive ability of a bank's risk estimates and the use of ratings in credit processes.
- **Principle 2:** The bank has primary responsibility for validation.
- **Principle 3:** Validation is an iterative process and should have a regular cycle.
- **Principle 4:** There is no single validation method.
- **Principle 5:** Validation should encompass both quantitative and qualitative elements.
- **Principle 6:** Validation processes and outcomes should be subject to independent review.

The above principles set up a broad framework for model validation. This covers the goal of validation, the responsibility for validation, regulatory expectations pertaining to validation and control environment. Principles 3–5 give a comprehensive understanding on validation of IRB rating systems. The Basel Committee Accord Implementation Group Validation sub-group (AIGV) of BCBS was established in 2004 to share and exchange views related to the validation of IRB systems. The AIGV has set several criteria for model validation which has been subsequently adopted by supervisors of many countries (e.g. Hong Kong Monetary Authority, Monetary Authority of Singapore, etc.). In India, banks send model validation report to RBI in their Internal Capital Adequacy Process (ICAAP) document. It comes under Pillar II risks. As per the RBI's ICAAP guidelines, banks must conduct periodic review of their risk management processes and validate the model inputs and outputs (NCAF, RBI, 8 February 2010). Both result-based quantitative validation (also called back testing) and process-based qualitative validation are equally necessary to get the regulatory approval. Besides quantitative validation, how the rating system is integrated into the bank's overall risk management processes needs to be evaluated properly. Banks must have established policies, procedures and controls to ensure the integrity of the model and modelling process used to derive regulatory capital under IRB (Basel II IRB Circular of RBI, December 2011, paragraph 109). Moreover, banks are expected to have in place a robust system to validate the accuracy and consistency of the model and its inputs (RBI, 2011, Paragraph 180).

A. Qualitative validation

Validation itself is a process, not just statistical tests. The regulator expects IRB banks to have in place a robust system to validate the accuracy and consistency of the model outputs. Banks need to fully document all material elements of their internal models and modelling process which will be finally reviewed by the regulator. A complete validation process includes (a) selecting standard tests and analyses to be performed, (b) documentation and reporting of findings, (c) proof of actions taken in response to findings, (d) independent review and board and management oversight. If banks are using vendor models, they have to ensure that they understand the model designs, data used, assumptions, limitations and usefulness in business. It is important that the users be able to acquire full knowledge support from the vendors to inherit those (BIS, 2010). These generic models should be appropriately customized and the entire customization process should be properly documented and justified. Banks should also conduct the ongoing monitoring and outcome analysis of model performance using internal data. In this context, clear documentation and description of the methods are essential. The regulator presumes that it is the responsibility of the bank to verify suitability and appropriateness of the model in all respects, in relation to its business at the time of adopting the model (RBI, 2011, Paragraphs 33 and 34). Qualitative validation, therefore, mainly focuses on evaluating the bank's understanding of the model (both internal and external) and its application in taking credit decisions, pricing, portfolio management, capital estimation, etc. It has the following important elements:

1. **Model design:** The purpose, scope, transparency and completeness of documentation are the essential validation criteria for checking model design. Model documentation assists independent review of the model development as well as creates a corporate memory about the methods, data and assumptions implanted in the model. It is necessary to ensure the transparency of the assumptions and/or evaluations which forms the basis of the rating model's design. Full description about model assumption, conceptual foundations, methodology, reason for selecting a specific model type, model architecture, data set used to construct the model, logical selection of parameters, model outcomes and limitations are the essential components of model documentation report. As per RBI's expectations, during supervisory query, bank should be able to interpret the output of the models. While discussing the development of statistical PD and LGD models in Chapters 3 and 4, we have shown how to report various model architectures in an organized manner. An independent review by a peer team can further help the bank to reduce model risk.

2. **Data:** As per validation requirements, an IRB bank should be able to demonstrate the regulator that data used for model development is the representative of the underlying population and is consistent

through time. Volume and quality of availability of data is the most important validation requirement. The IRB approach requires banks to collect at least 5 years of PD data, 7 years of LGD and EAD data and 3 years of minimum use to get the regulatory approval. When the underlying observation period is less than five years, banks are allowed to use external data to estimate the model. However, they have to apply conservatism in estimating the critical risk parameters. A comprehensive and robust data set is an essential precondition for quantitative validation. All standard statistical methods require complete data set. Completeness of data is absolutely necessary to ensure that the model results are comprehensible and present the reality. Banks need to establish a good IT system to capture accurate and relevant account level historical data to build as well as test their IRB models. Data sources and representative of the samples used for model development and validation need to be clearly mentioned in the validation report. Regulator may also want to know what measures were taken to ensure quality and cleansing raw data as a further validation check.

3. **Use test:** Finally, banks will have to provide sufficient evidence of how rating models are used in actual credit decision-making, risk-based pricing, rating-based limit systems, forecasting credit losses, portfolio monitoring, etc. This requires preparation of complete and verifiable documentation of the process for supervisory examination. This is an essential qualitative criteria to get passed through the regulatory validation test. The documentation should demonstrate banks' compliance with the minimum quantitative and qualitative standards and should address the application of the model to different segments of the portfolio, estimation methodologies, responsibilities of parties involved in the modelling, and the model approval and model review process.

The questions bankers and supervisors might ask about ratings assignments are mainly principle based:
- What are the assumptions in the ratings "model" and the effect of each assumption?
- What raw data was used? What was done to clean it?
- What is the interpretation of the output?
- How robust (or stable) are the ratings? What happens if some of the data is removed? What if the time horizon is changed? What if industry is altered?

- What results do other models give? Why the difference? Whether any comparison has been made?
- What is the actual loss experience versus predicted result?
- What is the relevance of model output in taking business decisions?
- Is the model's risk similar to that viewed by the management? Whether the management is involved in the rating design and implementation process?

Banks are required to demonstrate the use of the internal models for credit approval, credit monitoring and reporting to the senior management and board of directors. As per the IRB qualitative criteria set by BCBS (2006), there should be sufficient human judgement and oversight in the development and use of bank rating systems. Rating systems should be subject to corporate governance, credit risk control and internal audit. Moreover, there should be a credible track record for the use of internal ratings and loss estimates in the bank's credit risk management processes. Chart 5.2 illustrates an internal model validation course of action in a bank.

Chart 5.2: Example of an Internal Model Validation Process

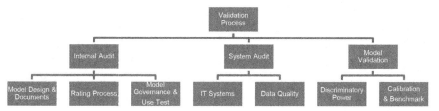

Source: Validation process in a bank.

Internal audit, systems audit and feedback of the model validation committee play a vital role in the rating validation process. The model validation committee can act as a control function and their independent views may be effectively used in financial reporting, management reporting and regulatory reporting. For example, in the above example, the entire validation reports may be submitted to the Chief Risk Officer (CRO) of the bank. The minutes of committee meetings are to be signed by the Head of Validation committee and should be informed to the CRO. Model governance minimizes the risks associated with depending on models to take informed decisions. A good model governance structure requires senior managements' insight, involvement and support.

The general regulatory expectation is that the IRB banks must have in place robust documented processes designed to validate the accuracy of its IRB models and must ensure the operational integrity and consistency of those systems and estimates. This documentation must be current and consistent with their actual practices. Consistent with this, the institutions are expected to have in place a suitably robust model risk policy that documents detailed model development, validation and control processes. The internal audit function should assess the overall effectiveness of model risk management framework. Validation is an ongoing process and banks must regularly check the conformity of the rating procedures with the credit risk strategy mentioned in the policy. The validation exercise should be done by people independent of model developers to ensure integrity. Further, the process for resolution of model deficiencies must also be addressed in the report. There is also a need for functional separation of responsibility of business units accountable for rating systems from those in charge for loan origination. An independent internal audit team must assess that the development, implementation and validation processes are operating as intended and are effective. Finally, the board and senior management have the ultimate responsibility for the performance of IRB rating system. They must actively discuss the appropriateness and effectiveness of the bank's risk estimates. Therefore, they should receive the results of the model validation process including details of "use tests" and remedial measures. As per regulatory norms (RBI, 2011), banks which intend to use an IRB approach will be required to document these sets of criteria completely and in a verifiable way.

Chart 5.3 illustrates the linkage between IRB credit risk models and its usage in credit risk management and loan sanctioning process that may be followed by banks. Establishing such linkage is an important validation criteria set by the regulator. The rating process has many interlinked elements which should be properly displayed in the validation report to pass the regulatory use test. A bank must provide evidence whether the risk components are used for capital calculations, portfolio management and RAROC calculation. This structure may, however, vary from bank to bank.

Validating a rating process requires analyzing the extent to which an internal rating system was used in daily banking business. For this, understanding the rating system and adequate corporate governance are crucial for banks. Chart 5.4 shows a broad structure of a bank's internal loan rating process in India and its use in taking crucial business decisions.

Chart 5.3: Linking the Models to Credit Risk Management Process

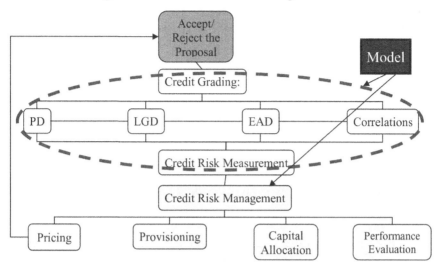

Source: Author's illustration.

Chart 5.4: Risk Rating Process of a Scheduled Commercial Bank

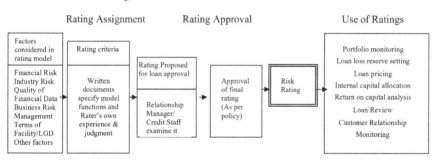

Source: Adapted from Treacy and Carey (1998).
Note: For illustration purpose.

The bank's internal statistical or judgemental rating model uses the account level data (financials, past record, business and management information) to determine the potential borrower's credit risk. The estimated credit score is then mapped to a rating grade and corresponding PD and LGDs (based on collateral and facility assessments) are estimated. Borrowers with broadly similar risk characteristics are typically allocated to a risk grade. For rating assignment, generally banks must have a well-written document (rating manual) that defines the model functions and the rater's own experience and judgement. Here, the relationship manager originates the loan proposal and does the rating. Then, the rating goes to a separate rating approval team for their approval and credit department approves the credit (as per the bank policy). This rating approval team is a part of risk department.

B. Quantitative validation

Quantitative validation is required for all rating models (judgemental as well as statistical). For this purpose, validation should primarily use the data gained during practical operation of the model. Comparison or benchmark data can also be included as a supplement. To determine the accuracy of the model, several statistical tests are available in the literature.

Quantitative aspects of validation mainly address statistical and mathematical aspects of validation and uses techniques such as:

1. **Back testing:** Measuring the forecasting ability of a rating process/ model by comparing actual historical data to forecasted variables.
2. **Stress testing:** Measuring rating process/model outcome(s) to extreme scenarios that might not be within a given rating process/ model structure. This is discussed separately in this chapter.
3. **Sensitivity analysis:** Assessing the responsiveness and sensitivity of a rating process/model outcome(s) to changes in key variables.
4. **Benchmarking:** Checking the robustness of power vis-à-vis industry models. Benchmarking compares a model's results to those of an alternative industry model that predicts the similar outcome.

Various statistical measures are available to check

1. **Model's discriminatory power**: Several quantitative tools such as Gini coefficient (Accuracy Ratio), Kolmogorov-Smirnov Test (K-S statistics), Area under Receiver Operating Characteristic (AUROC), Power Curve (or CAP) and Chi-square statistics may be used to test the predictive power (or accuracy) of rating models.
2. **Model calibration:** Reviewing the calibration of the rating model is also called back testing. This is like comparing the risk grades (both PD and LGD) with actual default or loss experiences. Calibration process involves testing correlation between actual and predicted values. Mean Square Error (MSE) or Chi-square tests are two popular calibration tools. Calibration can be done through benchmarking as well.

3. **Stability/robustness check:** This necessitates checking the robustness of the models with changing sample observations and macroeconomic cycle, etc. This involves stress testing and sensitivity analysis. This will be discussed at the end of the chapter.

We will now go into each statistical validation aspect in great detail. Assessing the discriminatory power and examining the calibration of credit risk models are two different important tasks of validation. Various performance measures are used to assess the quality of scoring models.

1. Discriminatory power

In practice, the quality of a rating model is very often expressed by means of their discriminatory power. The term "discriminatory power" refers to the ability of a rating model to identify ex-ante bad (defaulting) and bad (non-defaulting) borrowers. This is also termed as "classification accuracy" or separation power of a model. The validation process assesses the discriminatory power of a rating model using numerous statistical techniques. These tests check whether predicted ranks are in order of actual risks. Measures of discriminatory power can be meaningfully applied when we are comparing different rating systems on the same portfolio. Checking discriminatory power is a relative concept. Generally, it is done on a separate validation or holdout sample during model development stage when the model developer has to select one specific rating model among several. The relevant metrics applied are Wilk's Lamda test, type I/type II error checks, Kolmogorov-Smirnov (K–S) statistic, Gini coefficient, root mean square error check (or Chi-square test or Brier score) for credit risk predictor models.

Method 1: Descriptive statistics

Table 5.1 shows the review of rating performance of an external credit rating agency. See the ratio average per rating.

It can be noticed that, ratios across rating grade significantly differ. Like the operating cash flow is higher in better rated companies and low in risky grades. Similarly, the median leverage position is also high in risky grades and low in safe grades. On the other hand, profitability is higher in better grades and significantly low in risky grades. This clearly proves that the key financial ratios which are generally used by the agency are able to discriminate between good borrowers against the bad ones.

Table 5.1: Validation of CRAs Ratings through Descriptive Statistics

	AAA	AA	A	BBB	BB	B	CCC	D
WK/Asset	0.147	0.148	0.166	0.070	0.092	0.024	−0.009	−0.064
RETPROF/Asset	0.057	0.039	0.018	0.004	−0.007	−0.043	−0.051	−0.061
PBIT/Asset	0.153	0.114	0.095	0.070	0.065	0.055	0.020	0.019
CASHPROF/ Asset	0.137	0.098	0.072	0.043	0.029	−0.003	−0.012	−0.025
MVE/Asset	1.625	0.733	0.298	0.252	0.852	0.171	0.182	0.123
Sales/Asset	1.276	0.924	0.871	0.777	0.634	0.707	0.652	0.606
Total debt/Asset	0.167	0.343	0.397	0.703	0.506	0.566	0.509	0.595
Solvency Ratio	2.463	2.209	1.856	1.507	1.781	1.317	1.399	1.229
No. of Observations	181	295	129	57	53	17	31	281

Source: Author's own analysis using CRISIL's published bond rating data of total 150 corporates over 8 years.

Note: WK/Asset-networking capital to assets ratio; RETPROF/Asset: Retained profit to assets; PBIT/Asset: Profit before interest and tax to total assets; CASHPROF/Asset: Cash profit to assets; MVE/Asset: Market value of equity to assets. Solvency ratio is the same ratio used in Eq. 2.4 in Chapter 2.

One can also plot scatter graphs or line graphs to understand the relationship between key financial variables (say return on asset (ROA), sales growth (GRSALES), debt to equity ratio (DE), etc. and average default rate (PD).

Another simple test pertains to checking the difference of the means of the two groups (solvent vs. defaulted). Besides mean difference, Wilk's Lambda and F-tests test the inequality between the two groups of borrowers. This is shown in Table 5.2 group statistics.

F-statistic and Wilk's Lambda are used for discriminating the solvent group from defaulted group. The higher value of F and lower value of Wilk's Lambda indicate greater chance for the null of equal means of the two groups to be rejected. One can also use parametric mean comparison t-test in checking group difference.

Wilk's lambda is the ratio of the within groups sum of squares to the total sum of squares (Wilk's lambda = SS_{within}/SS_{total}). It provides information regarding difference among groups (solvent vs. defaulted).

Table 5.2: Group Statistics – Solvent vs. Defaulted Firms

Ratios	Solvent		Defaulted		Wilk's Lambda	F-Stat
	Mean	SD	Mean	SD		
NWK/TA	0.19	0.15	–0.07	0.33	0.80	153.3
CASHPROF/TA	0.10	0.07	–0.03	0.10	0.63	347.3
SOLVR	2.32	1.30	1.27	0.37	0.76	185.26
OPPROF/TA	0.10	0.08	–0.03	0.084	0.62	353.56
SALES/TA	1.06	0.60	0.57	0.33	0.80	152.81

Source: Bandyopadhyay (2006).
Note: Total number of observations = 600.

The closer the Wilk's lambda is to zero, better the defaulting borrowers are separated from non-defaulting ones. The F-statistic is the ratio of between groups variability to the within groups variability ($SS_{between}/SS_{within}$). It is equivalent to the square of a t-statistic for a two sample pooled variance t-test. It assumes that both the groups are normally distributed.

Method 2: Classification error calculation

The rating model validation has to be tested both on a within and a hold-out sample to check the percentage of correct prediction for bad accounts (otherwise type I error) and percentage correct prediction for good accounts (otherwise type II error). This may be applied for both PD and LGD models. A score is always connected with a default probability estimate (PD score). One can manually check the difference in prediction and count the classification error rates. For validating a statistical PD score model, one can set a cut-off score (say $Z < 1.81$ for Altman (1968) model; or EPD < 50% for a logit model) for bad (defaulting) firms. Similarly, the borrowers above this cut-off score are grouped as good (non-defaulting) firms. The predicted states of borrowers are coded as 1 for bad firms and 0 for solvent firms (captured by a dummy variable EPD). Now obtain the actual status of the firms from the credit history and again give codes. The firms with NPA flags can be coded as 1 and firms in standard categories to be coded as 0. The actual state of the firms is captured by a dummy called DDEF. Now, check the difference between the predicted status and the actual status of the borrowers. This classification test may be conducted for both within sample (used for the analysis) as well as out of sample (hold out sample). Table 5.3 illustrates the classification test on a sample of 300 borrowers.

Table 5.3: Classification Power of the Model (Within Sample Test)

		Predicted State		Total
		Bad	Good	
Actual State	Bad	141 (94%)	9 (6%)	150 (100%)
	Good	18 (12%)	132 (88%)	150 (100%)
	Total			

Source: Bandyopadhyay (2006).

The type I error rate for the above model is 6 per cent and type II error rate is 12 per cent. Overall 91 per cent of original grouped cases correctly specified. A proper balance between the two error rates is desirable. Optimum error (OE = (type I + type II error rate)/2) is also used to balance the discriminant classification error. The closer the OE is to zero, the better the discriminatory power of the model. Such validation tests are required to be conducted independently to remove biasness. To make the validation process robust, the persons involved in model development should not be involved in testing the models' predictive power.

Other statistical measures

Banks can use non-parametric measure like power curve or cumulative accuracy profile (CAP) to check the discriminatory power of their rating models. These tests focus on a scoring (PD) model's ability to discriminate "good" outcomes from "bad" outcomes; also referred to as a model's power. Similarly, when assessing the accuracy of an LGD model, how well it ranks orders higher-than-average losses versus lower-than average losses is important. There are two accepted non-parametric statistical rank correlation measures: Kendall's tau and Spearman's rho which are popularly used for validation check. Kendall's tau and Spearman's rank correlation coefficient assess statistical associations between the ranking of the predicted LGD (or PD) with the observed LGD (or PD) both arranged in terms of rating buckets. The higher the correlation, better is the model's predictive accuracy. A financial institution's ability to correctly predict when losses are going to be higher than the average will be the key for their business success, especially during downtime. Sobehart et al. (2000), De Servigny and Renualt (2004), Fritz, Poken and Wagner (2002); and Fritz, Luxenburger and Miehe (2007) have shown many statistical measures of discriminatory power. The validation team of BCBS in a BIS (2005) working paper surveyed various validation practices in the US banking industry. While exploring a broad range of qualitative and quantitative validation techniques, the group formed by the research task force considered contributions from the literature and the results from a bank survey. The study recommends that besides validation and calibration, benchmarking is also an important part of validation process under IRB.

Power Curve and Gini Coefficient Approach

The power of a rating model to discriminate credit risk between good and bad debtors is often highlighted as the main criterion for assessing the quality of a rating system. To measure the discriminatory power, Power Curve and Gini coefficient are popularly used by risk management analysts. Gini coefficient (or ratio) is a popular measure of the relative ability of ratings to differentiate risk. It can be estimated by drawing a Power Curve.

The Cumulative Accuracy Profile (CAP) curves are successfully used to make visual assessment of model performance. Power curve can successfully show the discriminatory power of scoring function. The predicted scores (either from judgemental or a statistical model) are ranked in order of riskiness, and then the actual number of good and bad cases are counted. Following this procedure, a set of CAP curve is generated over entire population of borrowers ordered in terms of PD predicted from the tested models. The steeper the curve, the better is the model's power in differentiating between defaulting and non-defaulting obligor. Larger the area under the curve (AUC), more accurate is the model. CAP curve simultaneously provides information on Type I and Type II errors. Ideally, power curves give best results if two (or many) rating models are validated on the same data.

To check the performance of rating system, we have studied the historical rating migration from 2003 till 2009 of 3,000 accounts of a mid-sized public sector bank. We have used six rating cohorts for 2003–04, 2004–05,…, and 2008–09. This transition study has helped us to test whether the ranking of debtors is in line with the assessment of their risk as predicted by the rating models. From each of these six rating cohorts, we track and count the number of accounts assigned different grades and their migration to default (D) grades. The frequency of the rated and defaulted borrowers are then ranked in line with their risk grades in descending order from safest (AAA) to riskiest grade (C). Next, the relative percentage share of borrowers in each grade and their share of defaults are estimated and presented in Table 5.4.

Table 5.4: Validation Report of a Bank's Internal Rating System for Commercial Loans, 2003–09

(1)	(2)	(3)	(4)	(5)	(6)	(7)	(8)	(9)	(10)
Rating	No. Defaults	Relative Default % (100 pi)	Cum. Default %	Total Rated A/cs	% Rated A/cs	Cum % Rated A/cs (100 z_i)	$100\times$ $(z_i + z_i - 1)$	10^4 pi $\times$ $(z_i + z_{i-1})$	Diagram Area
AAA	2	2.7397	100.00	1783	39.45	100.0	160.55	439.87	219.936
AA	3	4.1096	97.26	1278	28.27	60.55	92.83	381.50	190.750
A	7	9.5890	93.15	820	18.14	32.28	46.42	445.08	222.542
BBB	12	16.4384	83.56	390	8.63	14.14	19.65	322.95	161.474
BB	8	10.9589	67.12	135	2.99	5.51	8.03	88.01	44.0053
B	16	21.9178	56.16	64	1.42	2.52	3.63	79.52	39.7624
C	25	34.2466	34.25	50	1.11	1.11	1.11	37.88	18.9417
	73	0.0000	0.00	4520	0.00	0.00	0.00	0.00	
Total								1794.82	897.412
Gini								**0.8205**	
Y area									0.0897
X area									0.4103
Gini= X/ (X+Y)									**0.8205**

Source: Rating Data of a Bank, For illustration purpose.

The cumulative relative percentage shares of the borrowers (in terms of numbers) are then estimated across ranking (of grades) and are plotted on the abscissa (X-axis) and cumulative relative share of all default events is marked off on the ordinate (Y-axis) in a chart. This produces the power curve or CAP curve (or Lorenz curve) as shown in Table 5.4 and Chart 5.5.

The frequency density distributions and the cumulative frequencies of debtors in seven grades and their incidents have been documented in Table 5.4. It can be clearly seen that the default rate for each rating class increases steadily from safest AAA grade to riskiest C grade. The cumulative probability of default is also significantly higher in lowest three grades (BB–C). This provides an evidence of good discriminatory power of the rating system.

Exploiting the bank's seven years' historical rating migration data, we also estimate average one-year transition matrix capturing grade-wise rating movements including slippage to D category.

Chart 5.5: Overall Discriminatory Power of Commercial Loan Rating Model of a Bank

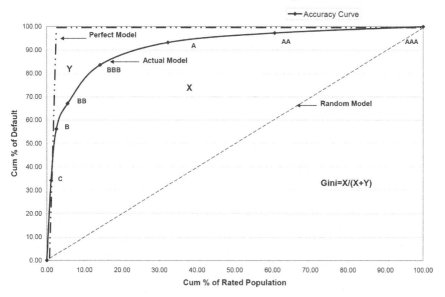

Power Curve for Internal Bank Rating

Source: Input obtained from Table 5.4.

In an extremely best situation, all defaults should accumulate among the borrowers classified as the riskiest debtors (grade C) and the power curve would then hit the top horizontal line (in case of a perfect model). On the other hand, in a very rarely worst case, if the rating system has zero discriminatory power, the CAP curve will resemble to diagonal 45° lines. Greater the area between the curve and 45° lines, higher is the discriminatory power of the rating model. The plotted actual CAP curve obtained from the bank rating history lies between these two extremes. One can clearly see from Chart 5.5 that the lowest three grades C, B and BB capture almost 70 per cent (estimated at 67.2 per cent in Table 5.4) of the total 73 defaults in the portfolio.

To measure the discriminatory power of the rating system, the area between the power curve and the diagonal (area X) is placed in relation to the area between the maximum power curve and the diagonal ($X + \Upsilon$). This gives the Gini coefficient or accuracy ratio (AR) or Power Stat. Also see the Gini coefficient value that has been obtained diagrammatically in the last column of Table 5.4.

Using Table 5.4 and Chart 5.5, we obtain Gini coefficient as a measure of model's discriminatory power. In case of discrete observations, Gini coefficient is calculated by:

$$G = 1 - \Sigma p_i \times (z_i + z_{i-1}) \qquad \text{Eq. 5.1}$$

Where Z_i is cumulative per cent share in total default and P_i is relative default per cent share (this is documented in Table 5.4).

From 9th column of Table 5.4, we obtain:
$$10^4 \times \Sigma p_i \times (z_i + z_{i-1}) = 1,794.82$$
$$\Rightarrow \Sigma p_i \times (z_i + z_{i-1}) = 0.179482$$
Therefore, $G = 1 - \Sigma p_i \times (z_i + z_{i-1})$
$$= 1 - 0.179482$$
$$= 0.8205 \text{ (approximately)}$$

Here, Gini measures inequality amongst grades in predicting bad debtors. Hence, higher Gini value is good for increasing the predictive power of the rating model. Gini coefficient ranges between 0 and 1. The closer the Gini is to one, the better the discriminatory power of the model. For continuous Gini computation framework, read Fritz, Popken and Wagner (2002).

Power curve can also be used to assess the ability of a LGD model to discriminate between good LGDs (those below historical average) vs. bad LGDs (above historical average). The more accurately an LGD model assigns its lowest (worst) scores to cases that are truly poor, the more rapidly the power curve will ascend. A perfect model will cover the entire area. A random model will have no discriminatory power and will be a diagonal line.

The error rate of LGD model can also be tested with an estimate of the mean square error rate (MSE).

$$MSE = \frac{\sum (L_i - \hat{L}_i)^2}{n - 1} \qquad \text{Eq. 5.2}$$

Where L_i and $\hat{L}_i$ are the actual and estimated LGDs, respectively, for each loan facility i. The variable n is the number of facilities (or borrowers) in the tested sample.

Models with lower MSE have smaller difference between the actual and predicted values and thus have forecasting power.

It is sensible to know that these measures of discriminatory power can be meaningfully applied in situations where different rating systems (or models) can be compared on the same portfolio in the same period (that means for relative comparison). This is usually the case when rating systems are in their development phase when the developer has to select one rating function among several (Blochwitz et al., 2005, Wilmott). Many academicians and risk management experts have provided empirical evidence that the absolute measure of discriminatory power gives sub-optimal result in comparison to the relative measure because of portfolio dependency of such measures.

Table 5.4 can also be used to estimate rating wise PD for a low default pool (LDP) of assets. This can be done through CAP curve optimization technique as suggested by van der Burgt (2008). Let us consider that a hypothetical low default portfolio (e.g. sovereign or bank exposure) that has an industry average default rate of 2 per cent. Therefore, we can assume that 5 out of 250 borrowers may default in the next year. In the earlier case, we have seen how we can draw a set of CAP curves and obtain accuracy ratios (Gini coefficient, G) and concavity. Note that concavity is measured by using the formula: $1/(1 - G)$. A high concavity corresponds to a rating system with high discriminatory power. However, we have to obtain the grade-wise relative default rates by fixing accuracy (or Gini coefficient) by an optimization method. This can be done by using excel solver. In this reverse optimization method, we will have to set the desired Gini coefficient (e.g. $G = 0.75$) and then by changing the variable cells in columns 3 and 6, we can obtain the grade-wise default rates. Van der Burgt (2008) had found a concavity of 8.03 and Gini = 0.875 as optimal values that can best discriminate the grades. If we fix $G = 0.875$, we can obtain the grade-wise distribution of defaulted accounts and the default rates. A bank's top management can also decide the desired accuracy and concavity of the grades for the pool.

Next, we will now compare the discriminatory power of two rating models and will try to know which model is better. Let's assume that a bank is conducting a validation test to compare predictive power of two alternative internal credit scoring models. Both these models (models 1 and 2) have produced the predicted scores (or expected probability of default, EPD) and accordingly borrowers have been arranged in terms of deciles orders (highest to lowest scores). Suppose 200 borrowers have actually defaulted. The validation outcome has been summarized in the Table 5.5 below. The column inputs are generated with the cumulative fraction of defaults over the entire population of obligors ordered by the default probability predicted by the models.

Table 5.5: Comparison of Discriminatory Power of Two-rating Models

Deciles Groups of no. of Borrowers from Top	Cumulative % of Rated Borrowers	Average Credit Score	Model 1: % Share in Default	Model 2: %Share in Default
10	100%	387.5	0.5%	0%
9	90%	362.5	1.5%	2%
8	80%	337.5	2%	2%
7	70%	312.5	2.5%	2.5%
6	60%	287.5	3.5%	3.5%
5	50%	262.5	6%	5%
4	40%	237.5	10%	8%
3	30%	212.5	15%	17%
2	20%	187.5	24%	22%
1	10%	162.5	35%	38%
Total			100%	100%

Source: Author's own created example for illustration purpose only.

Note: Quantiles are the scoring points taken at regular intervals from the cumulative distribution function (CDF) of predicted scores. Dividing ordered data into q essentially equal-sized data subsets is the motivation for q-quantiles. The 2-quantile is called median, 4-quantile is called quartiles (Q), 10-quantile is called deciles (D) and 100-quantile is called percentiles (P). Total number of defaults = 200.

Now, we will draw cumulative accuracy profile (CAP) graphs to fit the two models and compare their predictive powers. The CAP curves in Chart 5.6 have been constructed using Table 5.5 values.

We can make visual comparison of model performance using cumulative accuracy profiles. The steeper is the graph, better the model is able to discriminate between defaulters and solvent firms.

Clearly, Model 2 outperforms Model 1 in terms of discriminatory power. One can notice that Model 2 covers greater area above the 45 degree line than Model 1.

Chart 5.6: Comparison of Model Performance Using CAP Curves

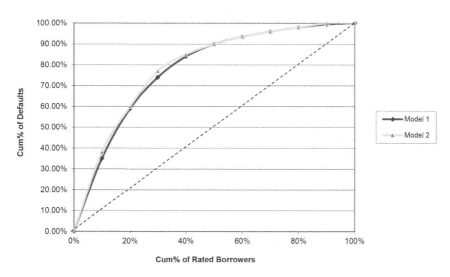

Source: Input obtained from Table 5.5.

The discriminatory power of the two-rating models can be measured by estimating their Gini coefficients. This has been demonstrated in Table 5.6.

Table 5.6: Comparing Model Gini Coefficients

Deciles groups of no. of Borrowers from Top	Cumulative % of Rated Borrowers (z_i)	Model 1: Cum% Share in Default (p_i)	Model 2: Cum% Share in Default (p_i)	Model 1: $p_i \times (z_i + z_{i-1})$	Model 2: $p_i \times (z_i + z_{i-1})$
10	100%	0.5%	0%	0.95%	0.00%
9	90%	1.5%	2%	2.55%	3.40%
8	80%	2%	2%	3.00%	3.00%
7	70%	2.5%	2.5%	3.25%	3.25%
6	60%	3.5%	3.5%	3.85%	3.85%
5	50%	6%	5%	5.40%	4.50%
4	40%	10%	8%	7.00%	5.60%
3	30%	15%	17%	7.50%	8.50%
2	20%	24%	22%	7.20%	6.60%
1	10%	35%	38%	3.50%	3.80%
Total		100%	100%	44.20%	42.50%
Gini				0.5580	0.5750

Source: Input obtained from Table 5.5.

The Receiver-operating Characteristic (ROC) Approach

Receiver-operating characteristic is a popular tool to measure discriminatory power of a credit-scoring model. It is another form of representation which is similar to the CAP curve or Power curve in which the cumulative frequencies of good cases are placed on the X-axis instead of the cumulative frequencies of all the cases. Both the ROC and CAP curves are identical in terms of information content. The ROC and CAP curves are based on rank ordering and deal with relative classification power. The area below ROC curve is widely used as a measure of model performance.

Traditionally, an ROC curve shows the true positive rate sensitivity on the Y-axis and false positive prediction rate 1 – specificity on the X-axis. The proportion of correctly predicted defaulters is called sensitivity (or hit rate) and the proportion of correctly predicted non-defaulters is called specificity. Thus, the false alarm rate is 1 – specificity.

In statistics, the false positive prediction (1 – specificity) is also called type I error, which is the error of rejecting a null hypothesis that should have been accepted. The false negative prediction (1 – sensitivity) is called type II error, which means the error of accepting a null hypothesis that should have been rejected.

Chart 5.7: ROC Curve

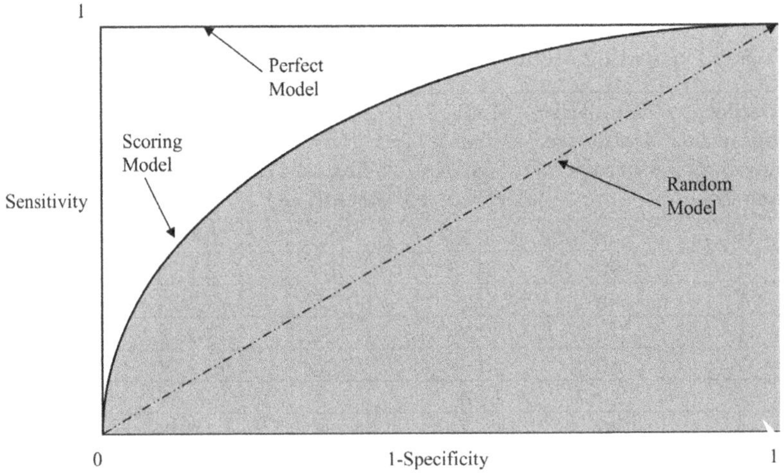

Source: Author's illustration.

ROC curve of the ideal procedure would run vertically from the lower left point (0, 0) upwards to point (0, 100) and from there to the right to point

(100, 100). The x and y values of the ROC curve are always equal if the frequency distributions of good and bad cases are identical. The ROC curve for a rating procedure which cannot distinguish between good and bad cases will run along the diagonal.

The slope of the ROC curve in each section reflects the ratio of bad cases to good cases in the respective rating class. On this basis, we can conclude that the ROC curve for rating procedures should be concave (i.e. curved to the right) over the entire range. A violation of this condition will occur when the expected default probabilities do not differ sufficiently. The greater the area below the curve, the better is the discriminatory power of the rating model.

Model Comparison

Chart 5.8 shows the ROC curves for three alternative corporate default prediction models. These models are (a) Original Altman Z score model, (b) New Indian Z score model and (c) the stock market-based structural Merton model. The performances of these three models have been back-tested using a sample data of 150 Indian listed firms. A detailed description of these default prediction models have already been given in Chapter 2. The diagonal line represents the random model. It is quite clear that all the three models perform considerably better than the random model. Overall, New Z score model (2005) has the highest discriminatory power. The area under the ROC (AUROC) curve measures the model's discriminatory power. The AUROCs for the three alternate scoring models are 0.873 (New Z score), 0.87 (Altman Z score) and 0.853 (Merton Model).

These ROC curves can be generated using statistical packages like SPSS and STATA. One has to compare the actual state of the borrowers (take it as control group, using a dummy ddef = 1 if the borrower is a defaulting firm and ddef = 0 if it is a solvent firm) with the predicted probability of default generated by these model scores (convert Z score to expected probability of default; or use predicted EDF like Merton model does).

In practice, the procedure which shows a steeper curve in the lower range of scores on the left would be preferable because fewer type I errors occur at the same level of type II error in this range.

ROC curve can also be used to compare the performance of internal rating models. Suppose a bank has three different models to rate its corporate customers. Model 1 is for private firms, Model 3 evaluates creditworthiness of public sector firms and Model 4 is used to rate the wholesale Traders. Model 2 (for infrastructure loans) is a new model which has not yet been tested.

Chart 5.8: Comparing Discriminatory Power of Default Prediction Models
ROC Curve

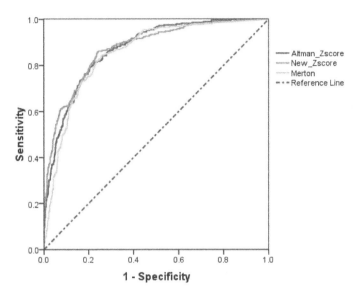

Source: Author's own analysis.

We find that out of total 19 corporate defaults in 2008–09 in a bank, seven defaults are generated by Model 1, nine from Model 3 and three from Model 4. Now, we can draw the ROC chart to compare predictive power of Models 1, 3 and 4. As we have already said, Model 2 has not been compared due to insufficient number of observations.

Chart 5.9 shows an example of three ROC curves generated by the three internal rating models. Clearly, rating Model 4 has the highest predictive power than Models 1 and 3. The industrial model (Model 1) ranks second in terms of predictive power and Model 3 (trader model) has the least predictive power.

The following relation applies to the ROC and CAP curves' measures of discriminatory power:

Gini Coefficient = 2 × AUC – 1   Eq. 5.3

AUC (area under curve) is a graphic measure of a rating procedure's discriminatory power derived from the ROC curve and refers to the area under the ROC curve. Gini coefficient for Model 1: 0.87; Model 3: 0.62 and Model 4: 0.92

Chart 5.9: Comparative Performance of Rating Models

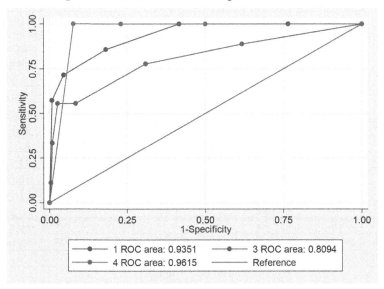

Source: Validation of Internal Rating Models of a bank.

Besides, its geometric interpretation as the area under the ROC curve, AUC can also be interpreted as the probability that a bad case randomly selected from the given sample will actually have a lower rating than a randomly drawn good case. Therefore, the information contained in the summary measures of discriminatory power derived from the CAP and ROC curves is equivalent.

Error area = 1 – AUC.

Therefore, AUC and the error area are equivalent measures of discriminatory power. The smaller the error area is, the higher the discriminatory power of the rating model. In this case, Model 1 has the greatest area and also the steepest and, hence, is better in terms of the other two models.

There are also other measures of discriminatory power like Pietra Index, Kolmogorov-Smirnov Test, Entropy Measure, etc. which are not being discussed here. Useful graphs include the lift chart, Kolmogorov Smirnov chart and other ways to assess the predictive power of the model. For example, the following graph shows the Kolmogorov Smirnov (KS) graph for a credit scorecard model.

In Table 5.7, we have computed the K–S values as a measure of accuracy by taking the maximum difference between columns 6 and 7 figures. The K–S value can range between 0 and 100. A high value indicates better model power in separating the two populations. The score band where we obtain the maximum K–S is the point of maximum separation.

Table 5.7: Example of KS Test

(1) Score (z) Interval	(2) Bad	(3) Good	(4) Relative % Bad	(5) Relative % Good	(6) Cum % Bad	(7) Cum % Good	(8) Difference in % Cum.
z>575 & z<=590	0	3	0.00	8.82	100.00	100.00	0.00
z>560 & z<=575	0	3	0.00	8.82	100.00	91.18	8.82
z>545 & z<=560	0	2	0.00	5.88	100.00	82.35	17.65
z>530 & z<=545	0	3	0.00	8.82	100.00	76.47	23.53
z>515 & z<=530	0	3	0.00	8.82	100.00	67.65	32.35
z>500 & z<515	0	3	0.00	8.82	100.00	58.82	41.18
z>485 & z<=500	0	4	0.00	11.76	100.00	50.00	50.00
z>470 & z<=485	1	4	6.25	11.76	100.00	38.24	61.76
z>455 & z<=470	1	3	6.25	8.82	93.75	26.47	67.28
z>440 & z<=455	3	2	18.75	5.88	87.50	17.65	69.85
z>425 & z<=440	5	2	31.25	5.88	68.75	11.76	56.99
z>410 & z<=425	6	2	37.50	5.88	37.50	5.88	31.62
Total	16	34	100.00	100.00			

Source: Author's own illustration.

Next, we produce graph in Chart 5.10 by plotting columns 7 and 8 from Table 5.7.

Chart 5.10: KS Graph

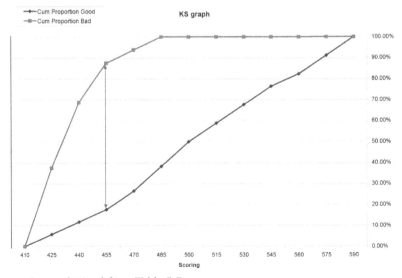

Source: Input obtained from Table 5.7.

In KS graph, the X-axis shows the credit score values (sums) and the Y-axis denotes the cumulative proportions of observations in each outcome class (good credit vs. bad credit) in the holdout or within sample. The further apart are the two lines, the greater is the degree of differentiation between the good credit and bad credit cases in the holdout sample, and thus, the better (more accurate) is the model. As shown in column 8 of Table 5.7 and green line in Chart 5.10, the maximum K–S value in this exercise is 69.85 and it occurs at the score band 440–455 (10th bucket).

1. Model calibration

Credit scores reflect the borrower's creditworthiness. However, it is necessary to assign default probabilities to score values by means of calibration. This assignment converts ordinal ranking (or scoring) into cardinal measure. The process of mapping a borrower's credit score to a rating class and the PD percentage is called calibration. Default probabilities are to be classified into as many as risk grades in order to meet the minimum requirements of the IRB approach of Basel II. Whether achieved through statistical methods, expert judgement, business line expertise or a combination thereof, rating systems of an IRB bank should result in rank ordering of risk by counterparty. This is an important IRB qualifying criteria in the Basel II credit risk measurement framework.

The objective of calibration is to assign default probability for each predicted credit scores or rating buckets. Calibration technique allows us to assign a borrower's score obtained from internal rating model to an implied PD percentage and then look up the "master scale of grades" (lower range, median/mode and upper range) and obtain a Basel II/III PD estimate. Calibration process should ultimately compare the relationship between the estimated default probabilities and the actual default outcome. Therefore, calibration of a rating model is frequently referred to as back testing. Recalibration or rescaling may be necessary if sample default rate deviates a lot from the predicted ones.

Table 5.8 gives an example of score distribution produced by an internal IRB retail-scoring model. It illustrates the simple calibration process. In standard calibration exercise, the rating model's score values are divided into several intervals according to rank order (in terms of deciles or percentiles) on a large sample data. For examining calibration, the differences of forecast PDs and realized default rates must be considered. The quality of calibration depends on the degree to which the default probabilities predicted by rating model match the default rates actually realized. This can be done through back testing.

A bank has obtained Table 5.8 information during customization of an internal-rating model for all retail loans. One can notice that as we move down to the master rating scale, the odd ratio in favour of good decreases, but the default rate increases. Hence, the underlying rating system is obviously able to classify cases by default probability. This way a bank can calibrate its rating systems and ultimately fix its rating grades to take pricing decisions.

Table 5.8: A Retail-rating Model Calibration

Credit Score Range	Number of good cases	Number of bad cases	Total	Default Rates (%)	Odd Ratio: (Good/ Bad)
>300	791	9	800	1.13	87.9
276–300	1480	20	1500	1.33	74.0
251–275	2450	50	2500	2.00	49.0
223–250	2910	90	3000	3.00	32.3
213–222	2400	100	2500	4.00	24.0
202–212	1683	117	1800	6.50	14.4
195–201	1472	128	1600	8.00	11.5
180–194	890	110	1000	11.00	8.1
170–179	680	120	800	15.00	5.7
<170	304	96	400	24.00	3.2
Total	15060	840	15900		

Source: Author's own illustration.

Following the same exercise shown here, IRB bank can also decide its hurdle grade and the cut-off score which can be linked to its credit policy. Cut-off scores are taken such that default rate is contained at 15 per cent or less (say corresponding cut-off score = 170). All applicants scoring 170 or above would be accepted. However, all applicants scoring below 170 would be rejected even if they meet the eligibility criteria. If rating buckets are not in proper cardinal order, bank will have to re-calibrate the grades. Comparing the internal model score range with overlay risk criteria (lower risk band, moderate risk, higher risk segment, etc.) and finally linking it with approval distribution enables the lender to accept a limited number of loans with lower credit scores provided they are within the acceptable lower risk segment. Similarly, they can approve a smaller number of high risk loans and can earn higher spread as well if the borrowers' credit scores are high. Following this calibration strategy, banks can pass the "use test" model validation criteria set by the regulator.

Similarly, statistical regression models output scores can be ranked and ordered into various buckets and determine default probabilities directly from the model function. One essential benefit of statistical model like logistic PD scoring model has the fact that it directly computes the expected default probabilities from the scoring function (EPDs = $1/(1 + \exp(-z))$). This characteristic facilitates the calibration of the rating model. It is in this context that the logistic model is superior to MDA-based Z score model. However, the rating buckets (or EPD intervals) must be defined in such a way that the differences between the corresponding average default probabilities are sufficiently large, and at the same time the corresponding classes contain an adequately large number of cases (both good and bad).

In terms of discriminatory power and calibration, statistical models demonstrate clearly superior performance in practice compared to heuristic models. Therefore, banks are increasingly replacing or supplementing judgemental models with statistical models in IRB framework. This is true where sufficient data set is available for the development of those statistical models and conduct back testing.

Rescaling default probabilities is necessary whenever the proportion of good and bad cases in the sample does not match the actual composition of the portfolio where the rating model will be finally used. Accordingly, in order to perform calibration, it is necessary to know the segment's average default rate. Once the default probabilities have been assigned to grades in the rating scale, the calibration is complete.

As per the IRB validation principle set by the Basel committee, back-testing risk rating system predictions against realised defaults has to be done by employing a variety of validation tools. This also includes the review of developmental evidence, process verification and benchmarking, which can satisfy both itself and its supervisor that its rating estimates are reasonable.

The calibration process concludes the actual rating development process. Hence, it is done at the last stage. Sometimes, additional external data is also necessary for the calibration of default rates. A bank can also use credit bureau data along with internal data to calibrate its grades. Besides statistical testing, management oversight is also required to finally decide how many grades are necessary.

Chi-square test

For conducting chi-square test, one has to place the borrowers into quintile groups or decile groups. The null hypothesis is set depending upon the requirement of the test. Then, we compare the deviation between actual outcome and predicted outcome.

The table below illustrates some simple Chi-squared validations applicable for both PD and LGD models. By comparing the expected defaults per grade (E) and comparing them with the actual defaults (A), one can obtain the estimated Chi-square value:

$$\tilde{T} = \sum_{i=1}^{k}(A_i - E_i)^2 \,/\, E_i \qquad \text{Eq. 5.4}$$

The degrees of freedom for this test is the total number of grades (or quantiles) less one. For example, with eight rating grades (n = 8) in the rows, we will have 7 degrees of freedom (d.f = n – k – 1) as no parameters to be estimated (k = 0).

In relative terms, we can compare the predictive power of rating models through Chi-squared calibration test. One has to compare the computed Chi-square value with the table value at a certain level of confidence (say at 5 per cent level of significance) and degrees of freedom. The following exercises will help us to better understand Chi-squared statistical test.

Chi-squared test 1: PD rating model

Consider a scoring system with 8,000 scores classified in 8 rating scales, 1 being the safest (best) grade and 8 being the riskiestgrade. Suppose 360 borrowers have actually defaulted. We will now use Chi-square test to check the predictive power of two competing scoring models from the information set given in Table 5.9.

Chi-square values are estimated in columns 5 and 6. If we use 5 per cent (=alpha) significance level (or confidence level of 95%); Chi-square table gives us the critical value of 14.07 for degree of freedom of 8 – 1 = 7. One can either check the statistical table or use excel function "=chiinv(5 per cent, 7)" to obtain the critical values. The computed Chi-squared values for two models have been estimated by summing up (A – E)^2/E values in column 5 and column 6. The null hypothesis (H$_0$) is: scoring model correctly predicts the actual default rates (i.e. there is no problem with the rating model).

Table 5.9: Chi-square Test for Model Comparison

Rating Class/ Score Quantiles	Actual Defaults	Model 1: Expected Defaults	Model 2: Expected Defaults	Model 1: (A − E)^2/E	Model 2: (A − E)^2/E
1	10	9	5	0.11	2.78
2	20	18	10	0.22	5.56
3	30	25	29	1.00	0.04
4	40	35	30	0.71	2.86
5	50	45	50	0.56	0.00
6	55	60	60	0.42	0.42
7	65	68	62	0.13	0.13
8	90	100	114	1.00	5.76
Total	360	360	360	4.15	17.54

Source: Author's own illustration.

Since computed Chi-square value is less than the table value for Model 1, the model fitness is good. However Model 2 is comparatively a bad model since Chi-square deviation is very high and the null hypothesis of good fit is rejected.

Similarly, Brier score and Mean square error tests are also used to compare the default probability of a rating class with the observed default frequency of this class.

If we have only two categories: default and solvent type of customers,

$$\text{Brier score} = \frac{2}{n}\sum_{i=1}^{n}(EPD_i - ODP)^2 \qquad \text{Eq. 5.5}$$

where n denotes the number of rating classes.

One can also use non-parametric Kolmogorov-Smirnov (KS) test or Mann-Whitney rank-sum tests to check the empirical difference in the distribution of two series. Brier scores are also used as calibration test.

Chi-squared test 2: LGD rating model

The Chi-square test is useful to calibrate the IRB LGD models as well. For this, one has to collect data in the following order (Table 5.10).

Using 5 per cent level of significance and degree of freedom of 10 – 1 = 9, the table (or critical) Chi-square value is 16.92. Again, the null (H_0) hypothesis is that the model correctly reflects the actual loss pattern. If the estimated Chi-square value (Σ $(A - E)^2/E$) is lesser than the critical value (16.92), then the null hypothesis will be rejected and model fitness will be good. Hence, we can conclude that Model B is able to predict LGD more accurately than Model A. The calibration test also reveals that Model B has greater monotonic ascending sequence in LGD rating class than Model A. Thus, Model B has higher classification accuracy in comparison to Model A.

Table 5.10: Calibration Test for LGD Rating Model

LGD Class	Observed Actual Numbers (A)	Model X: Predicted Numbers (E)	Model Y: Predicted Numbers (E)	Model A: $(A - E)^2/E$	Model B: $(A - E)^2/E$
LGD1	5	5	6	0.00	0.17
LGD2	15	12	15	0.75	0.00
LGD3	25	24	20	0.04	1.25
LGD4	30	16	20	12.25	5.00
LGD5	50	33	40	8.76	2.50
LGD6	40	45	40	0.56	0.00
LGD7	40	40	55	0.00	4.09
LGD8	30	40	35	2.50	0.71
LGD9	15	20	17	1.25	0.24
LGD10	20	35	22	6.43	0.18
Total	270	270	270	32.53	14.14

Source: Author's own illustration.

Table 5.10a has been constructed to orderly report the predicted LGDs produced by these two models. This table will help us to compare the discriminatory power of two models.

Table 5.10a: Comparing the Discriminatory Power of Models

Deciles groups of LGD Range	Cumulative % of Rated Facilities	Model A: Percentage Share in Bad LGD	Model B: Percentage Share in Bad LGD
0–10%	100%	1.00%	0.60%
10–20%	90%	2.00%	1.00%
20–30%	80%	2.50%	1.40%
30–40%	70%	4.00%	1.50%
40–50%	60%	10.50%	4.50%
50–60%	50%	12.00%	9.00%
60–70%	40%	13.00%	12.00%
70–80%	30%	15.00%	15.00%
80–90%	20%	15.00%	25.00%
90–100%	10%	25.00%	30.00%
Total		100.00%	100.00%

Source: Author's own illustration.

Chart 5.11 has been drawn using the inputs from Table 5.10a. The power curves for LGD graphically portray and compare the ability of two LGD models to discriminate between Good LGDs (those below historical average) vs. Bad LGDs (above historical average). The more accurately an LGD model assigns its lowest (worst) scores to cases that truly are poor, the more rapidly the power curve will ascend. A perfect model will cover the entire area. A random model will have no discriminatory power and will be a diagonal line. As the area of graph for Model B is larger than the area of graph for Model A, Model B is more accurate than Model A. The ROC area for Model A is 0.699 and for Model B is 0.7683. Thus, Model B performance is comparatively better.

The IRB banks will have to ensure whether the granularity of the rating scales is consistent for describing actual LGD risks. The LGD rating model's predicted value range should sufficiently be divided into several intervals according to the quantity of data available. The intervals should be defined in the same way as we have done in the earlier PD model case.

Chart 5.11: Power Curve Comparison of Two Different LGD Models

Power Curve for LGD

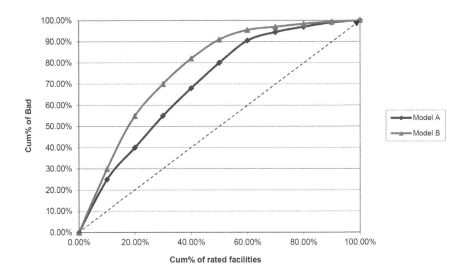

Source: Based on input obtained from Table 5.10a.

Benchmarking tools for validation

Benchmarking the rating model through internal calibration or through external comparison (such as agency ratings) is helpful in maintaining the integrity of internal ratings.

Certain loan portfolios may have limited number of defaults (e.g. exposures to sovereign, banks, insurance companies, etc.). The scarcity of internal historical default data makes it difficult to meaningfully back-test risk-rating predictions against the realized defaults. In such cases, banks may have to use various benchmarking tools for validation. Basel committee has suggested the following tools that could be potentially used by the banks:

- Compare internal rating migration matrices with the ratings and migrations of third parties such as rating agencies or data pools or results from other internal models.
- Internal ratings could be compared with market-based proxies for credit quality such as equity prices (e.g. KMV-type model for bank PD estimation), bond spreads, etc.
- An analysis of the rating characteristics of similarly rated exposures could be undertaken.

- The average rating output for the portfolio as a whole could be compared with the actual experience for the portfolio.

Source: BCBS newsletter no. 6 (September 2005).

There are also other validation tests like confidence interval-based Binomial test and Hosmer–Lemeshow test that are used by risk domain experts. The Hosmer and Lemeshow (HL) test actually checks how close the predicted probabilities are to the actual rate of events through a Chi-square test. This is done by splitting the data into 10 sections based on ascending order of probabilities (or rating grades).

c. Model stability

The rating system should be robust against the ageing of the loans rated and against changes in general conditions (e.g. regional factors, industry and macroeconomic conditions, etc.). This requires an in-depth analysis of the model parameters and should, therefore, accompany the ongoing development of the model. Rating models have to undergo further development whenever their performance decreases due to change in general conditions.

Testing the discriminatory power of rating models over a longer time horizon is an important validation check. Banks should know how far their rating models can predict borrower default. A robustness check on the model performance must be done by changing the sample observations and also the time period.

In terms of discriminatory power and calibration, statistical models demonstrate clearly superior performance in practice compared to heuristic (e.g. expert-based systems) models. Therefore, banks are now increasingly replacing or supplementing heuristic models with statistical models in practice. The model validation and calibration results are affected by the credit cycle. Therefore, the impact of business cycle on rating model output needs to be taken care of. Ratings should be reviewed at least annually. Generally, an appropriate validation cycle for rating models consists of two to three years at most.

Basel committee desires that even if IRB estimates are grounded in historical experience, they are intended to be forward looking for all portfolios. This is consistent with the first IRB validation principle. This is why stress testing and scenario analysis are important.

Stress testing the credit risk parameters

Banks' loan business tends to follow the same cyclical pattern as that of the real economy (pro-cyclicality). Hence, loans typically show strong growth in an economic upturn and slow growth or even contraction in an economic downturn and so is their capital structure. Basel II IRB approach may give rise to pro-cyclical problems owing to the fact that the three main input parameters (PD, LGD and Correlation) are themselves – albeit to different degrees – influenced by cyclical movements. Pro-cyclicality involves the regulatory capital impact for expected and unexpected losses based on the rating distribution of bank portfolios. The issue is that ratings and default rates respond to the cycle, the banks need to protect its capital and limit the credit supply. To counter pro-cyclicality effect, Basel II committee suggests that banks should have a strong stress-testing framework for scenario analysis. A system of stress testing the model parameters ensures that the model remains valid and stable even under extreme conditions. Simultaneously, banks need to perform stress test to ensure bank's capital adequacy in times of shocks. A credit institution shall regularly perform a credit risk stress test to assess the effect of certain specific conditions on its total capital requirements for credit risk.

The most crucial input for stress-testing and capital simulation exercise depends upon choosing/identifying realistic scenarios. By scenario, we mean an event (for example, an increase in interest rates, unemployment rate, inflation, etc.) and, possibly, its broader implications that are believed to represent abnormal operating conditions (fall in profit, growth and rise in volatility). Scenarios can be chosen based on historical experience, or they can be hypothetical. Since credit risk models predict the future outcomes, a series of scenario-based model sensitivity analysis should be designed at the bank level so that results can be combined across portfolios. Sensitivity analysis to such scenarios show how model output (e.g. rating, PD, LGD, etc.) is impacted by variations in one or more parameters (e.g. leverage, profitability, sales volatility, fall in collateral value, etc.) due to changing macroeconomic conditions.

Usefulness of stress testing

Stress tests have received much attention worldwide after the financial crisis. The usefulness of stress-test exercises is to assess the impact of specific macroeconomic shocks, such as specific industry downturn or a country recession, which finally penalizes portfolio risk concentrations. Stress testing is a very useful reference in the process of assessing capital adequacy under Pillar II. Under Pillar II, banks are expected to perform "rigorous, forward-looking stress testing that identifies possible events or changes in the market conditions that could adversely impact the bank". For this, banks are required to have a routine, robust process for stress testing and scenario analyses to support its measures of capital adequacy are sufficient to resist a "range of severe but plausible" events.

Stress-testing process

Stress testing is the process of determining the effect of a change on a port-folio or sub-portfolio due to extreme, realistic events. This can be done through scenario analysis through parameterization of credit risk drivers. For example, express PD in terms of macroeconomic variables. This will translate the shocks of a stress scenario into credit risk. The full shock effect transferred when LGD and EAD are also expressed in terms of macro-variables.

The relevant macro-variables are housing prices, interest rates, GDP growth rate, industrial growth rate, etc. However, for such stress-testing exercise, banks should have relevant data covering at least a full cycle (may be 5–10 years). Basel II stipulates the performance of stress test to determine capital adequacy. This implies the involvement of supervisory authorities in design, calibration and analysis of impact, adequate approach to test credit risk to see whether the excess capital is large enough to weather an adverse shock and development and integration of stress test as prudential tools.

Stress testing PD

Default probabilities are driven primarily by how firms are tied to business cycles, both domestic and foreign. Macroeconomic conditions can have great impact on the sales and profitability of firms and as such they influence the risk profile of the corporate sector. In general, in an expansionary phase, demand is high, higher profitability and fewer defaults will happen. Whereas during a recession, keeping a business profitable is more challenging and it is more likely for a firm to default. There is considerable evidence that macroeconomic conditions impact the probability of corporate default and corporate capital structure choice.

A Point-in-Time (PIT) philosophy group's obligors according to one-period-ahead predicted default frequencies. A Through-the-Cycle (TTC) philosophy group's obligors according to stress-scenario default probabilities. The stressed pooled PD for a point-in-time bucket will rise (or little bit higher) during economic upturns and fall (or smaller) during economic downturns. So, we need to adjust PIT PD to get a stable estimate for the credit risk capital number.

Academicians as well as risk management experts worldwide have proved that default probabilities depend strongly on the stage in the business cycle, and transition matrices tend to exhibit a higher frequency of downgrades during a recession and a higher occurrence of upgrades during boom. Through a regression analysis, we have empirically found that a 1 per cent fall in GDP growth rate in India increases the corporate PD by 65 basis points. This linkage has been shown in Chart 5.12. A regression analysis of Indian corporate bond default rates and yearly GDP growth rate yields important information: a 1 per cent fall in GDP growth rate in India increases the corporate PD by 65 basis points.

Chart 5.12: Link between Corporate PD and GDP Growth Rate in India

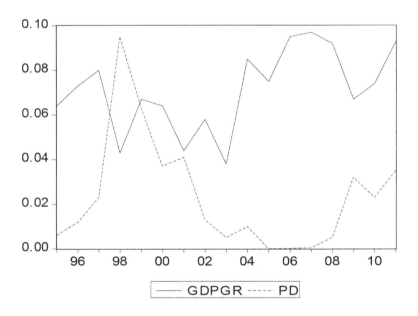

Source: CRISIL bond default data and CMIE data.

The unstressed pooled PD associated with a PIT risk bucket can be expected to move in a systematic way over the business cycle. This pooled PD should be highest at the trough of the business cycle and lowest at the peak of a business cycle. The stressed pooled PD associated with a TTC risk bucket should remain more stable throughout the business cycle (see Chart 5.13).

Chart 5.13: PIT PD vs. TTC PD

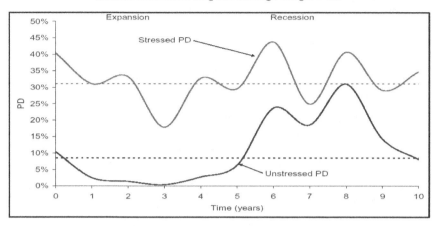

Source: BIS (2005).

One solution of this is to have both PIT and TTC rating and know the art of extracting TTC PD from PIT PD. This can be done through a mapping process (either internally or through external mapping) or through stress testing. Chart 5.14 illustrates the adjustment approach. This is because TTC rating is a combination of PIT PD and time.

Chart 5.14: Approach for Extracting TTC PD from PIT PD

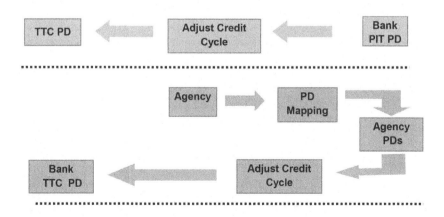

Source: Adapted from ISDA/PRIMA, March 2007, London.
Note: For illustration purpose.

An unstressed PD is an unbiased estimate of the likelihood that an obligor will default over the next year given all currently available information. Unstressed PD is likely to fall as macroeconomic conditions improve and rise as they deteriorate.

A stressed PD measures the likelihood that an obligor will default over the next year using all available obligor information, but assuming adverse stress-scenario economic conditions. Because this PD makes use of dynamic obligor characteristics, it will change as an obligor's individual characteristics change, but it will tend not to be highly correlated with the business cycle. One can observe that the new default rates of scheduled commercial banks in India are cyclical in nature (Chart 5.15). A fall in annual GDP growth rates in recent years has resulted in sharp increase in the rate default rates in Indian banks (especially in public sector banks, PSBs). The rise in NPA has further resulted in deceleration in the system level credit growth rate.

Chart 5.15: Pro-cyclical Movements of Fresh NPA Slippage Rates of Scheduled Commercial Banks in India

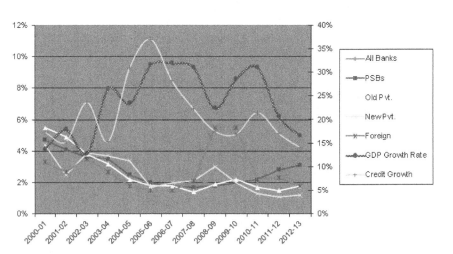

Source: RBI and audited data on NPA movements of Indian banks.

A credit institution shall assess migration in its ratings or NPA slippage movements under the stress test scenarios and adjust its grade-wise PDs. A common approach is to apply a TTC PD scalar to the PIT PD estimate. Let's assume that the loan portfolio's PIT PD estimate in good time is around 0.60 per cent and using historical data (through internal or external mapping) the long run TTC PD estimate is 2 per cent. Hence, the TTC scalar is =2%/0.60%=3.33. Similarly, in a down time period as well, PD needs to be adjusted downward. PIT PD also need to be Please note that this scalar approach must be forward looking as the portfolio mix and the credit growth would actually change going forward. Once scalar is worked out, it can be used to convert PIT PD into TTC PD. During good time, we multiply this scalar to the segment PIT PD to obtain more conservative long run estimate. This way, the variable scalar approach (suggested by the FSA, UK, 2006) can reduce the cyclicality of the IRB regulatory capital requirements in respect of PD.

Another way of conversion is to use a log odd ratio adjustment. In our example, the log odd ratio for PIT PD is=ln(99/0.60)=ln(165.67)=5.110. For long run PD, the same log odd value would be=ln(Good/Bad)=ln(98/2)=ln(49)=3.892 approx. One can notice that there is an overall shift in odd from PIT 5.110 to TTC 3.892 by -1.218 factor. The same shift factor can be applied to individual PD of each account within the portfolio to derive long run PD for each account. Suppose, a borrower account has obtained a credit score of 350 which is again mapped to a PIT PD of 0.90 per cent. The log odd ratio value would be=ln(99.10/0.90)=ln(110)=4.70. We now follow the shift adjustment of -1.218 on this and re-estimate the log of value=3.48. This new log odd score can be further mapped back to a PD estimate by using the exponential function: $1/(1+\exp(3.48))$=3% (approx.). The derived PD is the long run adjusted stable PD estimate for the concerned borrower. Though it is based on past data, a scalar adjustment would at least give a degree of conservatism in the immediate period by adjusting PD. This can be at least used as a benchmark. Note that the scalar adjustment should be properly calibrated at risk grade level. The Basel Committee suggest banks to use cycle adjusted long run stable PD to calculate the IRB regulatory capital.

As a more advanced approach, time series or panel regression methods can be used to incorporate macro-conditions to conduct cycle adjustments on the PD. Aguias et al. (2007) provided such mapping methodology to separate the PIT from the TTC effects. Jakubik (2008) in FSI award-winning paper has numerically explained the methods for credit risk modelling with macroeconomic variables.

Stress-testing LGD: Link between LGD and macroeconomic cycle

When the Basel II IRB formula was first developed, it was based on assuming an infinitely granular, homogenous portfolio. It was further assumed that the volatility of LGD, if any, would be fully diversified and would not contribute to the capital requirements. However, if it was found that LGDs are correlated to systematic default rates, then the volatility of LGD would add to capital requirements. Basel II's AIRB requirements now include estimating "downturn LGDs". It is based on the theoretical arguments and empirical evidence that LGDs are positively correlated with the economic cycle and default rates. That is, among other reasons, during periods of high defaults, one might expect that market conditions are such that buyers of distressed assets or of companies can bargain more effectively. Thus, yield requirements by buyers are elevated, leading to lower recovery values.

A significant body of academic and practitioner research suggests that systematic volatility in recovery rates is a potentially important source of unexpected credit losses for some asset classes. Hence, banks and other financial institutions are recommended to calculate "Downturn LGD" (Downturn Loss Given Default), which reflects the losses occurring during a "Downturn" in a business cycle for regulatory purposes.

Chart 5.16 gives empirical evidence that LGDs are positively correlated with the economic cycle. This chart has been derived from our commercial loan LGD survey of Indian banks that is discussed in Chapter 4.

Chart 5.16: Trend in the Commercial Loan Loss Rate (LGD) by Default Year

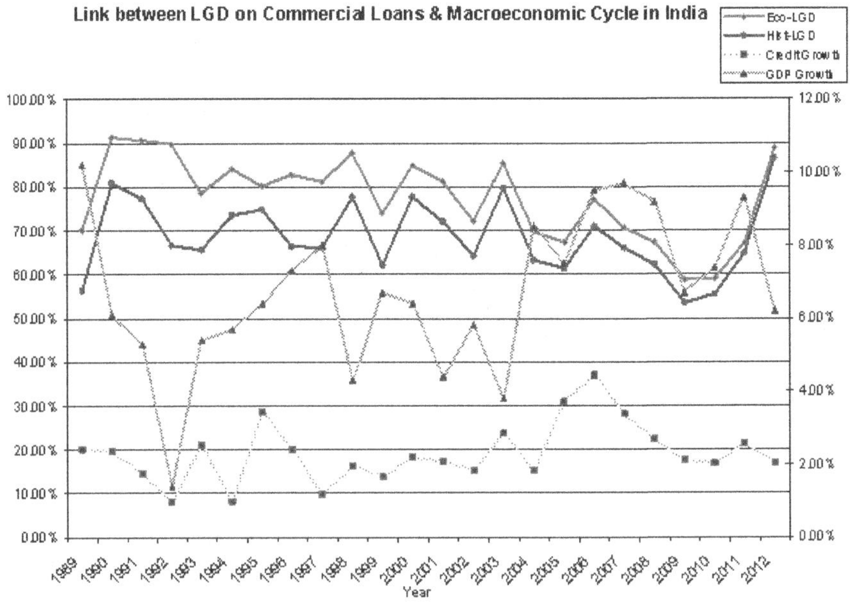

Source: Author's own LGD survey analysis of Indian banks.

As can be seen from the chart, LGD for commercial loans in India is lower during the upturn of the business cycle and higher during the downtime. This may be because the value of the collaterals fall and recoveries are much lesser than in the upturn of the business cycle. Among other reasons, during the periods of low growth and high defaults, one might expect that the market conditions are such that buyers of distressed assets or borrowing companies can bargain more effectively.

The higher provisioning and capital requirements will induce the bank to cut down the credit growth. A bank must estimate LGD for each facility that aims to reflect economic downturn conditions. Several international incidents suggest that the value of collateral falls in recessions when industry default rates are high. Recovery rates on collateralized facilities therefore decline sharply as a results of the fall in the value of their collateral. Hence, the link between macro-economic cycle and LGD needs to be well understood by banks to be better prepared during adverse economic condition. For this, the bank should be able to link its yearly default rates with yearly LGD estimates. For example, JP Morgan & Chase (JPMC) in Araten et al. (2004) has used the following regression equation using 15 years data points:

$$LGD = 1.16 + 0.16 \times \ln(\text{default rate}) \qquad \text{Eq. 5.6}$$

The draft NPF (Notice on Public Rulemaking) issued by the US regulatory agencies suggests a fallback formula based on the expected (non-downturn) LGD or ELGD if there was limited data linking LGDs and systematic default rates. It sets the LGD as follows (*Source*: BIS):

$$LGD = 0.08 + 0.92 \times ELGD \qquad \text{Eq. 5.7}$$

Thus, if one had a 40 per cent ELGD, the LGD to be used would be 12 per cent higher.

Thus, a bank should properly weight their LGD estimates with the number of defaults to take a more conservative view of LGD. In addition, a bank must take into account the potential for the LGD of the facility to be higher than the default-weighted average during a period when credit losses are substantially higher than average. This can be done through a regression analysis as shown in Eq. 5.6 and Eq. 5.7. More advanced bank capital models allow for a systematic overall default rate variable to affect the LGD chosen through an estimated historical correlation. The percentage of increase in the capital can be used as a "mark up" of LGD in the Basel II/III IRB risk-weighted asset (RWA) formula for LGD for all exposures to achieve the downturn effect desired.

Summary

Indian banks need to establish an integrated risk management framework, culture and system to reap the benefits of increased sophistication in measuring and understanding risk and managing the effect of risk. A better rating model allows credit officers to avoid defaults and to increase business with lower risk borrowers. It can also be used to technically know the correct price for risk. Accordingly, banks must have a robust process to validate its important credit risk parameters: PD, EAD and LGD to adopt the IRB approach. A regular model performance tracking and validation process can assure the regulator that consistent and optimal model based decisions are being made.

Validation focuses on comparing credit outcomes against predictions. In order to meet the supervisory expectation, bank's rating system needs to ensure that the rating grade PD and LGD values are correctly calculated and are consistent with the actual default experiences. Many statistical model validation exercises have been illustrated in this chapter. These measures of discriminatory power can be meaningfully applied when we are comparing the performance of different types of alternate rating models on the same portfolio. This usually takes place during model development process and the model builder has to select one rating function among several.

Model validation is not a purely statistical exercise although statistical analysis is necessary. Validation process should encompass both quantitative (discriminatory power, calibration, stability and stress testing) and qualitative elements (model design, data quality and internal application). The onus is on banks to demonstrate to their supervisors that their internal validation process enables them to assess the performance of internal rating and risk estimation systems consistently and meaningfully.

The scoring function which reflects the creditworthiness of the borrower should be mapped to the default probabilities by means of calibration. An internal PD mapping process converts ordinal ratings into cardinal PD equivalents. Such mapping exercise actually facilitates the PD validation process when it comes to comparing different types of rating models. In external mapping, the PD buckets are set by comparing with an established external rating system. In this case, one has to ensure that the bank's rating criteria is similar to those published by rating agencies.

The IRB banks should give attention to the choice of optimal bucket structure for better loan pricing and reduce adverse selection phenomenon. Different borrowers are evaluated by using credit scoring models on an individual basis and then grouped into rating classes or buckets with similar pooled PDs. Finally, the regulatory capital charge against credit risk is computed based on the bucket-wise pooled PD. Both the number and the width of the risk buckets should be chosen carefully so that model's predictive power is retained and individual credit risk is not overestimated.

It is worthwhile to mention that the validation and calibration results may change with time. Banks should carefully examine whether portfolio composition and the model's predictive power are changing over time or not. Model performance will change if significant shifts of the portfolio structure might happen. Because credit cycles exist, distinctions between PIT and TTC PDs have a meaning. Satisfying both Basel II/Basel III and sophisticated credit risk management objectives requires an integrated PIT/TTC rating framework. In Basel IRB regime, the rating quality will strongly influence the output quality and, hence, the credit risk weights. Therefore, banks must have a system to perform model validation and calibration checks at a regular time interval.

Key learning outcomes

After studying the chapter and the relevant reading, you should be able to understand:
- Importance of rating model validation for banks
- Predictive power of a rating model
- Basel II IRB validation principles
- Quantitative vs. qualitative validation
- Rating validation techniques
- Discriminatory power of rating models
- Calibration methods
- Through the cycle adjustments of credit risk parameters

Review questions

1. What is validation? Why is it important for banks?
2. What are the key validation principles?
3. What is model risk? How can it be managed?

4. What is discriminatory power of a rating model? How can it be measured?
5. Is there any difference between granularity and discriminatory power?
6. What are the differences between qualitative validation and statistical validation?
7. What is the difference between CAP and ROC approach of validation?
8. How do you use Gini coefficient in measuring the rating discriminatory power?
9. How Chi-square test is applied for model calibration?
10. What is scenario analysis?
11. What is down-turn LGD? How it can be estimated?

References

Agarwal, V. and R. Taffler. 2008. "Comparing the Performance of Market-based and Accounting-based Bankruptcy Prediction Models", *Journal of Banking and Finance* 32: 1541–51.

Aguais, S.D., L.R. Forest Jr., M. King, M.C. Lennon and B. Lordkipanindze. 2007. "Designing and Implementing a Basel II Compliant PIT-TTC Rating Framework", in *The Basel Handbook: A Guide for Financial Practitioners*, ed. Michael K. Ong (London: Risk Books).

Araten, M., M. Jacobs Jr. and P. Varshney. 2004. "Measuring LGD on Commercial Loans: An 18 Year Internal Study", *The RMA Journal* May.

Bandyopadhyay, A. 2006. "Predicting Probability of Default of Indian Corporate Bonds: Logistic and Z score Model Approaches", *The Journal of Risk Finance* 7(3): 255–72.

BCBS. 2005. "Update on Work of the Accord Implementation Group Related to Validation under the Basel II Framework", January.

———— 2006. "International Convergence of Capital Measurement and Capital Standards: A Revised Framework", Publication No. 128, Basel Committee on Banking Supervision, Bank for International Settlements, Basel, June.

BIS. 2005. "Studies on the Validation of Internal Rating Systems (revised)", BIS Working Paper No. 14, May 2005. Available at: http://www.bis.org/publ/bcbs_wp14.pdf

———— 2005. "Validation of Low Default Portfolios in the Basel II Framework", Basel Committee News Letter No. 6, September.

———— 2006. "The IRB Use Test: Background and Implementation", Basel Committee News Letter No. 9, September.

———— 2010. "Vendor Models for Credit Risk Measurement and Management", BIS Working Paper No. 17, February.

Blochwitz, S., A. Hamerle, S. Hohl, R. Rauhmeier and D. Rosch. 2005. "Myth and Reality of Discriminatory Power for Rating Systems", Technical Article, *Wilmott Magazine*.

Demyanyk, Y. and O.V. Hemert. 2008. "Understanding the Subprime Mortgage Crisis", Federal Reserve Bank of St. Louis Supervisory Policy Analysis Working Paper, August.

Galindo, J. and P. Tamayo. 2000. "Credit Risk Assessment Using Statistical and Machine Learning: Basic Methodology and Risk Modeling Applications", *Computational Economics* 15: 107–43.

Ellis, L. 2008. "The Housing Meltdown: Why Did it Happen in the United States?",

Working Paper, BIS No. 259.

Fritz, S.G., M. Luxenburger and T. Miehe. 2007. "Implementation of an IRB Compliant Rating System", in *The Basel Handbook: A Guide for Financial Practitioners*, ed. Michael K. Ong (London: Risk Books).

Fritz, S.G., L. Popken and C. Wagner. 2002. "Scoring and Validating Techniques for Credit Risk Rating Systems", in *Credit Ratings-Methodologies, Rationale and Default Risk*, ed. Michael K. Ong (London: Risk Books).

HKMA. 2006. "Validating Risk Rating Systems under the IRB Approaches", Supervisory Policy Manual, February.

——— 2006. "The Validation of Internal Rating Systems for Capital Adequacy Purposes", HKMA Bulletin, September.

Joseph, M.P. 2005. "A PD Validation Framework for Basel II Internal Ratings-Based Systems", Mimeo. Available at: http://www.business-school.ed.ac.uk/waf/crc_archive/2005/papers/joseph-maurice.pdf

Jakubik, P. 2008. "Stress Testing Credit Risk: Comparison of the Czech Republic and Germany", BIS Working Paper, September.

RBI. 2010. "Master Circular – Prudential Guidelines on Capital Adequacy and Market Discipline – New Capital Adequacy Framework (NCAF)", 8 February.

——— 2011. "Implementation of the Internal Rating Based (IRB) Approaches for Calculation of Capital Charge for Credit Risk", DBOD, 22 December.

Siddiqi, N. 2006. *Credit Risk Scorecards: Developing and Implementing Intelligent Credit Scoring* (New York: John Wiley & Sons).

Sobehart, J.R. and S.C. Keenan. 2007. "Hybrid Contingent Claims Models: A Practical Approach to Modelling Default Risk", in *The Basel Handbook: A Guide for Financial Practitioners*, ed. Michael K. Ong (London: Risk Books).

Tasche, D. 2003. "A Traffic Lights Approach to PD Validation", Available at: hrrp://www.gloriamundi.org/deltailpopup.asp?ID=453057435r

——— 2006. "Validation of Internal Rating Systems and PD Estimates", Working Paper, DefaultRisk.com.

———— 2009. "Estimating Discriminatory Power and PD Curves when the Number of Defaults is Small", Working Paper, Available at: DefaultRisk.com.

Treacy, W. F. and M. S. Carey. 1998. "Credit Risk Rating at Large US Banks", *Federal Reserve Bulletin,* November.

VantageScore. 2012. "Validating a Credit Score Model in Conjunction with Additional Underwriting Criteria", September.

Chapter **6**

Portfolio Assessment of Credit Risk
Default Correlation, Asset Correlation
and Loss Estimation

Portfolio credit risk is that loss which arises due to holding two or more assets in the portfolio. Concentration risk is the additional portfolio risk resulting from increased exposure to one obligor or groups of correlated obligors in related industries, sector and geographic area. International evidence suggests credit events are not independent – firms prosper or suffer in line with each other. When two or more borrowers default simultaneously, the losses are more severe. Correlation exists between firms in the same industry because of industry-specific common systematic factor. Correlation also exists among companies in different industries that rely on the same production inputs and among companies that rely on the same geographical market. Correlation may also arise due to systematic or macroeconomic conditions in the national or international economy.

The higher the correlation of default, the greater is the concentration risk of the portfolio. The lower the correlation of default, the more diversified the portfolio. Correlation of default adds to credit risk when a portfolio of loans and advances is in consideration vis-à-vis single loans or advances. When correlations are significant, they produce loss distributions that are highly skewed (tail measures of credit risk like value at risk captures this).

Risk can be measured along two dimensions: expected loss (EL) and unexpected loss (UL). While it is never possible to know in advance the losses a bank will suffer in a particular year, a bank can forecast the average level of credit losses (EL) it can reasonably expect to experience.

EL of an asset is the average loss the bank can expect to lose over 1-year horizon. During that time, the asset can fluctuate in value due to unexpected change in its credit quality. Such risk at the horizon can be conveniently measured using the standard deviation of the value at the horizon. This quantifies UL. Chart 6.1 illustrates EL and UL concepts of an asset.

Chart 6.1: EL and UL Concepts of an Asset

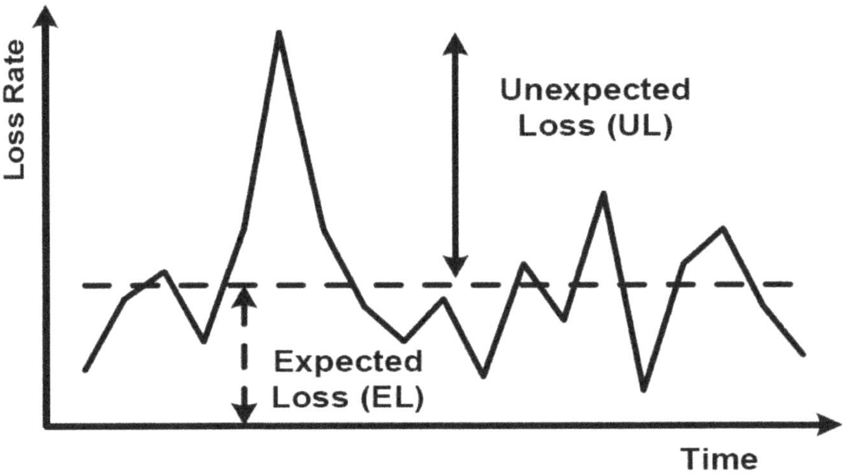

Source: BIS (2006).

In other words, UL is the estimated volatility of the potential loss in value of the asset around its EL. It is UL that creates the need for economic capital. Institutions know that these losses will occur now and then, but they cannot know in advance the time of their arrival and their severity.

For a single facility, we describe the credit-loss distribution by the mean and standard deviation of the loss over a year. The mean is commonly called the EL. The EL can be interpreted as being the amount that a lender could expect to lose on average over a number of years depending upon its creditworthiness, exposure and security. The EL can be viewed as the cost of doing business because the bank should expect to lose an amount equal to EL each year.

Expected credit risk loss (EL) is intended to set reserve requirements for doubtful accounts, calculation of PLR (default premium), pricing credit risky instruments (bonds and exotic options), and for calculation of risk-adjusted profitability (e.g. RAROC).

Expression for EL:

$$EL = EAD \times PD \times LGD \qquad \text{Eq. 6.1}$$

The bank can also suffer losses in excess of ELs, say, during economic downturns. These losses are called ULs or uncertain losses. The standard deviation of the loss is typically called the EL (see Chart 6.1).

Expression for UL:

$$UL = EAD \times LGD \times \sqrt{PD(1 - PD)} \qquad \text{Eq. 6.2}$$

We assume EAD and LGD are fixed. The standard deviation of default frequency is assumed to be similar to the standard deviation of a binomial distribution.

The capital base is required to absorb the UL, as and when they arise.

Suppose an FI manager gives $100 amount loan to a BB-rated company and PD of that company is 200 basis points (can be obtained from the bank's internal rating transition matrix or from rating agencies transition matrix). If the security provided for the loan ensures LGD = 50% (can be mapped with internal data), EL of the loan would be: 100 × 2% × 50% = $1 or 100 basis points.

The UL of the loan would be:

UL = $100 × 50% × $\sqrt{2\% \times (1 - 2\%)}$

= $50 × $\sqrt{2\% \times 98\%}$

$50 × 14%

= $7 or 7%

Portfolio Loss

Portfolio consists of many assets. Portfolio losses are of two types: Portfolio expected loss (EL_p) and Portfolio unexpected loss (UL_p). The EL grows linearly with risk elements of each asset in the pool (PD, LGD, etc.). Therefore, two different risky assets A and B that suffer average losses due to a credit event at some time during the analysis horizon have portfolio average loss (in rupees or dollars amount) equal to the sum of the two average losses. Mathematically, the portfolio expected loss for the two assets can be written as:

$EL_P = EL_A + EL_B$

Or more generally, for N risky assets/borrowers $i = 1, 2, ..., N$, we have

$$EL_p = \sum_i EL_i = \sum_i EAD_i \times PD_i \times LGD_i \qquad \text{Eq. 6.3}$$

Thus, EL_p (in nominal amount) is a simple sum of the individual ELs from all the risky assets in the portfolio. This is because of the linear and additive relationship and, hence, it is simple to estimate.

However, in order to estimate the EL_p in percentage term of the exposure, one has to make some adjustment:

$$EL_p\% = \frac{EL_p}{E_p} = \sum_i w_i EL_i \qquad \text{Eq. 6.3a}$$

Where w_i is the exposure weight: E_i/E_p ; E_i is the exposure or EAD for ith asset.[1] E_p is the portfolio exposure (total exposure).

Note that EL = EAD × PD × LGD

Actually, a bank is exposed to a portfolio of risky assets that are each subject to default risk of varying degrees and severity. Therefore, portfolio volatility (or UL) of two assets A and B can be expressed as:

$$UL_p^2 = VAR_p = VAR(A) + VAR(B) + 2Cov(X,Y)$$
Or
$$UL_{a+b}^2 = UL_a^2 + UL_b^2 + 2\rho_{ab} UL_a UL_b \qquad \text{Eq. 6.4}$$

Where $-1 \le \rho_{ab} \le +1$
note, VAR=Variance.

The correlation of default $\rho_{a,b}$ is very important when assessing the true risk of a portfolio as quantified by the UL_p.

If $\rho_{ab} = +1$,
$$UL_{a+b}^2 = UL_a^2 + UL_b^2 + 2 UL_a UL_b = (UL_a + UL_b)^2$$

---

[1] Remember for term loan, outstanding is also termed as exposure; however for off balance sheet facilities, one has to adjust the exposure by proper UGD percentage).

In this case, UL_p is maximum. However, this situation normally does not arise in a real portfolio case. Actually, $\rho < 1$ and hence:

$$UL_{a+b} < \; << \; = UL_a + UL_b$$

Actually banks will have thousands of assets in their credit portfolio. For many assets, we may write the portfolio unexpected formula (Eq. 6.4) in a generalized form:

$$UL_P = \sqrt{\sum_{i=1}^{n} \sum_{j=1}^{n} \rho_{i,j}^d \times UL_i \times UL_j}$$ Eq. 6.5

The sign Σ denotes the algebraic sum. Where $\rho_{i,j}^d$ is the default correlation between asset i and asset j.

It means the UL_p is much lower than the aggregate of individual asset's ULs. This is because of correlation and diversification effect.

If we expand the portfolio formula in Eq. 6.5, we get:

$$ULp = \sqrt{ \begin{aligned} &UL_1 UL_2 \rho_{11} + UL_1 UL_2 \rho_{12} + UL_1 UL_3 \rho_{13} + \ldots + UL_1 UL_n \rho_{1n} + UL_2 UL_1 \rho_{21} \\ &+ UL_2 UL_2 \rho_{22} + \ldots + UL_2 UL_n \rho_{2n} + \ldots + UL_n UL_1 \rho_{n1} + UL_n UL_2 \rho_{n2} + \ldots UL_n UL_n \rho_{nn} \end{aligned} }$$

Eq. 6.5a

Because of the diversification effect:

$$UL_P << \sum_i UL_i \quad \because \rho_{i,j}^d < 1$$

Hence, for N risky assets indexed by $i = 1,2,\ldots, N$, UL_p is not equal to the linear sum of the individual ULs of the risky assets that make up the aggregate portfolio. This is due to the presence of default correlation. Because of diversification effects, the UL_p is very much smaller than the sum of the individual ULs.

This implies that only a portion of each asset's UL (or volatility of loss) actually contributes to the portfolio's total risk of loss (or overall volatility of the portfolio). This portion is called the risk contribution.

Risk contribution

Risk contribution (RC) is that measure which can help the bank to understand the extent of diversification in their credit portfolios and help them in their strategic purpose. It just tells how much incremental risk a single risky asset contributes to the portfolio as a whole.

There are two risk contributions of a single loan to the portfolio loss: (a) average risk contribution and (b) marginal risk contribution (RC).

The marginal risk contribution of an asset i (RC_i) is the incremental risk that the exposure of a single asset contributes to the portfolio's risk. Marginal risk contribution helps in analyzing how much risk a particular borrower brings to the portfolio. It can be estimated at sub-portfolio level and hard limits can be set after evaluating the risk contribution of a particular grade/sector in the total portfolio of a bank.

$$RC_i \equiv UL_i \frac{\partial UL_p}{\partial UL_i}$$ Eq. 6.6

Marginal risk contribution (RC) is also termed as unexpected loss contribution (ULC). Observe that the risk contribution of asset i is measured in terms of the units of unexpected loss of asset i, or UL_i.

The above equation shows risk contribution of asset i, RC_i, is a sensitivity measure, as represented by the partial derivatives (shows partial changes), of the UL_p with respect to the UL of asset i.

By performing the actual differentiation on equation (6.2), it can be easily shown that:

$$RC_i = \frac{UL_i \sum_j UL_j \rho_{ij}}{UL_p}$$ Eq. 6.6a

This is the equation that is used in practice to measure UL contribution of an asset.

For a two assets portfolio case, equation (6.5) can be written as:

$$RC_1 = \frac{UL_1(UL_1 + \rho_{12}UL_2)}{UL_p}$$

This is the risk contribution of first asset.
Similarly, the risk contribution of the second asset would be:

$$RC_2 = \frac{UL_2(UL_2 + \rho_{21}UL_1)}{UL_p}$$

$\rho_{12} = \rho_{21} = \rho$ is the default correlation between two assets.
It can be proved that:

$$UL_p = RC_1 + RC_2$$ Eq.6.7

Thus, UL_p is the sum of all the risk contributions from all the assets in the portfolio.

Volatility of portfolio loss is driven by two factors: concentration and correlation. Concentration describes the lumpiness of the portfolio (specific risk); correlation describes the sensitivity of the portfolio to changes in underlying macroeconomic factors (systematic risk).

Table 6.1 explains the method for calculating portfolio losses and risk contributions with a numerical exercise.

Table 6.1: Portfolio Loss Calculations for Two-asset Example

Suppose an FI manager holds the following portfolio of assets:

Borrower X got sanction of a non-amortizing secured term loan of ₹100 crore for 1 year at 13 annual interest rate; Credit rating of the borrower is A and corresponding PD = 0.50; LGD for the facility is 40.

Borrower Y got sanction of a non-amortizing unsecured term loan of ₹50 crore for 1 year at 15 annual interest rate; Credit rating of the borrower is BBB and associated PD = 1; Facility LGD = 60.

Estimated default correlation between the borrower X and borrower Y is 10.

Solution:

Expected loss of X loan and Y loan would be:

EL_X (in ₹) = EAD × PD × LGD = 100 × 0.50 × 40
= 0.20 crore

EL_Y (in ₹) = 50 × 1 × 60
= 0.30 crore

Unexpected losses of two loans would be:

$UL_X = EAD \times LGD \times \sqrt{PD \times (1-PD)} = 100 \times 40 \times \sqrt{0.50\% \times (1 - 0.50\%)}$
= 100 × 40 × 7.05
= 2.82 crore

$UL_Y = 50 \times 60 \times \sqrt{1\% \times (1 - 1\%)}$
= 50 × 60 × $\sqrt{1\% \times 99\%}$
= 2.98 crore

The portfolio expected loss (EL_p):

$EL_X + EL_Y$ = 0.20 + 0.30 = 0.50 crore or 0.33 of total portfolio exposure of ₹150 crore.

Table 6.1 contd.

Table 6.1 contd.

The portfolio unexpected loss (UL_p) in ₹:
$\sqrt{UL_X^2 + UL_Y^2 + 2 \times \rho_{X,Y}^d UL_X UL_Y}$ $= \sqrt{2.82^2 + 2.98^2 + 2 \times 10\% \times 2.82 \times 2.98}$ $= 4.307$ crore
Or it is 2.87 of the total portfolio exposure (UL_p).
The average risk contribution of assets:
$ARC_X = \dfrac{EL_X}{EL_p} = 0.13$ $ARC_Y = \dfrac{EL_Y}{EL_p} = 0.20$
The marginal risk contribution of assets:
$MRC_X = \dfrac{2.82 \times (2.82 + 10\% \times 2.98)}{4.307} = 2.043$ crore
Note that this value is $< UL_X$
$MRC_Y = \dfrac{2.98 \times (2.98 + 10\% \times 2.82)}{4.307} = 2.264 < 2.98$ crore which is UL_Y
It is important to note that
$MRC_X + MRC_Y = 2.043 + 2.264 = 4.307$ crore which is the UL_p

Source: Author's illustration.

Concept of portfolio credit risk

The ability of the bank to manage its geographic or sectoral concentration depends on how it is able to manage the risk in its credit portfolio. This further depends on rating-wise allocation of assets in sub-pools (i.e. sectors, industries, regions, etc.). Chart 6.2 demonstrates business-wise loan portfolio categorization of a bank.

Chart 6.2: Portfolio View

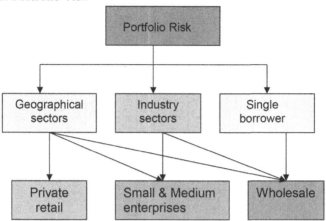

Source: Author's illustration.

A portfolio view enables a bank to monitor the movement of riskiness of the assets in a more granular way. Accordingly, the portfolio manager sitting at the central office should be able to compare the portfolio composition across regions or sectors and examine how this composition is changing over time. In order to better understand the portfolio risk characteristics, it is essential to collect the PD and LGD data at sub-portfolio levels and compare their positions in a risk return axis.

Establishing a clear risk profile and portfolio segmentation strategy will ensure appropriate risk diversification and limit downside risk potential. Risk management department can exploit techniques, like setting policy guidelines for fixing exposure limits, stipulating benchmark ratios in respect of financial risk (e.g. current ratio, debt equity ratio, debt service coverage ratio, etc.), monitoring portfolio quality across industry and regions and altering the bank's product mix time to time. The portfolio quality is evaluated by tracking the migration of borrowers from one rating category to another under various industries, business segments etc. The transition matrix provides the profile of credit quality changes or migrations that have taken place for the selected credit portfolio between any two years that are selected. It is an effective tool for credit portfolio capital allocation, loan monitoring and performance evaluation.

Next, an attempt has been made to understand the system level portfolio quality across industries in India. Table 6.2 depicts half-yearly rating position of various sectors in India during 2013–14 and 2014–15.

Table 6.2: Assessment Industry Rating Position and Sectoral Credit Growth

Industry Name	H1-2014-15			H1-2013-14			
	Upgrade Rate	Downgrade Rate	Credit Growth	Upgrade Rate	Downgrade Rate	Credit Growth	Comments
Heavy electrical equipment	5.04%	8%	6.22%	4.20%	23.50%	15.49%	Riskier
Auto Ancillaries	5.00%	6.50%	8.72%	5%	12.50%	8.57%	Moderate
Apparel & Luxury Goods	6%	7.52%	5.21%	–	–	21.52%	
Steel	9.20%	10.40%	8.05%	7.85%	10.20%	22.52%	Moderate
Industrial Machinery	10%	10%	9.44%	7.15%	15%	14.69%	
Construction & Engineering	10.50%	9.86%	14.95%	7.35%	22%	12.70%	Riskier
Real Estate Development	8.20%	7.90%	17.12%	8%	10.03%	17.93%	
Hotels & Resorts	10%	9.40%	13.84%	–	–	11.94%	
Pharmaceuticals	17%	9.40%	-6.62%	7.50%	8%	15.00%	Safer
Packaged Foods	20.60%	9.65%	26.24%	15%	5%	44.20%	Safer
Textiles	15%	5%	7.83%	8%	5.20%	14.75%	Safer
Agricultural Products	14.95%	4.85%	18.76%	11%	7.92%	9.94%	Safer
Power	–	–	14.44%	4.85%	16.30%	29.83%	Riskier
Transports	–	–	14.63%	6.30%	16.15%	21.48%	Riskier

Source: Compiled from CRISIL Report and RBI Data.

Note: June – Credit Growth rates are compared; some industries are mapped to near best to maintain consistency.

The upgrade and downgrade rates reflect the portfolio quality mix. Generally, the downgrades were due to sluggish demand or pressure on working capital (liquidity problem), poor financial position or due to default. The upgrades were the result of enhanced scale of operations or due to improvement in financial position, etc. If there are more downgrades than upgrades in an industry, it means the loan quality is deteriorating and there is an increase in perceived risk position in the industry. On the contrary, if the upgrade rate is higher than the downgrade rate, it means loan pool quality is improving in that industry segment. Degradation in credit rating adversely impacts the performance and credit availability of industrial sectors. An analysis of Table 6.2 reveals that an increase in the risk position in some industry segments (like heavy electrical equipment, power, auto ancillaries, and so on) has resulted in the slowdown in the credit growth rate. This signals some degree of concentration risk in these industries.

On the other hand, the asset quality of agricultural products and packaged foods has improved sharply, resulting in higher credit growth. Surprisingly, there is a significant fall in the credit growth rate in the pharmaceutical sector and the textile industry despite improvements in the loan quality in these segments. The changing portfolio mix has implications on the banks' aggregate credit risk weighted assets and, hence, capital adequacy ratio. This type of portfolio analysis may help our banks to understand the system level portfolio risk positions, which will ultimately guide them to design their business mix and target profitability and solvency in future. Establishing a clear risk profile and portfolio segmentation strategy will ensure appropriate risk diversification and limit downside risk potential.

Drivers of portfolio credit risk

The critical element in successfully managing a credit risk portfolio is that you must manage the dynamics of credit risk. Portfolio credit risk is the risk of changes in the market value of the portfolio over a specified time horizon as a result of changes in credit quality due to:

- Credit migration (upgrades/downgrades)
- Large loan default
- Simultaneous default (or default correlation)

A credit portfolio that is not well diversified will have higher portfolio risk in terms of both ELs and ULs relative to a more diversified portfolio. In order to take advantage of credit portfolio management opportunities, the answer to these technical questions is important:

- What is the risk of a given portfolio as opposed to individual credits comprising the portfolio?
- How do different macroeconomic scenarios at both the regional and the industry sector levels affect the portfolio's risk profile?
- What is the effect of changing the portfolio mix?

Chart 6.3 shows the key drivers of portfolio credit risk. Note that besides PD and LGD, exposure distribution (or weight) and default correlation among borrowers play an important role in measuring portfolio credit risk.

Chart 6.3: Portfolio Concept of Credit Risk

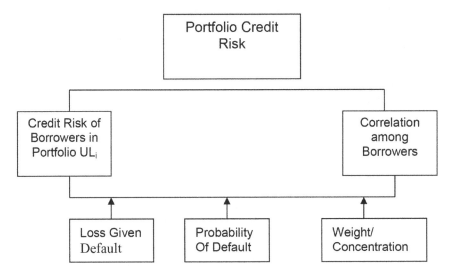

Source: Author's illustration.

Correlated credit deterioration has been the specific cause of many occurrences of financial distress in many countries (e.g. agricultural loans in US mid-west, oil loans in Texas, the Latin American debt crisis, recent US mortgage crisis). Internationally, there are a lot of incidents of clustered defaults (within industries as well as between industries). The reason being that in addition to very significant concentrations of lending in a particular industry (e.g. energy), there is regional dependence and a strong correlation between the health of the industries.

Lack of sufficient historic default data and data on credit quality co-movements makes it difficult to measure default correlation directly. However, rating agencies like Moody's, S&P have longer bond rating history that can be used to measure default correlation following the rating-based default correlation.

Default correlation

Default correlation among two assets or loans suggests the joint occurrence of their default. Default correlation or the pair-wise correlation between two assets is very important when assessing the totality of portfolio risk (UL_p). If default correlation is high, it suggests that there will be less diversification benefit. The glue that ties the risk contribution of a risky asset to the totality of the portfolio is "default correlation". The strength of the correlation is determined by macroeconomic, industrial, geographic and temporal factors. In turn, an aggregate of risk contributions from several risky assets indicate the level of concentration risk in the portfolio. Finally, the level of concentration risk decides on the degree of diversification in the portfolio. The correlation effects need to be considered carefully in the risk management and measurement of credit portfolios. However, measuring default correlation is very difficult.

We now explain few standard methods for calculating default correlation.

We first explain a simple method for computing default correlation that can be obtained from the bank's loss history. This method is also called single default correlation.

1. Loss history-based simple default correlation

Consider a simple case of a portfolio of two loans. The UL for this portfolio is given by the variance equation:

$$UL_p^2 = \rho_{11}UL_1^2 + \rho_{22}UL_2^2 + 2\rho_{11}UL_1UL_2$$

UL (loss volatility) of a loan can be expressed as:

$$UL_i = \overline{EAD} \times \overline{LGD} \times \sqrt{PD \times (1 - PD)}$$

Where, $\overline{EAD}$ is the average exposure at default, LGD is the average loss given default and PD is the probability of default.

If we consider a large number of loans in the pool, we can show that the portfolio UL_p will be:

$$UL_p^2 = \sum_{i=1}^{N}\sum_{j=1}^{N} \rho_{ij}UL_iUL_j \qquad \text{Eq. 6.8}$$

We can get an estimate for the correlation of default if we assume that the correlation between each loan is identical (i.e. $\rho_{ij} = \rho$):

$$UL_P^2 = \sum_{i=1}^{N}\sum_{j=1}^{N} \rho_{ij} UL_i UL_j$$

$$= \rho \sum_{i=1}^{N}\sum_{j=1}^{N} UL_i UL_j$$

Assuming each loan has the same UL (i.e. $UL_i = UL_j$), we can estimate the correlation as follows:

$$\rho = \frac{UL_P^2}{(\sum_{i=1}^{N} UL_i)^2} = \frac{UL_P^2}{(N^2 \times UL_i^2)} \qquad \text{Eq. 6.9}$$

Here, N is the number of loans in the portfolio. UL_P can be obtained from the volatility (standard deviation) of time series of observed portfolio losses (or default rates). Solving for ρ will yield a default rate volatility implied loss correlation number.

Note that, $UL_P = N \times \bar{E} \times UL\%_P$, where $\bar{E}$ = EAD average, $\bar{L}$ = LGD average

$$\therefore \rho = \frac{(N \times \bar{E} \times \bar{L} \times UL\%_P)^2}{(N \times \bar{E} \times \bar{L} \times UL\%_i)^2}$$

$$= \frac{UL\%_P^2}{UL\%_i^2} \qquad \text{Eq. 6.10}$$

$$= \frac{UL\%_P^2}{PD \times (1-PD)}$$

Using this approach, one can estimate the single default correlation (ρ) of a bank loan on an aggregate level. This has been shown in Table 6.3 for a bank case. The numerator of the above expression can be estimated from sample variance of time series of observations of historical default rates. The denominator values can be obtained straightforward from the long-run PD estimate for the entire pool (Bandyopadhyay and Ganguly, 2013).

The yearly default rates on bank loans are obtained from fresh slippage rate from the movement of non-performing assets (yearly additions in fresh NPA to 3 years' gross average advances).

The standard deviations are estimated from historical time series data (2001 to 2013) of fresh slippage rate which also expresses unexpected portfolio loss of the bank (refer to Table 6.3).

This correlation is a measure for the sensitivity of the bank's incremental risk of default of loans to the systematic factors which represents the state of the economy.

Table 6.3: Estimation of Single Default Correlation

Year	Gross Advances (₹ crore)	Additions in Gross NPA	Default Rate (PD)
1997–98	5,708		3.23%
1999–2000	6,956		4.89%
2000–01	9,326	236.59	5.22%
2001–02	11,076	446.32	4.53%
2002–03	14,158	601.02	3.08%
2003–04	16,524	630.28	9.02%
2004–05	20,612	527.10	1.37%
2005–06	25,299	1877.64	1.07%
2006–07	35,549	372.97	1.28%
2007–08	45,395	379.27	0.88%
2008–09	54,566	579.75	1.64%
2009–10	69,065	495.70	1.87%
2010–11	84,184	1133.10	3.98%
2011–12	96,839	1556.00	2.83%
2012–13	113,050	3,897.59	3.23%
PD			3.21%
PD volatility (UL $_\rho$)			2.23%
Total UL			17.62%
Single DC (ρ)			1.60%
Implicit AC (ρ_a)			8.30%

Source: Author's own computation-based audited annual reports of a bank.

The DC has been estimated by using equation 6.10. The implicit asset correlation (AC or ρ_a) can be extracted by using the variance equation:

$$V[\mathcal{g}(y)] - JDP(PD, \rho_a) + PD^2 = 0 \qquad \text{Eq. 6.11}$$

Wherge $V[\mathcal{g}(y)]$ = variance of historical fresh slippage rates (or UL_p^2) or variance of PD. It is estimated by sample variance of the time series of observed default rate reported in the last column of Table 6.2.

Strong sensitivity to the systematic factor implies a higher correlation of the obligor and higher volatility of the default rates. Notice that DC and AC estimates are not the same. DC estimate is much lower than the AC.

JDP in equation 6.11 is estimated using "BIVNOR" function in excel. It is a function that gives the cumulative bivariate standard normal distribution, and using this we can get an estimate of implicit AC through optimization method. This approach was also used by Gordy (2002) and Bluhm and Overbeck (2007).

Solving for ρ_a yields volatility implied asset correlation, which then has been used to estimate default correlation DC.

One can also take write-off percentage and estimate the single loss correlation using the same method. The similar approach can be extended to industry-level default correlation or regional level default correlation calculation.

Table 6.4 reports the DC and AC positions of selected Scheduled Commercial Banks in India. Their values have been derived from the variance of temporal default rates. These correlation numbers are measures for the sensitivity of the PD of a bank loan to the systematic risk factor that represents the state of the economy. The higher the correlation, the higher is the dependence to the systematic factor. The default correlation (DC) is used to compute economic capital (EC) but the asset correlation (AC) is used for calculating IRB regulatory capital (RC).

Table 6.4: Default and Asset Correlation of Indian Banks

Bank Name	Group	Probability of Default of a Loan (PD)	Default volatility of a Loan SD(PD)	Asset Correlation (AC)	Default Correlation (DC)
Allahabad Bank	Public Sector	3.13%	1.48%	4.13%	0.72%
Axis Bank	Private Sector	1.91%	1.01%	4.27%	0.54%
Bank of Baroda	Public Sector	1.65%	0.97%	4.98%	0.58%
Bank of India	Public Sector	2.02%	1.09%	4.49%	0.59%
Canara Bank	Public Sector	2.59%	1.03%	2.79%	0.42%
Central Bank	Public Sector	2.69%	0.88%	1.93%	0.30%
Corporation Bank	Public Sector	3.16%	1.55%	4.42%	0.79%

Table 6.4 contd.

Table 6.4 contd.

Dena Bank	Public Sector	3.90%	2.56%	8.15%	1.75%
Federal Bank	Private Sector	2.85%	1.45%	4.55%	0.76%
HDFC Bank	Private Sector	1.91%	0.97%	4.01%	0.51%
ICICI Bank	Private Sector	2.83%	2.58%	12.68%	2.42%
Indian Bank	Public Sector	1.28%	1.10%	8.95%	0.96%
Indian Overseas Bank	Public Sector	3.37%	1.42%	3.37%	0.62%
Indusind Bank	Private Sector	2.77%	2.51%	12.47%	2.34%
Karur Vysya Bank	Private Sector	1.57%	1.25%	8.36%	1.01%
Kotak Mahindra Bank	Private Sector	1.70%	1.16%	6.59%	0.81%
Oriental Bank of Commerce	Public Sector	3.25%	2.19%	7.95%	1.53%
Punjab National Bank	Public Sector	2.83%	1.14%	2.92%	0.47%
State Bank of India	Public Sector	3.06%	0.83%	1.39%	0.23%
Union Bank of India	Public Sector	2.35%	0.81%	2.05%	0.29%
United Bank of India	Public Sector	3.18%	2.83%	12.77%	2.61%
Yes Bank	Private Sector	0.55%	0.31%	3.25%	0.17%

Source: Audited Annual Reports of Banks.
Note: PD, Default Volatility and Asset Correlations are estimated based on their yearly NPA movements for last 15 years (2001-15).

Rating-Based Default Correlation

The rating-based default correlation approach has been shown in Lucas (1995), Nagpal and Bahar (2001), Servigny and Renault (2003), Bandyopadhyay et al. (2007), Bandyopadhyay and Ganguly (2013). These works mainly extract information about the joint behaviour of rating migrations and defaults directly from historical bond data to calculate joint default probabilities.

The correlation of default probability between two assets, i and j, can be derived by using the following expression:

$$\rho_{i,j}^{D,D} = \frac{JDP_{i,j} - PD_i PD_j}{\sqrt{PD_i(1 - PD_i)PD_j(1 - PD_j)}}$$ Eq. 6.12

The joint default probability between two industries, say i and j ($JDP_{i,j}$), is the probability that loans in both industries will default at the same time. It describes the joint movement of credit quality between two obligors in the portfolio. Clearly, the correlation will be positive if the JDP is larger than the product of the univariate probabilities. The main difficulty is to estimate the JDP.

Estimation of joint default probability by counting joint rating migration

Consider the joint migration of two obligors from the same class I (say, IG rating class: AAA to BBB graded borrowers) to default (D). Assume that at the beginning of the year t, we have N_t^i firms rated i (IG borrowers). From a given set with N_t^i accounts, we can create $N_t^i(N_t^i - 1)/2$ different pairs (through combination method). Using D_t^i, denote the number of accounts (or borrowers) migrating from this IG group to default D, we can create $D_t^i(D_t^i - 1)/2$ defaulting pairs. Taking the ratio of the number of pairs that defaulted to the number of pairs that can possibly default, we obtain an estimation of the joint probability if we do it over a longer history of n years of data.

$$JDP_{i,i} = \sum_t w_t \frac{D_t^i(D_t^i - 1)}{N_t^i(N_t^i - 1)} \qquad \text{Eq. 6.13}$$

This formula was used by Lucas (1995) and Bahar and Nagpal (2001) to estimate joint probability of default. Although quite logical, the above estimator has the drawback that it can generate spurious negative correlation when default incidents are very few (say $D = 1$ but $N = 10$).

Accordingly, to mitigate the spurious negative correlation, the JDP formula for same grades (i, i) has been modified below:

$$JDP_{i,i} = \sum_t w_t \frac{(D_t^i)^2}{(N_t^i)^2} \qquad \text{Eq. 6.13a}$$

Following the same approach, 1-year joint default probability of two obligors from different rating classes (say between IG and NIG class of assets) can also be estimated:

$$JDP_{ij} = \sum_t w_t \frac{D_t^i D_t^j}{N_t^i N_t^j} \qquad \text{Eq. 6.14}$$

D_i and D_j are the number of defaults in a given year t from respective grades (IG and NIG) and N_i and N_j are the corresponding number of borrowers in the beginning of the year in each grade, where $w_t = \dfrac{N_t^i N_t^j}{\sum N_i N_j}$; D_t^i & D_t^j are the number of defaults in a given year.

All these movements can be tracked from the rating transition history data of a bank.

We also have to estimate rating-wise long-run PDs by taking weighted average of obtaining the estimates of JDP and PDs across and between grades, finally default correlation (DC) can be derived using equation 6.12.

The rating grade-wise default correlation estimation method has been demonstrated in Table 6.5. This correlation analysis is based on a CRISIL rating Indian companies from 1992–93 to 2012–13.

Table 6.5: Estimation of Rating-wise Default Correlation

Year	Rating Grade: IG Count of D	Rating Grade: IG Count of N$	Rating Grade: NIG Count of D	Rating Grade: NIG Count of N	JDP IG–IG	Weight	JDP IG– NIG	Weight	JDP NIG– NIG	Weight
1992–93	0	96	0	3	0.00%	1.53%	0.00%	0.48%	0.00%	0.07%
1993–94	0	151	0	5	0.00%	3.80%	0.00%	1.25%	0.00%	0.20%
1994–95	0	184	0	1	0.00%	5.64%	0.00%	0.30%	0.00%	0.01%
1995–96	1	215	1	6	0.00%	7.69%	0.08%	2.13%	2.78%	0.29%
1996–97	3	266	2	12	0.01%	11.78%	0.19%	5.27%	2.78%	1.16%
1997–98	2	278	7	23	0.01%	12.86%	0.22%	10.56%	9.26%	4.26%
1998–99	15	243	20	40	0.38%	9.83%	3.09%	16.05%	25.00%	12.90%
1999–00	2	206	15	44	0.01%	7.06%	0.33%	14.97%	11.62%	15.61%
2000–01	3	181	8	32	0.03%	5.45%	0.41%	9.57%	6.25%	8.25%
2001–02	2	170	7	20	0.01%	4.81%	0.41%	5.62%	12.25%	3.22%
2002–03	1	129	4	11	0.01%	2.77%	0.28%	2.34%	13.22%	0.98%
2003–04	1	148	0	6	0.00%	3.65%	0.00%	1.47%	0.00%	0.29%

Table 6.5 contd.

Table 6.5 contd.

2004–05	0	149	2	3	0.00%	3.70%	0.00%	0.74%	44.44%	0.07%
2005–06	0	95	0	1	0.00%	1.50%	0.00%	0.16%	0.00%	0.01%
2006–07	0	128	0	1	0.00%	2.73%	0.00%	0.21%	0.00%	0.01%
2007–08	0	123	1	1	0.00%	2.52%	0.00%	0.20%	100.00%	0.01%
2008–09	2	191	0	9	0.01%	6.07%	0.00%	2.84%	0.00%	0.65%
2009–10	1	90	1	21	0.01%	1.35%	0.05%	3.12%	0.23%	3.56%
2010–11	0	100	11	41	0.00%	1.66%	0.00%	6.77%	7.20%	13.55%
2011–12	2	107	8	45	0.03%	1.91%	0.33%	7.95%	3.16%	16.32%
2012–13	1	101	8	48	0.01%	1.70%	0.17%	8.01%	2.78%	18.57%
Total	36	3351	95	373	100.00%		100.00%			
Avg. PD		1.07%		25.47%						
Avg. JDP					0.04%		0.69%		8.57%	
DC					3.11%		9.28%		10.97%	

Source: CRISIL bond rating data.
Note: Number of rated IG in the beginning of the year (withdrawal adjusted).

The estimated default correlation coefficients are further reported in Table 6.6.

Table 6.6: Overall IG–NIG Default Correlations (%), 1992–93 to 2012–13

	IG	NIG
IG	2.99	8.21
NIG	8.21	10.03

Source: CRISIL bond rating data.

Table 6.6 best captures the effect of the common macroeconomic environment on correlated defaults. As we move from IG–IG to NIG–NIG category (i.e. credit quality worsens as PD increases), default correlation also rises.

The results reflect that default correlation within IG group is lower than the default correlation within the NIG group over a 1-year horizon for all industries taken together. The values of significant positive default correlations are much higher than those quoted for developed economies that are reported in Servigny and Renault (2004) and Lucas (1995), respectively.

Table 6.7 and 6.7a report the default correlations across more granular rating scales (AAA to CCC) for Indian and global corporates. The second table has been reported for benchmarking purpose. It is quite evident that with declining credit quality, we see that, default correlation increases within the same rating grade. Both the tables also show that there is relatively lower default correlation between the lower grade categories than between the higher rating grades.

Table 6.7: Default Correlation across Rating Grades, 1992–93 to 2008–09

	AAA	AA	A	BBB	BB	B	CCC
AAA	0.00						
AA	0.00	1.46					
A	0.00	3.14	4.46				
BBB	0.00	3.90	3.90	6.23			
BB	0.00	10.24	14.16	20.49	32.93		
B	0.00	−2.02	−5.35	11.64	−2.88	30.02	
CCC	0.00	5.35	9.22	20.60	17.29	2.19	22.14

Source: Author's own estimates.

Table 6.7a: Global Rating-wise Default Correlations (%) – All Countries, All Industries, 1981–2002, S&P Credit Pro

Rating	AAA	AA	A	BBB	BB	B	CCC
AAA	NA						
AA	NA	0.16					
A	NA	0.02	0.12				
BBB	NA	−0.03	0.03	0.33			
BB	NA	0.00	0.19	0.35	0.94		
B	NA	0.10	0.22	0.30	0.84	1.55	
CCC	NA	0.06	0.26	0.89	1.45	1.67	8.97

Source: Servigny and Renault (2004), Using, S&P CreditPro database of 10,000 firms and 22 years' data, computed the above default correlation table.

The grade-wise correlation estimates provide us more detailed picture to understand the effect of concentration risk in the credit portfolio. As far as external rating grade-wise movements are concerned, default correlation monotonically increases as we move down to the rating scale. However, between grades correlation figures reveal that there is a diversification of risk between A–AA, AA–BBB, A–BBB, AA–B, A–B and even in B–BB. The above default correlation matrix may guide IRB banks to make portfolio selection to optimize return and save capital.

Equity Correlation as Proxy

Equity correlation can be used as a proxy approach for estimating asset correlation and default correlation. In this case, equity correlation of industry index return (ρ_e) can be taken as a substitute for asset correlation.

The correlation of asset returns between two industries (X and Y) is:

$$\rho(X, Y) = w_1^X \times w_2^Y \times \rho_e \qquad \text{Eq. 6.15}$$

The symbols w_1, w_2 are industry specific weights which can be represented either by their respective market size or exposure size. One can use regression equation on equity return of industry stock indexes over the market index (e.g. S&P CNX 500) return and estimate obligor-specific (or idiosyncratic) risk weight (w) by using: $1 - R^2$; where R^2 (captures systematic risk).

One can also use company beta and multiply their industry equity correlation to obtain asset correlation.

As a next step, in both the cases, use joint distribution function "bivnor" to convert asset correlation into joint default probability (JDP). For this, borrower (or industry) PD estimates have to be used as key inputs in JDP (or bivnor) function.

The relationship between joint default probability and asset correlation is expressed by the following equation:

$$JDP_{ij} = \Pr[A_i \leq K_i, A_j \leq K_j]$$

$$= N_2(K_i, K_j, \rho_{ij}^a) \qquad \text{Eq. 6.16}$$

where N_2 (.) denotes the cumulative bivariate standard normal distribution, ρ_{ij}^a denotes the asset correlation between firm i and firm j. The joint default probability is the probability that both obligors default at a fixed time horizon (of say 1 year) that means their assets fall below a certain threshold as depicted in Merton (1974) based KMV model.

This joint dependence in default (JDP) among borrowers may be triggered by common underlying factors (call it systematic factor like changes in unemployment rate, changes in raw material prices, input price changes, etc.). There is enough historical evidence that support the idea that credit events are correlated (like studies by Nagpal and Bahar, 2001; Servigny and Renault, 2003; Bandyopadhyay, et al., 2007).

The joint default probability (JDP) between borrowers can be estimated from equation 6.16. One can use bivariate normal cumulative density function: $BIVNOR[\phi^{-1}(PD_i), \phi^{-1}(PD_j) \cdot \rho_{ij}^a]$ function (see Crouhy et al., 2000; Gordy, 2000, Gordy and Heitfield, 2002). This "bivnor" function can be used in excel. In this case, equity correlation between industry index return (ρ_e) can be taken as proxy for asset correlation.

We assume that when the asset value of a firm A_i falls below a critical default threshold say K_i (popularly known as distance to default), default is triggered.

Thus,

$$PD_i = \Pr[A_i \leq K_i]$$
$$\Rightarrow K_i = N^{-1}(PD_i)$$

Eq. 6.16a

We substitute the asset correlation and default thresholds using industry PDs in the bivariate joint distribution function (Eq. 6.16) and find out joint default probabilities ($JDPs$).

Finally, given the values of JDP_{ij} (empirically derived), PD-implied default correlation (DC) between borrowers can be estimated using equation 6.12.

Numerical Illustration 1: Borrower-wise Correlation Estimation

Borrower X (Hero Moto Corp) and borrower Y (Tata Steel) are in automobile and metal industries, respectively, and let ρ_e be the industry correlation between industry equity returns. Both the borrowers are listed in the stock market and their respective bond ratings are AAA and BB.

We take their equity returns as proxy for asset return. We run two ordinary least square (OLS) regressions based on their daily equity returns. In each time series regression, the dependent variable is company stock return (R_{co}) and independent variable is industry return (R_{ind}). We thus obtain the following estimated beta regression equations:

$R_x = 0.0002 + 0.775\ R_{auto}$ Eq. 6.17

$R_Y = -0.0002 + 1.030\ R_{steel}$ Eq.6.17a

The intercept portions of the above equations capture the idiosyncratic borrower risk and the slope beta coefficients depict the industry effects. The asset return of each obligor is the weighted average of obligor-specific return (captured by the intercept) and industry return (captured by the beta coefficient).

Both are obtained from their daily equity returns (Co. vs. industry) for the period 1 January 2004 to 14 November 2013.

The obligor-specific returns are also known as idiosyncratic returns for the respective borrowers. Let's assume that idiosyncratic returns are independent – i.e. intercept terms are uncorrelated.

Next, we estimate that the industry equity correlation between the auto and steel sectors and the correlation coefficient is (ρ_e) 72.23 per cent.

We can immediately calculate the two firms' asset correlation:

Corr $(X,Y) = \text{Cov}(R_X, R_Y)$; assuming asset returns have unit variance.
$= 0.775 \times 1.030 \times \text{Cov}(R_{auto}, R_{metal})$
$= 0.775 \times 1.030 \times 0.7223$
$= 0.5764$

Note that with unit variance, correlation and covariance values are same.

Now, we can estimate the joint default probability by using equation 6.16. To complete the estimation process, we obtain the PD values for both the companies. The 1-year average default rates for issuers in AAA and BB categories (mapped from CRISIL's transition matrix), we find $PD_{AAA} = 0.03\%$ for company X and $PD_{BB} = 5.15\%$ for company Y.

Therefore, JDP $= N_2(PD_X, PD_Y, 5.4\%)$
$= N_2[N^{-1}(0.03\%), N^{-1}(5.15\%, 57.64\%)]$
$= \text{bivnor}(-3.43, -1.63, 57.64\%)]$
$= 0.02173\%$

Finally, the default correlation (DC) is obtained as 5.274 per cent (using the formula 6.12).

This way, one can estimate pair-wise asset correlations for publicly traded firms using the above factor model. In principle, pair-wise default correlations between obligors need to be calculated, but this is not practical given the fact that bank as thousands of individual assets in its portfolio. For a credit portfolio containing $N = 1,000$ borrowers, there are 499,500 possible pairs of obligors.

In order to obtain quick estimates, borrowers/firms are categorized into several industry groups according to their industry affiliation and then industry–industry default correlations are computed.

To estimate default correlation between industry indices, we need to determine asset correlation among them using equity proxy. For this, the required industry weights to capture obligor-specific indiosyncratic risk can be determined running a regression on industry equity index return (say auto, metal indices) vis-à-vis its market index return (e.g. S&PCNX500 index return). The regression results are summarized in Table 6.8.

Table 6.8: Industry Risk Weights

Industry	R^2	$1 - R^2$ (Idiosyncratic)	Industry Beta
Auto	0.741802	0.258198	0.871207
Bank	0.680956	0.319044	0.895398
Energy	0.774114	0.225886	0.888861
Finance	0.861354	0.138646	1.108489
FMCG	0.479641	0.520359	0.482059
IT	0.274336	0.725664	1.451868
Media	0.823936	0.176064	1.146431
Metal	0.812491	0.187509	1.402146
Pharma	0.554093	0.445907	0.581394
Realty	0.871751	0.128249	1.904402

Source: Author's own estimates based on CMIE Prowess Sectoral Equity Index (Monthly) data.

The industry-specific weights $(1 - R^2)$ are then used in equation 6.15 to convert equity correlation to proxy asset correlation between two industries.

Numerical Illustration 2: Industry correlation estimation

Here, we explain the process of extracting default correlation from asset correlation from industry groupings. We first estimate the equity return correlations of 25 industries by using the monthly industry stock index return from February 1999 to March 2009.

We have used regression equation on equity return of industry stock indexes over the market index (BSE 500) return and find obligor-specific risk weight (or idiosyncratic) by using: $1 - R^2$; where R^2 (captures systematic risk) is the ESS/TSS. For this, we have used 10 years of monthly equity returns data from February 1999 till March 2009.

Next, we convert the equity correlation into asset return correlation proxy by multiplying the respective industry-specific idiosyncratic risk weights. Then, along with asset correlation proxy, industry PDs are also used to derive their joint default probabilities (equations 6.15 and 6.16). The industry-wide PDs are obtained from CRISIL data.

Finally, the industry–industry default correlations are estimated from their JDPs and PDs. The estimated industry default correlation values are reported in Table 6.9.

It is important to note that default correlations within same industries are significantly higher than the between industry correlations. Higher the correlation values, greater is the concentration risk in the credit portfolio.

Default correlation describes the degree to which the default risk of one borrower one industry depends on the default risk of another borrower in another or same industry. Therefore, default correlation risk represents the risk that several borrowers default together in clusters.

Since two industry's risk position may be affected by common macroeconomic factors either because they are located in the same geography or purchase the raw material from the same source or serve the same market or due to input–output linkage effects, we have dependence between their defaults.

Here, default correlation is measuring clustered defaults within sector as well as across sector. The correlation coefficient is capturing the effect of one borrower default in one industry to another borrower default in the same industry (within sector correlation) or in the different industry (cross-sectoral correlation). Like cross-sectoral correlation between automobile and coal and lignite sectors (SL#1-SL#4) is 2.6 per cent, which means if one borrower defaults in SL#1 sector, the probability of another borrower default in SL#4 sector goes up by 260 basis points.

It is worthwhile to mention that default dependencies may be more pronounced during macroeconomic stress condition. Default correlations have a strong impact on the tail portion of the credit loss distribution for a large portfolio because of common systematic factors.

Table 6.9: The System Level Industry Default Correlation Estimates in India

SL# Industry	1	2	3	4	5	6	7	8	9	10	11	12	13	14	15	16	17	18	19	20	21	22	23	24	25
1 Auto	0.06																								
2 Cement	0.06	0.26																							
3 Chemical	0.00	0.00	0.00																						
4 Coal&Lignite	0.44	0.53	0.03	10.82																					
5 Computer	0.00	0.00	0.00	0.01	0.00																				
6 Construction	0.29	0.40	0.02	3.18	0.01	2.55																			
7 Electricity	0.16	0.21	0.01	2.06	0.00	1.19	0.93																		
8 Engineering	0.02	0.03	0.00	0.19	0.00	0.15	0.08	0.01																	
9 Ferrous Metal	0.29	0.48	0.02	3.08	0.01	2.06	1.14	0.16	2.61																
10 Gems&Jewellery	0.35	0.43	0.02	3.40	0.01	2.52	1.31	0.20	2.56	4.54															
11 Leather&Pdcts	0.14	0.25	0.01	1.27	0.01	1.12	0.47	0.10	1.01	1.60	1.67														
12 Misc.Manuf	0.28	0.42	0.02	2.81	0.01	2.16	1.06	0.16	2.08	2.65	1.31	2.47													
13 NBFCs	0.26	0.37	0.01	2.68	0.01	1.92	1.10	0.16	2.11	2.50	1.10	2.05	2.61												
14 Non-Ferrous Metal	0.06	0.11	0.00	0.43	0.00	0.36	0.20	0.03	0.41	0.44	0.24	0.37	0.35	0.13											
15 Paper&Pdcts	0.27	0.52	0.01	2.43	0.01	1.88	0.95	0.16	2.11	2.27	1.14	2.31	1.94	0.42	3.25										
16 Petroleum Pdcts	0.03	0.05	0.00	0.30	0.00	0.20	0.13	0.02	0.21	0.23	0.12	0.21	0.20	0.04	0.19	0.03									
17 Processed Food	0.34	0.57	0.02	3.81	0.01	2.76	1.35	0.22	2.55	3.74	1.95	3.09	2.76	0.42	2.71	0.24	8.65								
18 Rubber & Pdcts	0.38	0.54	0.02	4.00	0.01	2.82	1.32	0.23	2.87	3.26	1.48	3.11	2.94	0.56	3.07	0.25	3.87	14.32							
19 Sugar	0.48	0.80	0.03	5.15	0.01	3.69	2.05	0.24	3.73	4.26	1.85	3.64	3.47	0.63	3.21	0.37	4.22	5.04	13.73						
20 Tea	0.23	0.42	0.01	2.32	0.01	1.62	0.88	0.14	1.77	2.15	1.24	1.88	1.65	0.33	2.00	0.17	2.56	2.35	3.45	3.36					
21 Telecom	0.06	0.09	0.00	0.56	0.00	0.40	0.24	0.04	0.42	0.50	0.27	0.44	0.51	0.08	0.41	0.05	0.77	0.65	0.64	0.37	0.38				
22 Textiles	0.32	0.52	0.02	2.94	0.01	2.24	1.17	0.19	2.63	3.17	1.50	2.51	2.47	0.48	2.67	0.22	3.31	3.57	4.09	2.23	0.55	3.61			
23 Trading	0.03	0.05	0.00	0.20	0.00	0.19	0.10	0.02	0.22	0.28	0.16	0.23	0.24	0.05	0.24	0.02	0.33	0.33	0.29	0.20	0.07	0.28	0.05		
24 Transport Serv	0.22	0.24	0.02	2.97	0.00	1.50	0.98	0.10	1.40	1.60	0.66	1.40	1.32	0.23	1.15	0.17	1.68	2.01	2.65	1.02	0.28	1.43	0.11	1.92	
25 Veg Oil & Pdcts	0.39	0.48	0.02	4.18	0.01	2.68	1.47	0.18	2.46	2.62	1.29	2.61	2.40	0.43	2.05	0.24	3.55	3.48	5.13	2.21	0.49	2.74	0.23	1.74	11.98

Source: Author's own estimates based on 10 years' monthly industry equity index series and industry default data.

Measurement of portfolio concentration risk

As a matter of legacy, most banks have originated and are holding loan exposures that are the function of their geography and industry orientation. Banks tend to specialize in specific industries or geographical areas. As a result, they do hold concentration risk. Over time, credit portfolios might become increasingly concentrated in less creditworthy obligors not necessarily by choice but by chance. Furthermore, some banks maintain a close relationship with big clients/corporate groups in the hope of generating more business down the road. Subsequently, in meeting credit targets, many incur substantial concentration risk with specific borrowers (Michael Ong, 1999). These three situations, on which banks have little control, may make them more vulnerable to economic downturns. Hence, the measurement and monitoring of concentration risk by banks is a necessity for regulatory compliance under Pillar II of Basel II for IRB banks.

Credit concentrations in a lending portfolio can be viewed by borrower rating, credit product, industry and region-wise distribution of assets. The portfolio quality can be maintained by stipulation of exposure ceiling limit for individual borrower, group and industry, which is reviewed periodically on the basis of industry study. Banks have policies to establish a limit on how much the institution is willing to lend to an individual borrower or to an industry. These limits may vary from bank to bank. Limits can be established as an absolute amount or as a percentage of the entire portfolio. For example, bank management may mention in a policy that no more than 15 per cent of its total loan portfolio would be in construction lending. Bank can also stipulate quantitative ceiling on aggregate exposure in specified rating categories.

A bank can measure credit concentrations with widely used metrics like Hirschman Herfindahl Index (HHI), Gini coefficient (or Lorenz curve), Theil inequality index, etc.

The Herfindahl Index measures concentration as the sum of the squared business share of each loan in the pool (or portfolio), i.e.:

$$HHI = \frac{\sum_{n=1}^{N} E_n^2}{\sum_{n=1}^{N} E_n} = \sum_{n=1}^{N} s_n^2 \qquad \text{Eq. 6.18}$$

Where E = loan exposure amount (₹ crore) and s = loan share to total. The HHI is calculated by summing the squares of the portfolio share of each contributor.

HHI is a continuous measure with zero corresponding to the fully granular case (where each borrower has an infinitesimal share) and unity corresponds to maximum concentration (single exposure in the pool). Keeping everything else equal, the closer the HHI of a portfolio is to 1, the more concentrated the portfolio is and, hence, higher the appropriate granularity add-on charge in terms of capital/pricing will have to be imposed on the portfolio.

For example, consider a portfolio with six loans, with respective business share of 30 per cent, 20 per cent, 20 per cent, 10 per cent, 10 per cent and 10 per cent the Herfindahl index will be $(0.3 \times 0.3) + (0.2 \times 0.2) + (0.2 \times 0.2) + (0.1 \times 0.1) + (0.1 \times 0.1) + (0.1 \times 0.1) = 0.09 + 0.04 + 0.04 + 0.01 + 0.01 + 0.01 = 0.2$.

If all loans in an industry or loan pool have equal share, the reciprocal of the Herfindahl index $(1/H)$ will equal the number of loans in the industry/ loan pool. For portfolio in which loans have unequal share, the reciprocal of the Herfindahl indicates the "equivalent" number of loans. In this example, the six loans in the pool have the same level of concentration as an industry with $1/0.2 = 5$ competitors with equal business share.

Theoretically, a perfectly diversified portfolio of 500 borrowers would have HHI = 0.002. In contrast, if the bank portfolio is divided among five zones in the ratio of 5:2:1:1:1, then the implied HHI by sector is 0.32, indicating a significant level of concentration. However, the HHI of 0.32 does not hint at ways to lower the concentration. This is perhaps a major drawback of this method. As a general rule, an HHI below 0.1 signals low concentration, while an HHI above 0.18 signals high concentration. Between 0.1 and 0.18, the industry is moderately concentrated.

A more risk sensitive EL-based HHI may also be used to assess and compare concentration risk in rated corporate loan pools. In this approach, loss concentration measure is calculated using the expected rupee loss share (ELi) to portfolio loss share (EL_p). This EL-based measure is summarized in the following formula:

$$HHI = \sum \left(\frac{ELi}{ELp} \right)^2 \qquad \text{Eq.6.19}$$

EL = EAD × PD × LGD

EAD = Exposure at default; PD = Yearly probability of default calculated by a pooled method; LGD = Annualized loss given default obtained from bank's historical aggregate recovery data.

An alternative to measuring concentration relative to a theoretically fully diversified portfolio is to measure such concentration relative to a well-diversified benchmark portfolio through concentration entropy index of Theil (1976).

Theil entropy measure

We have used Entropy measure developed by the Theil (1967, 1977). Theil's entropy (Ex) statistic is a flexible, mathematically elegant and underutilized tool for measuring inequality in a credit portfolio across rating grades, industries, business, regions, etc.

To compute Theil's T-statistic, we simply multiply loan exposure share (x_i = L_i / L_T) and the natural logarithm of the quotient of exposure share (x_i) and the population share ($pi = N_i / N_T$); and then add these products for each year.

$$E_x = \sum_i^N x_i \ln(\frac{x_i}{p_i})$$

Where x = Exposure share
p = population share or number of borrowers share to total
i = grade or industry or regions
E_x is the measure of inequality in exposures. E_x takes a non-negative value. E_x = 0 if there is non-inequality. Thus, an equally distributed loan portfolio is denoted by zero Entropy (E_x = 0). This happens when the population share and the exposure share across rating grades or industries or regions are equal.

Geographic Concentration Measure: Gini-Lorenz Concentration Measure

Gini coefficient provides another method of measuring concentration. Diagrammatically, if the area between the line of perfect equality and the Lorenz curve is denoted by X and the area under the Lorenz curve is denoted by Y, then Gini coefficient is $G = X/(X + Y)$. This ratio can be interpreted as the concentration index. The Lorenz curve plots cumulative per cent share of loan amount to total pool (vertical axis) to per cent share of accounts number to total corporate pool (horizontal axis).

A value of Gini coefficient close to zero (the 45 degree diagonal line – no inequality) corresponds to a well-diversified portfolio where all exposures are more or less equally distributed and a value close to one corresponds to a highly concentrated portfolio. A Gini coefficient of 0.3 or less indicates substantial equality; 0.3 to 0.4 indicates the acceptable normality; and 0.4 or higher is considered too large. A gini range of 0.6 or higher is predictive of high inequality.

Longer the distance of the Lorenz curve from the diagonal line, greater is the presence of inequality (or higher is the concentration level of that region). Similarly, shorter the distance of the Lorenz curve from the 45° diagonal line, lower is the concentration ranking of that region. Using this as criteria, one can easily read Chart 6.4 and compare the zones in terms of concentration ranking. It is quite evident that loan distribution in the North Zone, Mumbai Zone and West Zone I are more unequal as compared to East Zone, Central Zone I, Central Zone II and West Zone II. Thus, the deciles-based inequality measure gives us more realistic measure of concentration.

Banks need to identify concentration based on common and/or correlated risk factors and assess its impact in terms of risk capital and bank solvency. There is an expectation on banks to measure concentration risks and explicitly consider the extent of credit risk concentrations in their assessment of capital adequacy under Pillar II of Basel II/III.

Chart 6.4: Gini-Lorenz Curve to Measure Zonal Concentration Risk

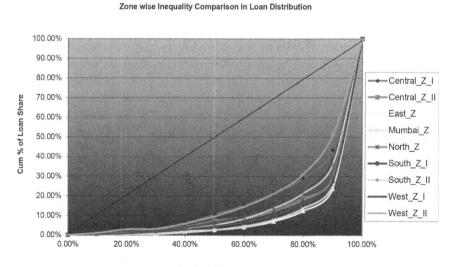

Source: Author's illustration.

Exposure vs. risk concentration

Credit concentrations in the lending portfolio can be examined from different angles by borrowers, regions, industry, rating, size, etc. The exposure inequality needs to be compared accordingly across many dimensions to better understand their extent of concentration in the bank's credit portfolio. Table 6.10 documents the industry-wise loan size distribution.

The size-wise distribution of loans and the quality of each industrial portfolio has been analyzed to ascertain the industries contributing to industry concentration. The average exposure and percentile values including maximum size of the loan gives idea about the allocation of various sizes of loans. To better compare the level of loan concentration (or inequality in the distribution of sizes) we measure the coefficient of variation (cv), skewness (sk), kurtosis (kurt), Gini coefficient and Theil inequality. The higher the value of these estimates, the greater the inequality in the loan allocation within the region and, hence, higher is the concentration.

This three dimensional view will help the central risk management department of a bank to identify the root cause of concentration risk contributing to the credit portfolio of the bank. Using this method, we can identify that industry concentration is higher in chemical, construction, gems and jewellery, NBFC and in coal and mining industries. The higher concentration arises due to the presence of few big size loans within the region. We have also examined the risk-wise concentration in the exposure distribution. To evaluate this, we find out and report the internal risk rating of three largest loan exposures (few cases all three ratings are not available). If grades are at risky side, then concentration risks in those industries/regions are effectively higher. In terms of risk consideration, concentration is higher in coal and mining, chemical, financial services and other metal industries. The regions granting such loans are also identified.

Estimation of concentration risk through marginal risk capital

The best way to measure the risk of a concentrated portfolio is to find correlation between the bank's loss volatility vis-à-vis segment's volatility and their increased capital requirements by estimating their marginal risk contributions.

In order to measure the marginal risk contribution (MRC) of each obligor, it is essential to know the default correlation (with the systematic factor) across rating grades (if rating is available). It is a measure to dependence among risks due to serial correlation with the common risk factor.

Table 6.10: Descriptive Statistics for Exposure Concentration of Large Borrowers (of A/Cs > Rs. 5 Crore exposure)

Units in ₹ crore

SL #	Industry	N	Mean	P50	P99	Max	CV	SK	Kurt	Gini	Theil	Rating	Region
1	Auto & parts	58	13.55	7.24	120.23	120.23	1.38	3.84	20.78	0.54	0.55	A, BBB	MUM, DEL
2	Cement	29	33.37	7.29	348.17	348.17	2.20	3.33	13.69	0.74	1.12	C,A+	HYD,ND
3	Chemical	66	25.92	6.18	399.96	399.96	2.37	4.14	23.00	0.76	1.13	C,B	MUM,DEL
4	Coal & Mining	197	25.16	4.85	961.28	1543.8	5.21	9.81	105.2	0.82	2.06	B,B+,C	MUM,ND
5	Construction	261	26.63	6.07	459.26	1000	3.10	7.93	82.34	0.76	1.36	A+,A+,A	UP, ND, MUM
6	Edu-Services	105	10.13	5.69	66.69	72.77	1.28	2.95	12.51	0.51	0.49	A, A+	BANG,PUN,CHEN
7	Engineering	94	9.44	4.62	77.50	77.50	1.46	2.82	11.64	0.58	0.61	AA,A,BBB	ND,GUJ, MUM
8	Film	7	36.54	10.68	85.73	85.73	1.02	0.33	1.21	0.50	0.49	A, A+	MUM, ND
9	Fin. Services	31	64.91	0.22	1000.4	1000.4	2.87	4.35	22.05	0.75	1.16	C,B+, BB	MUM
10	Food	143	16.2	7.54	174.99	183.43	1.58	4.18	24.80	0.58	0.65	B+,B+	ND
11	Gems & Jewel	36	9.73	6.47	49.16	49.16	1.18	2.01	7.01	0.45	0.36	BBB,BB	AHM,ND
12	Infrastructure	181	93.05	36.39	1012.8	1164	1.76	3.61	19.01	0.43	0.30	B+,B+,A	PAT,CHAND,JAIP
13	Iron & Steel	230	20.65	7.54	198.01	497.38	2.23	6.58	59.22	0.66	0.93	B+,B+,A+	BIH,BANG,RAJ
14	IT Software	16	10.20	6.57	32.25	32.25	0.99	1.19	3.10	0.68	0.89	A,A+	ND
15	Leather	7	5.16	5.83	14.87	14.87	1.02	0.75	2.63	0.31	0.18	B+,A	KOL,AGRA
16	NBFCs	34	118.54	36.93	1700	1700	2.62	4.34	21.72	0.74	1.24	A,A++,A+	MUM,ND
17	Other Metal	27	18.72	6.79	273.79	273.79	2.75	4.76	24.13	0.68	1.24	C, B+	MUM
18	Paper	54	17.08	8.86	164.01	164.01	1.54	3.69	19.53	0.59	0.66	BB, B+	AMRIT
19	Plastic	38	8.06	5.56	36.14	36.14	0.99	1.72	5.72	0.47	0.38	A+,A	KOL,HYD
20	Services	72	17.44	10.62	71.16	71.16	1.01	1.29	3.79	0.51	0.44	A, A+	MUM
21	Sugar	18	63.88	25.68	500.04	500.04	1.85	3.06	11.66	0.67	0.92	A,C	GHAZ,ND
22	Textiles	170	21.64	7.92	154.08	215.99	1.52	3.03	13.71	0.62	0.72	BBB, BB	ND
23	Other	28	2.78	1.37	21.44	21.44	1.46	3.63	17.25	0.54	0.57	BBB, B+	CHAND
	Total	1902	29.43	7.01	450	1700	3.22	9.67	126.5	0.75	1.34		

Source: Author's illustration.

Note: AHM: Ahmedabad, AMRIT: Amritsar, BANG: Bangalore, BIH: Bihar, CHAND: Chandigarh, CHEN: Chennai, DEL: Delhi, GHAZ: Ghaziabad, GUJ: Gujarat, HYD: Hyderabad, JAIP: Jaipur, KOL: Kolkata, MUM: Mumbai, ND: New Delhi, PAT: Patna, PUN: Pune, RAJ: Rajasthan, and UP: Uttar Pradesh.

Marginal risk contribution $MRC_i = \sqrt{r_i} \times UL_i \times Exposure_i$ $\qquad$ Eq.6.20

MRC is also termed as UL contribution. The correlation value r_i is the average default correlation, UL_i is the UL of the obligor and $Exposure_i$ is the amount of loan outstanding with the obligor.

We first estimate the rating-wise average default correlation (r_i) of a leading Indian public sector bank. For this, rating-wise yearly default rate information has been obtained for its all internally rated corporate accounts (see Table 6.9). These corporate loans are generally large loans whose exposures are above ₹100 million.

Rating-wise single default correlation values have been estimated using equation 6.10 that has been worked out in the previous section. Next, the implied asset correlation (AC) values have been extracted using variance equation 6.11.

Note that AC can be extracted using variance equation 6.11:

$$V[g(y)] - JDP(PD, \rho) + PD^2 = 0$$

where $V[g(y)]$ = variance of historical fresh slippage rates (or $UL_p{}^2$)

It is important to note that conceptually, there is a difference between default correlation (DC) and asset correlation (AC). Default correlations are generally lower than the asset correlations. Asset correlations (ACs) are used for estimating IRB risk weights and regulatory capital, whereas default correlations (DCs) are used to estimate economic capital.

Table 6.11 estimates reveal that up to LR6 grade, DC does not monotonically increase with PD. The bank can derive some diversification benefits due to less DC across LR2–LR6 grades. This result is of significance for Indian banks. It implies that poor credit quality commercial loan portfolios would have to be supported by a higher level of economic capital. This is not just because the default probabilities in such portfolios will be high, but also because of higher inherent DCs between poor credit quality borrowers.

Table 6.11: Estimation of Rating-wise Single Default Correlation

Yearly Cohort	LR1	LR2	LR3	LR4	LR5	LR6	LR7	LR8
2002–03	0.00%	0.00%	0.00%	0.00%	0.63%	5.35%	8.57%	30.00%
2003–04	0.00%	0.00%	0.00%	0.00%	0.59%	3.24%	21.33%	30.77%
2004–05	1.37%	0.72%	0.29%	0.27%	0.26%	3.76%	8.47%	25.93%

Table 6.11 contd.

Table 6.11 contd.

2005–06	0.00%	0.60%	0.52%	0.00%	0.70%	3.30%	5.90%	12.50%
2006–07	0.00%	0.42%	0.21%	1.24%	2.16%	3.04%	10.71%	16.67%
2007–08	1.20%	0.00%	0.68%	1.06%	0.66%	2.10%	6.00%	50.00%
2008–09	0.00%	0.00%	0.83%	1.01%	1.56%	4.99%	7.69%	14.29%
2009–10	0.00%	0.97%	0.73%	1.24%	1.37%	2.82%	17.81%	18.75%
2010–11	0.00%	1.05%	1.54%	2.30%	2.79%	5.28%	12.77%	38.10%
2011–12	0.00%	0.63%	1.26%	1.27%	2.29%	4.29%	10.96%	25.00%
2012–13	0.00%	0.75%	1.07%	1.79%	2.69%	5.44%	5.26%	8.11%
Avg. PD	0.21%	0.46%	0.67%	1.00%	1.54%	4.53%	10.60%	23.90%
$UL_p\left(\sigma_{PD}^{P}\right)$	0.50%	0.39%	0.49%	0.78%	0.96%	2.24%	4.88%	11.97%
$UL_i\left(\sigma_{PD}^{i}\right)$	4.62%	6.78%	8.18%	9.94%	12.31%	20.79%	30.79%	42.65%
Derived AC	22.00%	6.47%	5.58%	7.01%	5.42%	5.16%	6.75%	14.35%
Derived DC	1.13%	0.32%	0.35%	0.61%	0.61%	1.16%	2.51%	7.87%

Source: Author's own computation using the corporate rating movements of a large bank.

Note: UL_p: Portfolio unexpected loss=std. deviation of PD; UL_i: Unexpected loss of an obligor; AC: Asset correlation; DC: Default correlation.

The magnitude of ACs is relatively higher in top grades LR1, LR2 and LR3. However, AC values are not necessarily decreasing with decreasing credit quality. If we ignore AC number at LR4 grade, then we get to see that AC decreases with increase in PD up to LR5 grade; thereafter it increases with increase in PD.

Estimation of concentration risk capital for top 20 borrower accounts

One commonly used concentration ratio is the n-firm concentration ratio, or Cn, which consists of the market share, as a percentage, of the n largest firms in the industry. Accordingly, the 20-borrower concentration ratio C20 reported in Table 6.12 is the percentage of loan shared by the 20 largest borrowers in the bank's loan book. The bank's exposures to individuals are ranked in descending order to find the 20 firm concentration ratios.

Table 6.12: Exposure to Top 20 Borrower Accounts of a Mid-sized Bank in India

SL #	Industry Name	Limit % to capital funds	Total Credit Exposure (₹ crore)	Rating	% to Total Credit Risk Exposure	UL%	DC%	MRC in ₹ crore
1	Trading	12.16%	2,200	LR-3	1.99%	5.31%	0.35%	6.92
2	Transport Equipment	15.91%	2,000	LR-2	1.71%	4.41%	0.32%	4.97
3	Trading	11.75%	1,800	LR-4	1.37%	6.46%	0.61%	9.05
4	Housing Finance Services	11.74%	1,600	LR-2	1.33%	4.41%	0.32%	3.97
5	Refinery	12.36%	1,400	LR-4	1.33%	6.46%	0.61%	7.04
6	Refinery	8.56%	1,350	LR-3	1.31%	14.92%	0.35%	11.92
7	Infrastructure	9.74%	1,280	LR-3	1.30%	5.31%	0.35%	4.03
8	Infrastructure	11.92%	1,240	LR-3	1.29%	5.31%	0.35%	3.90
9	Refinery	12.11%	1,230	LR-3	1.28%	5.31%	0.35%	3.87
10	Refinery	18.49%	1,210	LR-3	1.26%	5.31%	0.35%	3.80
11	Construction	12.74%	1,207	LR-2.	1.26%	4.41%	0.32%	3.00
12	Trading	7.56%	1,200	LR-5	1.26%	8.00%	0.61%	7.49
13	Iron & Steel	11.98%	1,150	LR-5	1.16%	8.00%	0.61%	7.17
14	Telecommunications	10.10%	1,080	LR-4	1.09%	6.46%	0.61%	5.43
15	Telecommunications	12.35%	1,200	LR-2	1.05%	4.41%	0.32%	2.98
16	Telecommunications	7.22%	1,100	LR-5	0.94%	8.00%	0.61%	6.86
17	Housing Finance Services	11.68%	950	LR-4	0.92%	6.46%	0.61%	4.77
18	Telecommunications	10.75%	870	LR-1	0.82%	3.00%	1.13%	2.78
19	Electricity Generation	7.67%	820	LR-6	0.81%	13.51%	1.16%	11.96
20	Infrastructure	8.77%	780	LR-6	0.78%	13.51%	1.16%	11.37
	Total		25,667		24.30%			123.28

Source: Author's own illustration.

Note: The overall LGD for the entire pool is 65%.

The top 20 big borrowers' exposure contributes 24.30 per cent of total credit exposure of the bank, indicating significant amount of exposure concentration. However, as far as prudential limits in terms of capital funds are concerned, these exposures are within the regulatory/prudential ceilings fixed by the bank except borrower SL no. 2 and 10 (limits exceed 15 per cent of capital funds). It is also important to note that some borrowers exceeding 12 per cent limit need to be monitored very closely. Some of these top exposures have lower rating LR5 and LR6 which are increasing the chance of concentration risk in the credit portfolio. These loans should also be monitored very cautiously. Bank's risk management or ICAAP policies reflect the extent to which the institution is willing to lend to an individual borrower (RBI, 1999, 2010).

Next, we add a dimension that incorporates a measure of risk sensitivity estimating the marginal risk contribution of each borrower to total UL. This was possible since we have rating information for each borrower and that rating gives us default correlation to total bank portfolio. Using MRC equation 6.20 and Correlation Table 6.9, we obtain the borrower level marginal risk contribution of loans. If we add all the rupees value of marginal risk contribution, we get total risk contribution for the pool, which is approximately ₹123.28 crore. Now, multiplying this amount by 3, we obtain additional economic capital (EC) amount of ₹369.84 crore that needs to be kept by the bank to counter concentration risk of these top 20 exposures. This amount gives an additional net profit target of approximately ₹48.82 crore (EC × ROE × (1–34%)) in the next financial year to cover this concentration risk. We have assumed that ROE is the cost of raising this additional pillar II capital (ROE = 20% assumed).

Risk adjusted limits either based on limits or on economic capital can be imposed on loans to management concentrations in credit portfolio. How much should the bank charge/earn from a specific obligor to reward him for holding larger amounts of credit risk with the same obligor should be worked out. The tool discussed here is called the technical loan pricing calculator which is used to determine the required spread the bank should charge as compensation for taking on additional credits into an existing portfolio. This aggregate amount of Rs. 369.84 crore may also be considered as additional pillar II capital while assessing its own capital adequacy ratio in their annual Internal Capital Adequacy Assessment Process (ICAAP) report.

Bank might also decree economic capital-based limit that allows the business manager to make some relatively risky deals that are profitable on a risk-adjusted basis but ensures that the portfolio as a whole fits within the bank's risk profile.

Summary

Banks are actually exposed to a portfolio risk due to holding of many risky assets that are subject to default risk of varying degrees and severity. Therefore, it is necessary to measure portfolio risk and understand the risk correlation between various assets. In this chapter, we have explained various methods for empirically estimating default and asset correlations for loan accounts. We have also seen how correlation estimates are useful for calculating portfolio risk, risk contribution of a loan and economic capital. From portfolio management point of view, these are the most important risk measures for assessing credit risk. The unexpected loss contribution (ULC or termed as MRC) is very useful to allocate economic capital of the whole portfolio to the individual loan.

Credit portfolio management aims to increase efficiency and return by identifying credit concentrations, calculate the exposure arising from these risks and assist management in allocating scarce economic capital to internal business. Efforts by bank to limit exposures to particular economic sectors or to rating grades or to individual obligors are intended to reduce unexpected loss (UL), thereby lessening the need for costly capital. Accordingly, risk-based exposure limits may be set to manage portfolio concentration risk. For example, at the sub-portfolio level (e.g. sector, borrower, etc.), hard limits can be placed on notional exposure such that the economic capital as a percentage of exposure does not exceed a certain threshold. Risk criteria should be used in limiting borrower/sector concentration rather than size criteria should be the basis.

Because default events are not independent, the correlation effects need to be considered carefully in managing and measuring concentration risks in credit portfolios. Using default and asset correlations, banks have to compare their IRB regulatory capital with their economic capital to understand the capital gap. Using the correlation matrices, risk contribution of loans can easily be computed by broadly classifying borrowers under various sub-portfolio industry/rating groups. Correlations vary across rating grades, industries and macroeconomic cycles. Different correlation estimates provide an incentive to optimize the portfolio's risk profile by investing in different classes of assets.

Key learning outcomes

After studying the chapter and the relevant reading, you should be able to understand:

- Computation of portfolio unexpected loss (UL_p)
- Concept of default correlation and asset correlation in portfolio risk assessment
- Marginal risk contribution and portfolio unexpected loss
- Joint default probability
- Difference between default correlation and asset correlation
- Measures of credit concentration risk
- Concept of portfolio diversification

Review questions

1. What are the major causes of credit concentration risk?
2. What is Top 20 borrower concentration? What is Theil index of credit concentration?
3. What are the key differences between the default correlation and the asset correlation?
4. Explain the expected loss based HHI measure of concentration risk.
5. What is the difference between the average risk contribution and the unexpected loss contribution?
6. What is the difference between the risks of an individual asset versus a portfolio of assets?
7. What is the link between correlation and portfolio risk?
8. What is single default correlation measure? If the average PD in a pool of 200 assets in 1.70 per cent and joint default probability within similar assets class is 0.07 per cent, calculate the default correlation for the pool.
9. How will you estimate the concentration risk capital?
10. If the expected loss of a loan is 1.2 per cent and the expected recovery rate (RR) for the same is 40 per cent, what is your estimate of the probability of default (PD) and the unexpected loss of the loan?
11. Prove that $UL_P = MRC_1 + MRC_2$
12. Assume that in case of a term loan of exposure $1.8 million, we have determined that the correlation between the individual facility and the overall portfolio loss is 0.10. Estimate the marginal risk contribution of the loan to the total portfolio.

References

Bandyopadhyay A. 2010. "Understanding the Effect of Concentration Risk in the Banks' Credit Portfolio: Indian Cases", MPRA Working Paper No. 24822. Available at: http://mpra.ub.uni-muenchen.de/24822/1/MPRA_paper_24822.pdf

Bandyopadhyay, A., T. Chherawala and A. Saha. 2007. "Calibrating Asset Correlation for Indian Corporate Exposures: Implications for Regulatory Capital", *The Journal of Risk Finance* 8 (4): 330–48.

Bandyopadhyay, A. and S. Ganguly. 2013. "Empirical Estimation of Default and Asset Correlation of Large Corporates and Banks in India", *Journal of Risk Finance* 14 (1): 87–99.

Basel Committee on Banking Supervision (BCBS). 2006. International Convergence of Capital Measurement and Capital Standards: A Revised Framework, Publication No. 128, Bank for International Settlements, Basel, June.

Bluhm, C. and L. Overbeck. 2003. "Systemic Risk in Homogeneous Credit Portfolios", in *Contributions to Economics*, eds. G. Bol et al., (Heidelberg. Physica: Verlag/Springer).

———. 2007. "Explaining the Correlation in Basel II: Derivation and Evaluation", in *The Basel Handbook: A Guide for Financial Practitioners*, ed. O. Michael, (London: Risk Books).

De Servigny, A. and O. Renault. 2003. "Correlations Evidence", *RISK* July: 90–4.

——— 2004. Measuring and Managing Credit Risk, Chapter 5, Standard & Poor's (New York, NY: McGraw-Hill Companies).

Gordy, M. and E. Heitfield. 2002. "Estimating Default Correlations from Short Panels of Credit Rating Performance Data", Working Paper, Federal Reserve Board, Washington DC.

Gordy, M.B. 2000. "A Comparative Anatomy of Credit Risk Models", *Journal of Banking and Finance* 24 (1/2): 119–49.

Ong, M.K. 1999. *Internal Credit Risk Models: Capital Allocation and Performance Measurement* (London: Risk Books).

Lopez, J.A. 2004. "The Empirical Relationship between Average Asset Correlation, Firm Probability of Default, and Firm Size", *Journal of Financial Intermediation* 13 (2): 265–83.

Lucas, D.J. 1995. "Default Correlation and Credit Analysis", *Journal of Fixed Income* 4 (4): 76–87.

Nagpal, K. and R. Bahar. 2001. "Measuring Default Correlation", *RISK* 14 (March): 129–32.

RBI. 1999. "Risk Management Systems in Banks", DBOD, 7 October.

——— 2010. "Master Circular – Prudential Guidelines on Capital Adequacy and Market Discipline – New Capital Adequacy Framework (NCAF)", 8 February.

Zhang, J., F. Zhu and J. Lee. 2008. Asset Correlation, Realized Default Correlation, and Portfolio Credit Risk. Moody's KMV Technical Working Paper. Available at: http://www.moodyskmv.com/research/files/wp/Asset_Correlation_and_Portfolio_Risk.pdf

Zhou, C. 1997. "Default Correlation: An Analytical Result", Mimeo, Federal Reserve Board, Washington, DC.

## Chapter 7

Economic Capital and RAROC

B anks ultimately need to assess the cushion that protects them against various business risks, which is economic capital. The process by which a bank assigns economic capital to transactions, products, customers and business lines is known as risk-based capital allocation. In order to maximize shareholder value, business strategies in banks should be based on risk-based capital allocation and performance incentives. Risk-adjusted return on capital (RAROC) and economic capital (EC) are two powerful risk management tools that assist banks and financial institutions (FIs) in both measuring solvency and evaluating performance of different business activities.

EC is the amount of capital needed to provide a cushion against the unexpected loss incurred in the credit portfolio. It checks whether a bank's available capital equals or exceeds the capital necessary to ensure survival with a given level of confidence. While regulatory capital focuses on satisfying the objectives of the regulator, economic capital looks at internal management of the business to maximize the shareholder return. The amount of EC depends on the bank's target debt rating in the market. To achieve the proper capitalization for any line of business, it is necessary for the bank to identify a confidence level that is consistent with the bank's desired credit rating. This is because a desired debt rating for the bank corresponds to a given probability of capital exhaustion. Credit value at risk method (C-VaR) is considered worldwide as a standard approach to estimate risk capital. Economic capital is the difference between this worst-case loss and the expected loss. It is the estimate of the level of capital that a bank requires to operate its business with a desired target solvency level.

In financial mathematics, value at risk (VaR) is a widely used measure of the risk of loss on a specific portfolio of financial assets. VaR summarizes in a single number the downside risk of an institution, under normal conditions, from borrower risk movements. By definition, VaR is maximum loss over a target horizon such that there is a low, pre-specified probability that the actual loss will be larger.

Credit VaR and EC

EC is typically defined as the difference between some given percentile of a loss distribution and the expected loss. It is sometimes referred to as the unexpected loss at the confidence level. It is measured through the value at risk metric.

By definition, VaR is maximum loss over a target horizon such that there is a low, pre-specified probability that the actual loss will be larger. EC for a given confidence level k is defined as the value-at-risk at level k of the portfolio unexpected loss (UL_p) minus the expected loss (EL_p) of the portfolio.[1]

Credit VaR or EC = $k \times ULp - ELp$ Eq. 7.1

Expected losses (EL_p) are the losses expected on a credit portfolio. These losses are 'expected', i.e. we know that these will happen, and even if they do not fully materialize in one year, they should be fully provided for as they would show up in future periods. Unexpected losses (UL_p) measure loss volatility and are calculated at a given confidence interval. Both portfolio EL and UL measurement techniques already have been discussed in the previous chapter.

Credit VaR is the distance from the mean to the percentile of the loss distribution. For credit risk VaR, the time horizon is normally 1 year. From credit VaR, we arrive at capital at risk, which is also termed as "Economic Capital". It is thus the amount of capital needed to provide a cushion against the unexpected loss incurred in the credit portfolio.

The confidence level threshold (k) is established by bank management and can be viewed as the risk of insolvency during a defined time period at which management has chosen to operate. Thus, EC for a given confidence level k is defined as the value-at-risk at the level k of the portfolio unexpected loss (UL_p) minus the expected loss (EL_p) of the portfolio. Using the historical

---

[1] Even under standard normal assumption of loss distribution series, ELp = 0; however, we will adjust if the bank is making any provisions for standard assets and we have deducted this percentage $k \times$ ULp.

regional portfolio/industry portfolio of a bank, one can estimate the amount of true risk capital.

We can calculate the value-at-risk if we have a distribution of future portfolio losses. The loss distribution shows that there is a certain level of expected loss that will be realized with a high probability, and as we go further away from the expected loss, the probability keeps going down (see Chart 7.1).

Chart 7.1: Credit Loss Allocation (at Portfolio Level)

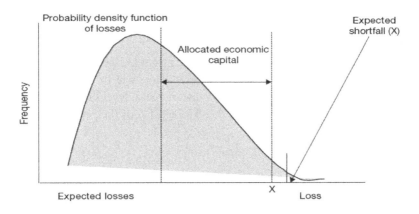

Source: Author's illustration.

Note: Economic capital = VaR (X) – Expected loss;

VaR = Value at risk at a particular confidence interval (multiplier, k); Expected shortfall is the average loss conditional on the loss being occurred above the VaR level.

Once the definition of loss and the planning horizon have been selected, the credit VaR model generates a distribution – a probability density function (PDF) – of future losses that can be used to calculate the losses associated with any given percentile of the distribution.

The above loss distribution shows (Chart 7.1) that there is a certain level of expected loss that will be realized with a high probability, and as we go further away from the expected loss, the probability keeps going down. EC is the tail percentile (as illustrated in the above chart) that represents the total amount of risk (value-at- risk) less the expected loss covered by the loan-loss reserve.

In practice, banks concentrate on two such loss figures: expected loss and unexpected loss. Expected loss is the mean of the loss distribution and represents the amount that a bank expects to lose on average on its credit portfolio. Unexpected loss, in contrast, is a measure of the variability in credit losses, or the credit risk inherent in the portfolio. Unexpected loss is computed as the losses associated with some high percentile of the loss distribution (for example, the 99.9th percentile) minus expected loss. A high percentile of the distribution is chosen so that the resulting risk estimates will cover all but the most extreme events.

The choice of confidence level is established by bank management and can be viewed as the risk of insolvency during a defined time period at which management has chosen to operate. The higher the confidence level selected, the lower the probability of insolvency. For a confidence level CI = 99.9%, the EC can be interpreted as the appropriate capital the bank has to keep for the next year to cover unexpected losses in 999 events out of 1000 possible events of losses. Economic capital (EC) is estimated from a set of Credit VaR models. The value at risk (VaR) is the difference between the maximum possible standard deviation of loss over and above the average loss in a portfolio. The degree of standard deviation, however, depends on the actual nature of the credit loss distribution. Under normal condition, a multiplier $k = 3$ can be used for a confidence level of 99.9 per cent. Under the Basel IRB approach, regulatory capital (RC) is set to maintain a supervisory fixed confidence level of 99.9 per cent. This capital multiplier value is the normal inverse of 99.9 per cent that can be derived from a standard normal table. However, to estimate economic capital in case of non-normal loss distribution, higher multiplier ($k = 5$ or 6) should be used since deviation will be larger. At Bank of America (BoA), the total amount of economic capital attributed to all of the business units is the amount that is estimated to guarantee the solvency of the bank at a 99. 97 per cent confidence level. The multiplication factor "k" may also be set through back-testing of the model. Many banks using economic capital models have selected a confidence level between 99.96 and 99.98 per cent, equivalent to the insolvency rate expected for an AA or Aa credit rating.

Bank-wide portfolio unexpected loss can also be estimated by adding the marginal risk contribution of all the regions of the bank:

$$MRC_i = \sqrt{\rho_i} UL_i$$

Eq. 7.2

It can be mathematically proved that $\Sigma MRC = ULP$

This we have shown later in a separate exercise.

Estimation of Portfolio EC: Top-down Approach

Bank level economic capital can be estimated from its historical yearly or quarterly NPA movement data.

Estimation of EC through Simulation-based C-VaR Model

Here, we study the temporal NPA movements of a north-based Indian public sector bank and develop a simulation base credit VaR model to estimate EC. The overall advances position and movement of assets of the bank are documented in Table 7.1. The marginal PDs are estimated from the fresh slippage rates and then the average PD is computed. Similarly, we also estimate the historical cash loss given default (LGD) from their yearly cash recovery rates. The EC method relates a bank's whole portfolio of risk to the amount of capital that the bank must hold if it is to achieve a particular solvency target. Here, we are inferring VaR from a distribution of the losses in education loan portfolio.

Three types of distributions (normal, log normal and beta distributions) have been used to define and fit the aggregate loss trend and derive VaR estimates. Excel functions have been used to define the properties of distributions (=norminv(prob, mean, sd); loginv(.) and betainv(.) functions are used). Note that both log normal and beta distributions are typically highly skewed and, hence, very useful in describing credit losses.

Ten thousand simulations have been run excel using random number generator (i.e. using rand() function) and linking it with the properties of these distributions. These simulated values are the likely loss values in percentage form. Charts 7.2 and 7.2a depict such loss distributions.

The distribution graphs are drawn in "Best fit" package of Palisade. There are many possible choices of probability distributions to fit the tail of the distribution which is the most important information for estimating credit VaR. From the simulated loss fractions, VaR estimates have been obtained using the function "Percentile (simulated loss data, confidence level)". This way, three alternative VaR models have been estimated. From our VaR calculation, we obtain the EC amount to cover the unexpected loss in the entire credit portfolio. The VaR number and EC estimates have been reported in Table 7.2.

Table 7.1: Aggregate NPA Movements of a Large Indian Public Sector Bank

Year	Gross Advances	Opening GNPA	Additions in GNPA	Total Recovery	Closing GNPA	Recovery Rate %	GNPA%	Marginal PD
1997–98	5,708							
1998–99	6,956							
1999–2000	9,326		236.59		527.51			3.23%
2000–01	11,076	527.51	446.32	95.74	585.76	16.34%	5.29%	4.89%
2001–02	14,158	585.76	601.02	259.97	951.79	27.31%	6.72%	5.22%
2002–03	16,524	951.79	630.28	305.23	1,146.25	26.63%	6.94%	4.53%
2003–04	20,612	1,146.25	527.10	461.07	1,210.91	38.08%	5.87%	3.08%
2004–05	25,299	1,210.91	1,877.64	482.16	2,492.27	19.35%	9.85%	9.02%
2005–06	35,549	2,492.27	372.97	469.71	2,116.31	22.19%	5.95%	1.37%
2006–07	45,395	2,116.31	379.27	641.65	1,454.05	44.13%	3.20%	1.07%
2007–08	54,566	1,454.05	579.75	512.67	1,280.11	40.05%	2.35%	1.28%
2008–09	69,065	1,280.10	495.70	488.35	1,058.12	46.15%	1.53%	0.88%
2009–10	84,184	1,058.12	1,133.10	399.34	1,468.75	27.19%	1.74%	1.64%
2010–11	96,839	1,468.75	1,556.00	512.72	1,920.54	26.70%	1.98%	1.87%
2011–12	113,050	1,920.54	3,897.59	1,660	3,580.49	46.36%	3.17%	3.98%
2012–13	130,186	3,580.49	3,213.30	1,526	4,183.96	36.47%	3.21%	2.83%
Avg. PD								3.21%
Std. Dev. of PD (σ_{PD})								2.23%
Avg. LGD								67.93%
ELp%								**2.18%**
ULp%								**1.51%**
$UL_T\%$								11.97%

Source: Bank's audited annual reports.

Note: SD-PD is standard deviation of yearly marginal PDs. Similarly, SD–LGD is standard deviation of LGD. The portfolio volatility is:

$$UL_P = Avg.LGD \times \sqrt{Avg.PD \times (1 - AvgPD)} \,.$$

Chart 7.2: Simulated Log Normal Credit Loss Distribution

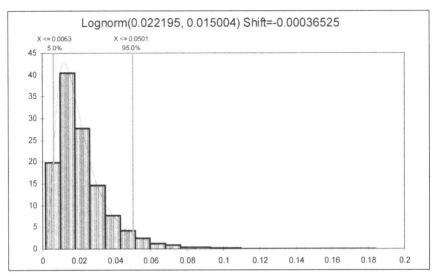

Source: Author's own computation based on figures obtained from Table 7.1.

Chart 7.2a: Beta Simulated Credit Loss Distribution

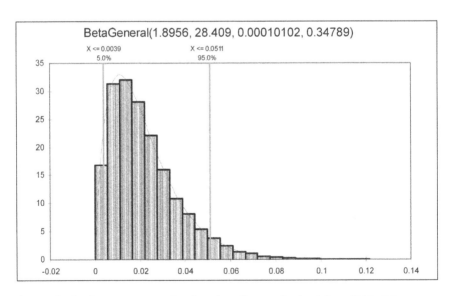

Source: Author's own computation based on figures obtained from Table 7.1.

Table 7.2: Credit VaR and EC Estimates

Confidence Interval	EL =PD × LGD	Provision	Normal VaR	Economic Capital (EC)	Beta VaR	Economic Capital (EC)	Log Normal VaR	Economic Capital (EC)
99.97%	2.18%	1.21%	7.20%	5.99%	10.57%	9.36%	14.35%	13.14%
99.9%	2.18%	1.21%	6.73%	5.52%	9.41%	8.20%	11.84%	10.63%
99.5%	2.18%	1.21%	6.01%	4.80%	7.74%	6.53%	8.76%	7.55%
99%	2.18%	1.21%	5.64%	4.43%	6.96%	5.75%	7.52%	6.31%
95%	2.18%	1.21%	6.01%	3.46%	5.11%	3.90%	5.02%	3.81%

Source: Author's own estimation using Table 7.1 figures.

Note: The property of a generalized beta distribution has been specified by estimating its location (alpha) and scale (beta) parameters. Alpha = 2.005 and Beta = 90.07. The log normal distribution is fitted after estimating location (meu) and scale parameter (sigma).

The EL portion has been compared with the provision percentage and has been deducted from VaR number to estimate EC. General rule is that the EL_p portion should be either provided or priced and remaining portion is to be covered by capital funds. The EC computation relates a bank's whole portfolio of risk to the amount of capital the bank must hold as a buffer, if it is to achieve a particular solvency target. If a bank is targeting to achieve higher rating, it should assign a higher confidence level to reserve the capital to limit the loss. Now the question is: how much protection is sufficient against unexpected losses? At Bank of America, a 99.97 per cent coverage level was sufficient to reduce the risk of the bank to the average levels for AA-rated companies. This corresponds to a distance to default of 3.43 specified by MKMV model. Table 7.2 illustrates how EC obtained from credit VaR varies over the choice of coverage level. If a bank targets higher rating, it will have to keep 13.14 per cent as EC against unexpected loss. Note that the median tier I per cent in AA-rated US banks was 9.2 per cent on average during 2010 (Jokivuolle and Peura, 2010). It is expected that Eco-cap/RWA would be higher than Tier I per cent for a better-rated risk conscious bank. The reported Table 7.2 result is based on Monte Carlo simulation using historical loss data of a bank described in Table 7.1. The key drivers of portfolio risk are thus: correlation, exposure, PD, LGD and volatility of PD which are in-built in simulation-based EC modelling.

EC Estimation at a Sub-portfolio Level

The above method can be applied in estimating EC at a retail pool (e.g. education loan) as well. Here, we have followed a similar VaR technique to estimate EC for education loan portfolio. The major risk elements PD, LGD, DC and UL of the aggregate pool have been estimated and reported in the upper panel of Table 7.3. These portfolio risk elements have been obtained from the risk elements of some leading public sector banks in India who have significant share of advances in education loan segment. However, instead of simulation, we have directly used a multiplier of 6 (k = 6) to capture the possibility of non-normal losses which is very much realistic. Bank has to hold sufficient capital to be able to absorb future losses up to a certain confidence. Typically, this confidence interval is set with regard to the risk appetite of the entity.

From our VaR calculation, we obtain the EC amount to cover the unexpected loss in the entire credit portfolio. Thus, EC in percentage amount of credit exposure is 5.66. This means, for each Rs. 100 loan outstanding, Rs. 5.66 should be set aside as a protection for unexpected loss of a loan. This is a system level estimate as many banks' education loan portfolio data has been pooled down together to derive a VaR estimate.

Table 7.3: Estimation of EC for a Retail Loan Portfolio

Items#	Portfolio Risk Elements	Values
1	Portfolio PD%	2.57%
2	LGD%	72.48%
3	EL_p%	1.86%
4	PD Volatility: SD(PD)	1.18%
5	Portfolio Unexpected Loss (ULP%)=4×2	0.85%
6	UL of an individual loan (ULi%)	11.17%
7	Default Correlation (DC): $(UL_p\%)^2/(UL_i\%)^2$	1.94%
8	Marginal Risk Contribution of a loan (MRC):	1.56%
	Estimation of EC to Cover Portfolio Risk:	
9	Capital Multiplier (k)	6
10	Economic Capital (EC) through Credit VaR: $k \times UL\text{-}EL_p$	5.66%
11	Total Advances of SCBs (Rs. Crore): 2011-12	50190
12	Economic Capital (Rs. Crore)	2841.46

Source: Author's own illustration.

Thus, if the system level total credit (education loan) exposure is ₹50,190 crore (as on the year end, 2012), the credit risk protection fund (or economic capital cover for unexpected loss in education loans) requirement will be of ₹2131 crore for 2012–13. This estimated capital requirement is for one year, i.e. 2012–13. However, as the credit volume goes up, the fund requirement in future will also be higher depending upon the credit growth and portfolio risk behaviour.

Estimation of Portfolio EC using Regional Data: A Case of Two Banks

Table 7.4 compares regional portfolio composition of two public sector banks in India. The region-wise unexpected loss shares and marginal risk contributions are estimated using regional PDs and LGDs and single default correlations (DCs) obtained from their historical time series observations. The single default correlation has been estimated using their yearly loss variance that we have already discussed in the previous section (equation 6.10 has been used). As can be seen from Table 7.4, the two bank's regional portfolio risk in terms of their marginal risk contributions are significantly different which is affecting their total portfolio risk position.

Table 7.4: Linkage between Concentration and with Risk Capital: Marginal Risk Contribution and Zonal Unexpected Loss (Large Bank Case)

Units in ₹ crore, others in numbers

	Large Bank (Western India)					Mid-sized Bank (Southern India)				
SL#	Region Name	Expos. wtd. UL (%)	Region MRC	Region MRC	Region-wide UL (%)	Region Name	Expos. wtd. UL (%)	Region MRC	Region MRC	Region wide UL (%)
1	Agra	0.20	2.62	37.56	11.77	Pune	0.33	3.11	11.53	8.09
2	Ahmedabad	0.27	1.72	51.65	7.74	Hyderabad	0.49	6.33	14.88	11.39
3	Bhopal	0.37	1.97	70.86	8.84	Bangalore	0.72	2.05	22.95	6.76
4	Chandigarh	0.41	2.08	78.96	9.33	Chennai	0.47	4.25	15.34	9.76
5	Chennai	0.91	2.72	175.02	12.22	Hubli	0.13	3.25	7.38	11.09
6	Delhi	0.84	0.84	160.45	3.77	Udupi	0.22	2.37	8.52	7.76
7	Guwahati	0.09	3.01	16.34	13.52	Kerala	0.19	3.48	13.77	12.91
8	Hyderabad	0.65	2.29	124.66	10.30	Kolkata	0.19	2.40	4.92	6.63
9	Kolkata	0.89	3.93	169.92	17.65	Delhi	1.40	2.40	36.50	6.52
10	Lucknow	0.58	3.44	110.79	15.44	Goa	0.04	1.14	0.91	4.27
11	Mumbai Main Region	0.03	0.32	5.51	1.43	Gujarat	0.39	3.03	14.56	9.08
12	Mumbai Metro Region	0.66	1.24	126.06	5.58	Hassan	0.30	3.80	17.49	12.82

Table 7.4 contd.

Table 7.4 contd.

#	Region					Region				
13	Muzaffarpur	0.28	2.98	53.45	13.37	Vijaywada	0.19	4.83	12.47	15.16
14	Nagpur	0.13	2.73	25.09	12.28	Greater Mumbai	1.46	1.85	24.95	5.10
15	Patna	0.25	3.53	48.18	15.85	Belgaum	0.13	3.68	7.85	11.95
16	Pune	0.35	3.37	67.16	15.14	Coimbatore	0.37	2.59	13.44	7.69
17	Raipur	0.31	3.49	59.80	15.67	Lucknow	0.07	4.46	3.02	12.16
18	Corporate Region	0.04	0.05	7.18	0.21	Chandigarh	0.12	2.97	4.22	8.93
19	Card Region	0.002	5.29	0.34	23.76	Bhopal	0.13	6.17	4.09	11.89
	Total	7.26		1389.00			7.34		743.36	
	Default Correlation (DC)	0.0495					0.0438			
	Portfolio UL (%)	1.62					1.54			
	Multiplier (k)	5					5			
	Provisioning (%)	0.80					0.92			
	Portfolio EL (%)	0.97					0.49			
	Economic Capital (%)	7.28					6.88			
	Regulatory Capital	5571.30					4305.22			
	Deficit of Regulatory Capital (%)	12.31					-22.66			

Source: Author's own computation based on regional credit portfolio data of two banks.

It is important to remind you that the portfolio unexpected loss of the bank is the summation of regional marginal risk contributions. Next, using credit VaR method, we get bank level EC estimates. Here, instead of simulation, we have directly applied a capital multiplier of 5 ($k = 5$) on portfolio unexpected loss and deducted the provision amount to estimate the EC. We have chosen the capital multiplier of 5 because credit losses are generally not normally distributed. The VaR results are reported in Table 7.4.

Next, we compare the EC numbers with the Basel II minimum regulatory capital position (under standardized approach) of these two banks. We find that the capital gap is significantly high for the large bank (the gap between EC and the existing Basel II credit risk regulatory capital is 12.31 per cent of the regulatory capital). On the other hand, the mid-sized bank having a capital surplus as its Basel II credit risk regulatory capital (under the standardized approach) is 22.66 per cent higher than the EC.

Our large bank case, even if it may not be able to cover up such a high capital gap, gives some idea about largeness of the loss size the bank may incur in most unlikely but plausible events. If the actual credit losses are of this nature, targeting AA in such stress time would mean they have to keep enough surpluses to cover losses and it is a challenging exercise and accordingly they have to plan their business growth and plan to raise further capital. For example, if the large bank decides to meet additional 12.31 per cent capital which amounts to ₹686 crore (as estimated in Table 7.12), it should be aware that if they target a 15.27 per cent return on equity (ROE), the minimum targeted net profit for the entire portfolio would be at least ₹955.5 crore (ROE × Eco – cap = 15.27% × ₹6257.30 crore). This is because future earnings also get added to the core Tier I capital.

In this context, adoption of a risk assessment and performance management (RAPM) framework will enable the top management to meet this profit target. Accordingly, we estimate the unexpected losses and marginal risk contribution of various regions of the two banks. The region-wise risk position (in terms of unexpected loss) would help us to compare performance and allocate capital to minimize concentration risk. The regions whose risk contributions are higher should ensure adequate return to ensure stability in the bank's overall solvency position.

Estimation of portfolio EC: Bottom-up approach

Under the bottom up approach, the portfolio EC is estimated using more granular data. For this, a bank may have to develop a portfolio risk template to obtain the borrower level segment-wise risk data (PD, EAD, LGD, correlations). Then, using the portfolio structure (e.g. rating-wise or industry-wise), credit exposures can be segmented. Next, using the rating–rating or industry–industry default correlation estimates (presented in Tables 6.6, 6.7, 6.7a and 6.9 in Chapter 6), the portfolio expected loss (EL_p) and unexpected loss (UL_p) are to be estimated. The portfolio loss calculation formulas are shown in equations 6.5 and 6.5a in the previous chapter. From portfolio loss, EC can be estimated using credit VaR method.

The Pro-Cyclicality Issue Under Basel II IRB Approach: Stress Testing Economic/Regulatory Capital as Offset

Pro-cyclicality refers to the empirical observation that banks' loan business tends to follow the same cyclical pattern as that of the real economy. Hence, loans typically show strong growth in an economic upturn and slow growth or even contraction in an economic downturn and so does their capital structure. Basel II IRB may give rise to pro-cyclical effects owing to the fact that the three main input parameters (PD, LGD and correlation), especially under the AIRB approach, are themselves influenced by cyclical movements. If IRB capital requirement becomes more dependent on the business cycle, bank's regulatory capital will increase, which will limit the credit supply when the economy is slowing down and may further aggravate the condition. To counter pro-cyclicality effect, Basel II committee suggests that banks should have a strong stress-testing framework for scenario analysis. Therefore, IRB banks need to perform stress test to ensure bank's capital adequacy in times of shocks.

Stress testing is an important risk management tool that can be used by banks as part of their internal risk management practices. This has already been suggested by the Reserve Bank of India (RBI) under internal capital adequacy assessment process (ICAAP) guidelines under the Basel II (especially, for fulfilling the pillar II requirements). Stress-testing alerts bank management to adverse unexpected outcomes related to a variety of risks and provides an indication of how much capital might be needed to absorb shocks should large losses occur.

The most crucial input to do stress testing and capital simulation exercise depends upon choosing/identifying realistic scenarios. By scenario, we mean an event (for example, an increase in interest rates) and, possibly, its broader implications that are believed to represent abnormal operating conditions. Scenarios can be chosen based on historical experience, or they can be hypothetical. Incidents like increase in new NPAs, slippage in restructured assets, downgrade in borrower rating (hence, increase in PD), depletion in collateral value (i.e. increase in LTV ratio), increase in LGD, correlated defaults and exposure concentrations leading to higher defaults during downturn of the business cycle are the examples of such scenarios. Rating transitions also tend to exhibit a higher frequency of downgrades during a recession and a higher occurrence of upgrades during booms. In either case, the objective is to select as scenarios those rare but plausible events that have caused abnormal operating conditions in the past, or that could cause them in the future. How the credit stress test scenario analysis is actually done in a bank has been summarized in Chart 7.3.

Chart 7.3: Credit Risk Stress Testing Framework

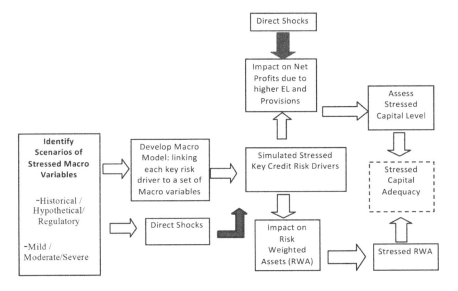

Source: Author's summary.

Multivariate regression analysis may be used to link macro-variables to credit risk stress drivers.

Change in credit risk between t and $t + 1$ period based on risk-weighted asset (RWA) calculations can be linked to the one of the standardized approach/IRB approach/EC models.

Capital adequacy under stress can be measured as:

$$\text{Capital Adequacy } (t+1) = \frac{\text{Capital } (t)}{\text{Current RWA} + \text{Stressed RWA } (t+1)}$$

Eq. 7.3

The RWA $(t + 1)$ calculation is subject to credit growth between t and $t + 1$, change in credit risk portfolio position between t and $t + 1$ based on RWA calculations linked to one of the standardized approach/IRB approach/ EC models. Further, if net income of the bank in $t + 1$ period becomes negative under a stress scenario due to higher EL and provisions, capital (in the numerator of CRAR) will take a hit.

The internal economic model should be run under both with PD, LGD (and obviously default correlation) stress scenarios to observe the increase in capital at the Basel II imposed 99.9 per cent confidence interval. The percentage of increase in the capital can be used as a "mark up" in the Basel II IRB risk-weighted asset (RWA) formula to achieve the downturn effect desired.

One such scenario analysis has been presented in Table 7.5.

Table 7.5 demonstrates the effect of change in PD and LGD on Basel II IRB risk weight functions for various categories of exposures. One can see that IRB risk weights are more sensitive to changes in LGD than PD. Interestingly, the sensitivity of RWA to PD is more pronounced in the corporate exposure class than the retail asset class. Hence, the required capital may go up during downturn period of the economic cycle. These business cycle effects need to be assessed properly to work out the desired capital to have a more stable Tier I capital adequacy ratio. The IRB risk weight computation formula has been explained in Chapter 8. The IRB banks must conduct such stress analysis to test the impact of changing risk weighted assets on its overall capital adequacy ratio.

In response to the recent global financial crisis in US that has virtually crippled the health of the US financial market, the Basel Committee on Banking Supervision (BCBS) issued the principles for sound stress-testing practices and supervision in May 2009. BCBS strongly advocates raising the standard and sophistication of stress-testing programmes to make them more realistic and meaningful. Accordingly, RBI has also updated its existing guidelines on stress testing through a new circular in December 2013. The regulator expects that the degree of sophistication adopted by banks in stress-testing analysis would be dependent upon the degree of complexity in the nature of their business operations.

To counter pro-cyclicality effect, it is recommended that banks should have a strong stress-testing framework for realistic scenario analysis. Scenarios can be chosen based on historical experience, or they can be hypothetical. One such scenario analysis has been shown in Chart 7.4.

Table 7.5: Scenario Analysis to Examine the Sensitivity of IRB Risk Weights to PD and LGD

(Figures in %)

Asset Class:	Corporate		SME as Corporate		Other Retail (or SME as Retail)		Residential Mortgage			Qualifying Revolving Retail	
LGD:	50.00	75.00	50.00	75.00	50.00	85.00	25.00	45.00	75.00	45.00	85.00
PD					IRB Risk weighted assets (RWA)						
0.03	16.05	24.05	12.55	18.83	4.95	8.41	2.31	4.15	6.92	0.98	1.85
0.05	21.83	32.75	17.11	25.66	7.37	12.52	3.46	6.23	10.38	1.51	2.86
0.10	32.95	49.42	25.89	38.83	12.40	21.09	5.94	10.69	17.82	2.71	5.12
0.25	54.97	82.45	43.34	65.02	23.50	39.96	11.83	21.30	35.50	5.76	10.88
0.50	77.35	116.02	61.01	91.52	35.96	61.13	19.49	35.08	58.47	10.04	18.97
0.75	91.98	137.96	72.38	108.57	44.55	75.74	25.81	46.46	77.44	13.80	26.06
1.00	102.57	153.86	80.44	120.66	50.86	86.46	31.33	56.40	94.00	17.22	32.54
2.00	127.62	191.42	98.38	147.58	64.43	109.53	48.85	87.94	146.56	28.92	54.63
2.50	135.73	203.59	103.81	155.72	67.66	115.03	55.91	100.64	167.73	33.98	64.18
5.00	166.50	249.76	124.74	187.11	73.79	125.45	82.35	148.22	247.04	54.74	103.41
7.00	187.63	281.44	140.70	211.04	76.95	130.82	97.22	175.00	291.67	67.88	128.21
9.00	206.26	309.39	155.81	233.71	81.33	138.25	108.74	195.74	326.23	78.96	149.15
10.00	214.54	321.81	162.79	244.19	83.94	142.69	113.56	204.41	34.68	83.89	158.47
12.00	229.05	343.57	175.41	263.12	89.64	152.39	121.71	219.07	365.12	92.74	175.18
15.00	246.15	369.22	191.01	286.51	98.45	167.36	130.96	235.72	392.87	103.88	196.23
20.00	264.70	397.05	209.35	314.03	111.42	189.41	140.62	253.12	421.86	117.89	222.86

Source: BCBS (2006).

Note: Maturity of the above exposure is assumed to be 2.5 years. This is for illustration purpose only.

Chart 7.4: Business Cycle Effects on Indian Corporate Risk Profile

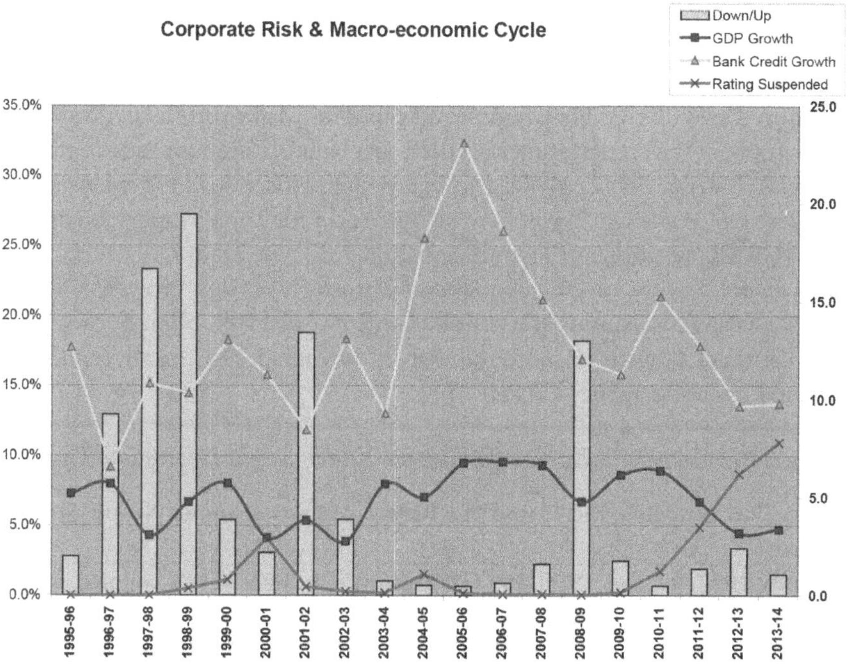

Corporate Risk & Macro-economic Cycle

Source: Based on Centre for Monitoring Indian Economy (CMIE) data.

It can be seen in Chart 7.4 that whenever GDP growth rate was high, corporate rating downgrade to upgrade ratio was low and when GDP growth rate was down, the downgrade–upgrade ratio also peaked up. One can also notice that the rating suspension rate peaks up when growth decelerates. These ratings are assigned by external credit rating agencies (CRAs). As a result, the risk-weighted assets go up, which puts a downward pressure on the capital adequacy ratio (CRAR). This finally may lead to slow down in the credit growth causing pro-cyclicality problem for the economic system. It has been observed that a concentrated loan portfolio in a bank under stress situation would result in large losses relative to a more diversified portfolio.

The portfolio risk dimension of a bank may change during economic downtime and a bank may experience capital erosion because of increase in concentration of lower quality of assets as well as increase in the number of new defaults. Consequently, using three historically generated scenarios, a bank might stress test the large corporate loan pool of the bank and it also examines their impact on capital erosion and bank's capital adequacy ratio.

We have created three scenarios to assess the corporate credit risk capital of a large-sized public sector bank in India (see Tables 7.6–7.8). These three scenario analyses have been assessed by incorporating the impact of an economic downturn as well as upturn on their capital adequacy position (measured by CRAR). For example, an economic downturn could lead to a downgrade in the credit ratings awarded to a bank's counterparties by rating agencies (CRAs). This might lead to a consequent increase in the risk weights for these exposures which will have an impact on the bank's capital adequacy ratio (CRAR) position as shown in equation 7.3.

Scenario 1 is the severe economic downturn (low GDP growth coupled by East Asian Crisis during the period from 1997 to 1999. Notice downtime 1 scenario actually led to more number of downgrades in corporate ratings awarded by rating agency CRISIL.

Scenario 1: Corporate Rating Transition under Severe Depression Time

Table: 7.6 Studying the Corporate Rating Migration under Severe Stress Scenario

Period: 1997–98 and 1998–99; GDP growth @ 4.21–6.47% coupled with East Asian Crisis

	AAA	AA	A	BBB	BB	B	CCC	D
AAA	91.30%	8.70%	0.00%	0.00%	0.00%	0.00%	0.00%	0.00%
AA	1.91%	73.89%	17.83%	3.18%	2.55%	0.00%	0.00%	0.64%
A	0.00%	2.07%	70.95%	14.11%	7.05%	0.83%	0.83%	4.15%
BBB	0.00%	0.00%	2.60%	54.55%	24.68%	2.60%	7.79%	7.79%
BB	0.00%	0.00%	0.00%	0.00%	45.65%	4.35%	6.52%	43.48%
B	0.00%	0.00%	0.00%	0.00%	0.00%	80.00%	0.00%	20.00%
CCC	0.00%	0.00%	0.00%	0.00%	0.00%	0.00%	50.00%	50.00%

Source: Author's own computation based on CRISIL's monthly bond rating data.

Table: 7.6a Rating-wise Slippage Statistics

	Downgrade (%)	Upgrade (%)	Net-Downgrade (%)	Rated to Unrated (%)	Slippage to D (%)
AAA	8.70%	0.00%	8.70%	8.70%	0.00%
AA	24.20%	1.91%	22.29%	8.28%	0.64%
A	26.97%	2.07%	24.90%	14.11%	4.15%
BBB	42.86%	2.60%	40.26%	37.66%	7.79%
BB & Below	50.79%	0.00%	50.79%	7.94%	42.86%

Source: Author's own computation based on CRISIL's monthly bond rating data.

Downtime 2 captures period 2000–02 when GDP growth rate was again down at around 4.35–5.81 per cent; but that the crisis was over and government had also undertaken stabilization policies to improve the growth rate. One can notice that the net slippage rate (downgrade rate minus upgrade rate) was not as severe as downtime 1. This situation can be taken as moderately severe scenario.

Scenario2: Corporate Rating Transition under Moderate Depression Time

Table: 7.7 Studying the Corporate Rating Migration under Moderate Stress Scenario

Period: 2000–01 and 2001–02; GDP growth @ 4.26–5.65% coupled with Stabilization Policy Announced by the Indian Government

	AAA	AA	A	BBB	BB	B	CCC	D
AAA	96.51%	3.49%	0.00%	0.00%	0.00%	0.00%	0.00%	0.00%
AA	3.79%	89.39%	6.06%	0.76%	0.00%	0.00%	0.00%	0.00%
A	0.00%	7.53%	81.72%	6.45%	1.08%	0.00%	2.15%	1.08%
BBB	0.00%	2.50%	5.00%	72.50%	2.50%	7.50%	0.00%	10.00%
BB	0.00%	4.00%	0.00%	4.00%	72.00%	4.00%	0.00%	16.00%
B	0.00%	0.00%	0.00%	18.18%	0.00%	45.45%	0.00%	36.36%
CCC	0.00%	0.00%	0.00%	0.00%	0.00%	0.00%	56.25%	43.75%

Source: Author's own computation based on CRISIL's monthly bond rating data.

Table: 7.7a Slippage Statistics

	Downgrade (%)	Upgrade (%)	Net-Downgrade (%)	Rated to Unrated (%)	Slippage to D (%)
AAA	3.49%	0.00%	3.49%	2.33%	0.00%
AA	6.82%	3.79%	3.03%	10.61%	0.00%
A	10.75%	7.53%	3.23%	31.18%	1.08%
BBB	20.00%	7.50%	12.50%	45.00%	10.00%
BB & Below	30.77%	7.69%	23.08%	28.85%	28.85%

Source: Author's own computation based on CRISIL's monthly bond rating data.

The third scenario captures the economic condition which prevailed during 2007–09 and GDP growth rate was 8.62 per cent which fell down to

6.8 per cent in the aftermath of US sub-prime crisis. Notice that the movements from rated to unrated category and net downgrades rate were quite high in this phase of economic cycle.

Scenario 3: Indian Corporate Rating Transition in Recent Downtime

Table 7.8: Studying the Corporate Rating Migration under Recent Downtime Scenario

Post Sub-prime Crisis Period: 2007–08 and 2008–09

GDP growth @ 8.62% and fell down to 6.8% along with Sub-prime crisis

	AAA	AA	A	BBB	BB	B	CCC	D
AAA	91.18%	8.82%	0.00%	0.00%	0.00%	0.00%	0.00%	0.00%
AA	2.73%	95.45%	1.82%	0.00%	0.00%	0.00%	0.00%	0.00%
A	0.00%	10.53%	84.21%	5.26%	0.00%	0.00%	0.00%	0.00%
BBB	0.00%	0.00%	0.00%	80.00%	20.00%	0.00%	0.00%	0.00%
BB	0.00%	0.00%	0.00%	0.00%	66.67%	0.00%	0.00%	33.33%

Source: Author's own computation based on CRISIL's monthly bond rating data.

Table: 7.8a Slippage Statistics

	Downgrade (%)	Upgrade (%)	Net-Downgrade (%)	Rated to Unrated (%)	Slippage to D (%)
AAA	8.82%	0.00%	8.82%	9.80%	0.00%
AA	1.82%	2.73%	-0.91%	10.00%	0.00%
A	5.26%	10.53%	-5.26%	21.05%	0.00%
BBB	20.00%	0.00%	20.00%	40.00%	0.00%
BB & Below	33.33%	0.00%	33.33%	0.00%	33.33%

Source: Author's own computation based on CRISIL's monthly bond rating data.

It is quite evident from the above set of tables that the severe depression time in Indian economy in scenario 1 has actually led to more number of downgrades in corporate ratings awarded by rating agency CRISIL during 1997–99 (See Tables 7.6 and 7.6a) in comparison to their average migration pattern by CRAs. Scenario 2 captures period 2000–02 when GDP growth rate was again down at around 4.35–5.81%; but that the crisis was over and government had also undertaken stabilization policies to improve the growth rate. One can notice that the net slippage rate (downgrade rate minus upgrade rate) was not as severe as in scenario 1 (compare Table 7.7a with Table 7.6a). This situation has been taken as moderate stress scenario. Table 7.8 shows (scenario 3) the recent economic condition which prevailed during 2007–09 and GDP growth rate was 8.62 per cent which fell down to 6.8 per cent in the aftermath of US sub-prime crisis. The slippage statistics have been documented in Table 7.8a. These are all published bond ratings of 572 corporates given by CRISIL.

As a next step, we will take the moderate and severe stress scenarios and examine how they impact on a bank's corporate credit portfolio risk composition, risk weights and finally on capital adequacy (CRAR). For example, an economic downturn could lead to a downgrade in the credit ratings awarded to a bank's counterparties by rating agencies. This might lead to a consequent increase in the risk weights for these exposures which will have an impact on the bank's capital adequacy (CRAR) position. The stress-testing exercise shown in Table 7.9 is for illustration purpose only.

In Scenario 1, it is assumed that unrated category (i.e. not rated by external rating agency) could consist of a mix of categories and 15 per cent of unrated categories go down to BB and below category or NIG category (150 per cent RW) including 6 per cent of which go to D. The stress capital position has been shown in Table 7.9. It is observed that in a mild stress Scenario 1, slightly tilting the risk position of the corporate portfolio that results in additional capital requirement of ₹18.24 crore that changes CRAR by marginal 3 basis point and it comes down to 14.20 per cent from 14.23 per cent of March 2011 position. However in moderate stress scenario 1, an exposure shock of 5 per cent has been assumed, which results in additional capital requirement of ₹197.21 crore that changes CRAR by marginal 31 basis point and it comes down to 13.92 per cent from 14.23 per cent of March 2011 position for this bank.

Further, under severe stress Scenario 2 with an exposure shock of 5 per cent and assumption that 25 per cent of unrated moves down to NIG (150 per cent RW) including 15 per cent of them go to D, then the position would be as shown in the last two columns of Table 7.9. Under severe stress, bank's corporate portfolio rating distribution of assets is assumed to change significantly, which results in additional minimum capital requirement of ₹687.37 crore. This reduces the CRAR position approximately by 103 basis points (from the existing 14.23 per cent to 13.20 per cent) as a result of capital erosion. Similarly, one can also check the effect of third scenario on CRAR position of the bank.

Table 7.9: Stress Testing Bank's Corporate Credit Portfolio

Units in ₹ crore, others in %

Grades	Original Corporate Portfolio of the Bank				Scenario 1				Scenario 2	
	Exposure Shock				Mild Stress		Moderate Stress		Severe Stress	
					Nil		5%		5%	
	Exposure (E)	Expos. % share	RW	RWA	Changed Exposure %	Changed RWA	Changed Exposure %	Changed RWA	Changed Exposure %	Changed RWA
AAA	3358	5.51%	20%	206	2.56%	223.53	2.56%	234.70	2.12%	194.30
AA	5844	9.60%	30%	1170	8.65%	1133.45	8.65%	1190.12	6.30%	867.02
A	6640	10.90%	50%	2532	7.73%	1687.20	7.73%	1771.56	8.87%	2034.39
BBB	14866	24.41%	100%	11569	9.04%	3945.99	9.04%	4143.29	6.39%	2931.47
BB & Below	6431	10.56%	150%	7962	10.69%	7003.89	10.53%	7240.71	19.21%	13210.19
D	0	0.00%								
D with <20% prov.	0	0.00%	150%		1.80%	1181.32	1.78%	1224.51	11.42%	7852.30
D with prov.>20% of O/s but<50%	0	0.00%	100%		3.44%	1500.09	3.39%	1554.94	2.14%	981.54
D with prov. at least 50%	0	0.00%	50%		3.35%	731.29	3.31%	758.03	0.71%	163.59
Unrated (UR)	23770	39.03%	100%	16796	52.74%	23030.86	53.02%	24308.38	42.83%	19637.68
Total	60909	100.00%		40235	100%	40437.62	100%	42426.25	100%	47872.47
Basel II min, Regulatory Capital (9%×RWA)	3621.2					3639.39		3818.36		4308.52
Additional Capital Requirement						18.24		197.21		687.37
						0.50%		5.45%		18.98%
Effect on Bank's overall CRAR	14.23%					14.20%		13.92%		13.20%
						-0.03%		-0.31%		-1.03%

Source: Author's illustration.

This way, every bank needs to perform stress test to ensure bank's capital adequacy in times of shocks. Stress-test modelling is a forward-looking approach which complements other risk management tools like credit value at risk (C-VaR) or economic capital (EC). Servigny and Renault (2003) have given a nice illustration on scenario-based credit VaR computation in growth and recession situations. They considered a growth scenario that has a low PD (4.31 per cent) and lower default correlation (0.77 per cent) compared to a recession scenario that has high PD (8.88 per cent) as well as high default correlation (1.5 per cent). A third scenario is a hybrid one with high PD (8.88 per cent) but with low correlation (0.77 per cent). All these three scenarios were applied on a VaR analysis to assess the contribution of correlation on EC. Stress-testing model allows a risk manager to test the capital safety cushion during stress events caused by business cycle undulations. This way, stress testing enables the bank to absorb the unexpected systematic shocks during trough phase of the economic cycle and will eventually make the bank's capital more stable (i.e. through the cycle).

The meaningful stress tests should tie back into the management decision-making process. The regulatory authorities are also involved in monitoring the systemic risk and set various macro-prudential policies (e.g. in the form of counter-cyclical buffer, dynamic provisioning norms, monetary policy measures, setting stress-testing guidelines, prudential limits, etc.) to check these pro-cyclical behaviours and ensure economic stability.

It is important to remember that stress capital acts as shock absorber for banks to maintain a steady growth in the lending business. Stress tests actually complement the standard capital adequacy and economic capital measures and help the management to plan responses to stress scenarios and facilitate communication of the same internally and to regulators.

RAROC, Hurdle Rate and EVA

The RAROC is the risk-adjusted post tax income divided by economic capital or credit VaR. It measures the performance of a business unit on a risk-adjusted basis. It is calculated as the economic return divided by economic capital. RAROC helps determine if a financial entity has the right balance between capital, returns and risk. The central concept in risk-adjusted return on capital (RAROC) is economic capital: the amount of capital a company should put aside it needed based on the risk it runs. It helps banks to evaluate the performance of business units and strategies on a risk-adjusted basis by enabling the implementation of risk-adjusted performance measures (RAPM).

The ultimate goal of a risk-based capital allocation system like RAROC is to provide a uniform measure of performance. Management can use this measure to evaluate performance for capital budgeting and as an input to the compensation system. The term "allocation" of capital refers to the process whereby a notional or pro forma calculation of the amount of capital underpinning a business is made.

The RAROC for a loan or business unit or a region can be estimated using the following formula:

$$RAROC = \frac{(Intr\_Inc + Fee\_Inc - CoF - CoO - EL) \times (1-t)}{EC} \qquad \text{Eq. 7.4}$$

where $Intr\_Inc$: Interest income on advances; Fee_Inc: Fee income related to advances; CoF: Cost of funds (mainly deposit cost); CoO: Cost of operations; EL = Expected loss = $EAD \times PD \times LGD$; EC = Economic capital and t = Corporate tax rate (e.g. t = 34% in India).

The above expression can be used to compute the post-tax RAROC. The numerator portion within bracket is also called pre-tax risk-adjusted income.

Where the numerator is:
Risk-adjusted net income (in absolute rupee terms) =
+   Expected revenues (Gross interest income + Other revenues, e.g. fees)
–   Cost of funds
–   Non-interest operating expenses
+   Other transfer pricing allocations
–   Expected credit losses

The formulation of the numerator assumes that the expected risk-adjusted net income is a good proxy for the free cash flows to the shareholders at the end of the period. The numerator can be expressed either in absolute rupee terms or in percentage.

The denominator is:
Economic capital (in absolute rupee terms or in percentage)
= Amount of risk capital required for the bank as a whole/business/ product line/customer/transaction

For example, a 1-year bullet loan has yield of 9.5 per cent, cost of funds 5.5 per cent and operating expenses 2.5 per cent, EL of 0.50 per cent and EC of 4 per cent. The hurdle rate (HR) is 15 per cent. The post-tax RAROC (assuming tax rate of 34 per cent) of the loan is estimated as 16.50 per cent. Once calculated, the RAROC is to be compared with some hurdle rate reflecting the bank's cost of funds or the opportunity cost of stockholders in holding equity in the bank.

First generation RAROC compares RAROC to a hurdle rate; i.e. if RAROC is above a firm-wide hurdle rate (e.g. cost of equity capital), then the project is accepted. But its flaw is that it will reward risky projects: projects that have a higher RAROC but add to the firm's total risk (which is not incorporated).

Second generation RAROC fixes this by requiring that the project's RAROC exceeds the firm's expected return; i.e. projects are accepted if RAROC > [Market return – Riskless rate] × Beta + Riskless rate.

In RAROC models, the hurdle rate may also be proxied by the expected return on equity (ROE) or post-tax cost of equity capital (risk premium attached). If RAROC > Hurdle rate, then loan or project or business unit is viewed as value adding (i.e. Economic value added or EVA > 0).

$$\therefore\ Economic\ profit = Risk\text{-}adjusted\ Income - HR \times EC \qquad \text{Eq. 7.5}$$

Where, risk-adjusted income is the first component within the bracket of the numerator of RAROC expression as depicted in equation 7.3. HR is the hurdle rate which defines the opportunity cost of losing capital for a project.

All can be estimated either pre-tax or post-tax basis. It is important to note that pre-tax risk-adjusted income should be compared with pre-tax cost of capital (HR × EC). This way, economic profit gives us an estimate of the amount of the dollar (or rupee) amounts of the contribution to shareholder value. In terms of shareholder value, the management can decide the businesses that generate the most shareholder value in dollar denomination.

Thus, economic profits are neither accounting profits nor cash flows. They rather represent the contribution of a business or transaction to the value of the firm by considering the opportunity cost of the capital that finances the business or transaction. If the economic profit is positive, shareholder value is enhanced by the business. If the economic profit is negative, shareholder value is eroded by the business.

This "economic profit concept" is increasingly used to measure the efficiency of a project. This new concept is an extension of the technique to the valuation of different strategic options within companies (or FIs) so as to ensure that the maximum value is created for the shareholders.

It can also be expressed as RARORAC (risk-adjusted return on risk-adjusted capital):

$$= \frac{(\text{Risk Adjusted Income} - HR \times EC)}{EC}$$

RAROC can be also estimated as post-tax basis.

Hurdle rate is computed using capital asset pricing model (CAPM):

$$HR = r_f + \beta \times (\pi - r_f) \qquad \text{Eq. 7.6}$$

Where r_f is the risk-free rate (we have used 364 T bills rate as risk-free rate); β = equity beta estimated for the bank using the daily closing stock price data of the bank vis-à-vis the index return (BSE 500 index closing), π = average market index return over 10 years. For example, if we find annualized average stock market return = 12.16 per cent on an annual basis and bank beta = 1 and risk-free rate 8 per cent, the hurdle rate (HR) would be 8% + 1 × 4.16 % = 12.16%.

The beta coefficient (β) of bank stocks can be calculated by time series regression of the bank's stock returns and the returns on the equity index selected. One can use ordinary least square regression to estimate the beta.

Finally, post tax RAROC of a project is compared with its hurdle rate. The project is viable or acceptable when RAROC is greater than its hurdle rate. One can also estimate the expected return of the project that should be generated if the project has to contribute to the shareholder value.

This way, RAROC attempts to address the issue of capital allocation from the perspective of improving performance measured from both inside the bank as well from the outside. It is argued that RAROC-based capital allocation process can improve returns earned on that capital. The use of RAROC as a performance measurement tool helps the management to maximize the return for shareholders by bringing risk considerations in the calculation of return and choosing business strategy on the basis of risk-adjusted returns.

Risk-based Pricing Model

RAROC metric also enables the pricing of products on the basis of risk-adjusted return for different segments of customers. For a credit customer of the bank, RAROC calculations become very important in the light of pricing the underlying loan products to the customer. To ensure that a loan to a credit customer adds value to the bank, the loan should be priced such that the RAROC as estimated for the customer is at least not below the hurdle rate of the bank. Pricing a credit customer of the bank as per the RAROC framework would ensure that each credit asset of the bank would at least not erode shareholder value at the margin and that the economic profit generated by the credit asset would be non-negative.

Let us consider an example where a loan of $10,000 for 1 year to a borrower-rated BBB gives collateral such that the loss in the event of default (LGD) is 30 per cent with no uncertainty. The average default correlation with the rest of the portfolio is 4 per cent. The EL for the loan is $60 (see equation 6.1 for the formula). Now, one can estimate the UL and UL contribution (or Marginal Risk Contribution, MRC) of the loan in $ amount. Using equation 6.2 and equation 6.20 worked out in Chapter 6, we obtain: UL = $420 and ULC = $84.

Next, using a capital multiplier of 6, one can get an estimate of the economic capital (EC) for the loan in $ amount. The estimated EC value is $504.

Now, if the customer is charged an interest of 9 per cent (yield); and cost of fund (CoF) is worked out to be 5 per cent and average operating cost (CoO) of the loan is 2 per cent, we can now calculate the pre-tax RAROC of the loan as: 27.78 per cent (using expression 7.3, without tax deduction). Here, RAROC is defined as the expected net profit divided by the economic capital. If the pre-tax hurdle rate is 27 per cent, the estimated economic value addition (EVA) of this loan would be 0.78 per cent. This amount is also termed as the economic profit of the loan.

The risk-based pricing framework has been summarized in Chart 7.5. The main purpose of risk-adjusted pricing is to ensure optimal allocation of capital funds and earn adequate return on it. Mispricing of loans results in adverse selection of assets and non-achievement of the desired return on net worth. Risk-adjusted pricing has achieved global acceptance as a tool to maintain proactive provisioning and earn adequate return on the capital. This concept acts as a basis for our calculation of credit risk protection fee.

Risk charge (or risk spread or premium) of a loan takes care of two different types of losses that a risk manager has to bear: expected loss (EL) and unexpected loss (UL). Expected loss is the long-run average loss. Unexpected loss necessitates the allocation of capital (economic capital or capital at risk), which is assumed to be at least invested in risk-free securities. The opportunity cost of the capital thus allocated would need to be priced adequately. This is done by multiplying the economic capital with a factor called hurdle rate. The hurdle rate is the difference between the desired return on net worth and the risk-free rate (e.g. return on equity can be a proxy).

Chart 7.5: Risk-based Loan Pricing Framework

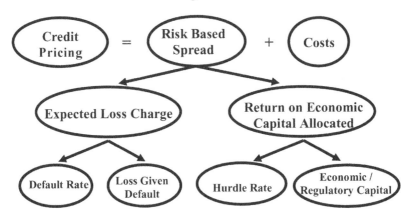

Source: Author's illustration.

The following steps are generally undertaken to estimate the total credit risk premium:

Total risk charge = EL charge + UL charge   Eq. 7.7

EL charge = PD × LGD   Eq. 7.8

UL charge = EC Charge = Return on EC   Eq. 7.9

Return on EC = EC of a Loan × Hurdle rate   Eq. 7.10

Economic capital of a loan = ECi = k × MRCi   Eq. 7.11

Here, k = 6 has been used to capture non-normal credit loss tail.

Marginal risk contribution of a loan (MRCi) is the unexpected loss contribution of that loan to the entire portfolio of education loans. Using the default correlation, we can now determine the marginal risk contribution of that loan to the portfolio as a whole:

$$MRC_i = \sqrt{\rho_i} UL_i$$ Eq. 7.12

This relationship is used for the calculation of unexpected loss spread.

Let us explain the "risk charge calculation" of a loan with a numerical example. Suppose that we are pricing a CR4 rated 1-year retail loan with an expected probability of default (PD) = 2.57 per cent, LGD of 72.48 per cent and standard deviation of PD is 1.18 per cent. These figures are obtained from the retail pool average (let's consider education loan pool). The average spread based on expected loss (EL) = 1.86 per cent. These numbers are obtained from Table 7.3. The average cost of funds (CoF) is 7 per cent and cost of operations (CoO) is 1.2 per cent.

Next, we have to estimate the unexpected loss charge as well to derive the total credit risk spread for the loan. The UL of the loan is estimated as 0.85 per cent (=SD(PD) × LGD). The EC of the loan is 0.71 per cent, which has been derived by using a capital multiplier of 6 on marginal risk contribution of the loan (Eq. 7.12). Next, assume that the minimum return one should earn from the project for taking risk (and hence holding EC) is 20 per cent. This is termed as hurdle rate which represents the opportunity cost of risk capital. This may be represented by borrowing cost or return on equity. A bank can also use capital asset pricing model (CAPM) to estimate the hurdle rate. Therefore, the cost of EC is: 20% × 0.71% = 0.14% (or 14 basis points). Therefore, total credit spread for the loan = 1.86% + 0.14% = 2% (or 200 basis points). Thus, the prime lending rate for the loan works out to be 7.00% + 1.20% + 2.00% = 10.20%. Note that the EL charge needs to be properly adjusted to EC charge to avoid double counting problem. Table 7.10 illustrates how risk-based loan pricing based on a target return can be practically applied across risk grades in a bank.

Table 7.10: Risk-based Loan Pricing Chart

Credit Score Band	750–800+	700–750	650–700	600–650	550–699
Base Rate	10%	10%	10%	10%	10%
Risk Premium	(0.20%)	0.1%	0.7%	1.6%	2.6%
Rate to Borrower	9.8%	10.1%	10.7%	11.6%	12.6%
Cost of Funds	(6.5%)	(6.5%)	(6.5%)	(6.5%)	(6.5%)
Operating Expenses	(2.5%)	(2.5%)	(2.5%)	(2.5%)	(2.5%)
Loan Loss Charge	(0.30%)	(0.6%)	(1.2%)	(2.1%)	(3.1%)
Target Net Return	0.50%	0.50%	0.50%	0.50%	0.50%

Source: Author's illustration.
Note: For illustration purpose only.

It is important to note that for long duration loan pricing (say a 2-year loan), the bank will have to use cumulative PD or chain-based two-year measure of LGD and the changing amount of EC to estimate the RAROC for the loan.

Portfolio Optimization

Portfolio theory describes how portfolio risk and return are determined from the risk and return of the instruments in the portfolio. The returns can be added up, however, risks do not. Correlations between assets determine how risks combine in a portfolio. We have seen how risk contribution measures the risk of an instrument in the portfolio. Portfolio optimization requires bringing risk contributions into line with returns.

In order to take advantage of credit portfolio management opportunities, the answer to the following technical questions is important:

- What is the risk of a given portfolio as opposed to individual exposures comprising the portfolio?
- What is the risk and return implications of changing the portfolio mix?

In portfolio optimization exercise, we have to set some objective functions:

- Objective Function 1: Minimize credit risk (i.e. unexpected loss: UL_p) subject to a target yield (expected yield, e.g. hurdle rate).
- Objective Function 2: Maximize portfolio yield subject to a target credit risk.
- Objective Function 3: Maximize RAROC.

The portfolio optimization and return comparison exercise has been illustrated in the following numerical example:

A portfolio manager holds two loans with the following return and risk characteristics presented in Table 7.11.

Table 7.11: Return and Risk of a Two-asset Portfolio Case

Loans	Exposure Share	Rating	Annual Yield of the loan over cost of funds	Annual Fees	Facility LGD	Borrower PD	Default Correlation
1	60%	BBB	5.50%	1.50%	40.00%	2.00%	
2	40%	BB	7.50%	1.00%	20.00%	10.00%	8.21%[$]

Source: Author created example.

Note: [$] Default correlation value has been taken from Table 6.5.

Using the above table inputs, one can estimate the expected net return and unexpected risk of both the loans in the following manner:

$E(R_1)=(5.50\%+1.50\%)-(2\%\times40\%)=6.20\%$

$UL_1=40\% \times \sqrt{2\%\times98\%} =5.60\%$

Similarly, for second loan:

$E(R_2)=(7.50\%+1.00\%)-(10\%\times20\%)=6.50\%$

$UL_2=20\% \times \sqrt{10\%\times90\%} =6.00\%$

The overall expected return and unexpected risk of the portfolio is:

$E(R_P)=60\%\times(6.20\%)+40\%\times(6.50\%)=6.32\%$

$UL_P=$

$$\sqrt{(60\%)^2 \times (5.60\%)^2 +(40\%)^2 \times (6.00\%)^2 + 2\times(60\%)\times(40\%)\times8.21\%\times(5.60\%)\times(6.00\%)}$$

$=4.29\%$

One can check that the portfolio unexpected loss is significantly lower than the unexpected losses of each loan. This is due to the correlation effect.

We can also work out the marginal risk contribution (or termed as unexpected loss contribution) of each loan:

$$RC_1 = \frac{60\%\times5.60\%\times(60\%\times5.60\% + 40\%\times8.21\%\times6.00\%)}{4.29\%} =2.79\%$$

$$RC_2 = \frac{40\%\times6.00\%\times(40\%\times6.00\% + 60\%\times8.21\%\times5.60\%)}{4.29\%} =1.50\%$$

Note that $RC_1 + RC_2 = UL_P = 4.29\%$

Portfolio management ultimately consists of changing weights to bring risks in line with expected returns. Optimization requires bringing risk contributions into line with returns. A template for computation of credit VaR for a multiple assets loan portfolio along its technical assessment of RAROC has been illustrated in Annexure 7.1A and 7.1B at the end of this chapter. This template can be used to measure how a variation in the industry correlation factor is significantly changing the EC and RAROC number even if PD and LGD are held constant. Several simulations can be run based on various scenarios to check their impact on EC and RAROC. Hence, default correlation and concentrations can extensively drive the results of EC modelling.

Estimation of RAROC for a Bank as a Whole

A bank should necessarily assess its risk-adjusted profitability by comparing its post-tax RAROC with its cost of capital. Accordingly, we first estimate the RAROC for a bank as a whole. This exercise has been shown in Table 7.12.

Table 7.12: Risk-adjusted Returns of a Large Public Sector Bank

Year	2011-12	2012-13
Yield on Advances (%)	12.16	12.27
Cost of Funds (%)	7.36	7.56
Operating Expenses (%)	1.31	1.36
Provisions for NPA (%)	0.95	1.21
EL% (Estimated)	2.18	2.18
Pre-tax net income (%)	1.87	1.77
Credit-VaR (%)	9.81	9.81
Economic Capital (%)	8.86	8.60
Corporate Tax Rate (%)	34.00	34.00
RAROC (%)	13.93	13.58
Hurdle Rate (ROE%)	11.91	9.91
EVA (%)	2.02	3.67

Source: Audited balance sheet data of a bank.

In order to calculate bank level RAROC, we have collected information about income and cost estimates of the same bank whose NPA movements and economic capital estimations are shown in Tables 7.1 and 7.2. The income and cost estimates are obtained from the bank's audited annual reports and RBI database.

Regional RAROC Estimates

The region-wise RAROC estimation (in terms of unexpected loss) would help the top management in banks to compare performance and allocate capital to minimize concentration risk. Charts 7.6 and 7.7 compare the regional RAROC position of two banks studied by us.

Chart 7.6: Regional RAROC Position: Large Bank Case

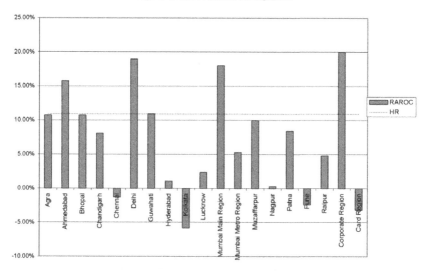

Regional RAROC Position of the Large Bank

Source: Author's illustration.

Chart 7.7: Regional RAROC Position: Mid-sized Bank Case

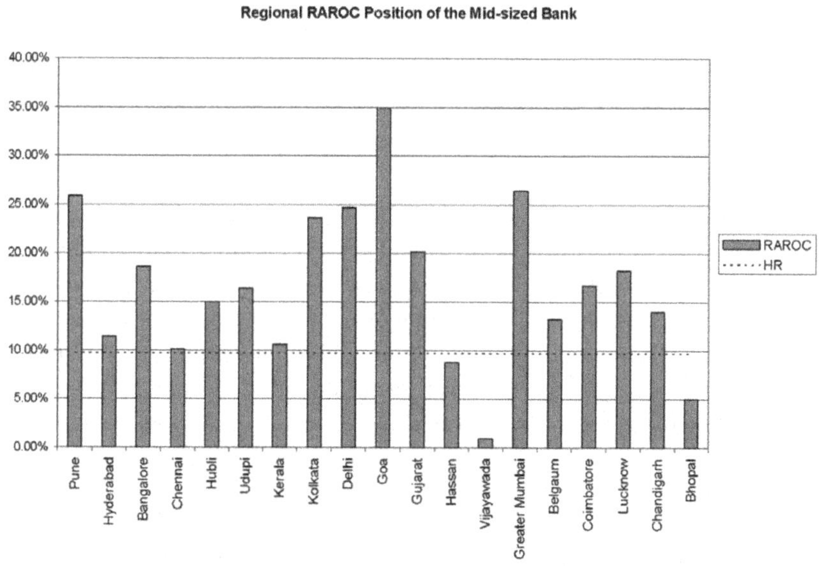

Regional RAROC Position of the Mid-sized Bank

Source: Author's illustration.

The regions, whose risk contributions are higher, should ensure adequate return to ensure stability in the bank's overall solvency position. Consequently, we compute the risk-adjusted return on economic capital or RAROC for all the regions of these two banks to identify the regions that are having higher RAROC in comparison to a hurdle rate.

We have taken the regional unexpected losses in the denominator of RAROC formula as expressed in equation 7.3 and also use region-wide income and expenditure obtained from regional balance sheet data of these two banks to compute region-wide RAROC numbers. The regional ECs have been computed in Table 7.4.

The bank is making economic profits in regions where RAROC is above the hurdle rate of the bank. The bank can use this analysis to target the performance of individual regions and may attempt to bring them above the hurdle. Such RAROC–EVA exercise also facilitates the bank in setting return targets, deposit mix, rates and volumes, advance, mix, rates and volumes, target other income, set recovery targets while planning their business growth. It also prods the bank to move away from the traditional "Transfer Pricing Mechanism" (TPM) to "Fund Transfer Pricing Mechanism" (FTP) to generate the desired business profile to augment its performance.

This way, the performance of various business segments, zones, regions and branches can be aligned to the overall corporate expectations in terms of RAROC and EVA. To successfully implement this, the vocabulary of risk management has to percolate down to the individual unit level of a bank. New performance benchmarks in the form of RAROC and EVA should form the unifying cord in every bank.

Estimating RAROC for a Business Unit/Product Line

The methodology for estimating RAROC for a business unit (for example, treasury/credit operations) or a particular product line (for example, retail credit products/wholesale credit products) is exactly the same as outlined for the bank as a whole. The first step would be to estimate the risk-adjusted returns for the business unit/product line. This will entail the allocation of revenues, cost of funds and operating costs to the business unit/product line. It would also require the estimation of the expected credit loss pertaining to the business unit/product line using a similar approach as outlined for the bank as a whole. The next step would be to internally allocate EC or Tier I capital to the business unit/product line. This can be done by first estimating the risk-adjusted assets of the business unit (by considering mainly credit risk) as a proportion of the total risk-adjusted assets of the bank. Tier I capital can be allocated in the same proportion. Otherwise, marginal risk contribution (MRC) of the loan needs to be estimated to calculate the EC of the loan. This has been already shown in the section, "risk-based pricing model".

The ratio of the risk-adjusted assets to the allocated EC (or Tier I Capital[2]) would give the RAROC for the business unit/product line. RAROC can be then compared to the hurdle rate estimated for the bank as a whole to determine whether the business or product adds to shareholder value or not. A bank can also determine different hurdle rates to set target returns for different business units. However, defining different target returns need for a differentiated beta for different businesses. The capital budgeting rule would be to increase capital allocation to those business units/product lines where the RAROC exceeds the hurdle rate. This way, capital allocation can be linked to the business planning process.

Summary

In this chapter we have explained how EC and RAROC can be estimated for the bank as a whole as well as at sub-portfolio level. EC method relates a bank's actual portfolio of risk to the amount of capital that the bank must hold if it is to achieve a particular solvency target. EC is the amount of capital a bank should put aside needed based on the risk it actually runs. After the US subprime crisis, it has been realized that stress-testing techniques need to be combined with economic and regulatory capital to better capture fat tail risks. During parallel run phase of IRB journey, supervisor therefore expects an EC approach to the internal capital adequacy assessment process (ICAAP) exercise. Adoption of an EC-based risk-adjusted performance measurement (RAPM) system should be driven primarily by business demands guided by the top management in bank. As banks become "capital-hungry" to meet their growth expectations and simultaneously meet the regulatory requirements in the more sophisticated Basel III era, they would have to remain responsive to the expectations of the market on a risk-adjusted basis to ensure the continued supply of financial capital from shareholders and human capital from the ultimate stakeholders. Through the RAMP framework, a bank can

---

[2] Tier I capital in a bank mainly comprises (a) retained earnings, (b) paid up equity capital and (c) free reserves (together called common equity). The innovative perpetual debt instruments (IPDI) and perpetual non-cumulative preference shares (PNCPS) are also eligible Tier I capital. The IPDI and PNCPS should not exceed 40 per cent of Tier I capital.

align the performance of individual zones/regions/branches to the overall corporate expectations in terms of RAROC and EVA.

The RAROC approach to evaluating performance of the bank, its business units, products lines, customers and transactions is well accepted and implemented by many internationally best-practiced banks (e.g. Bank of America). Perhaps the most important use of EC and RAROC at a bank is in guiding strategic decisions about growing, shrinking or fixing businesses. RAROC helps the top management to determine if a financial entity has the right balance between capital, returns and risk. At the sub-portfolio level, hard limits can be placed on notional exposure such that the EC as a percentage of exposure does not exceed a certain threshold (risk criteria rather than size criteria should be the basis). This way, banks can manage concentration risk in their credit portfolio as well.

RAROC tool can be also used to accept or reject a loan decision, compare profitability across business segments and workout a risk-based pricing framework. The RAROC calculation permits a bank not only to determine whether it is pricing an individual loan correctly, but also to check whether its overall portfolio of loans is priced adequately. A good transfer pricing mechanism can further strengthen the risk-adjusted performance measurement process to incentivize the performance of business units (e.g. credit, deposit and treasury) and thereby contribute to business growth of a bank. Adoption of RAPM system may enable Indian banks to make the difficult transition from mere regulatory compliance to internal business modelling. Risk-based capital allocation and performance measurement system focuses on tools to achieve shareholder value maximization through portfolio optimization.

Key learning outcomes

After studying the chapter and the relevant reading, you should be able to understand:

- Methodology for estimating credit VaR and EC
- Credit risk stress testing and scenario analysis
- Stress testing and bank capital
- Risk-adjusted return on capital (RAROC) and economic value addition (EVA)
- Use of RAPM framework in banking business
- Risk-based loan pricing

Review questions

1. Differentiate between regulatory capital (RC) and economic capital (EC).
2. What is the economic foundation of Basel II IRB capital?
3. How can stress testing on bank capital be conducted?
4. What is credit VaR and economic capital (EC)?
5. Do you think credit VaR varies with the size of the loan portfolio?
6. What is the difference between RAROC and RARORAC?
7. How can credit risk spread of a loan be estimated?
8. How can RAROC, Hurdle Rate and EVA of a business unit be estimated?
9. If the yield, expenses, cost of fund and expected loss of a loan are 9%, 1.5%, 6% and 1.5%, respectively, calculate the pre-tax income of the loan. If the economic capital is estimated as 4.5% and tax rate is 34%, what will be your estimate of the loan's RAROC?
10. Mention at least three uses of RAPM in an organization.
11. Do you think that economic capital number can be applied to tactical and competitive decisions by the top management?

References

Bandyopadhyay, A. and A. Saha. 2007. "New Drivers of Business Growth", *Business Standard,* November.

Bangia, A., F. Diebold, A. Kronimus, C. Schagen and T. Schuermann. 2002. "Ratings Migration and the Business Cycle, with Application to Credit Portfolio Stress Testing", *Journal of Banking and Finance* 26: 445–74.

BCBS. 2006. "International Convergence of Capital Measurement and Capital Standards: A Revised Framework", Publication No. 128, Basel Committee on Banking Supervision, Bank for International Settlements, Basel, June.

Borio, C., M. Drehmann and K. Tsatsaroris. 2012. "Stress-testing Macro Stress Testing: Does it Live up to Expectations? BIS Working Paper, No. 369.

De Servigny and O. Renault. 2003. "Default Correlation: Empirical Evidence", S&P Working Paper.

Haubenstock, M.J. 1998. "Linking RAROC to Strategic Planning", *The Journal of Lending and Credit Risk Management*, October: 26–31.

Helbekkmo, H. 2006. "Retail Banks and Economic Capital: Special Issues and Opportunities", *RMA Journal* 89(2): 62–68.

Jakubik, P. and C. Schmieder. 2008. "Stress Testing Credit Risk: Comparison of the Czech Republic and Germany". BIS Working Paper. FSI.

Jakubik, P. and G.D. Sutton. 2011. "Thoughts on the Proper Design of Macro Stress Tests", BIS Working Paper, No. 60.

James, C. 1996. "RAROC Based Capital Budgeting and Performance Evaluation: A Case Study of Bank Capital Allocation", Wharton Working Paper, No. 96–40.

Jokivuolle, E. and S. Peura. 2010. "Rating Targeting and Dynamic Economic Capital", *The Journal of Risk* 12 (4): 3–13.

Matten, C. 2003. *Managing Bank Capital: Capital Allocation and Performance Measurement* (New York: John Wiley).

Nickell, P., W. Perraudin and S. Varotto. 2000. "Stability of Rating Transitions" *Journal of Banking and Finance* 24: 203–27.

Saunders, A. 1999. Credit Risk Measurement: New Approaches to Value at Risk and Other Paradigms, 1st edition, Chapter 13 (New York: John Wiley & Sons).

Wilhite, G. 2006. "Stressed LGDs in Capital Analysis", *The RMA Journal* October: 56–61.

Annexure 7.1A: Template for Estimating Portfolio Economic Capital

Values are in $ unit

Obligor Details			Default rate		Loss%	Sector split				Expected Loss	Unexp Loss
Company Name	Exposure	Credit Rating	Mean Def. Rate	Std. Dev.	LGD	Sector A	Sector B	Sector C	Total	Expected Loss	Unexp Loss
1	358,475	H	15.00%	35.71%	45%	100%	0%	0%	100%	24197	57601
2	1,089,819	H	15.00%	35.71%	45%	0%	100%	0%	100%	73563	175114
3	1,799,710	F	5.00%	21.79%	35%	0%	100%	0%	100%	31495	137283
4	1,933,116	G	10.00%	30.00%	40%	100%	0%	0%	100%	77325	231974
5	2,317,327	G	10.00%	30.00%	40%	0%	0%	100%	100%	92693	278079
6	2,410,929	G	10.00%	30.00%	40%	0%	100%	0%	100%	96437	289311
7	2,652,184	H	15.00%	35.71%	45%	100%	0%	0%	100%	179022	426159
8	2,957,685	G	10.00%	30.00%	40%	0%	100%	0%	100%	118307	354922
9	3,137,989	D	2.00%	14.00%	25%	0%	0%	100%	100%	15690	109830
10	3,204,044	D	2.00%	14.00%	25%	0%	0%	100%	100%	16020	112142
11	4,727,724	A	0.10%	3.16%	10%	100%	0%	0%	100%	473	14943
12	4,830,517	D	2.00%	14.00%	25%	0%	0%	100%	100%	24153	169068
13	4,912,097	D	2.00%	14.00%	25%	0%	0%	100%	100%	24560	171923
14	4,928,989	H	15.00%	35.71%	45%	0%	100%	0%	100%	332707	792000
15	5,042,312	F	5.00%	21.79%	35%	0%	100%	0%	100%	88240	384631
16	5,320,364	E	3.00%	17.06%	30%	0%	100%	0%	100%	47883	272276
17	5,435,457	D	2.00%	14.00%	25%	100%	0%	0%	100%	27177	190241
18	5,517,586	C	1.00%	9.95%	20%	100%	0%	0%	100%	11035	109799
19	5,764,596	E	3.00%	17.06%	30%	100%	0%	0%	100%	51881	295010
20	5,847,845	C	1.00%	9.95%	20%	100%	0%	0%	100%	11696	116371
21	6,466,533	H	15.00%	35.71%	45%	100%	0%	0%	100%	436491	1039056
22	6,480,322	H	15.00%	35.71%	45%	0%	0%	100%	100%	437422	1041272

Annexure 7.1A contd.

Annexure 7.1A contd.

23	7,727,651	B	0.50%	7.05%	15%	100%	100%	0%	100%	5796	81759
24	15,410,906	F	5.00%	21.79%	35%	0%	0%	100%	100%	269691	1175555
25	20,238,895	E	3.00%	17.06%	30%	100%	0%	0%	100%	182150	1035749
Total	130,513,072									2676105	9062068

$Million 1,305

	Exposure	EL	UL
Sector A	58942411	1001447	3516901.504
Sector B	18503854	561867.6	1541079.292
Sector C	53066807	1112790	4004087.633
Total	130513072	2676105	9062068.43

Sector	Industry
A	Auto
B	Building Material
C	Chemicals

Correlation	Sector A	Sector B	Sector C
Sector A	11%	9.00%	4.00%
Sector B		10.60%	3.00%
Sector C			13%

Multiplication Factor	5
VAR	7.46%
Economic Capital ($)	9742535
Economic Capital ($Mn)	9.7425

Source: Author's excel illustration

Annexure 7.1B: Template for Estimating RAROC and EVA

Units in $

Name	Obligor Exposure	Risk & Earning Details Credit Rating	Int. Rate	Expected Loss	Interest Income
1	358,475	H	14.00%	24197.0625	50186.5
2	1,089,819	H	14.00%	73562.7825	152574.66
3	1,799,710	F	13.00%	31494.925	233962.3
4	1,933,116	G	13.50%	77324.64	260970.66
5	2,317,327	G	13.50%	92693.08	312839.145
6	2,410,929	G	13.50%	96437.16	325475.415
7	2,652,184	H	14.00%	179022.42	371305.76
8	2,957,685	G	13.50%	118307.4	399287.475
9	3,137,989	D	12.00%	15689.945	376558.68
10	3,204,044	D	12.00%	16020.22	384485.28
11	4,727,724	A	11.00%	472.7724	520049.64
12	4,830,517	D	12.00%	24152.585	579662.04
13	4,912,097	D	12.00%	24560.485	589451.64
14	4,928,989	H	14.00%	332706.7575	690058.46
15	5,042,312	F	13.00%	88240.46	655500.56
16	5,320,364	E	12.50%	47883.276	665045.5
17	5,435,457	D	12.00%	27177.285	652254.84
18	5,517,586	C	11.50%	11035.172	634522.39
19	5,764,596	E	12.50%	51881.364	720574.5
20	5,847,845	C	11.50%	11695.69	672502.175
21	6,466,533	H	14.00%	436490.9775	905314.62
22	6,480,322	H	14.00%	437421.735	907245.08
23	7,727,651	B	11.25%	5795.73825	869360.7375
24	15,410,906	F	13.00%	269690.855	2003417.78
25	20,238,895	E	12.50%	182150.055	2529861.875
Total	130,513,072			2676105	16462468
				2.05%	12.61%

Economic Capital	9742535
Interest Income	16462468
Expected Loss	2676105
Cost of Funds	7.5%
Net Interest Income	6673987
Operating Expenses (@2%)	2610261
Revenue less Expenses	4063726
RAROC	14.24%
HR	14%
EVA	0.24%

Source: Author's excel illustration.

## Chapter 8

Basel II IRB Approach of Measuring Credit Risk Regulatory Capital

The Basel Committee on Banking Supervision (BCBS) issued its revised framework on "International Convergence of Capital Measurement and Capital Standards" in June 2006. This Basel II capital norm intends to foster a strong emphasis on risk management practices and encourage the ongoing improvements in banks' internal risk assessment capabilities. The Reserve Bank of India released its Revised Draft Guidelines for implementation of the New Capital Adequacy Framework (NCAF) in April, 2007. Following the release of RBI NCAF guidelines, Indian banks started implementing the Basel II regulatory norms. First, Indian banks with overseas presence and branches of foreign banks in India implemented the Basel II standardized approach for credit risk on 31 March 2008. The other banks were also in the Basel II regime by March end 2009. Indian banks were encouraged to maintain, at both solo and consolidated level, a Tier I CRAR of at least 6 per cent.[1] Banks which were below this level were asked to achieve this ratio on or before 31 March 2010. The purpose of the Basel II framework was to ensure that the

---

[1] $Total\ CRAR = \dfrac{Eligible\ Tier\ 1\ +\ Tier\ 2\ Capital\ Funds}{Credit\ Risk\ RWA\ +\ Market\ Risk\ RWA\ +\ Operational\ Risk\ RWA}$

Where RWA means Risk-weighted Assets; CRAR means Capital to Risk-weighted Assets Ratio.

minimum levels of capital are held by internationally active banks against their exposures to ensure solvency and financial stability.

The revised capital rules, especially the codifications of the Basel II IRB Formulations, represent a dramatic change as compared to Basel I and Basel II Standardized Approach. The new regulations recognize the advances in the science of credit risk management and provide incentives by allowing users of more sophisticated credit risk management techniques. Basel II is designed to extend and refine the regulatory approach outlined in Basel I used in measuring credit and operational risk. Its main goals are:

- to maintain the current level of capital in the financial system while creating incentives for a risk-sensitive management and
- to reduce the possibility for regulatory capital arbitrage (cherry picking by banks-incentive to minimize their capital cost by applying approach with least capital cost for each single exposure in their loan portfolio).

As a member of G20, the Reserve Bank of India (RBI) has now also issued final norms for Basel II IRB migration in December 2011.[2] The RBI in its Basel II IRB guidelines has advised the banks intending to move to IRB approaches for credit risk to assess their preparedness for the same with reference to the guidelines. The internal ratings-based approach (IRB) to credit risk is one of the most innovative elements of the new framework because it allows the banks to themselves determine certain key elements in the calculation of their capital requirements.

The time line for earliest application for Basel II IRB approach is set at 1 April 2012 and earliest approval possible by 1 April 2014. Journey should have already begun for Indian banks.

The introduction of Basel II has incentivized many of the best practices banks, both internationally and in the Indian economy to adopt better risk management techniques and to reconsider the analyses that must be carried out to evaluate their performance relative to market expectations and relative to competitors.

---

[2] See "Implementation of the Internal Rating Based (IRB) Approaches for Calculation of Capital Charge for Credit Risk" released by RBI through DBOD circular BP.BC.67/21.06.202/2011–12, dated 22 December 2011 which is also called Basel II IRB circular in India by RBI.

Basel II Capital Charge for Credit Risk

Basel II proposes three different approaches to calculating regulatory capital to cover credit risk:

1. **The standardized approach:** It allows banks to use external ratings to estimate risk weights and rules are prescribed for credit risk mitigation.
2. **The foundation internal ratings-based (IRB) approach:** It is a methodology permitting a bank to use its own internal risk-rating system, including its own calculation of PD, but with the LGD and EAD factors provided by the supervisors.
3. **The advanced IRB approach:** It bases capital calculations on a bank's own supervisory-validated models, including bank-calculated PD, EAD and LGDs.

Chart 8.1 depicts various stages of progress in measurement and management of credit risk under Basel regime. As the banks move towards a more sophisticated approach, they will be able to more accurately measure the credit risk inherent in their business. This is capital saving in terms of regulatory requirements.

Chart 8.1: Credit Risk Measurement Approaches under Basel II/III

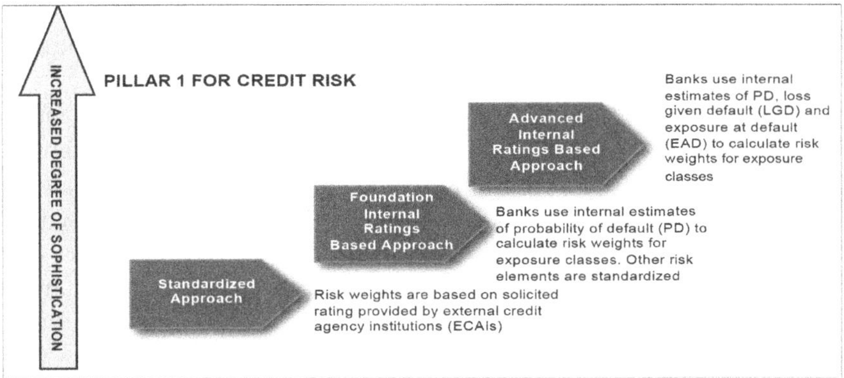

Source: BCBS, 2006.

The simplest is the standardized approach in which all rules pertaining to the estimation of PD, EAD and LGD are set by the regulator. This circular was issued by RBI in April 2007. Alternatively, banks may use own risk estimation systems by introducing an internal ratings-based approach (IRB approach) to measure credit risk. The ratings must comprise at minimum five years data for the probability of default (PD), seven years data for loss given default (LGD) and the exposure at default (EAD) and maturity of the credit (M). Banks which make use of the IRB foundation (FIRB) approach have to determine the PD and are to obtain operational values for the EAD, LGD and M from the national supervisory authority (in India, the RBI). Banks which apply the IRB advanced approach have to estimate the LGD, EAD and M, in addition to the PD using their internal data history.

For the two IRB approaches, the capital requirement is calculated from the pre-set supervisory formulas, using the banks own input. It is important to note that the risk-weight function developed by the Basel committee is used to calculate the unexpected losses (UL) only. Banks must calculate and manage the expected loss (EL) through pricing and provisioning.

EL and economic capital for credit risk are conceptually comparable to loan loss provisions and regulatory capital. Basel II advanced approaches align regulatory capital for credit risk more in line with economic capital (reflects the actual risk position of a bank), which has also implications for the relation between EL and loan loss provisions.

A. *The Standardized Approach*

The standardized approach is conceptually the same as the Basel I Accord, but is more risk sensitive as it is intended to adequately reflect credit risk. The new accord is supposed to make credit supply more risk sensitive than it was under the old arrangement. The bank allocates a risk weight to each of its assets and off-balance sheet positions and produces a sum of risk-weighted asset values. The risk-weights are assigned based on external credit agency ratings of borrowers (ECAIs) as given by the regulator. A risk weight of 100 per cent means that an exposure is included in the calculation of risk-weighted assets at its full value, which translates into a capital charge equal to 8 per cent of that value (in India it is 9 per cent). Similarly, a risk-weight of 20 per cent results in a capital charge of 1.6 per cent (i.e. one-fifth of 8 per cent).

Individual risk weights currently depend on the broad category of borrower (i.e. sovereigns, banks or corporates). Under Basel II, the risk weights are to be refined by reference to a rating provided by an external credit assessment institution (such as a rating agency or ECAIs) that meets strict standards. For example, for corporate lending, the existing Accord provides only one risk-weight category of 100 per cent but the new Accord will provide five categories in India (20 per cent for AAA corporates, 30 per cent for AA, 50 per cent for A, 100 per cent for BBB and 150 per cent for BB and below categories of assets). For details on risk weights, see Table 8.1. The risk-weighted assets for a loan exposure are estimated as follows:

Amount of loan (EAD) × *Risk weight (RW)* × 9%
= the capital required to be held against any given loan   Eq. 8.1

A major difference in the new standardized approach for credit risk is that it uses rating agency grades to determine risk buckets for claims, instead of the current regulatory buckets of sovereign, bank, residential real estate and corporate. Also new in the standardized approach are capital requirements for repo liabilities and undrawn commitments of one year and under in maturity. And the standardized approach gives retail exposures and claims backed by residential real estate lower risk weightings.

A snapshot of the risk weights for various categories of assets as stipulated by RBI under Basel II standardized approach has been summarized in Table 8.1. These risk weights have been used by the banks in estimating their regulatory capital requirements under the Basel II standardized approach.

Table 8.1: Risk weights under the Basel II Standardized Approach as per RBI's prescriptions

Portfolio	Standardized Approach Risk Weight (RW)
Sovereign Exposures	0% risk weight for domestic sovereign exposure, 20% for state govt., claims on foreign sovereign exposure depend on external credit rating: AAA to AA=0%, A=10%, BBB=50%, BB-B=100%, <B=150%.
Exposures to Banks	For scheduled commercial banks (SCBs) in India with minimum CRAR of 9%, RW=20%; non scheduled=100% with minimum 9% CRAR; for others, RW depends on capital adequacy positions (higher the CRAR, lower is the risk weight).
Corporate Exposures	Risk weights depend on the external credit rating agency (CRA) given solicited long term credit rating: AAA= 20%, AA=30%, A=50%, BBB=100%, <BB=150% & Unrated = 100% risk weight.
Commercial Real Estate; capital market exposure	100% risk weight; 125% risk weight respectively & standard provisions=1%.
Regulatory Retail	75% risk weight subject to four criteria: (1. individual, 2 small business-SME: turnover<50 Cr, 3 granularity-exposure<0.2 of total RR portfolio and low exposure limit<Rs. 5 Lakh)-it also includes Educational Loan.

Table 8.1 contd.

Table 8.1 contd.

Retail: Residential Mortgage	35% risk weight for housing loan exposures<Rs.30 Lac sanctioned to individual against the mortgage of residential housing property having LTV<=80% & for loan exposures >Rs.30 Lac but <Rs. 75 Lac & LTV<=75%; 50% risk weight for exposures <Rs.30 Lac & 80%<LTV<=90% and for exposures >Rs.30 Lac & <Rs.75 Lac with LTV>75% and <=80%. A higher 75% risk weight is stipulated for exposures >Rs. 75 Lac & LTV<=75% on properties that will be occupied by the borrower or rented; Std. Provisions= 0.40%; additional 25% RW & higher prov. 2% if restructured
Retail: Consumer credit-personal loans & credit card	Overall 125% risk weight; Loans up to Rs. 1 lac against gold & silver ornaments have confessional RW of 50%.
Loans Past Due 90 Days or More	150% risk weight for unsecured portions if specific provisions <20% of outstanding amount of NPA; RW 100% when provisions=20% & RWA 50% if provisions>=50%
Off-Balance Sheet Items	0% CCF for unused commitments under one year in maturity if unconditionally cancellable; 20% CCF for collateralized trade letters, stand by facilities maturity < 1 yr., 50% for performance bonds, 100% CCF for guarantees, repo style transactions.
Credit Risk Mitigation	Recognition of range of collateral, guarantees and credit derivatives netting approaches and use regulatory haircuts.

Source: RBI (2014) & Recent RBI Circular in October 8, 2015 on "Individual Housing Loans: Rationalization of Risk-Weights and LTV Ratios".

It is worthwhile to mention that the credit risk weight for unrated customers under the standardized approach is 100 per cent, whereas it is 150 per cent for BB and below rated customers. This difference may lead to regulatory arbitrage if banks wish to optimize their regulatory risk weights in seeking only compliance. In such cases, banks will have to depend on their internal rating to assess the actual credit risk position of such loans. Otherwise, the supervisor may ask the bank to keep additional capital as part of supervisory review process under pillar II (or ICAAP).

Credit risk mitigants are recognized for regulatory capital purpose as long as minimum conditions relating to collateral treatment are observed, are not double counted, general requirements for legal certainty are satisfied and remaining residual risks are properly accounted for. When the business cycle turns and economic condition changes, RBI as regulator changes the risk weights and provisioning norms for housing loans from time to time to check the loan growth and to limit pro-cyclicality in a proactive manner. Further, the internal rating-based approach (IRB) model of measuring credit risk advocates to the expected loss-based dynamic provisioning and unexpected loss-based capital buffer for banks.

IRB Approach

The IRB approach under Basel II is a more sophisticated methodology for calculating credit risk regulatory capital as it is primarily based on the bank's internal estimates of risk parameters subject to certain minimum conditions and disclosure requirements. Under the IRB approach, all banking book exposures must be categorized into broad asset classes using specific definitions and criteria provided by the Committee. For each of these asset classes, there are distinct risk components – PD, EAD, LGD, effective maturity, asset correlations and size adjustments which can be calculated by banks themselves or provided by supervisors.

Foundation IRB (FIRB)

The term "Foundation IRB" or "F-IRB" is an abbreviation of "Foundation Internal Rating Based Approach", and it refers to a set of credit risk measurement techniques proposed under Basel II capital adequacy rules for banking institutions. Under this approach, the banks are allowed to develop their own empirical model to estimate the PD (probability of default) for their obligors. Banks can use this approach only subject to approval from their local regulators.

Under F-IRB, banks are required to use regulator's prescribed LGD (loss given default) and other parameters required for calculating the RWA (risk-weighted asset). Then, total required capital is calculated as a fixed percentage of the estimated RWA.

Advanced IRB (AIRB)

The term "Advanced IRB" or "A-IRB" is an abbreviation of "Advanced Internal Rating Based Approach" and it refers to a set of credit risk measurement techniques proposed under Basel II capital adequacy rules for banking institutions. Under this approach, the banks are allowed to develop their own empirical model to quantify the required capital for credit risk. Banks can use this approach only subject to approval from their local regulators. Under A-IRB, banks are supposed to use their own quantitative models to estimate

PD (probability of default), EAD (exposure at default), LGD (loss given default) and other parameters required for calculating the RWA (risk-weighted asset). Then, the total required capital is calculated as a fixed percentage of the estimated RWA.

Table 8.2 summarizes the Basel IRB implementation status of various countries for managing credit risk.

The internal ratings-based approach (IRB) to credit risk is one of the most innovative elements of the New Framework because it allows the banks to themselves determine certain key elements in the calculation of their capital requirements. This is based on a portfolio invariant (or granular) credit VaR approach (similar to economic capital). A standardized approach to modelling credit risk across all types of banks is used for supervisory purpose for the first time. In this approach, banks can determine their own estimation for some components of risk measure: the probability of default (PD), exposure at default (EAD) and effective maturity (M). The goal is to define risk-weights by determining the cut-off points between and within the areas of the expected loss (EL) and the unexpected loss (UL), where the regulatory capital should be held, in the probability of default. Then, the risk weights for individual exposures are calculated based on the function provided by the local regulator (RBI). This has been discussed in the subsequent section.

Basel II IRB Exposure Categories

Under the IRB approach, banks must categorize banking-book exposures into broad classes of assets with different underlying risk characteristics according to definitions set out in Basel II. The classes of assets are (a) corporate, (b) sovereign, (c) bank, (d) retail and (e) equity. Within the retail asset class, three sub-classes are separately identified. Within the corporate asset class, banks are permitted to distinguish separately the exposures to small- and medium-sized entities ("SMEs"), as defined in Basel II. Banks adopting the IRB approach should implement the retail asset and sub-asset class definitions and distinguish SME exposures from corporate exposures in general. Banks are also permitted to group their loan exposures to small corporate clients to a retail portfolio, provided the regulatory criteria are met.

Under retail pool criteria, banks will have to calculate the capital requirement for credit risk of these portfolios instead of the individual loans. In creating the pools, banks must test that the pooling process provides for a meaningful differentiation of risks and each pool contains sufficiently homogenous exposures. Accordingly, banks are required to estimate PD,

Table 8.2: The Global Implementation of Basel IRB Approach

Country	Regulator	Implementation status	Std. Approach	FIRB	AIRB
Australia	APRA	Approved 5 internally active large banks (ADIs) to adopt AIRB (2013 status)	01.01.2008	01.01.2008	01.01.2008
Indonesia	BI		Q1 2009	Q1 2010	Q4 2010
Hong Kong	HKMA	Extends capital floor beyond 2009 (2013 status)	01.01.2007	01.01.2007	01.01.2008
Malaysia	BNM	At the moment, following std. approach	01.01.2008		
Singapore	MAS	Three local banking groups adopted FIRB since '08	01.01.2007	01.01.2008	
Thailand	BOT		31.12.2008	31.12.2008	31.12.2008
Japan	BOJ	87 per cent of internationally active banks under the IRB (2012 position)	31.03.2007	31.03.2007	31.03.2008
S Korea	BOK	Std. approach banks: 7 and IRB banks :11 (as of April 2014)	31.12.2007	31.12.2007	31.12.2007
USA	FED	Slower implementation, AIRB for large banks, SREP published in July-08. Amendments to be finalized in 2nd quarter of 2015	2009	Parallel run started in 2009	3 yrs transitional period

Table 8.2 contd.

Table 8.2 contd.

China	CBRC	New Capital Adequacy effective from 01/01/2013. All banks in China are on std. approach.	0.01.2013	Applications of 6 internationally active banks under review	Not approved
Europe	ECB	EU banks have broadly implemented IRB advanced approaches	2007	2008 (parallel run completed)	19 banks are using advanced IRB (by end 2014)
Russia	CBR	Prior project on IRB for 8 banks started in 2011	2012	2015 (recommended for banks with high quality internal database & risk management system)	
India	RBI	Final guidelines issued in Dec 2011	31.03.2008/ '09	2015 (parallel run is on for systematically important banks)	2016/17

Source: BCBS updates, RCAP reports, various countries' central bank websites and from global consultants' published reports. Also check http://www.bis.org/publ/bcbs/b3prog_dom_impl.htm

EAD and LGD at the pool level to derive the capital requirement. The qualifying criteria for retail assets for Indian IRB banks are given below:

Orientation criterion: The exposure (both fund-based and non-fund-based) is to an individual person or persons (regardless of the size of exposure) or to a small business.

Product criterion: The exposure (both fund-based and non-fund-based) takes the form of any of the following: revolving credits and lines of credit (including overdrafts), term loan and leases (e.g. instalment loans, leases and educational loans) and small business facilities and commitments.

Granularity criterion: Banks must ensure that the regulatory retail portfolio is sufficiently diversified; No aggregate exposure to one counterpart should exceed 0.2 per cent of the overall regulatory retail portfolio.

Low value of individual exposures: The maximum aggregated retail exposure to one counterpart, except for individual person or persons should be less than the threshold limit of ₹5 crore.

Source: RBI (2011).

Within the retail asset class category, banks are further required to identify separately three sub-classes of exposures: (a) exposures secured by residential properties, (b) qualifying revolving retail exposures and (c) all other retail exposures subject to the condition that these exposures broadly meet the retail assets criteria as specified in the Basel II IRB guidelines of RBI.

Chart 8.2 explains how the assets under Basel II IRB need to be classified into various exposure categories. Exposure categorization has major implications on the estimation of risk-weighted assets. Grouping exposures into homogenous pools is the essential feature of Basel's retail IRB. In case of retail pooling, supervisory segmentation is a more popular approach as it ensures homogeneity in terms of risk parameter.

In creating, homogeneous sub-retail pools, banks need to test risk-wise homogeneity within the pool and heterogeneity across pools through various validation methods.[3] The term homogeneity is used to refer to the risk characteristics or default behaviour. These pools then form the basis for estimating PD, EAD and LGD for exposures in the pool. The primary uses of retail homogeneous pooling exercises are for computation of minimum capital requirements under Basel II IRB advanced approach and monitoring

---

[3] A leading private sector bank in India uses a decision tree algorithm like Chi square Automatic Interaction Detector (CHAID) as a risk pooling methodology. This is a decision tree based on the adjusted significance testing where default status is the dependent and risk factors are independent variables.

of pool performance. More granular is the risk differentiation, greater will be the diversification benefits.

Chart 8.2: Basel II IRB Asset Categories

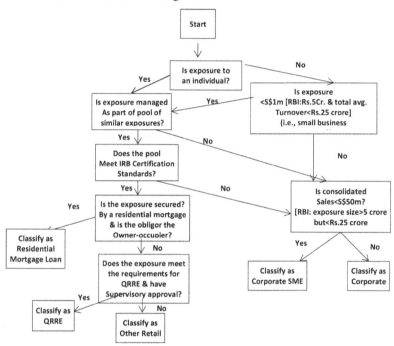

Source: Author's own illustration adopted from Monetary Authority of Singapore (MAS) guidelines on IRB Approach.

Basel II IRB risk weight computations for various exposure categories

Risk weights under IRB approach need to be estimated as capital per unit of exposure following a standardized Value at Risk (VaR) formula given by the supervisor:

$$K = LGD \times \left| N\left(\frac{N^{-1}(PD) + \sqrt{R}N^{-1}(0.999)}{\sqrt{1-R}} \right) - PD \right|$$ Eq. 8.2

The first portion of the above expression is LGD-weighted default tail at 99.9 confidence level which has been worked out using an asymptotically fine-grained portfolio (assuming perfect granularity or diversified) global portfolio data. The $K(PD)$ formula is the quantile function of the loss distribution associated with a one-factor (systematic risk) model. This model assumes that default probability of a loan is conditional on the common macroeconomic factor. The factor R is the asset correlation which is the association between the asset return and for client i and the common factor. $N^{-1}(PD)$ is the normal inverse of PD, which is the distance to default of a borrower used in MKMV model. $N(.)$ is the cumulative standard normal distribution. It is assumed that the credit loss follows standard normal distribution. The first portion of the capital (K) formula is also termed as "default tail" multiplied by LGD. The second portion PD × LGD is the expected loss (EL). It is assumed that banks will make provisions of each loan based on their expected loss (EL). The term $N^{-1}(0.999)$ is the VaR tail threshold with respect to a level of confidence $\alpha = 99.9$ per cent. The quantile function has been obtained from the seminal works of Gordy (2001) and Bluhm, Overbeck and Wagner (2003). The principal form of the IRB capital formula depicted in equation 8.2 comes from considering that the default probability is conditional on the macroeconomic factor. The correlation factor, thus, links the asset pool with the systematic factor.

Conceptually, the above capital formula, which captures the likelihood that the bank will remain solvent over a 1-year horizon, is equal to the confidence level, meaning that the needed capital per rupee (or dollar) amount of exposure against unexpected losses. Under the Asymptotic Single Risk Factor (ASRF) framework that underpins the IRB approach, it is assumed that bank portfolios are perfectly fine grained, that is, that idiosyncratic risk has been fully diversified away so that the regulatory capital depends only on systematic risk. The main objective of the capital formula is to ensure that regulatory capital requirements are more in line with economic capital requirements of banks and by this, make capital allocation of banks more risk sensitive.

Once, the critical elements PD, EAD, LGD, correlation and Maturity (M, which is present for corporate long term loans) have been calculated and proper exposure category has been obtained, it is relatively simple to determine the expected loss (EL), the regulatory capital requirements (K) and the risk-weighted assets (RWA) under the Basel II IRB approach using the above expression.

Though the original structure of the risk-weight function is the same, however, risk-weight formula varies for different exposures as correlation assumption differs.

Correlation for Corporate and Banking Exposures

$$R = 0.12\left(\frac{1 - e^{-50PD}}{1 - e^{-50}}\right) + 0.24\left(1 - \frac{1 - e^{-50PD}}{1 - e^{-50}}\right) \qquad \text{Eq. 8.3}$$

Where e = exponential, inverse of log whose value is 2.71828 (approximately)

Residential Mortgages

$R = 0.15$ Eq. 8.3a

Revolving Credit Exposures

$R = 0.04$ Eq. 8.3b

Other Retail Credit Exposures

$$R = 0.03\left(\frac{1 - e^{-35PD}}{1 - e^{-35}}\right) + 0.16\left(1 - \frac{1 - e^{-35PD}}{1 - e^{-35}}\right)$$ Eq. 8.3c

The effect of systematic factor on an individual loan in a portfolio is captured through the asset correlation value (R). It is a key input to construct the IRB regulatory capital risk weights for banks. The link between borrower PD and asset correlation also depends on the size of the firm's assets. The correlation effect is stronger for low PD, bigger firms (or larger exposure). This relationship arises because high credit quality firms are more likely to be influenced by common macroeconomic conditions. On the other hand, asset correlations for poor credit quality, large-sized companies are low because defaults of such firms are subject to firm-specific problems. The inverse relationship between PD and asset correlation (R) across IRB exposure categories has been illustrated in Chart 8.3. Basel IRB correlation formula has given greater correlation benefits to SME and other retail loans.

Chart 8.3: The Relationship between PD and Asset Correlation for Different IRB Asset Classes

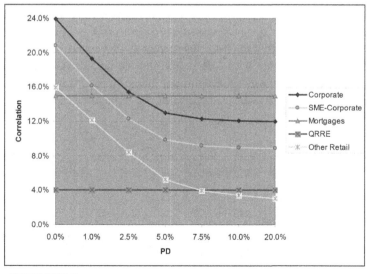

Source: BCBS (2006).

Besides the correlation factor, there are maturity adjustment and size adjustment factors for corporate and SME exposures. To better understand the risk-weight functions, we now take a closer look at different exposure categories:

1. IRB Risk Weight Formula for Corporate/Sovereign/Bank Exposure

Correlation (R)=0.12×(1–EXP(–50×PD))/(1–EXP(–50))+
0.24×[1–(1–EXP(–50×PD))/(1–EXP(–50))]

Maturity adjustment (b) = (0.11852-0.05478×ln(PD))^2

ln is the natural log function

Capital requirement (K) =
[LGD×N{(1–R)^–0.5×G(PD)+(R/(1–R))^0.5×G(0.999)}–
PD×LGD] ×(1–1.5×b(PD))^–1×(1+(M–2.5) ×b (PD))

Risk-weighted assets (RWA) = K×12.5×EAD

12.5 is the inverse of 8 min. capital adequacy requirement

Maturity adjustment is present for IRB corporate exposure to capture long-term effects. Credit portfolios consist of instruments with different maturities. Empirical evidence indicates that long-term credits are riskier than short-term credits. For instance, downgrades from one rating category to a lower one are more likely for long-term credits. Moreover, maturity effects are stronger for obligors with low probability of default. Consistent with these considerations, the Basel Committee has proposed a maturity adjustment m_i to be multiplied with each term of the regulatory capital computed from the equation.

$$m_i = \frac{1+(M-2.5)b(p_i)}{1-1.5b(p_i)}$$
Eq. 8.4

and slope adjustment:

$$b(p_i) = (0.11852 - 0.05478 \times \ln(p_i))^2$$
Eq. 8.4a

M is the effective maturity. In Basel II, M is set to 2.5 years for all rating grades. The effective maturity is calculated as the longest possible remaining time before the borrower is scheduled to fulfil its obligations. It is generally estimated through the loan cash flow duration method. As per the RBI norm, M will not be greater than 5 years. If the cash flow schedule of a loan is known, the effective maturity can be estimated by using the following formula as specified by BCBS:

$$\text{Effective maturity } (M) = \sum_t t \times CF_t \bigg/ \sum_t CF_t \qquad\qquad \text{Eq. 8.5}$$

Where, CF_t denotes the cash flows (principal and interest due) contractually payable by the borrower in period t number of years as per the loan contract.

The maturity adjustment is only done for corporate borrower portfolio and SMEs if treated as corporate.

2. Corporate exposure adjustment for SME

Mainly, correlation function has incorporated size adjustment factor

Correlation (R) = 0.12×(1–EXP(–50×PD))/(1–EXP(–50))+0.24× [1–(1–EXP(–50×PD)) /(1–EXP(–50))]–0.04×(1–(S–5)/45)

Note that RBI has made firm size adjustment more conservative for SME corporates that results in higher correlation number. RBI's prescribed size adjustment: (S–5)/20 where S=total exposure to the entity instead of the turnover mentioned in the original BCBS document]

The size adjustment has been introduced to provide some diversification benefit to the SMEs if considered as corporate. The bank can save capital if it lends to good SMEs.

The maturity adjustment factor is still there for this exposure category of loans.

3. Risk-weight function for residential mortgage exposures

For residential mortgage exposures defined earlier, those are not in default and are secured or partly secured by residential mortgages, risk-weights will be assigned based on the following formula:

Correlation (R) = 0.15
Capital requirement (K) = LGD × N[(1 – R)^–0.5 × G(PD) + (R/(1 – R))^0.5 × G(0.999)] – PD × LGD
Risk-weighted assets = K × 12.5 × EAD

The capital requirement (K) for a defaulted exposure is equal to the greater of zero and the difference between its LGD and the bank's estimate of expected loss [i.e., K=Max (0, LGD-EL)]. The risk-weighted asset amount for the defaulted exposure is the product of K, 12.5, and the EAD. There is no maturity adjustment or size adjustment in this case. The term N is the cumulative standard normal distribution, or normsdist(.). The term G is normal inverse N^{-1} or normsinv(.). This is as per the Basel II IRB formula as specified in BCBS (2006) document.

Risk-weight function for qualifying revolving retail exposures (QRRE)

For qualifying the revolving retail exposures (e.g. credit card products) as defined earlier that are not in default, risk weights are defined based on the following formula:

> Correlation (R) = 0.04
> Capital requirement (K) = LGD × N[(1 − R)^−0.5 × G(PD) + (R/(1 − R))^0.5 × G(0.999)] − PD × LGD
> Risk-weighted assets = K × 12.5 × EAD

The capital requirement (K) for a defaulted exposure is equal to the greater of zero and the difference between its LGD and the bank's best estimate of expected loss. The risk-weighted asset amount for the defaulted exposure is the product of K, 12.5, and the EAD. There is no maturity adjustment or size adjustment in this case.

Risk-weight function for other retail exposures

For all other retail exposures that are not in default, risk weights are assigned based on the following function, which also allows correlation to vary with PD:

> Correlation (R) = 0.03 × (1 − EXP(−35 × PD))/(1 − EXP(−35)) + 0.16 × [1 − (1 − EXP(−35 × PD))/(1 − EXP(−35))]
> Capital requirement (K) = LGD × N[(1 − R)^−0.5 × G(PD) + (R/(1 − R))^0.5 × G(0.999)] − PD x LGD
> Risk-weighted assets = K × 12.5 × EAD

The capital requirement (K) for a defaulted exposure is equal to the greater of zero and the difference between its LGD and the bank's best estimate of expected loss. The risk-weighted asset amount for the defaulted exposure is the product of K, 12.5, and the EAD.

Note, "G" function is the normal inverse of a cumulative normal distribution (N^{-1} (.)). It is also termed as inverse Gaussian.

Functions are taken from original BCBS document (June, 2006 document) and RBI's Basel II IRB guidelines for Indian banks (released in December 2011)

PD = the probability of default; LGD = loss given default; EAD = exposure at default; M = effective maturity

Illustrative Example

Assume that the bank has a Housing Loans Pool (Residential Mortgage Exposures) and estimating the RWA for an exposure of ₹80 lakh with LTV ratio of 75 per cent:

The pooled PD of the Housing Loans Portfolio = 1.5 per cent (the geographic diversification may be incorporated)

Pooled LGD of the Housing Loans Portfolio = 40 per cent (same diversification effect may be incorporated)

Table 8.3 demonstrates the Risk-weighted assets of the Housing Loans Portfolio as per the AIRB Approach.

Table 8.3: Computation of Risk-weighted Assets for Loans in Retail Residential Mortgage/Housing Loans Portfolio

Housing Loans Pooled PD	1.5%	(estimated by the bank)
Housing Loans LGD	40%	(estimated by the bank)
EAD (₹ lakh)	80 lakh	(taken as balance outstanding as on date of estimation)
Correlation (R)	0.15	(given under the IRB Approach)
K (per ₹ Exposure.)	0.052	(derived using the Capital Requirement Formula)
Risk-Weight (in per cent)	65.28	= K × 12.5
Risk-Weighted Assets (₹ lac)	52.23 lakh	(product of risk-weight and EAD)
Min. Regulatory Capital (₹ lac)	4.7004 lakh	(9%×RWA)

Source: Author's own illustration based on Basel IRB formula prescribed by BCBS (2006)

Here, RWA in value is much lower than the 65.28 per cent RW number prescribed under the Basel II Standardized Approach (Refer to Table 8.1, RW=75 per cent). In this illustration, the bank is able to save capital due to better recovery and low PD in comparison to fixed RW under the Standardized Approach. Banks will be able to save capital under IRB if there is better recovery and lower PD in a diversified Housing Loan Pool.

However, there is a prudential capital floor restriction which will be controlled by RBI and this has been mentioned in RBI (2011) circular. This prevents a sudden fall in banks' regulatory capital due to the use of IRB approach and thereby provides enough time for supervisors to ensure its prudent implementation. The purpose of keeping prudential floor is to ensure soundness and safety of banking sector and restrict capital arbitrage.

Estimation of EAD under the Basel II standardized approach

In case of off balance-sheet exposures like a cash credit facility of ₹100 lakh (which is not unconditionally cancellable), where the drawn portion is ₹60 lakh, the undrawn portion of ₹40 lakh will attract a lower CCF of 20 per cent. The reason is that the cash credit facility is subject to review/renewal normally once a year and thus has relatively less drawal uncertainty. The credit equivalent amount of ₹8 lakh (20 per cent of ₹40 lakh) will be assigned the appropriate risk weight as applicable to the counterparty/rating to arrive at the risk-weighted asset for the undrawn portion. The drawn portion (₹60 lakh) will attract a risk weight as applicable to the counterparty/rating.

If a large ticket term loan of ₹700 crore sanctioned for a big project which can be drawn down in stages over a 3-year period, still a CCF will be applicable to counter the exposure risk. The terms of sanction allow draw down in three stages – ₹150 crore in Stage I, ₹200 crore in Stage II and ₹350 crore in Stage III, where the borrower needs the bank's explicit approval for draw down under Stages II and III after completion of certain formalities. If the borrower has drawn already ₹50 crore under Stage I, then the undrawn portion would be computed with reference to Stage I alone, i.e. it will be ₹100 crore. If Stage I is scheduled to be completed within one year, the CCF will be 20 per cent and if it is more than one year, then the applicable CCF will be 50 per cent (these illustrations are given by RBI).

Similar Credit Conversion Factors (CCFs) are followed in Basel II standardized approach (Appendix 6, Basel II IRB guidelines, RBI, 2011).

CCF as per RBI rule under Basel II standardized approach and in FIRB approach

- For direct credit substitutes like LCs, guarantees of loans, CCF = 100 per cent.
- For bonds, warrants, standby letters of credit related to particular transactions, CCF = 50 per cent.
- Short-term self-liquidating trade letters, documentary credits collateralized by the underlying shipment for both issuing bank and confirming bank, CCF = 20 per cent.
- Sale and repurchase agreement and asset sales recourse where credit risk remains with the bank, CCF = 100 per cent.
- Forward asset purchases, forward deposits and party paid shares and securities, which represent commitments with certain drawdown, CCF = 100 per cent
- Lending of banks' securities including repo-type transactions, CCF = 100 per cent.
- Note issuance facilities and revolving underwriting facilities, CCF = 50 per cent.
- Commitments with certain drawdown, CCF = 100 per cent.
- Other commitments (e.g. formal standby facilities and credit lines) with original maturity of <=1 year, CCF=20%, >1 year, CCF=50%
- Similar commitments that are unconditionally cancellable at any time by the bank without prior notice or that effectively provide for automatic cancellation due to deterioration in a borrower's credit worthiness, CCF = 0 per cent.

Under A-IRB, the bank itself determines the appropriate EAD to be applied to each exposure. This method has already been explained in the earlier section.

Estimation of LGD under the Basel II standardized approach

Banks are currently using standard supervisory prescribed haircut approach for eligible collaterals depending upon the instruments rating or borrower rating. The following exercise illustrates the Haircut Calculation for Exposure:

Illustration: Suppose exposure of ₹110 working capital limit has been given to a corporate with a residual maturity of 1 year and a rating A+

Thus, supervisory exposure haircut = 2% (see Table 8.4)

The collateral value (C) = ₹100 which is a 4-year debt security issued by AAA issuer.

Thus, supervisory collateral haircut = 4% (see Table 8.4)

Table 8.4: Supervisory Haircut (%)

Issue rating for debt securities	Residual Maturity	Sovereigns	Other issues
AAA to AA PR1/P1/F1/A1	≤ 1 year	0.5	1
	>1 year, ≤ 5 years	2	4
	>5 years	4	8
A+ to BBB- PR2/P2/F2/A2; PR3/P3/F3/A3 and Unrated bank securities (as specified below)	≤ 1 year	1	2
	>1 year, ≤ 5 years	3	6
	> 5 years	6	12
Main index equities (including convertible bonds) and Gold			15
Other equities (including convertible bonds) listed on a recognized exchange			25
Mutual funds			Highest haircut applicable to any security in which the fund can invest
Cash in the same currency			0

Source: BCBS (2006), RBI (2011).

Now, one has to use the exposure haircut formula as prescribed by RBI (and BCBS):

$$E^* = \max [0, \{E \times (1+H_e) - C \times (1-H_c-F_{fx})\}] \qquad \text{Eq. 8.6}$$
$$= ₹16.2$$

Where H_e is the exposure haircut; H_c is the collateral haircut; F_{fx} is the haircut for currency mismatch (it can be assumed = 0 in this case).

Finally, this exposure needs to be multiplied by corresponding risk weight depending on the external solicited rating of the borrower (e.g. here, it will be 50 per cent) to calculate the risk weight.

Note that, there is a simple adjustment formula suggested by the regulator to take care of maturity mismatch between exposure and collateral (Page 64, RBI 2013, NCAF guidelines).

Estimation of LGD under the Basel II FIRB Approach

As per the original Basel II IRB document (issued by BCBS), Under FIRB, senior claims on corporate, sovereigns and banks not secured by recognized collateral will be assigned a 45 per cent LGD. A subordinated claims on corporates, sovereigns and banks will be assigned a 75 per cent LGD (Paragraph 287–88 of BCBS document, June 2006).

In addition to the eligible financial collateral recognized in the standardized approach, under the FIRB approach some other forms of collateral, known as eligible IRB collateral, are also recognized. These include receivables, specified commercial and residential real estate (CRE/RRE), and other collateral, where they meet the minimum requirements set out in paragraph 509–524 of original BCBS document.

LGD under Basel II FIRB of RBI

RBI's Basel II IRB (2011) circular paragraph 47–49 has prescribed the following rule for calculating LGD. The maximum benefit a bank can get for secured exposure is 140 per cent. For unsecured loans, the prescribed minimum LGD is 65 per cent. However, if the claim is subordinated unsecured, the applicable LGD would be 75 per cent.

Suppose the exposure is ₹100 crore (E) and is collateralized with eligible CRE/RRE of the value of ₹105 crore (C). In this case, one can find out the effective secured portion of the exposure by using the following formula:

$E^* = C \times (1/140\%)$
$= 105 \times 0.7143$
$= 75$ crore (approximately)

The fully collateralized portion of ₹75 crore will then be assigned an LGD of 50 per cent to calculate the risk-weighted assets (RWA) under FIRB approach. The LGD value has been obtained from Table 8.5. The remaining ₹25 crore portion will be treated as unsecured and should be assigned an LGD = 65 per cent (if senior loan) as per the RBI (2011) circular. Hence, the exposure weighted LGD for the loan works out to be = 75%×50%+25%×65%=53.75%. Note that an RBI estimate shows that the average LGD for Scheduled Commercial Banks (SCBs) in India is around 60 per cent.

Table 8.5: Prescribed LGD for FIRB banks – for Unsecured and Non-recognized Collateralized Exposures

Type of Collateral	Minimum LGD%	Threshold level of collateralization required for partial recognition of collateral for the exposure (C*)	Required level of (over) collateralization for full recognition of collateral for the exposure (C**)
Eligible financial collateral@	–	–	–
Eligible financial receivable	50	0	125
Eligible Commercial Real Estate (CRE)/ Residential Real Estate (RRE)	50	30	140
Other physical collateral$	60	30	140

Source: RBI (2011)
Note: @treatment has been dealt with in detail in para 56 and 57 of the guidelines and Appendix 3.
$may include industrial properties, land, etc.

LGD under Basel II AIRB approach

For the advanced IRB approach, the bank itself determines the appropriate LGD to be applied to each exposure, on the basis of robust data and analysis. Such values would be expected to represent a conservative estimate of long-run estimates. Subject to certain additional minimum requirements, supervisors may permit banks to use their own internal estimates of LGD for corporate, sovereign and bank exposures (and for retail loans also). This methodology has been already discussed in EAD and LGD sections.

Basel IRB approach and position of Indian banks

Fifteen Scheduled Commercial Banks in India have applied for graduating towards Basel II IRB credit risk standards in 2013. Out of these applications, RBI has considered four large systematically important nationalized banks and three leading private sector banks in India to work together as parallel phase. Robust data management process to develop internal models, model predictive power assessment (i.e. validation), incorporating model outputs in business decision-making are the pre-requisites for adoption of advanced approach. The entire exercise should be seen as not only an exercise in determining regulatory capital but also a sophisticated risk management tool to reduce loan losses.

A survey of 10 banks was conducted by the author to understand the preparedness of Indian banks in implementing IRB approach. The survey suggests that even though banks are eagerly planning for IRB implementation, the preparation level of banks is highly skewed. Some banks still depend on external models, whereas others have their own. Moreover, data storage and pooling is another issue that needs to be sorted out internally by most of the banks. Many banks do not have rating-wise PD history even for five years. Unlike corporates, update of ratings of retail loans is not done regularly. Estimation of facility-wise EAD and LGD and using these risk inputs in taking credit decisions, portfolio monitoring and risk-based pricing is also not prevalent practice among banks. However, the top management of few leading banks in India thinks that moving into more advanced IRB process is rewarding, since increased sophistication in the risk assessment process will provide business advantages in the long run.

Essentials for Moving towards IRB Adherence

Before a bank can start thinking of adhering to capital requirements for credit risk as outlined in BASEL II IRB, the following essential support systems are required:

- Credit rating system (dual rating system: borrower rating and facility rating);
- Robust rating methodology for all exposures including specialized lending (e.g. infrastructure loans);
- Credit risk models for assessing PD, EAD and LGD and also maintain data history;
- Master data management and regular data quality checks of key fields used in modelling;

- Benchmark and stabilize the models for computation of regulatory/ economic capital;
- Formulate policy on credit risk mitigation techniques and collateral management system duly approved by the board. Bank shall consider valuation, liquidity, price volatility, liquidation cost, legal enforceability of the collaterals received on the loans to use them for risk mitigation;
- Adopt regular model validation process through back-testing and ensuring route for resolution of model deficiencies. The bank should have the requisite skillsets and ensure board and senior management involvement;
- Implement appropriate model validation strategy to support the risk-rating process and ensure correctness of PD, EAD, LGD and capital estimates for credit risk;
- Integrating model-based outputs capital calculations with banks' day-to-day business operations (e.g. credit decisions, pricing, etc.) of the bank;
- Establish risk sensitive credit limit-based system (followed by internal policy) to mitigate concentration risk;
- Take a portfolio approach in managing risk in all segments and
- Ensure corporate governance, internal audit and controls.

It is virtually impossible to embark on Basel IRB journey without a robust data warehouse. Hence, moving over to Basel IRB era could imply banks to make fullest use of their newly created IT backbone to capture relevant granular data on timely and ongoing basis. In this context, it is important for banks and FIs to understand the IRB formulations exhaustively so that they can efficiently migrate to the new system in a phased manner.

ICAAP Under IRB

The internal capital adequacy assessment process (ICAAP) is a framework for an IRB bank to perform a comprehensive self-assessment of the risks they face and to relate capital adequacy to these risks. The supervisor in its ICAAP circular is encouraging banks to develop and use better risk management techniques in monitoring and managing their risks. Banks that adopt the IRB approach are expected to conduct extensive risk profile analysis and their documentation to ensure comprehensiveness and reliability of their internal credit risk assessment capabilities. Based on risk profile analysis, banks will have to assess overall capital adequacy and develop strategy for maintaining capital levels consistent with risk appetite and business plans. Risk appetite considers the quantum of risk a bank is willing to accept within its overall capacity. IRB banks are also subject to a stringent set of minimum standards. Accordingly, compliance with the IRB regime requires considerable internal resources. The board is the ultimate owner of the ICAAP and the management body must take its responsibility. A satisfactory ICAAP comprises a complete process with proper oversight and controls, and not just an ability to carry out certain capital calculations.

Bank-wide risk identification and assessment, capital assessment, stress testing, forward capital planning and proper documentation of risk management process adopted in the business by the top management are the key components of ICAAP report. Banks should have in place policies that require all aspects of a bank's IRB rating and quantification system to be well documented (e.g. policies and procedures and other documents relating to the rating system's development, operation, control and oversight etc.). ICAAP is a process that requires Board and Senior Management oversight for ensuring the availability of appropriate level and quality of capital for bank's risk profile and business plan. A regular review of risk management and capital management processes is also necessary to ensure integrity, objectivity and consistent application of the advanced risk management system.

The supervisor review process (SREP) expects that the whole IRB system should be seen as not only an exercise in determining regulatory capital but also a sophisticated risk management tool to better manage their business. The IRB bank has to check whether their risk and governance framework is sufficiently robust. For example, a bank must demonstrate to its supervisor that it has been using a rating system broadly in line with the IRB minimum requirements for at least three years prior to qualification. The ICAAP document of banks should also reflect how well capital management is linked to the bank's risk profile and its risk appetite. The involvement of top management in the IRB process is necessary for incorporating model outputs in business decision-making (e.g. credit planning, pricing, capital planning, etc.), thereby establishing a strong risk culture within the organization.

Basel III Regulatory Changes

In response to the US sub-prime crisis that has caused lenders to write off huge losses, BCBS (in December 2010) announced a substantial revision in the capital and liquidity standards in the form of Basel III regulation. This was a proactive effort from the G20 leaders that aimed at reinforcing the regulatory framework and to ensure a safe and stable global banking system. Since then the need for strengthening the capital position of banks has emerged prominently. Basel III urges banks to raise the quality of capital to absorb the unexpected losses to reduce the chance of another financial crisis. The Reserve Bank of India (RBI) on 2 May 2012 had released its guidelines on implementation of Basel III capital regulation in India. These guidelines became effective from 1 April 2013 in India in a phased manner. Recently, an updated Basel III guideline was issued by RBI on 1 July 2014. The Basel III capital regulation will be fully implemented as on 31 March 2019.

Basel III is not a replacement of Basel II but a series of amendments and enhancements to the existing Basel II framework (NCAF in India) with the objective of improving the banking sector's ability to absorb shocks arising from financial and economic stress. It has enhanced risk coverage, though its focus is on capital charge for complex securitization and re-securitization positions, counterparty risk in Over the Counter (OTC) derivative positions and mark-to-market losses in the trading book. For OTC derivatives, the counterparty to a transaction could default on or before the final settlement of the cash flows, thereby causing loss to the other party. This is known as "counterparty credit risk". Under Basel III, banks are required to maintain adequate capital to absorb CVA losses. Besides covering the counterparty default risk, the current regulatory reform package includes an additional capital requirement for Credit Value Adjustment (CVA) risk to cover mark to market losses due to deterioration in the credit worthiness of counterparty.

The portfolio capital charge for CVA risk for the counterparties is determined using a standardized formula that has been prescribed by RBI in its latest Basel III 2015 document. This has been clearly mentioned in RBI (2015) Basel III master circular in paragraph "Capitalization of mark-to-market counterparty risk losses (CVA capital charge)". This capital charge can be interpreted as the 99 per cent confidence interval for a portfolio of normally distributed assets. The existing rules for IRB approach will be the same in Basel III regime. The regulator wants to ensure that banks are better able to absorb losses on both Tier I and Tier II capital basis. The new accord seeks to improve banks' ability to withstand periods of economic and financial stress by prescribing more stringent capital and liquidity requirement.

Basel III mainly focuses on the numerator part of the bank's capital adequacy ratio (CRAR). A key element of new definition is the greater focus on "common equity" (paid up equity capital, reserves, retained earnings, etc.). In order to improve the quality of regulatory capital, many of the deductions from capital under Basel II which were made either from Tier I or from both Tier I and Tier II, will be made from minimum common equity Tier I (CET1) under Basel III. Many new items have been introduced for deduction from CET1 directly under Basel III. In addition to raising the quality of the capital base, banks need to ensure that all material risks are captured in the capital framework. Basel III capital rule is, thus, raising the level of the minimum capital requirements to safeguard the banks. This includes gradual increase in the minimum common equity requirement (i.e. Tier I (CET1)) from 4.5 per cent of risk-weighted assets in 2013 to 5.5 per cent since 2015 along with an increase in capital conservation buffer (CCB) of 0.625 per cent from 31 March 2016 to 2.5 per cent in a phased manner by 31 March 2019. This will bring the total common equity requirement to 8 per cent by 2019. The banks in India are subject to the capital adequacy guidelines stipulated by RBI, which are based on the framework of the Basel Committee on Banking Supervision (BCBS). The Basel III transitional schedule applicable for SCBs in India has been shown in Table 8.6.

Table 8.6: Basel III Transitional Arrangements for Scheduled Commercial Banks in India

Minimum Capital Ratios:	(% of RWAs)						
	1st Apr- 2013	31st Mar- 2014	31st Mar- 2015	31st Mar- 2016	31st Mar- 2017	31st Mar- 2018	31st Mar- 2019
Minimum Common Equity Tier I (CET1) ratio	4.5	5	5.5	5.5	5.5	5.5	5.5
Capital Conservation Buffer (CCB)	0	0	0	0.625	1.25	1.875	2.5
Minimum CET 1 + CCB	**4.5**	**5**	**5.5**	**6.125**	**6.75**	**7.375**	**8**
Additional Tier I ratio	1.50	1.50	1.50	1.50	1.50	1.50	1.50
Minimum Tier I Capital-CCB	6	6.5	7	7	7	7	7
Minimum Tier I ratio +CCB	**6**	**6.5**	**7**	**7.625**	**8.25**	**8.875**	**9.50**
Tier II ratio	3	2.5	2	2	2	2	2
Minimum Total Capital	9	9	9	9	9	9	9
Minimum Total Capital + CCB	**9**	**9**	**9**	**9.625**	**10.25**	**10.875**	**11.5**
Phase-in of all Deductions from CET1 (in %)	20	40	60	80	100	100	100

Source: RBI Notification, March 27, 2014

The capital conservation buffer (CCB) will ensure that banks maintain a capital buffer that can be used to absorb losses during the periods of financial and economic stress. The overall minimum Tier I capital requirement (common equity plus other qualifying financial instruments) has been gradually raised to 7 per cent in 2015 (without conservative buffer). Hence, even though risk-based capital ratios are technically 9 per cent, the actual minimum risk-based capital ratio is higher because of CCB restriction. Upon full implementation, Basel III guidelines target minimum CRAR including CCB to be 11.5 per cent. Banks should maintain prudent earning retention policies with a vision to meeting the conservation buffer during the transition phase shown in Table 8.6.

Banks will also have to keep countercyclical buffers (CB) besides CCB. Countercyclical buffers (CB) will only be required when excessive credit growth builds up systemic risks. RBI has recently (5 February 2015) issued guidelines for implementation of countercyclical capital buffer (in RBI's terminology, CCCB). The main aim of countercyclical buffer is to encourage banks to build up a capital buffer in good times which will be helpful to sustain the flow of credit to the real sector in difficult times. It also prevents a bank from reckless lending in the good time when the system level credit growth is already high along with higher private sector leverage in the economy (Drehmann and Tsatsaronis, 2014). A time-trend deviation of credit-to-GDP ratio has been considered by both Basel committee and RBI as a good measure to base banks' countercyclical capital buffer. Jokivuolle, Pesola and Viren (2015) have empirically examined the banks' loan losses pattern of nine European countries during 1982 to 2012 that includes two waves of banking crises. Their unbalanced panel regression results reveal that banks' loan losses (loss to advance ratio) in bad times depend on the situation of three crucial macro-factors: output growth (or GDP growth rate), corporate indebtedness (debt to GDP ratio) and interest rate behaviour. They have suggested that since output growth is beyond the direct control of economic policies, banks' loss rate may be alleviated by accommodative monetary policy and control over firms' excessive indebtedness. Their empirical findings of non-linear relationship between loan losses and output shocks during the regime of high indebtedness provide empirical support for the Basel III's recommendation for CB. The basic logic for countercyclical buffer is that this additional capital buffer may help to check system level excessive credit growth. The CCCB will have to be maintained in the form of common equity Tier I (CET1) capital or other fully loss absorbing capital only. The CCCB decision would normally be pre-announced with a lead time of four quarters. This has been prescribed in the recent RBI guidelines (5 February 2015).

Capital contingency planning under Basel III's "loss absorbency" requirement is an important international development that has attracted the significant attention of banking as well as investor community worldwide. In a crisis situation, a bank will be allowed to let its common equity Tier I capital ratio (CET 1) drop temporarily to as low as 5.5 per cent. But then, the bank will be limited from paying bonuses and dividends to shareholders until it has rebuild this ratio above the regulatory minimum that includes CCB. The capital conservation buffer will begin in a phased manner from 31 March 2015 and will be fully phased in as of 31 March 2019.

The requirement of additional core capital may impact the Indian banking sector's competitiveness significantly. However, by retaining greater proportion of earnings during a downturn, banks will be able to support the ongoing banking operations and sustain the steady credit flow to the system. The new capital rule thus demands a lot of emphasis on internal management of risk, earnings and distribution of earnings. Table 8.7 documents the group-wise Basel III Tier I capital adequacy ratios, default risk, default correlation and return on risk-weighted asset (RORWA) estimates of Scheduled Commercial Banks in India. The default probabilities and default correlations are capturing credit portfolio risk (both idiosyncratic and systematic). These have been estimated from the historical trend and volatility of their yearly NPA movements for last 15 years (2001–15). Higher the correlation factor, higher is the economic or regulatory buffer needed as a protection against the unexpected loss due to rise in systematic risk. Strong positive correlation would mean that very large portions of the portfolio would go into default at the same time. Default correlation has significant impact on portfolio loss distribution. The risk-adjusted return on risk-weighted assets (RORWA) measures if a financial entity has the right balance between risk and return. The higher the ratio, the better is the banks' ability to balance shareholders' return (ROE) and Basel III Tier I capital requirement.

Table 8.7: Risk, Capital and Risk-adjusted Return Position of Scheduled Commercial Banks in India as on 31 March 2015

Bank Group	Basel III Tier I Ratio	Avg. Loan Default Rate	Std. Dev. of PD	Default Correlation	RORWA
Large PSB	8.70%	2.59%	0.96%	0.38%	0.69%
Medium PSB	8.11%	2.61%	1.29%	0.77%	0.54%
Small PSB	9.40%	2.69%	1.61%	1.14%	0.71%
New Pvt.	12.91%	2.32%	2.04%	2.49%	2.10%
Old Pvt.	11.78%	1.85%	1.09%	0.70%	1.34%

Source: Author derived estimates based on annual audited report of Indian Banks. Tier 1 ratios are obtained from Basel III disclosure of banks.

Basel III regulation expects that banks for its survival in future must understand the importance of people's perception about a bank's liquidity condition (short term as well as long term) besides internal management of liquidity. It emphasized that banks' liquid assets should be sufficient enough to cover net cash outflow. It focuses on stable funding sources and high quality liquid assets to reduce the short-term vulnerabilityof the maturity structure of bank's assets and liabilities.

Basel III also wants to ensure that banks' leverage ratio (Tier I capital divided by all on and off balance sheet items) should be at least greater than 3 per cent (in India, 4.5 per cent). The countercyclical and capital conservation buffers have been introduced to dampen the cyclical effect of the minimum capital requirements and provisioning standards. The capital conservation buffer should be built in the form of common equity in phased manner (2.5 per cent or RWA) over and above the minimum capital requirement so that it can be drawn during the periods of economic stress. The counter cyclical buffer (0–2.5 per cent of RWA) has been kept to adjust the bank credit growth to macroeconomic growth. These ensure the availability of credit during economic downturn to reduce pro-cyclical effects. It is expected that more conservative capital estimate under Basel III will provide more stability in the bank's capital structure by restricting the banks to take on excessive leverage (or more risky) positions.

Recent Regulatory Developments in Assessing Credit Risk Capital

Conceptually, the IRB framework is intended to ensure accuracy and risk sensitivity of capital requirements and thereby motivate the banks to implement better risk management practices. As part of regulatory efforts in ensuring level playing field among internationally active banks, the Basel Committee on Banking Supervision has established the Regulatory Consistency Assessment Programme (RCAP) in 2012 to assess the consistency of Basel IRB standards. Lately, BCBS July 2013 RCAP study has highlighted that different PD methodologies used by banks lead to significant variations in PD estimates and risk-weighted assets (RWAs). The European Banking Authority (EBA) has also reviewed the validity of IRB framework since its implementation over the 8 years. The forum has accepted that the more risk sensitive IRB system has actually encouraged the institutions to adopt more sound and sophisticated internal risk management practices. However, both EBA and RCAP forum have also noted that there is a significant divergence in the risk estimates due to IRB. Both the regulatory bodies have opined that this difference can be remedied through proper benchmarking exercises, delegation of a number of technical standards and planned regulatory developments through seeking industry opinion. They have also recommended harmonization of methodologies and publication of supervisory benchmarks in due course. Recently, Basel Committee has suggested certain revisions to the standardized approach to credit risk to properly balance risk sensitivity and complexity in risk weighted assets across banks and jurisdictions (BCBS, 22 December 2015). However, these changes will be consistent with the existing set of norms. The second consultative document has come in response to the extensive industry feedback on its first consultative document that was published in December 14 (BSBCS, 22 December, 2014). The main aim is to further strengthen the link between the standardized approach and the internal ratings based (IRB) approach by increasing risk sensitivity and improve consistency and congruity of capital requirements across banks. The US agencies have also proposed some additional regulatory initiatives to improve the level of compliance with the Basel IRB minimum standards. Still, it is under consultation process as the regulator is now awaiting comments from the banking industry. The amendments to the final rule are expected to be released in the middle of 2016 (see BIS website).

Lately, the Reserve Bank of India (RBI, 31 March 2015) has made certain modifications to the guidelines on implementation of advanced model-based approaches for credit risk. The regulator expects that once IRB is adopted by Indian banks, it will be extended across all material asset classes within the bank and for the entire banking group. Only the exposures to Central Counter Parties (CCPs) arising from OTC derivatives will be treated separately under Basel III. However, in some bank cases, RBI may permit a phased transition to IRB approach. During the transition period, the IRB regulatory capital will be subject to prudential floor which shall be 100 per cent of the existing standardized approach for one year and 90 per cent for second year and onwards. As part of quantitative disclosures, now banks will have to report NPA movements by major industry or counterparty type. In addition, banks will have to reveal the amount of NPAs and past due loans by significant geographic areas including provisions related to each area. It has also been indicated that the IRB banks will have to make additional disclosures in comparison to banks under the standardized approach. It is expected that the improved disclosures will bring more transparency to the entire banking system and enhance stakeholders' value.

Summary

Broadly speaking, the objectives of internal rating-based approach under Basel II and Basel III are to encourage better and more systematic risk management practices, especially in the area of credit risk, and to provide improved measures of capital adequacy for the benefit of supervisors and the marketplace more generally. The details about regulatory capital requirements for various exposure categories have been explained in this chapter. The regulatory and supervisory aspects pertaining to the adoption of internal rating-based approach are also discussed in detail. Basel IRB approach wants to ensure that regulatory capital requirements are more in line with economic capital requirements of banks and by this, make capital allocation of banks more risk sensitive and accurate. The advanced risk management system will make the banks aware of the risks inherent in the business activities and take advantage of this knowledge to gain competitive advantage and enhance shareholder value. Supervisors too need to develop skills to validate the internal models developed by the banks, in conjunction with enhanced disclosure requirements that reveal more detailed risk information to the market at an aggregate level.

Integrated implementation of advanced credit risk measurement approaches in banks with wide geographical coverage is a phenomenal challenge. Major IRB implementation challenges for banks are building a robust and accurate credit risk data system, model development, combine the model outputs, obtain human resource and skills, train the business people to familiarize with the system, and finally, involve the top management to implement the process successfully. The IRB approaches require banks to formulate their own internal-rating models to calculate the credit risk capital. It should be seen as not only an exercise in determining regulatory capital but also a sophisticated risk management tool.

Senior bank management may have legitimate concern about IRB approaches due to the potentially high-implementation cost (develop models, IT system, maintain database, develop skillsets, etc.). For example, at the top level, retail pooling logic involves business judgement and, hence, is subjective. It is difficult to determine which product variant or customer segment should be treated separately (for example, different models for auto loan and used auto loan). Moreover, not all factors may be captured in a scoring model and subjectivity in applying application or behavioural scorecards may further lead to risk weight variation across banks. However, the benefits of IRB compliance are manifold. The IRB approach seeks to differentiate risk on an asset-by-asset level in direct contrast to the "grouping" method in the standardized approach. This risk differentiation is intended to add transparency to the decision-making process at many levels in the bank: by asset, customer, business unit, portfolio and organization wide. Then, the IRB approach urges banks to apply the sophisticated risk methodologies consistently across the organization. The IRB advanced approach provides banks the opportunity to significantly reduce their credit risk-weights and reduce their required regulatory capital if they suitably adjust their portfolio by lending to rated but strong corporates, increase their retail lending, provide mortgage loans with higher margins and adopt diversification strategies. It may lead to the realignment of business models as banks will seek to optimize risk reward and return on capital. As the banks progress towards increased sophisticated risk measurement framework, in the long run they will be able to reduce their capital requirement in a controlled way and maximize its return through better capital management.

Finally, the more recent Basel III capital standard expects that bank should create a buffer in good time so that it can be used in bad time. It urges banks to maintain high credit ratings to ensure greater solvency and to avoid costs in raising additional capital under unavoidable market conditions. The regulator may take credit to GDP ratio as a measure of balancing factor and calibrating measure. The RBI has recently identified some systemically important banks and suggests that these banks should have orderly resolution criteria so that the effect on the system in case of crisis is lessened. Basel III also emphasizes on better, more transparent disclosure requirements for banks to conform to the Pillar III market discipline. In this context, ICAAP policy of a bank plays a very important role as a risk management progress report of banks to the regulator. The purpose of the ICAAP is to inform the board about the ongoing assessment of the bank's risks, how management intends to mitigate those risks and how much current and future capital is necessary for long-term survival. It is expected that by attaining more sophisticated IRB status, banks will be able to align their capital more favorably to the Basel III measures and can accomplish higher levels of core capital.

Key learning outcomes

After studying the chapter and the relevant reading, you should be able to understand:

- Risk weights and CRAR calculations under the Basel II standardized approach.
- Basel II IRB risk weight functions for various categories of assets.

- Major differences between the Basel II standardized approach and internal rating based approach (IRB).
- Haircut approach and CCF applications for various credit exposures.
- Challenges under FIRB and AIRB approaches.
- Implications of ICAAP and SREP on business benefits of banks.
- Basel III regulatory expectations.

Review questions

1. Do you think that Basel II IRB approach is a more risk-sensitive approach than the Basel II standardized approach?
2. What is the basis of risk-weight functions under the Basel II standardized approach?
3. What is capital arbitrage? Why is this problematic from the supervisory angle?
4. Explain the exposure classification under the IRB approach
5. What is portfolio invariance?
6. Is Basel II IRB risk-weight function more sensitive to LGD than the PD?
7. Do you think IRB maturity effects are stronger for obligors with low probability of default and why?
8. Does the association between the correlation factor and the PD values vary across asset classes?
9. What are the major challenges for banks under Basel II IRB approach?
10. Mention the key IRB challenges for supervisors.
11. Do you understand the exposure classification process under the Basel II IRB approach? Why has it been suggested?
12. What is ICAAP? Why is it important for banks?
13. Who owns the risk appetite statement in a bank? State three indicators to explain the risk appetite statement of a bank
14. What is a loan loss provision?
15. What is pro-cyclicality problem?
16. What is Basel III capital regulation?
17. What is the purpose of capital conservation buffer (CCB)?
18. What is countercyclical capital buffer (CCCB)?

References

Aas, K. 2005. "The Basel II IRB Approach for Credit Portfolios: A Survey", Norsk Regnesentral.

BCBS. 2005. "An Explanatory Note on the Basel II IRB Risk Weight Functions", BIS, July.

——— 2006. "International Convergence of Capital Measurement and Capital Standards: A Revised Framework", Publication No. 128, Basel Committee on Banking Supervision, Bank for International Settlements, Basel, June.

——— 2010. "Basel III: A Global Regulatory Framework for More Resilient Banks and Banking Systems", 10 December.

——— 2011. "Basel III: A Global Regulatory Framework for More Resilient Banks and Banking Systems", June (revised).

——— 2012. "Basel III Counterparty Credit Risk and Exposures to Central Counterparties: Frequently Asked Questions", December.

——— 2013. "Analysis of Risk-weighted Assets for Credit Risk in the Banking Book", BIS, July.

——— 2013. "Regulatory Consistency Assessment Programme (RCAAP): Analysis of Risk-weighted Asset for Credit Risk in Banking Book", July.

——— 2014. "Revisions to the Standardized Approach for Credit Risk", Consultative Document, 22 December.

——— 2015. "Revisions to the Standardized Approach for Credit Risk", Second Consultative Document, 22 December.

Bluhm, C., L. Overbeck and C. Wagner. 2003. *An Introduction to Credit Risk Modeling* (Boca Raton, Florida: Chapman Hall/CRC).

Drehmann, M. and K. Tsatsaronis. 2014. "The Credit to GDP Gap and Countercyclical Buffers: Questions and Answers", *BIS Quarterly Review*, March.

EBA. 2015. "Future of the IRB Approach", Discussion Paper, 4 March, European Banking Authority.

Gordy, M. 2001. "A Risk Factor Model Foundation for Ratings-based Bank Capital Rules", Working Paper, February.

Ong M. 2003. *The Basel Handbook: A Guide for Financial Practitioners* (London: RISK Books).

Jokivuolle, E., J. Pesola and M. Viren. 2015. "Why is Credit-to-GDP a Good Measure for Setting Countercyclical Buffers?" *Journal of Financial Stability* 18: 117–26.

RBI. 1999. "Risk Management Systems in Banks", DBOD, 7 October.

——— 2007. "Guidelines for Implementation of the New Capital Adequacy Framework", April.

——— 2008. "Master Circular – Prudential Guidelines on Capital Adequacy and Market Discipline – Implementation of the New Capital Adequacy Framework (NCAF)", 26 March.

——— 2010. "Master Circular–Prudential Guidelines on Capital Adequacy and Market Discipline – New Capital Adequacy Framework (NCAF)", 8 February.

——— 2011. "Implementation of the Internal Rating Based (IRB) Approaches for Calculation of Capital Charge for Credit Risk", DBOD, 22 December.

——— 2012. "Guidelines on Implementation of Basel III Capital Regulations in India", 2 May.

——— 2013. "Master Circular – Prudential Guidelines on Capital Adequacy and Market Discipline – New Capital Adequacy Framework (NCAF)", 1 July.

——— 2013. "Master Circular – Basel III Capital Regulations", 1 July.

——— 2014. "Implementation of Basel III Capital Regulations in India – Capital Planning", 24 March.

——— 2014. "Master Circular – Basel III Capital Regulations", 1 July.

——— 2014. "Mater Circular – Prudential Guidelines on Capital Adequacy and Market Discipline – New Capital Adequacy Framework (NCAF), 1 July.

——— 2015. "Prudential Guidelines on Capital Adequacy and Liquidity Standards – Amendments", 31 March.

——— 2015. "Guidelines for Implementation of Countercyclical Capital Buffer (CCCB)", 5 February 2015.

——— 2015. "Master Circular-Basel III Capital Regulations", 1 July.

Index

Printed in the United States
by Baker & Taylor Publisher Services